Greek Byways

GREEK BYWAYS

BY

T. R. GLOVER

CAMBRIDGE
AT THE UNIVERSITY PRESS
1932

CAMBRIDGE
UNIVERSITY PRESS

University Printing House, Cambridge CB2 8BS, United Kingdom

Cambridge University Press is part of the University of Cambridge.

It furthers the University's mission by disseminating knowledge in the pursuit of education, learning and research at the highest international levels of excellence.

www.cambridge.org
Information on this title: www.cambridge.org/9781107438491

First published 1932
First paperback edition 2014

A catalogue record for this publication is available from the British Library

ISBN 978-1-107-43849-1 Paperback

To

The Reverend Frederick John Foakes Jackson, D.D.

Fellow of Jesus College, Cambridge, Briggs Graduate Professor of Christian Institutions in Union Theological Seminary, New York

My dear Foakes,

I can never recall our first meeting. Probably it was at a Cambridge Review *tea. We often met there; and how often we went on to Jesus College, I can't guess. And the encounters on the street—strolling together or sitting in your rooms—I listening, and you (as you have so often reminded me) trying to teach me a little sense ("I have no man so* un-*like-minded", you once misquoted), and firing off nonsense at me, to my great delight; for Cambridge is a serious place.*

I have been luckier than most of your friends here; for, in spite of the gap your going has meant and still means, I have happy memories of you over there—the club, the college and the shops in New York, the little house at Englewood, the garden at Montclair, the community at New Haven, the lakeside at Silver Bay—the Latin verses you wrote me, Tertullian, Josephus, endless things. So I send you my Byways, *to be sure of one reader who is not a candidate for a Tripos and who will realize that they were written for people bred like you and me on the Classics, and fond of them, and in no great hurry to do something else. What a world the others miss!*

There are things one Cambridge man can't say to another in print any more than face to face; but perhaps you will guess them.

Yours

T. R. Glover

Cambridge
7 *April*, 1932

CONTENTS

The elephant on the title page comes from a Carthaginian coin, struck, we are told, in Spain. It will be seen that the artist commits himself to joints, at least in the forelegs. (See page 143.) The ear is decisively African, and the angle of the tusk also suggests reference to Nature. The garb and pose of the *mahout* hardly reveal his race; perhaps in life he was rather smaller, or the elephant larger, than the coin suggests.

THE GREEK ON THE SEA[1]

It is not of small importance, whether man's views of the world that he inhabits were such as to cramp his energies and terrorize his mind, or the reverse. SIR RAYMOND BEAZLEY, *Dawn of Modern Geography*, vol. I, p. 391.

But ever, night and day,
Rings in my ears the windy sea's deep note.

THE phrase, from one of the last of Classical poets, suggests one enduring characteristic of the Greek mind, of Greek life and art and literature. Hero, in this poem of Musaeus, says what they all felt from the first. Euripides, we are told, wrote his tragedies in a cavern, grim and gloomy, on the isle of Salamis; "I have seen it", adds Gellius; and that is why, says the writer of his life, "he draws the greater part of his similes from the sea".[2]

αἰεὶ δ' ἀνὰ νυκτὰ καὶ ἠῶ
ἐξ ἁλὸς ἠνεμόεντος ἐπιβρέμει οὔασιν ἠχή.

The Greek does not sentimentalize about the sea; he has so little in fact to say of enjoyment of the sea that some moderns assure us that the Greek never liked the sea at all. Hesiod tells his brother how their father was wont to sail in ships, for that he lacked a livelihood sufficient, and came at last to Boeotia from Aeolian Cyme in his black ship, over a great stretch of sea, flying not from wealth nor riches and substance, but from poverty; and he settled near Helicon in that miserable hamlet Ascra, bad in winter, hard in summer, never good.[3] He implies only one reason for sea-faring. Hesiod made one voyage himself, one only voyage, a sea-passage to be measured by yards, across the Euripus to Chalcis; the Boeotians eventually bridged it. "Full is the land of evils and full the sea", he says; so perhaps his gloomy view

1 A paper read to the Hellenic Travellers on the *Théophile Gautier*, 14 September, 1929, off Naples.

2 Cf. Gellius, *Noct. Attic.* xv, 20, 5; and *Vit. Eurip.* 59 ff.

3 Hesiod, *Works and Days*, 633 ff.; cf. p. 82. The Euripus is 120 feet across, Tozer says.

of the sea need not prejudice our conclusion, when the land is no better. We shall have to return to him for instructions—a landsman's advice.[1]

Meanwhile some readers of Homer hold that the Achaean heroes too were very dubious about the sea; which, if they really were the kin of the Celts and came from mid-Europe or mid-Russia, need not much surprise us. Hephaistos wrought many pictures of common life on the shield he made for Achilles, but no scene was taken from the sea or ships. The heroes, when Troy fell, "pondered over the long voyage" homeward, whether they should cross the open Aegaean to the south end of Euboea, some 110 miles, with the island of Psyria "for their encouragement about midway", or should skirt the Asian coast southward and thence by Crete make their way to the Peloponnese.[2] None of them sailed for pleasure; indeed we hardly find a hint of such a thing in Greek literature, but do we in Icelandic saga? Yet it is plain that, whether they said so or not, the old Norse did enjoy the sea; and it is arguable that, if not the Achaeans, nor Homer himself (whether from Scio's rocky isle or not), there were Greeks who could as little keep off the sea as the Norse, even if they too abstained from talking about their feelings. After all, that form of relief is a late development of literature—perhaps decadent, too.

On the other hand Homer is evidence that Greeks enjoyed stories of the sea, of long wanderings, and strange lands and adventures. To-day, at all events, that is the part of the *Odyssey* that most captures us. Perhaps the return and the slaying of the suitors was as pleasing to the first hearers and to the poet; perhaps; but he also gives us a hint that there was another saga of the travels of Menelaus. Both his epics have allusions to the tale of Jason; and Odysseus tells how Jason before him ran his ship, the *Argo*, by the blessing of Hera, safely through between the Wandering Rocks. *Argo*,

1 *Works and Days*, 101.

2 See T. D. Seymour, *Life in the Homeric Age*, chapter XI, "Sea Life and Ships"; and *Odyssey*, III, 169. H. F. Tozer, *Geography of Greece*, p. 19, picks out this passage as "almost the only really reliable piece of Geography" in the *Odyssey*.

the sea-faring ship, πᾶσι μέλουσα—she indeed interests all men from the tellers of tales before Homer to the curious late poet who wrote the Orphic *Argonautica*—the last of the three epics on the hero and the Northward voyage that survive from antiquity.

Perhaps even when we are dealing with myth and legend, there is something to be said for a chronological order, if there is one, and Odysseus concedes priority to Jason. In a very interesting volume[1] Miss Janet Bacon has traced the growth of the *Argo* story, with a strong implication that the *Argo* interests men more than the Argonauts. In Apollonius Rhodius she finds Jason only "passively agreeable", and "except for his youth and beauty he is as unheroic as Aeneas".[2] An old gentleman may take a kinder view of Aeneas, I hope, in the belief that middle age, queer as youth may think it, can also have its heroism. Pindar gives us our oldest surviving tale of Jason[3], and a splendid one it is, splendid in Pindar's way with the great figure gloriously imagined and the great moment, the great outcome in fame and achievement; and you (he seems to say), who may hereafter have the Alexandrian or Cambridge mind, can fill in date and detail for yourselves.

"Tell me, what was it that first befel them in their seafaring? What was the peril that bound them with strong bolts of adamant? To Pelias came a prophecy, cold on his cunning heart, spoken at the central stone of tree-clad mother-earth—by every means to hold guard against the man of one sandal, whensoever, from the homesteads in the mountains, he shall come to the sunny land of glorious Iolcos, whether stranger or man of the city. So in the fulness of time he came, wielding two spears, a wondrous man. Raiment of two kinds was upon him, the garb of his Magnesian home close fitting to his splendid limbs; but above it the skin of a panther kept from him the lashing rain. Nor had the bright locks of his hair been shorn from him, but over his back ran rippling down. Swiftly he came and straight on, and took his stand, making trial of his dauntless soul, in the market-

1 J. R. Bacon, *The Voyage of the Argonauts*. 2 *Ib.* p. 91. 3 *Pythian*, 4.

place when the crowd was thronging it. Now they knew him not; howbeit, as they looked on him with awe, one spake to another and said: 'Surely this is not Apollo, nor verily Aphrodite's lord, of the brazen chariot....' Thus spake they; and thereon, in headlong haste of mules and polished car, came Pelias; and he was astonied as he gazed at the sandal, the one sandal, plain to see on his right foot."

So the quest is laid upon him—the sailing of the ship, the gathering of the heroes; and to the Euxine they fared, to Aietes and Medea his daughter, the fire-breathing bulls, and the stealing of the king's daughter, the passionate child, queen of Colchians. But, from old admiration of the hero with the one sandal, I have broken the course of Pindar's tale, or he broke it himself, starting it in the middle, as poets do, Ὁμηρικῶς. For he begins with a speech of Medea, far from Colchis or Greece, telling how "we had left the Ocean, and by my counsel had carried our seafaring ship twelve days over desolate ridges of land" to the waters of Lake Tritonis in Libya. At the end of his story—"Long were it for me to go by the beaten track, for the time is nigh out, and I know a certain short path and many others look to me for skill. The glaring speckled dragon he slew by subtlety, and by her own aid he stole away Medea. And they went down into the deep of Ocean, and into the Red Sea, and to the Lemnian race of wives that slay their men".

North Africa and the Indian Ocean (for that in those days, as we see in Herodotus, was the Red Sea) seem far enough from the eastern end of the Black Sea, and hardly the natural route back to Pelias and Greece; nor do days and distances seem to tally with modern Geography. But why should they? Legend brought Jason and his heroes home four different ways.[1] The obvious way was the one they took outward bound. But Apollonius sent them up the Danube, from which they portaged or somehow else got to the Adriatic, whence by the Eridanos (which, if not a poetic invention as Herodotus maintained[2], might in Jason's day have been the Po) to the

1 Cf. Scholiast to Apoll. Rhod. IV, 259; J. R. Bacon, *Voyage of Argonauts*, p. 114; Strabo, c. 46.

2 Herodotus, III, 115.

Rhone, and down the Etruscan coast, round to Corcyra, and off to Lake Tritonis. They also sailed, another tells us, through Russia up the Don to the Baltic and homeward by Gibraltar. And we have seen Pindar's route. Miss Bacon rebuts Rawlinson's conclusion that these inconsistent and wild stories prove "the unreal and poetic character of the whole". The routes, she urges, are not incredible; Pindar's is the oldest and is refuted most eagerly by the ancients; and a vessel of fifty oars would seem hard to carry so far over such ground. But some of the routes—the Rhone, the Danube, central Russia—were the trade routes by which amber came from the Baltic to the Mediterranean.[1] Possible routes for trade—or for wandering; but for one ship one route must suffice for one voyage. The Argonauts, says an ancient critic, sailed not with one ship, but with a considerable fleet. In other words, there gathered round the *Argo* the stories of many and many a pioneer voyage. That is the way of the folk-tale; the variants gravitate to the hero, and once he has begun to accumulate legend, there is no end to it, and the other great motives and stories are gradually woven in—the strange princess, the fiery bulls, the Rocks, the dragon—every strand of romance; and the saga grows and grows in wonder and interest, till at last it is too much for geographer and historian. "I think", says Pindar himself, "that the tale of Odysseus is more than ever he suffered, and all because of sweet-voiced Homer."[2]

There was great discussion in antiquity as to the historical and geographical value of what Homer wrote. Eratosthenes said:[3] "You will find the scene of the wanderings of Odysseus, when you find the cobbler who stitched up the bag of the winds". Polybius laid down a sounder canon: "To invent everything carries no persuasion, and it is not Homeric".[4] How much did he invent, then? how much did he know? Were the wonderful places, that Odysseus saw, out in the

1 J. R. Bacon, *op. cit.* chapter IX; H. F. Tozer, *History of Ancient Geography*, pp. 31 ff.

2 Pindar, *Nem.* 7, 20.

3 Strabo, c. 24.

4 Quoted by Strabo, c. 25, who has a very long discussion of Homer's geography and tries to accept as much of it as possible.

Ocean, or mostly in the Mediterranean—Sicily, Corcyra, the Straits of Messina? There was a divergence between Charybdis as described by Circe and as observed in nature. "So Circe lied"[1]—more than once, unless you call it hyperbole; and now we touch upon Circe, perhaps it was an invention of Homer's to make her sister of King Aietes of Colchis, and aunt of Medea—an invention which indeed illustrates his knowledge of Colchis and of Jason's expedition but raises questions as to how it was brother and sister lived so far apart.[2] And the Cyclops tribe suggests some free use of knowledge of Scythian Arimaspoi, about whom Aristeas wrote an epic,[3] and of whom Herodotus tells us that they were said to be one-eyed and stole gold from griffins.

The travels of Menelaus raised further questions. "The man who told Homer about Pharos, or rather the common report", put it much too far from the shore—a day's run; and nowadays it has no water on it.[4] Menelaus says he visited among other peoples Ethiopians and Erembians; but "no Ethiopians live on our sea, and it was impossible to take ships up the cataracts of the Nile". Could it be, some asked, that Menelaus made a coasting voyage by Gades (and Gibraltar) as far as India, that he was the precursor of Vasco da Gama in fact? This might explain his seven years of wandering. Or, asked others, did he sail *over* the isthmus of Suez? Eratosthenes, at least, fancied that, before the channel at the Pillars of Hercules had been burst open, the Mediterranean might have had a higher level, in which case there might have been no isthmus at Suez at all. This might allow you with Zeno to explain the Erembians as Arabs. Strabo urges that Homer did not know of India, for, if he had, he would have mentioned it. But here Strabo perhaps forgot what he said a few pages earlier[5] (as writers do[6]) to the

1 Strabo, c. 44. 2 Strabo, c. 21.
3 Strabo, c. 21; Herodotus, IV, 14.
4 Strabo, c. 37–42. 5 Strabo, c. 36.
6 If the reader thinks that the writer of this book is unaware that the same passage is sometimes quoted in more essays than one, the writer himself has noticed it. He would also plead Strabo's excuse for Homer's omissions, which Servius too made for Virgil. See p. 195.

effect that, in general, silence is no sign of ignorance; for Homer does not allude to the ebb and flow of the Euripus, nor to Thermopylae and other well-known things in Greece, which you must suppose he knew quite well. He did not even mention his own native place, which would have saved endless dispute. But whether the camel-drivers and spice-mongers of Arabia, now known as Blest,[1] were rich enough in Homer's day to make fine presents to Menelaus, and whether Erembians are etymologically derived from *eran embainein*, a name which later peoples for the sake of greater clearness changed to Troglodytes, we may perhaps postpone to another inquiry. We may conclude with Strabo that no one should quarrel with Hesiod for speaking of men who are half-dogs (he does not in his surviving works) nor with Homer for his pygmies;[2] we can allow with him that a poet may write of the wanderings of Odysseus and Jason, and insert for practical people sound lessons from the hardships these heroes underwent, while at the same time he concedes them (in moderation) no mean entertainment in the element of myth—the places being famous and the legends charming; but we shall agree that the geographer has a sterner task—and he must give us what is useful and reliable rather than what is famous and charming.

Modern students of Homer are often less worried about the Erembians. They are content to let them go, and with them the Oceanos with which the poet surrounded the world; but they note that Homer's knowledge even of the lands we call Greece has surprising limits.[3] That he does not mention Europe, and only thinks of Asia as one plain of Asia Minor, matters little. Why does he call Ithaca low-lying? they ask, and where was it? A great German would have us look for it in Leucas. Even the Argolid seems confused.

Before we leave Homer and Jason, a word or two from more modern stories of exploration may lend some light to

1 See p. 240.

2 Strabo, c. 43.

3 H. F. Tozer, *History of Ancient Geography*, pp. 20–25; T. D. Seymour, *Life in the Homeric Age*, chapter II, pp. 53, 66; cf. note on p. 2. The traveller Leake identified the Styx from Homer's description.

form our judgment. Where were the Indies, for instance? What lands did Columbus think he discovered? Distinguishing East and West Indies by and by, you would perhaps exclude Virginia from the West Indies; yet Mr P. A. Bruce says English prisoners destined for the West Indies often went to Virginia, and not by mistake. Where was Quivira, the city of gold? Where the Strait of Anian that connected Atlantic and Pacific? Where the Armenian's islands of gold and of silver east of Japan and therefore toward America? Was one of them California, rich in gold? It obviously was not; for California is not an island and it was not known to have any gold till Sutter set Marshall to dig him a mill-sluice in 1848. Yet Lower California is shown in good maps of the eighteenth century as an island; and Anian long haunted the minds of geographers. How, too, we may ask, did the name California get out of the romance of chivalry and attach itself to that land which the China galleon skirted and even missionaries could hardly colonize? And, a parallel question, how came Brazil upon the map, and what had it ever to do with South America before Vespucci? The amazing portages of the Argonauts are not altogether ludicrous, when you read of the regular routes by river and portage up the Ottawa, and from Lake Erie to the Mississippi, and many more. Birch-bark canoes and the fifty-oared *Argo*—they are very different. But portages cannot have been quite unfamiliar,[1] and one returns to the views of Polybius and Miss Bacon; there is a basis of fact for the wildest of the geography. There is an Indian Ocean, there is a Rhone, Russia has its rivers, and trade has its unmapped routes, revealed to-day in buried treasures, stray lost coins and men's graves. The poet is not a geographer; but, in days before Geography became so strictly scientific and "profitable", there was a charm in it, as Aeschylus bears witness, a poet always ready to digress to it, as Strabo notes.[2] Perhaps too *The Golden Journey to Samarcand* may remind us that even isotherms have not

1 Of course there was in historical times a shiproad at Corinth for rolling ships from one sea to the other; but that is not quite the same thing.

2 Strabo, c. 33.

driven all the charm from the face of the earth. Quebec is still romance, and must be as long as its rivers surround it and the Île d'Orléans faces it, and Wolfe and Frontenac are remembered. But let us get back to the Greek on the sea.

What took him to sea—to Colchis, of all places? Strabo suggests that the wealth of the regions round Colchis, derived from mines of gold, silver, iron and copper, may have been the motive of the Argonauts as of Phrixus before them.[1] At a later point Strabo returns to this gold of the Colchis region—alluvial gold carried down by mountain torrents and caught by the barbarians by means of perforated troughs and fleeces; and there he thinks you may have the origin of the tale of the Golden Fleece.[2] Nor again can Herodotus and Polybius have been the only Greeks who went over sea and land because some craving within drove them—the impulse to see and to inquire.

Long before Homer, the men of the Greek lands, whether one dare so early call them Greeks or not, were busy with the sea. Cnossos in Crete implies a sea trade of importance. Works of men's hands from Egypt, both in Crete and on the Greek mainland, awaited the excavator, with the ostrich egg, the amber beads, and the jade. Amber is found in a natural state in Sicily and Italy, but the great source of it has always been the Baltic, and there is a chemical difference between the two ambers. I do not know what succinic acid is, but it is not found in the Mediterranean amber; the Baltic amber has it variously from 3 to 7 per cent.; and the amber found in the Mycenaean graves has 6 per cent.[3] So the legends of Eridanus and Phaethon's sad sisters are confirmed by chemistry, and one far-ranging trade is proved for an age long before Homer. Carved ivories are also found. It was remarked by the ancients that Homer constantly mentions ivory, but not the elephant.[4] The ivory must be African. Jade of various colours is found in various places, but it is urged that New Zealand and South America may be safely ruled out. White jade is Chinese: so that a celt of white jade,

1 Strabo, c. 46.
2 Strabo, c. 499.
3 Schuchhardt, *Schliemann's Excavations*, p. 196; cf. p. 153, n. 2.
4 See p. 143.

two inches long by one across, found at Troy, may have travelled from China.[1] Stray things and stray people turn up in the unlikeliest places, and no one will wish to plead for a China town in Troy, or a regular trade connection with Pekin. Yet the presence of the thing is a witness to man's restlessness and intercourse.

But, moving downstream again, we turn once more to Homer. Whatever his Achaeans felt about the sea, they lived in a world of shipping and seafaring, of Taphian sea rovers and Phoenician traders and kidnappers—and of ship-builders in Greek waters, or nobody would have listened to a poet who could count up 1200 ships at Troy. An exaggeration, a poetic exaggeration, no doubt, but evidence of much acquaintance with the sea; and stray details in the *Odyssey* confirm it. Here we catch a glimpse of colour on the black ship—red-cheeked, it may be, or purple-cheeked, or blue-prowed. Oak, white poplar and pine are used to build ships, and they may take twenty men, or even fifty to row them; but every man can row. Oars, decks, the mast and the sails and ropes, the rudder, the landing plank, the boarding pike, all are mentioned; the beaching of the ship, that the sailors may sleep ashore; the mariner's knowledge of the stars—one thing with another gives us a fair picture of the shipping; and, if it is not fanciful so to translate ἄνοσος, we are even told of voyages without sea-sickness.[2]

After Homer comes a dark age, as all historians know. But when we find an immense colonial development at the end of those dim centuries, and 1200 ships alleged to have borne warriors to Troy before them; when we find the whole vocabulary of sea-faring is genuinely Greek, while our own is full of borrowed words, Dutch and others; when we find a wide and very accurate geographical knowledge of the Mediterranean implied in all that activity and colonization; our dark age may lack recorded episode, but we should be

1 Schuchhardt, *Schliemann's Excavations*, p. 38; see also H. R. Hall, *Oldest Civilization of Greece*, pp. 108–9.

2 For all this and much more, see T. D. Seymour, *Life in the Homeric Age*, chapter XI, "Sea Life and Ships".

able to fill it with achievement. Homer knows no Ionian cities in Asia Minor; his Miletus was Carian. When recorded history begins, the Ionians are well established on the littoral, and Miletus is the founder herself of many Greek colonies in the Black Sea.

Somewhere about the eighth century B.C., when it was beginning, some say, and others, when it was ending, but the date is uncertain though in any case early, there was a war between Chalcis and Eretria on the island of Euboea. The Euripus, the narrow strait across which Hesiod successfully voyaged, was very shallow, and its bottom was for long the home of the murex, the shellfish which, as it putrefied, yielded the purple dye:

> that dye of dyes,
> Whereof one drop worked miracles
> And coloured like Astarte's eyes
> Raw silk the merchant sells.

Greece, however, was wearing wool, not silk; and the Lelantine plain that lay between the two Euboean cities was a great grazing ground for sheep. Whichever city held it controlled the trade in purple fabrics. So they fought, and commercial cities joined in the war, each against its neighbour; Megara sided with Eretria, Corinth with Chalcis; Samos supported Chalcis, so Miletus stood in with Eretria. Whether as a result of this division, or whether the cleavage followed from older feuds, the cities sought different areas for trade and colonization; Corinth's great foundation was Syracuse, while Miletus and Megara filled the Propontis and the Black Sea with new cities.

So much is easily said, and it does not tell us much till we think about it, in the light of more modern colonization. For there we learn that it is no easy thing to plant a successful colony. All round the American coast, from the Saint Lawrence to Florida, from La Plata to California, there are records of disaster and failure, caused often by ignorance of geography, carelessness as to climate and site and neighbours, and by sheer starvation. Even California had to be supplied by sea from Mexico. The Greeks knew as little about sanitation, diet and disease as the Elizabethans, and we are not told the whole story of their colonization. If an English scholar emphasizes that the first aim of the colony was agricultural land, he may very well be right, in measure; without land of that sort, where was the food? But to find such land was the task of the seaman, and he found it. Eighty Greek colonies are said to be the work of Miletus; and, if this is true, it gives us the right to suppose a long span of years between its own foundation and the beginning of our records. That span of years will be filled by the slow consolidation of Ionian and Carian in the conquered city, by agriculture, by the development of trade connections inland to central Asia Minor, a land rich in natural resources, wool, fruits, wheat, and some minerals. Outward we must imagine a slow growth of knowledge of the sea, its rocks, shoals and currents, of the general habits of the winds, and then of the shores and their inhabitants and possibilities. Probably the first colony hung fire for longer than we know; it resulted perhaps in failure, and was followed by other reluctant attempts, by failures and half successes. That this is not all guess-work is shown by the ups and downs of the colonists of Cyrene, of which Herodotus tells us, and by the remark of Strabo that Aeolians and Ionians would have had less ill luck with their colonies if they had known more about geography.[1] Virgil's story of Aeneas and his many attempts may be myth, brought into a legendary unity by scholars before him, but it must have closely resembled many a historical episode. At last there is a genuine movement; colonization catches the imagination, and at intervals of a year or two, or of decades, the great stream of population[2] finds its new homes, and the Inhospitable Sea becomes the Euxine, in hope and in fact. It is better to give the sea a lucky name that will encourage people and not bring ill-luck; and it proved hospitable.

These new activities of Miletus—and the same will be

1 Strabo, c. 10.

2 The birth-rate must have been more on the seventeenth-century scale than the twentieth, natural rather than artificial.

as true of Corinth—meant ceaseless ship-building, regular voyages and increasing knowledge. South Russia was geologically then what it is now, a land of endless plains where grain could be grown, a land that could feed ancient Greece or almost all modern England. If it be true, as we are now told, that there was not alluvial gold, but that the gold ornaments of the Scythians of many generations, stored 20,000 of them (it is said) in the Hermitage at Petrograd,[1] were made abroad or in the country of imported gold, there was gold in Transylvania, in the Urals, and in Colchis. The Black Sea has its own characteristics, a constant outward current, fed by the rivers that pour into it; a water less salt than some other seas; shallows, especially in the Sea of Azov; and feeding grounds for ever for fish, comparable with the cod-banks of Newfoundland. There was wealth there, but fully as significant were the needs which the land could not supply. The olive would hardly grow on the northern shore, though it did at Sinope and other places on the southern;[2] and the Greek depended on the olive. It gave him the equivalents of butter, soap and electric light, all in their way pleasant and contributive for a civilized life. The long severe frosts of winter were a very different story from the climate of Syracuse and Sicily in the warmer waters. From what the land produced and from what it did not, a great commerce might be guessed, but guessing is needless. The Russian fields fed Greece for centuries, and the shallow sea gave Athens dried fish to eat with her bread. Miletus was famous for her woollens; Turkey carpets and Angora should remind us of the pastures inland on the high Asian plateau;[3] and the famous story of Thales the philosopher "cornering" the oil-presses belongs to Miletus.[4]

Sea trade is a phase of Greek life that has not had much study. Here is a handful of statements from modern books on shipping, obvious and explicable enough when you realize them, and not more true to-day than of old. "A ship is nearly

1 See p. 96.
2 Strabo, c. 73.
3 Aristophanes, *Frogs*, 542, *ἐν στρώμασιν Μιλησίοις*; Virgil, *Georgics*, III, 306.
4 Aristotle, *Politics*, I, 11, 8–10.

as costly to run empty as full; so that, if paying cargo is available only in one direction, it must be charged a higher rate to cover the cost of the complete voyage out and home. This would be true, invariably, if all ships were tied, as railway waggons in this country, to more or less fixed lines; but a ship is more flexible: since the sea is free to all, it may return by the most devious routes carrying intermediate cargo on the way. Not all ships, however, are equally flexible. The tramp wanders at will over the face of the Ocean, going wherever profitable cargo is to be found at the moment."[1] "A port which can supply an unladen ship with an outward cargo, instead of sending her away in ballast to seek elsewhere, is a port which appeals to owners."[2] "Trade makes the harbour as often as the harbour makes the trade."[3] "A hundred or a thousand miles more or less count little in the cost of ocean transport, but on land the charges grow with every mile."[4] "In very early days the inland trade-routes were at the mercy of impenetrable forests, of deep-flowing rivers and of wide-extending marsh in low-lying grounds."[5] We are also reminded of two very important factors—the hinterland which must use the port, and the facilities which the port can offer as a centre of distribution. We have not to reckon with railways in ancient Greece, which when once established may give a port a monopoly immensely hard to break. But easy roads, and passes over mountain ranges, will do for an ancient port something of the same kind. We have to remember also that, in a tideless sea like the Mediterranean, a port is always a port, and there are no opportunities such as a tidal river gives to an Atlantic town. "The war", wrote Mr Sargent in 1918, "will not alter those ultimate geographical facts on which the interchange of commodities depends";[6] and with that we may link another of his observations, even if other factors come in: "an old-established centre possesses great power of re-

1 A. J. Sargent, *Seaways of the Empire*, p. 12.
2 Douglas Owen, *Ocean Trade and Shipping*, p. 11.
3 Sargent, *op. cit.* p. 41; Owen, *op. cit.* p. 11, cites Glasgow as an instance.
4 Owen, *op. cit.* p. 9.
5 Owen, *op. cit.* p. 7.
6 Sargent, *op. cit.* p. 3.

sistance to any shifting of its traffic".[1] So Greece found when the Peloponnesian War was over: Greek traders, conservative in habit, remembered—they had never forgotten—that Spartan victory or Athenian downfall did not alter the shape of the Peiraieus, nor shift it from the centre of the Greek world.

But to return to Miletus, an earlier centre of the Greek world, and her colonies. With woollens and oil-jars to go out, and wheat, fish and perhaps some gold to come back, the ships would have freight both ways—the first step to profit in ship-owning or broking. And this interchange of commodities was permanent—so far as things in a changing world are permanent—till the Persians destroyed Miletus. At each end there was something of a hinterland; emphatically there was one, with all civilized Asia behind it, to use Miletus. Nor were the Scythians without interest in Greek arts; at least the goldsmith's, and probably the cutler's, appealed to them. Frozen seas and winter storms must be remembered, the north wind of the Aegaean, and the total absence of lighthouses and of Admiralty charts. Navigation was an art indeed.

"When the Pleiades, to escape the rude strength of Orion, plunge into the misty sea," wrote Hesiod, indicating the period we call late October to early November, "then truly rage the blasts of all the winds. Then keep ships no longer on the wine-dark sea, but bethink you to till the soil as I bid you. Haul up your ship upon the dry land, and pack it closely with stones all round to keep off the power of wet winds, and draw out the bottom-plug so that the rain of Zeus may not rot it. Put away all the tackle and shipgear in your house, and stow the wings of the sea-going ship neatly, and hang up the well-shaped rudder over the smoke. ...For fifty days after the solstice (viz. July–August), when the weary season of harvest[2] is come to an end, sailing is seasonable for men. Then you will not wreck your ship, nor will the sea destroy the sailors, save only if Poseidon the

1 Sargent, *op. cit.* p. 54.
2 A good deal earlier in Greece and Carolina than we of the North expect.

Earth-Shaker be minded to destroy them, or Zeus, the King of the deathless; for the issues of good and evil alike are with them. At that time the winds are easy to judge and the sea is harmless. Then trust in the winds, and, without fear, haul your swift ship down to the sea, and put all the freight aboard. But make all haste you can to return home again; wait not till the time of new wine and autumn rain and oncoming winter."[1] So the landsman, from observation rather than experience; and he also concedes spring sailing, though "I praise it not". All Greece was with him in avoidance of winter sailing; in war or peace it must cease, as the reader of Thucydides will remember. Modern observers speak of the difficulties of the Aegaean in winter. Oddly enough, to quote the farm poet for the last time, he anticipates a modern judgment.

"Why does size mean cheapness?" asks Sir Douglas Owen, and he gives three reasons. The big ship means economy in space; in staff and management, officers as well as crew; and in building; "one big vessel costs less to build than four little ones aggregating in the same tonnage."[2] Mr Sargent adds speed to the factors, but perhaps thinks of steam.[3] We are reminded by Rye and Winchilsea and other quaint places that big ships, if cheap ships, require more depth of water in the docks, and concentrate trade in convenient harbours which can become good centres of distribution. We shall find all this illustrated in ancient Greece; dear little old ports of the early days[4] drop out of notice, and Corinth and Athens take the trade. Meanwhile here is Hesiod on the side of the men who set the ball rolling:[5] "Praise a small ship, but put your freight in a large one;[6] for the greater the lading, the greater will be your gain, if only the winds will keep back their evil gales".

1 Hesiod, *Works and Days*, 619–677, with omissions.

2 Owen, *Ocean Trade and Shipping*, p. 50.

3 Sargent, *Seaways of the Empire*, p. 39.

4 Look at the list in the Calaureian Amphictyony, at the towns that sent ships against Xerxes.

5 Hesiod, *Works and Days*, 643–5.

6 Virgil had this line in mind, but reversed it for farms; *Georgics*, II, 412.

If a ship has to be beached for the winter, if she is to be beached from time to time in summer, if she is to be rolled across the Isthmus of Corinth—as was frequently done—she will have to be built accordingly, more or less flat-bottomed and not too heavy. Warships might be daily beached. For everything that concerns building and equipment, Mr Cecil Torr's monograph, entitled *Ancient Ships*, is the fullest and most convenient authority—not less so for his giving his quotations in full instead of referring his reader to out-of-the-way books. For the moment we need not digress to ship-building, except to note this incessant beaching and its effects. Mr Torr points out[1] that "the timber for ships never was seasoned thoroughly, as it then became too stiff to bend into the needful shapes: but, as a rule, it was allowed some while for drying after it was felled, and then for settling after it was built into a ship; for otherwise the seams were liable to expand considerably and admit the water. The seams were calked by filling them with tow and other packing, and fixing this with wax or tar". Noah, if we may trust the Septuagint translators, calked the Ark with asphalt. One result of using this imperfectly seasoned timber was the rapid degeneration of a Greek war fleet unless in perpetual care; it explains the length of time that might be required to mobilize a fleet.

The Greeks, whether they liked the sea and said so or did neither, must have been very clever with their ships. Frank Bullen in his *Men of the Merchant Service* makes the point that a ship has its individuality; she may be well and staunchly built and never leak, and "act as viciously as any buck-jumping horse".[2] Some people still may remember the *Rolling Polly*, of the old Allan Line; *Polynesian* was her official name. Many tell us that two ships built to the same design will behave quite differently at sea. The master mariner must know, that is Bullen's thesis, the queer little tricks of his ship, which she does not display at the dockside; and he must more generally—even in this day of Admiralty

1 C. Torr, *Ancient Ships*, p. 34.
2 F. T. Bullen, *Men of the Merchant Service*, pp. 30, 31.

charts—have "personal acquaintance with the route pursued".[1] How much more in days when there were no charts! He must "nurse his ship under sail with never-ceasing care"; he must be quick to avail himself of every breath of wind that serves, and to guard himself and his ship as cannily; he needs the boldness to take real risks to avoid bigger dangers, and he must always be "learning by experience the weather-signs, and all the grammar of the language that the ocean speaks in to its intimate friends". "This knowledge it is that constitutes the fine flower of seamanship as it was." But to all that Bullen here says the ancient shipmaster had to add a great deal. He sailed unlighted seas without a chart, or with only the rudiments of a manuscript chart, if one may guess so much. The reader of Mark Twain's *Life on the Mississippi* will remember that the pilot of Mark Twain's youth had to navigate a river which it was impossible to chart, as it cut new channels through an alluvial plain, washed out huge trees and choked itself with them, and had to make détours to avoid the new islands it built upon the fallen trunks. The pilot had to steer by the shapes of surviving bluffs upon the banks; he had to know the look of them in every variety of light, half-light and darkness, whether he came at them from the North or the South; and he had to be prepared to find them missing altogether on a return trip. He had to have in mind a whole unwritten science of the water, to be able to tell from colour or ripple what new treachery his river had devised since he went down or up two weeks before. In the same way the ancient Greek had to know his Mediterranean "in profile", as the Austrian Empress Elizabeth once put it—to know the profile of the coast from either approach, whatever the light. He, too, had to know the ways of water and wind—ripple of wave, movement of cloud, the water's colour and the sky's reflection—if he was to avoid shoal; and stray rocks he

1 A P. and O. captain told me that, during the War, the Admiralty would send captains of his line to Montreal, while C.P.O.S. men who knew the Straits of Belle Île, Cape Race, Cape Ray, and the ways of fog and iceberg, had to experiment with the shoals of the Red Sea.

had to learn as best he could. "A new boat and old rocks", says the caustic proverb of the Gael. And the Greek did all this. "The wise", says Pindar,[1] with his eye on the sea, "know the wind that is to blow on the day after tomorrow, and are not wrecked through eagerness for gain."

Now let us take an actual voyage, which modern scholars tell us to date about 600 B.C. It comes incidentally in another story which Herodotus tells us.[2] A Samian sea captain, Kolaios, sailing for Egypt, was driven out of his course, and relieved a man marooned upon the island Platea near the shore of the eventual Cyrene, "and left him provision for a year. They then put out to sea from the island and would have voyaged to Egypt, but an easterly wind drove them from their course, and ceased not till they had passed through the Pillars of Herakles, and came (by heaven's providence) to Tartessos.[3] Now this was at that time a virgin port; wherefore the Samians brought back from it so great a profit on their wares as no Greeks ever did of whom we have any exact knowledge, save only Sostratos of Aegina, son of Laodamas; with him none could vie". And then the exasperating historian describes the monument Kolaios set up in the Heraeum at Samos, instead of digressing as he should have and telling us how and where Sostratos did so well. And that is all about Kolaios.

Unless, of course, you like to linger and understand the story, remembering the times and the geographical knowledge of the day and the obstacles to its extension. For much of this we must turn to Strabo. Strabo emphasizes the great gains to Geography from the wars of Alexander and the conquests of the Romans;[4] but in earlier days other ways prevailed. He quotes Eratosthenes as his authority for the barbarian's habit of expelling the foreigner, for Busiris, and the more historical Carthaginian plan of drowning any Greek caught sailing to Sardinia or to The Pillars; and that, said Eratosthenes, was why stories of the West were not

1 Pindar, *Nemean*, 7, 17.
2 Herodotus, IV, 152.
3 For Tartessos, cf. Strabo, C. 148.
4 Strabo, C. 14.

believed.[1] The Romans really had opened the West, he says. So Kolaios had blundered into danger and discovery, and, driven by his gale, had the chance that Drake sought in other Spanish waters; he was interloping, with his eyes open, being a Greek. And when one day the two huge rocks loomed up with the open sea between them, and something of a current, he divined where he was, and he used his chance.

He reached Tartessos where no Greek had ever been, a virgin port so far as they were concerned; and he sold his wares to some purpose. Is it possible to guess what he brought or what he took home? He was sailing from Samos and to Egypt. Herodotus tells us that earthen jars full of wine were brought from all Greece and from Phoenicia to Egypt;[2] yet you never, as you might say, see a single wine jar about the country; they are all used to carry water across the desert.[3] (One thinks of the great variety of uses to which old petrol tins are put in India.) Kolaios may have carried pottery too; we are told that ancient Italy was at one time full of Samian ware. Either commodity may well have sold at fabulous prices at Tartessos. We remember what the Cyclops and the King of the Ethiopians[4] thought of Greek wine. As to what he brought home, we may perhaps borrow a hint from his contemporary, Jeremiah, the prophet in Jerusalem, who says "silver spread into plates is brought from Tarshish".[5] All through antiquity Spain was noted for its mines; they were immensely productive, as Strabo tells us in his interesting section about the country, drawn largely from Polybius and Posidonius. The goods once sold, and the silver aboard, the next thing was to find the way back to Samos, to dodge the Carthaginians on the sea and to note landmarks for a future venture. Whether he went round by the mouth of the Rhone, for he was sure to coast—that was the sailor's habit, and it was landmarks he sought—or sailed along the North coast of Africa (three days for a modern

1 Strabo, c. 802.

2 See p. 90 for the story of another Greek who took wine to Egypt about this very time.

3 Herodotus, III, 6.

4 Herodotus, III, 22.

5 Jeremiah x. 9 (A.V.). The LXX προσβλητόν and the Vulgate *involutum* are not very clear.

tramp steamer), we cannot tell; but the latter, if not more dangerous, seems more probable. At all events he reached Samos, or Herodotus could not have seen the bronze crater of six talents (the tithe of their profits), with the griffins' heads on its rim, and the three colossi of bronze, seven cubits high, that supported it. Sixty talents, £15,000, and worth to-day some ten times as much—no wonder he wanted the landmarks!

Egypt was the destination of Kolaios, and, for centuries, of more of his countrymen than we can attempt to compute. They began by raiding along with Carians—"men of bronze", whose armour seemed to fulfil the oracle given to Psammetichos—and he enlisted them with such happy results, that down to the Persian conquest even nationalist kings of Egypt must have Greek mercenary troops. They came to trade, as we have seen, and at last had a city of their own, Naucratis. Of the reactions, many and various, of Egypt and its fauna and flora, its mysterious river, its strange inhabitants and their ancient religion, upon the Greek mind, it is hardly our present business to speak. But, as often in our own history, it was the seafaring man who brought home the incredible data that perplexed home-keeping minds and set them in their turn voyaging through strange seas of thought. And in Egypt tales were told of a Red Sea beyond the long and all but impossible Arabian Gulf. These are not our names; their Arabian Gulf is our Red Sea, a forty days' sail for them from North to South, for us three unsufferable days on a steamer. The Suez Canal made many changes—one, a big one, in the numbers of sailing ships that plied to the East. "The Red Sea", says Mr Sargent,[1] "was hardly a possible route for a sailing ship owing to the prevailing winds." It cannot have been much better in antiquity, but we must postpone the Eastward voyage.

Meanwhile here was the situation, with a new problem. Westward an Ocean had been found outside Spain and outside Africa, a huge open sea of colder water and heavier gales, reaching Northward—but how far? and Southward. "I know

1 A. J. Sargent, *Seaways of the Empire*, p. 52.

of no river Oceanos," says Herodotus,[1] "and I suppose that Homer or some older poet invented this name and brought it into his poetry"; nor could he speak exactly (ἀτρεκέως) of the farthest parts of Europe to the West, "nor have I knowledge of Cassiterides islands whence the tin comes to us."[2] The tin had been coming to them since Homer's time, or before; and, if we are truly informed as to its natural distribution in the Western world, it came from islands off the Atlantic coast of Spain or from Cornwall.[3] It is idle to say that Cornwall is not strictly an island; neither is California, as we saw. But Herodotus knew very well there was sea outside the Pillars; and, if others liked to guess that it was the original Oceanos, and ran round Northern Europe, to the bounds of which no man had gone or was to go for centuries, Herodotus did not wish to guess about Geography. Egypt had now made known that to the East of Africa there was another huge sea, their Red Sea, our Indian Ocean. Were they one sea, or two seas that met?

Herodotus is able to tell us that Africa is surrounded by sea,[4] save only at the Isthmus of Suez; "and this was first proved (so far as we know) by Necos, king of Egypt. When he had made an end of digging the canal which leads from the Nile to the Arabian Gulf,[5] he sent Phoenicians in ships, charging them to sail on their return voyage past the Pillars of Herakles, till they should come into the Northern sea (the Mediterranean) and so to Egypt. So the Phoenicians set out from the Red Sea and sailed the Southern sea; whenever autumn came, they would put in and sow the land, to whatever part of Libya they might come, and there await the harvest; and then, when they had gathered in the crop, they sailed on, so that, after two years had passed, it was in the third that they rounded the Pillars of Herakles and came to Egypt. There they said (what some may believe, though I

1 Herodotus, II, 23.

2 Herodotus, III, 115.

3 Strabo, c. 175, 176, quite clearly does *not* identify them with any British isles.

4 Herodotus, IV, 43.

5 Cf. Herodotus, II, 158; this canal was older than Necos; it was dug again by Darius and was restored by the Ptolemies and by Trajan.

do not) that in sailing round Libya they had the sun on their right hand"—i.e. to the North of them; and this incredible detail has convinced moderns that the circumnavigation was actually achieved, though Mr Tozer is sceptical.[1]

Another attempt from the West was an admitted failure. A Persian noble was ordered to do it, and he sailed out, and down the coast "along a country of little men who wore palm-leaf raiment", who always fled to the hills when the sailors landed; and the reason of his eventually turning back was that the ship could make no headway but was stopped. This Xerxes refused to believe;[2] for he at least could have no knowledge of trade winds which blow all summer without cessation on the coast of Guinea. But even if the Gorilla country discovered in West Africa by Hanno and his Carthaginians tempt us, we had better sail back with Sataspes, if we desert him in mid-Mediterranean.[3]

It has been remarked[4] that the Greeks kept away from the Adriatic and its coasts. Wind and sea were against their using it. One of the most prevalent winds blows directly down it; the sea is choppy about the entrance; the harbours on the Italian side were not inviting; on the Balkan side the mountains come down to meet the sea, they cut off any possible hinterland, they intercept the clouds and precipitate far too much rain and cold to please the Greeks or most other people. There was no need yet for a Venice to hold the gorgeous East in fee, and be the safeguard of the West. There were no German customers North of the Alps to develope either a Venice or a Genoa. Athens was so far the world's centre—the Greek world's centre, or Miletus, if we are still awaiting the Persian. The lands North of the Black Sea were no doubt colder than the Adriatic, as Canada is colder than Britain, but cold is less depressing than rain to anybody but Englishmen; and the Adriatic had not the wheat fields of the Euxine.

1 H. F. Tozer, *History of Ancient Geography*, pp. 99 ff.

2 Herodotus, IV, 43.

3 Yet other African voyages are mentioned on p. 245.

4 See J. L. Myres, "Geography and Greek Colonization," *Proceedings of Classical Association*, 1911.

But the name *Magna Graecia* tells of abundance of good land and good havens in a genial West, and reminds us of the early prosperity of Croton and Sybaris, and the longer greatness of Tarentum and the towns of Campania, and above all of Syracuse. Gradually, one would suppose, Syracuse became the gateway of the West, as New York did in virtue of the Hudson, and eclipsed its rivals almost as effectually as New York did Perth Amboy. A great port, a fortress, a seat of empire—it is not necessary here to try to rival Pindar, striving like crows against the divine bird of Zeus,[1] as he said in one of his Sicilian poems, nor to tell again in summary the story from the first Hiero to the last. City and story signalize the triumph of the Greek on the sea; and, even if ashore he failed to drive the Semite out of Sicily, he had his full share of control of the Western waters. Massilia is a more distant outpost on a more significant site, less important by far in the great days of Greece, in spite of its being the port for the overland trade through Gaul, the port to which British tin came on the backs of mules, or by river and portage, for shipment all over the Mediterranean; but with such a hinterland it was destined in time to surpass its Sicilian and Italian rivals.

One or two points, perhaps of minor interest, may be noted before we look at Massilia's greatest achievement in antiquity. Probably of all ancient dates, apart from eclipses which can be calculated to an hour, the years of the foundation of colonies are the most secure. Who knows when York was founded? But New York is another story—the occupation of Manhattan and the mouth of the Hudson, with its great waterways North and West[2] into the continent, implies thought and purpose based on real geographical knowledge, a design planned in detail by a group of commercial people in a highly developed community; and the settlers remembered well enough when they came. It is even on record that the sum of £5 was paid for Manhattan Island to the

1 *Olympian*, 2, 67.

2 The significance of the Mohawk river and valley for early settlement and trade and modern railroad is illuminative.

Indians; it has gone up in value. Year by year the colony had its troubles, its problems of food and war. Probably the dates were remembered with very much the same certainty and the same emotion in Greek colonies. Again, we have to note how food products, wheat, lard, hides and so forth, are sent from Sicily to Greece, and how manufactured articles travel back—glazed pottery for Italian tribes, fine woollens for Sybaris, Lydian slippers and other luxuries for all who begin to accumulate wealth and to care for looks or for comfort. There were intellectual reactions too. In New York twenty years after its foundation, so a Jesuit from Quebec tells us, eighteen languages were spoken. Probably Syracuse heard fewer; but its very mixed population had not the strong conservative traditions of a single old home-town. The presence on the island of a powerful enemy and trade rival, with impregnable fortresses, meant that, however far Syracusans plunged into reckless democracy, they were liable to swing back into autocratic government. Hiero and Agathocles were, in a sense, called out and created by the Carthaginian menace. They were extremely able men, and represented a type of tyranny different in the long run from that familiar even in Corinth, though the colonizing despot Periander and Pisistratus may suggest a likeness. The Syracusans, the Corinthians, the Athenians, all think of the sea, and handle its problems and opportunities with brilliant success. But Agathocles represents empire; and the experience of Syracuse was a constant reminder, or should have been, that different situations mean different forms of government, and that urban democracy is not the last word in politics.[1] The West anticipated what the East experienced under the Macedonian rulers. In another sphere, the Western offered to the Eastern Greek new conceptions of style—the sort of challenge that America has given England in Henry James and William Randolph Hearst. But Sicily may urge that, if we have had Gorgias from overseas, we are still waiting for Theocritus. We are accustomed to look on Athens as did

1 Readers, who have recently visited Syracuse, may at this point recall pictures of a more recent *duce* than Agathocles stuck upon the house walls.

the men criticized by Polybius,[1] and (six centuries later) by Synesius,[2]—as the very centre, origin, and home of all culture—the city that was (in Thucydides' phrase) "the education of Greece". But if Athens was the centre, much came in the way of intellectual stimulus from the circumference. It is Scythia, Egypt, Libya that suggest the criticisms to Herodotus; and Gelo of Syracuse made pungent criticism, too.

But the most amazing of all Western Greeks belonged to Marseilles. Pytheas went too far afield in genuine exploration, and offered his age far too much new geography, to be believed. His writings perished; those of his critics most luckily survived—for Polybius and Strabo would have been horrible losses—and they, the outstanding writers on the subject, condemn Pytheas. Pytheas, they tell us,[3] has misled many; for he asserts that he travelled over all of Britain that was accessible, that the island's coastline is 40,000 stades; he adds his story about Thule and the regions where there is no longer land, properly so-called, or sea, or air, but stuff like "sea-lungs", and he says he saw it himself; and on his way back he visited, he says, the whole coastline of Europe from Gades to the Tanais. Polybius would sooner believe Euhemerus' romance of Panchaea, rather than that Pytheas, a man without financial resources, explored in person the whole northern region of Europe to the world's ends—not even Hermes would be believed if he made such a claim. Thule, Pytheas says,[4] is a six days' sail North of Britain and is near the frozen sea; he is a liar *in excelsis*. He says Britain is 20,000 stades long, and that Kantion (Kent) is several days' sail from the Celtic country; and he lies about the Ostimians (Brittany) and about the land beyond the Rhine toward Scythia. So Strabo dismisses his contributions, and then drops a hint that Pytheas calculated the relation of the dial index (the gnomon) to the shadow for Massilia[5]—in other words the latitude, and got it right, moderns tell us.[6]

1 Polybius, XVIII, 4.

2 People who have seen Athens, wrote Synesius, *Ep.* 54, "move among us like demigods among demi-donkeys".

3 Strabo, c. 104.

4 Strabo, c. 63.

5 Strabo, c. 63; 71.

6 Cf. T. Rice Holmes, *Ancient Britain*, p. 219.

Strabo himself places Ireland to the North of Britain, which Pytheas had put to the West. From Strabo and from other sources we learn of other achievements or statements of Pytheas; he circumnavigated Britain; he maintained the connection of the tides with the moon (which Plutarch muddled up horribly); he was told in the extreme North that yet further North was the sleeping-place of the sun where the nights would be only two hours sometimes; he indicated the shape of the Bay of Biscay; he saw extraordinary tides either in Pentland Firth or the Severn, as you prefer to interpret; he was impressed with the gloominess of the British climate, where threshing had to be done under cover for fear of rain; he saw St Michael's Mount and talked of ingots of tin. Altogether he was too much for Polybius and Strabo, though he had friendlier readers in Eratosthenes and Hipparchus, and he fairly fascinates modern geographers and modern Britons, who after all know more than his critics about what he, spelling in an old style, calls the Pretanic Isles. Thule was the most northern of them, he said; and moderns are divided as to whether Mainland in the Shetlands, Iceland or Norway was meant. The history of exploration warns us to expect errors in distances, in names, and in explanation—and in quotation by the explorer's critics. But the amazing thing about Pytheas is not the occasional error, but the frequency of his being right, the freshness of his mind and the range of his observations.[1]

Once or twice so far we have alluded to Athens, and always swung off again. Her story it is needless to tell here; it is the very staple of our higher education. But one or two things in it must be recalled, which have only of late begun to gain the attention they deserve. The ancients thought of Solon as a sage, a teacher of morals, and a law-giver. To moderns he appears as a pioneer economist of great power, and they stress not so much his political as his economic work. He changed the basis of Attic currency; he turned the emphasis in Athenian life from agriculture to manufacture and

1 See H. F. Tozer, *History of Ancient Geography*, chapter VIII; and T. Rice Holmes, *Ancient Britain*, chapter IV; most interesting chapters, both.

commerce; he encouraged the settlement in his country of foreigners (Greeks mostly, we may presume) who could bring a trade, a craft, an industry with them, and would establish it there;[1] he did away with laws relating to interest and to the making of wills, which discouraged venture and activity and the use of brains, and in these ways he liberated Athenian energy from the bonds of sentimentalism and parochial morality. In all he realized that the Athenian mind was the chief asset of Athens. But it is emphasized that his other supreme discovery was that of a more general economic law—that a nation need not grow all its own food. On this discovery, as we all know, Athens lived for two centuries at all events, and probably more. It meant sea power; an open sea for Athenian trade, and free passage for wheat from the Black Sea to the Peiraieus. If the Suez Canal is the key of the British Empire, Byzantium was the key of the Athenian.[2]

The decline of Athens began when Pericles fell in with the vulgar opinion of his day, and put strict limits on Athenian citizenship, reversing the plan of Solon. The fall of Athens came when she lost control of the sea, at the Dardanelles. Her recovery she owed to the sea. The Peiraieus was still the great harbour, still approximately the centre of the world's trade. No Persia was there to destroy Athens as Miletus was destroyed—a destruction to which then, as in our days to the Turkish destruction of Smyrna, Athens had owed much. Sparta was not interested in the aggrandizement either of Corinth or of Thebes; she could not use the Peiraieus herself; so she left it to the Athenians, and Athens recovered—slowly but not ineffectually. The place was, as Isocrates said,[3] "an *emporion* in the very midst of Greece", where all commodities were brought and could be had—a centre of distribution. A nameless economist of his day, whose pamphlet entitled *Poroi* (Revenues) is usually printed with the shorter works of Xenophon, emphasizes the same point, writing much like

1 See pp. 52, 88.

2 On Byzantium see an interesting chapter in Polybius, II, 38: "as the Black Sea has many of the products which the rest of mankind need to live, the Byzantines control the whole of them".

3 Isocrates, *Panegyric*, 41, 42.

our own shipping experts. You can always get into the Peiraieus, whatever the wind, and it is handy when you are in. In most places you have to wait for a return freight; freight of all sorts is always available at the Peiraieus for the ports of all the seas; or, if none suits you, Athenian currency is good everywhere; cash or cargo, there need be no demurrage. And Athens is not a bad place, either, very pleasant and profitable; and he suggests that Athenians might develope their amenities and opportunities. More regard for merchants and traders, better hotels near the docks, more attention to foreigners who might domicile themselves in the place, above all a settled policy of peace—these are the true lines for Athens.

In earlier days conquest had been the plan—you must conquer to govern—as the Persians did. Or if not conquest, control; as the people who talked up Sicilian projects in the fifth century saw—a friendly government, a democracy helped from outside, was the thing. The new economist forswears these adventures; trust commerce, and make things right for the business world; if you can control commerce, you need no conquering expeditions, no subsidized revolutions.

A generation passed, and the whole balance of the world was changed. Alexander was king, and the Far East had been opened up. Politically, financially, commercially, it was a new world. Politically, because the new units of government were so large and so heterogeneous in blood, tradition, and interest, that no democracy was possible; monarchy was inevitable. Financially, because the age-long hoards of Persia were liberated[1], and gold and silver in unheard-of quantity moved Westward to new areas and new hands; Aetolia and Elis[2] are rich now, but the kings richest of all; and money gravitates to money. Commercially, because new trade-routes link up the Mediterranean and India, or old ones under new and better control, with new centres of distribution on the Euphrates, on the Orontes, and on the Nile delta. With the politics we are not here concerned, and much of the trade was overland.

1 See p. 74.
2 On the prosperity of Elis, cf. Polybius, IV, 73.

But Arrian tells us of Alexander's interest in the sea. If his one book was his Homer, he did not (shall we say?) forget that sea power sacked Troy. He definitely planned to control the Mediterranean by holding the big ports;[1] and he did it. He would not leave Tyre behind him in other hands, and he founded Alexandria. Once he held the coast, the Persian fleet could have no base, to replenish or to refit; and there was an end of it; it should henceforth make no trouble behind him by starting wars in Greece. But, arrived in India, after his long overland march, Alexander wishes to know where exactly he is. He reached and crossed the Indus—"the greatest river of Asia or Europe except the Ganges", Arrian tells us. He saw crocodiles in the Indus, brutes peculiar to that river and the Nile;[2] he saw on the banks of the Akesines beans familiar in Egypt; he learnt that the Akesines is a tributary of the Indus; could he really be on the upper waters of the Nile? It flows through deserts and might easily lose its name before it reaches Ethiopia and Egypt and the inward sea. He wrote to Olympias that he thought he had found the sources of the Nile.[3] But he inquired further into the river-system and learnt from the natives that the Indus flows into the Great Sea. And then Arrian tells the story of the king's voyage down the river, of his battles by the way, of the strong wind blowing upstream, and the surprise of the tides of the Indian Ocean. And it was like him not to return till he had sailed out on to that Ocean himself—chiefly for the sake of doing it, Arrian thinks, "that he might be able to say that he had navigated the great outer sea of India".[4] He next sailed down the other channel of the Indus to learn which was the easier.

Alexander had now another ambition—to sail back from the mouth of the Indus to Persia, coasting the lands between, a real voyage of exploration, though it had been done by Scylax of Caryanda, a notable Greek on the sea, at the

1 Cf. Arrian, *Anabasis*, I, 20, 1; II, 18, 4.

2 As to crocodiles, the same argument led Herodotus to conjecture the identity of the Nile and the Niger, Herodotus, II, 32; but he knew the Indus had them (IV, 44) on the authority of Scylax of Caryanda.

3 Arrian, *Anabasis*, VI, 1.

4 Arrian, *Anabasis*, VI, 19, 5.

command of Darius.[1] It was not feasible for Alexander; and his men in general shirked it, from cowardice, we are told, or homesickness, however much the king might plead, till Nearchus undertook it. He achieved it, too; and his story is epitomized in Arrian's book on India, and modern critics recognize the accuracy of the admiral's observation and the truth of his story.[2]

By Arrian's day exploration had gone further. The Ptolemies were naturally interested in the lands whose trade came to their great capital. They restored the old canal from the Nile to the sea we call Red, and founded colonies on the coast and as far as the island of Socotra. Indeed papyrus fragments have been found of a farce, in which shipwrecked Greek mariners on a barbarous coast are entertained by the king of the place. His speech was not immediately intelligible, but the Greeks took his remarks to be invitations to drink, and all went well. An Oriental scholar has recently maintained, though he has not quite convinced everybody, that this hospitable prince spoke Canarese, one of the four languages of Southern India and more especially of the Malabar coast.[3] A *Periplus* of the Red Sea is still extant, an anonymous work describing the coasts apparently from Pemba or Zanzibar to Nelcynda[4] in Malabar. It seems to be really a guide for travelling merchants, of a kind not unfamiliar in the Roman Empire, with information as to harbours and anchorages, winds and tides, and natives. There was a great deal of trade with India; Roman coins have been found at Ootacamund "by the coolie load", we are told, and we read of 120 ships in a season sailing from the African coast for India,[5] and bringing back parrots and pearls and pepper, jewels and Chinese silks.[6] In some ways the most interesting thing of all is the knowledge and use of the monsoon, which bore in ancient times a Greek name, the name

1 Herodotus, IV, 44.
2 Cf. H. F. Tozer, *History of Ancient Geography*, p. 141.
3 Cf. M. P. Charlesworth, *Trade Routes and Commerce of the Roman Empire*, p. 59.
4 Kottayam.
5 See p. 252.
6 See H. G. Rawlinson, *Intercourse between India and the Western World*; and E. H. Warmington, *The Commerce between the Roman Empire and India*.

of the man associated with its discovery. It is a matter of discussion how far Hippalos actually sailed himself in reliance on his wind, whether he only made Northern India, or whether by sailing closer to the wind (τραχηλίζειν) he went straight across to the Bombay coast. Later merchants found that the wind would allow them a still more direct passage, straight to the pepper country of Malabar, and in due season as straight back to their Arabian Gulf.[1] Pliny complains that a million sterling in gold and silver went from the Roman Empire every year to Indians and Chinese and "that peninsula;—so much our luxuries and our ladies cost us".[2]

It is not quite certain when Hippalos made his discovery. Strabo makes no allusion to it, writing in the reign of Augustus. Pliny and the author of the *Periplus*, writing after 50 A.D., both know of it; for the latter Hippalos is "a respected memory". In any case there is no geographical or commercial obstacle in the way of our accepting the most famous of all Eastern voyages. St Paul travelled freely about the Mediterranean, with one or two shipwrecks; St Thomas could as easily have had a passage to India in the same decades. But that hardly proves that he really went to India. His grave is shown outside Madras, and a little further off in an old church on a hill the cross that he carved. He certainly did not carve the inscription round the cross. King Gundaphar in his story was a real king, but a king in Northern India, far from Malabar or Madras. Dr J. N. Farquhar in the *Bulletin* of the Rylands Library[3] assembles the evidence, with a leaning toward belief. The most interesting of all apocryphal *Acts*, a Syriac production, perhaps of the end of the second century, more probably of the third, or perhaps even of later date, tells the amazing adventures of the saint, adventures so odd and so hard to link together as to perplex every reader, till Dr Rendel Harris suggested a clue; the ingenious author was transferring the

1 See Rawlinson, *op. cit.* p. 110; Warmington, *op. cit.* pp. 49 ff.; Pliny, *Nat. Hist.* VI, 26; *Periplus Maris Erythraei*, § 56. See also G. F. Hudson, *Europe and China*, pp. 98–101.

2 Pliny, *Nat. Hist.* XII, 84.

3 Volumes X and XI, Jan. 1926; Jan. 1927.

myths of the Heavenly Twins to the twin apostle and his divine brother Jesus Christ.[1] But here we may seem to be deserting from our ship.

But, before we leave our subject altogether, one more Greek voyage, a short voyage by a landsman, deserves note—not that any new discovery was made upon it or any supreme adventure, but that it gives in the liveliest language a true and vivid description of a very ordinary if rather stormy voyage from Alexandria to Cyrene. It was written by Synesius to his brother shortly after 400 A.D., and it is perhaps the only thing of the kind that survives from the ancient world, a cheery and amusing private document in which a letter-writer of genius tells over for family enjoyment the story of a real voyage. The captain was a Jew, so deep in debt that he did not care if he never made port; a downright Maccabee on the issue of Sabbath labour, he would not bestir himself in spite of the rising gale, whatever the soldier passengers said or did, till real peril burst on them, when his law, he said, permitted him to work. The announcement was received with screams by the women. Our letter-writer was haunted by a line of Homer—

> Ajax drank of the salt sea wave and utterly perished;

did it mean, he wondered, that death by drowning extinguished the soul as well as the breath? Meanwhile the soldiers stood with drawn swords, resolved not to drown; so instinct was evidently on Homer's side. And then some cheerful person urged all who had any gold to hang it round their necks; it was an old tradition that the dead washed up from a wreck should bring with him the price of his burial; it would not be canny for anybody to take the gold and not bury him. Synesius had borrowed money for the passage, and here they were racing under full sail to death; and what would the lender do? Perhaps he would be less ashamed if, like Ajax, he should utterly perish. But landsmen are not always drowned when they expect to be.

But it is time that we also left the sea—perhaps with a fresh

1 See *The Dioscuri in Christian Legends*, chapter II.

interest in the Greek's long centuries of adventure upon it, and some gratitude to him for his mastery of it, the cleverness that learnt to know the ways of wind and water, and, when all else failed, in the absence of chart and compass, could and did steer by the stars, and added astronomy to the gains brought home from the sea.

DIET IN HISTORY

πρῶτον μὲν οὖν ὑπάρχειν δεῖ τροφήν.
Aristotle, *Pol.* VIII, 8, 7, p. 1328 b.

"HE carried his victorious arms from Tobago to St Domingo, from St Domingo to St Lucia, from St Lucia to Guadeloupe. This was the traditional mode of making war on France." In these caustic sentences Goldwin Smith describes the operations of Pitt as war minister fighting Napoleon who made war on quite different lines, less traditional lines. Tradition emphasized the importance of the West Indies. Readers of Jane Austen remember how she sends Sir Thomas Bertram to Antigua, and brings him back at the wrong moment, thinner, with "the burnt, fagged, worn look of fatigue and a hot climate", but cheerful as one who had escaped the French privateer. Mr A. H. Norway, in his charming book, *The Post-office Packet Service*, has much to tell us of the Indies and the privateers,—worse still in 1812 when Mr Madison made that war upon us, which Heaven punished by giving a victory over the British and two presidencies over the Americans to Andrew Jackson. Atlantic trade before the American revolution had been on a three-cornered route, between Britain, New England and the West Indies; and the Americans were shocked to find what independence cost them in being cut out of the islands. Strangest of all, when one looks at the story of two and a half centuries, it is recorded that Oliver Cromwell suggested to the Puritan settlers in Massachusetts and Connecticut that they might with advantage remove to Jamaica. The centuries of our Empire have seen the West Indies in the very forefront of our possessions, in the very thick of our political struggles, and at last in the background of everyone's memory. What is the clue?

One great feature of History is that there are always more clues than one, that a variety of causes produces the significant movements. But in the study, if not in parliament, it is safe to isolate a factor, if one realizes that analysis is one thing and life quite another. There are many clues to great movements, many keys to every great issue, and all have to be used at once. But one key to a great deal of West Indian history, and to other phases of the world's history not unconnected with it, is Sugar.

The name and the thing come from the Orient.[1] That sugar goes with tea and coffee in having a name that you cannot translate but can only transliterate as best your language may allow, is evidence enough that it is a thoroughly foreign thing. The ancient world depended entirely on honey, if it wished its food sweetened: for you would hardly count isolated barbarians who do without bees—people like those of Callatêbos on the Maeander, where craftsmen make honey out of the tamarisk and wheat, and the Libyan Gyzantes "among whom much honey is made by bees and a great deal more, they say, by men". In Assyria the fruit of the palm was used for the same purpose.[2] Such occasional local exceptions do not disprove the main fact that the bee had a monopoly in the ancient world which it has not now, and was honourably entitled to the Fourth *Georgic*. There is physiologically, we are told, a slight advantage in honey over sugar, cane or beet.

The sugar cane was early introduced from India into Persia; and thence the plant was carried by the Arabs to Egypt,[3] North Africa and even to Spain.[4] The Portuguese took it to Madeira, the Spaniards to the Canary Islands; and thence, we are told variously, as early as 1505, or even by Columbus on his second voyage, the cane was transplanted to the islands with which we chiefly associate it—a historical fact which of

1 Indian sugar was known to the Hellenistic world, but only used as medicine; W. W. Tarn, *Hellenistic Civilization*, p. 205. Cf. Pliny, *Nat. Hist.* XII, 32; *saccharum*, white, fragile and medicinal. So the Crusaders regarded it (cf. W. Heyd, below), *e.g.* for chest troubles.

2 Herodotus, VII, 31; IV, 194; I, 193.

3 Cf. D. G. Hogarth, *The Nearer East*, pp. 202, 203, on sugar in Egypt: "The culture of both cotton and sugar has altered the conditions of *fellahin* life more than anything in six thousand years, except those railways which the profit of the new cultures has made profitable". He notes the growth of Alexandria from 5000 population in 1805 to a city of 300,000; and discusses the effect of sugar, which as a food has improved the vitality of the race, but the large flooded areas required are less obvious blessings, and criminals find the cane-beds convenient.

4 Cf. W. Heyd, *Histoire du Commerce au Levant au Moyen-Âge*, vol. II, pp. 680 ff.

itself should set us inquiring. The West Indies produced a better sugar, and in abundance, and captured the market. If the quest of gold was the spur of the Spaniard, native labour was wanted on the plantations as well as in gold-washing or gold-mining; and, as we all know, it gave out, and had to be supplemented, on the advice or with the approval of Las Casas, by negro labour. Sugar was not the sole cause of West Indian negro slavery, but it was among the initial causes, and came at last to be the supreme cause of the negro remaining in slavery. It was but a step from the Indies to the Southern colonies on the mainland which were also known for a while as the Indies; and negro slavery passed over to America, where indeed the crops to be produced by negro labour were not of sugar but of tobacco and rice, and eventually of course of cotton, after Eli Whitney of Connecticut had invented the cotton-gin, a machine to sever the seeds from the fibre which not even a negro slave could fail to work. Not all the consequences of African bondage must be put down to sugar, then, but on sugar the whole struggle for emancipation centred in the days of Clarkson and Wilberforce, and indirectly from sugar came the American Civil War, and the hideous troubles involved by the presence of the African in North and South America. Diet, it will be allowed, can have amazing consequences in history.

But we are not quite done with sugar. Pitt captured the sugar islands, and cut off from France her supplies of what had become in two or three centuries absolutely necessary to life. Napoleon, to meet the emergency, mobilized French botanists, horticulturists and chemists, to make France independent of Indies and sugar-cane together by giving her a new sugar and a new industry, whose staple was the beet. Later French economists of the type who safeguard, protect and stimulate industries, conceived the plan of encouraging this one, and gave a bounty for the manufacture of beet sugar which soon found an increasing market in England. The French taxpayer paid some part of the price of every pound of it, and the English purchaser found the balance, and it was less than the West Indian charged, for the West Indian taxpayer was less generous—or less foolish. Then arose an outcry, when the price of sugar fell and fell again, and the beet captured the market from the cane. An English government, anxious in a short-sighted way to help our dependencies, discriminated against the bounty-fed French beet-sugar, and then realized—or more probably failed to realize—how large a part in national life was held by cheap sugar, on the table, but far more in sweets, chocolates, other confectionery and jams—every one of which was hit by this method of fighting the bounty. French sugar was for English purposes the raw material—or an essential one among them—on which English industries depended, and with them English diet and English health, as the European war of 1914 was to teach us.

Politics, industry, human life, and human suffering, war and peace and prosperity—all affected by a single article of diet which was quite unknown to the ancients. On such trifles turn the fates of nations—if they are trifles. And the reflection rises how little interest in general through the centuries History or—to be more matter-of-fact—historians have taken in diet. They have recognized, of course, famine when they met it; they have seen what men will do in besieged fortresses; they have recorded bread riots; but, broadly, their attention has been occupied more by quantity than by quality; they have been content when the people have not complained of shortage, but not very curious as to the variety of their food, its sources, and the effects its consumption might have on health or its procurement on national policy. It is, on the whole, only in modern times that the economic historians have tried to redress the balance.

Yet Herodotus must escape this reproach. Few things are more surprising in the history of criticism than the casual and good-humoured contempt that critics have had for the most readable and lovable of all historians. He was so easy to read that they hardly noticed what they read. There is a Puritanism that has nothing to do with religion, or the love of truth—an instinctive feeling in every pedant (and they terrorize their disciples into believing it) that, if you enjoy an author, he cannot be really good. Now Herodotus travelled a great deal, and even if here and there people vexed him with chatter about tin islands and mythical rivers (Eridanos for instance and Oceanos), he was a much more leisurely and genial traveller than Thucydides or Polybius. One would not say that he cross-examined people less, but that they did not notice it; they were not forever being required to be "accurate", and they talked naturally about themselves; and the great man noticed their contradictions and used his eyes as well as his ears. And one thing which he constantly notes, and which he constantly records, is diet. He analyses the regimen of the Egyptians, healthiest of men—no doubt, partly because of their climate, but partly due to their monthly purges and emetics. Their land has no vines; so, when Sappho's brother and Kolaios and other Greek traders do not bring wine, or charge too much for it, they use a "drink made of barley"; they live on fish, sun-dried or preserved in brine, or quails and ducks and small birds salted and raw, and other fish and birds roasted or boiled. They also use the lotus root and castor oil, which they call *kiki*. And so he goes about the world, and in Babylonia finds tribes who use nothing but fish dried and pounded up; on the Araxes river, eaters of roots and dried fruit, who smoke what was perhaps hemp. The Scythians live on wheat, onions, garlic, and so on; the Libyans on locusts and dates, and some of them on monkeys; the Massagetae eat fish and live-stock and their aged relatives. On the other hand he marks taboos: the Egyptian will not eat beef, nor the Libyan the flesh of the pig, just as we Anglo-Saxons will not touch the horse, for a sacred reason.

It will be noted among these various diets, which Herodotus records, that a fairly large place has to be filled with preserved foods. Here, with the ancient world before us, and the changes evident in the last two centuries (particularly in America and other "new" countries), we are led to reflect that not all seasons of the year will yield food to the numbers of men who may want it. Some lands, like certain regions of South Africa, abound for a while in wild life. The western prairies in America were covered with bison at the right time of the year, and you had to make pemmican while the buffalo grazed.

But animals shift their pastures; birds migrate; and, as Labrador hunters point out, so small a thing as the field mouse, with its cycle of furious reproduction, will alter the whole balance of Nature. The caribou avoids mouse-polluted pastures; but game-birds abound in mouse years, because all their enemies, from the bear to the hawk and even the fish, find mice an easier prey.[1] So much for the uncertainties of the wild. But North America and South Africa remind us that man may kill off the wild animals quicker than they reproduce themselves; and when he has destroyed the obvious supply which wild Nature gave, he has to find something else. As human population spreads, the wild life recedes; and a land once abundant may become one of starvation. The preservation of food becomes a national problem; though assemblies will not often debate it, it comes into every family conclave. Gradually national habits of diet change and much more changes with them, which it is very difficult to detect and harder still to explain. What exactly are the relations between feeding and health? Even our British public has learnt the word *vitamins* and knows something of the relations of the thing (whatever it is) to such diseases as scurvy. But there are other questions. We eat, it seems, much less than our eighteenth-century ancestors ate—than those of them, at least, who were gentlemen and ladies. But the birth-rate is less. Choice may be the cause of that; but does diet affect it, and how? Are the under-fed more prolific than the over-fed? So far, one is inclined to think, we have paid more attention to food in relation to death than to birth. Of course we all can guess; for, I am told, the relation of diet to reproduction is not yet clearly ascertained; it is surmised that the eating of liver has some influence in promoting fertility. It is a saying among experts in farming that "half the pedigree goes in at the mouth".[2]

1 See the remarkable chapter (x) on Mice in W. B. Cabot's *Labrador*.

2 By the kindness of Sir Humphry Rolleston, I am permitted to add the following note: "Since their discovery in 1912 by Gowland Hopkins the vitamins, or accessory food factors, have multiplied and proceeded down the alphabet. The 'p.p.' or pellagra preventive factor, which Joseph Goldberger described, has by others been spoken of as vitamin G. From experiments on rats it has recently been shown that there is a vitamin E, the reproductive or anti-sterility vitamin, absence of which causes degeneration of the germ cells

In the history of the Greek world we have presented to us a singular change in national diet, which it may be worth while to discuss—if only to realize how very intermittent is our knowledge of antiquity, and perhaps of laws of food as well.

Polybius tells us[1] that Timaeus (it is one of the counts in his indictment) opined that poets and historians show their own natures in what they linger over; so Homer, at that rate, says Timaeus, must have been a bit of a glutton. Certainly there are a good many meals in Homer, but there are a good many people to eat them, and nearly every one of them has a healthy appetite—even Niobe, after losing twelve children, as the gloomy Palladas reminds us.[2] Athenaeus, about 200 A.D., compiled a masterpiece on our subject, his *Gastronomers*, as an American scholar renders the title. He is a kind of gastronomic Burton, not so pithy, nor so quaint, but as discursive, as learned, and as everlastingly reminiscent of lost authors who discussed the table and its delights, and everything else that might crop up at dinner. There never were sages so full of allusions for so extensive a menu; and wherever you open them, they are apt to combine infinite learning with a good deal of amusement, and enough scandal to keep you from being tired. Ancient life would be a duller story without Athenaeus; and he has a section on Homer. He takes a different view from Timaeus; Homer saw that moderation is the first and most appropriate virtue for the young, and he wished to encourage it; so he ascribes a simple manner of life to all, and it is the same for kings as for subjects, for the young and for the old. The meal is always roast, he notes—generally beef, he adds, though the modern reader of the *Odyssey*, perhaps from sympathy with Eumaeus, has a feeling that the pig played a large part in it. And, he notes, many as are the meals Agamemnon gives to his chieftains, whatever the occasion, the roast meat is the one big dish—"no entrées served in fig-leaves, no rare titbit, or milk-cakes, or honey-cakes, does

in male rats and death of the foetus in pregnant rats. The ordinary diet of man appears to contain it in quantities sufficient to prevent the recognition of a 'deficiency' disease due to its absence".

1 Polybius, XII, 24.

2 *Anth. Pal.* X, 47.

Homer serve as choice dainties for his kings, but only viands by which body and soul might enjoy strength". So with Alcinous (though he had a garden); so with Menelaus at his children's wedding; so with Nestor—"nay! then", says the old man, "let one go to the field for a heifer". Even the suitors, he continues, insolent though they were and recklessly given over to pleasure, are not represented as eating fish or birds or honey-cakes. Priam rebukes his sons for taking the lambs and kids of their countrymen. Even though Homer describes the Hellespont as teeming with fish, the Phaeacians as devoted to the sea, Ithaca as rich in creeks and islands full of fish and wild fowl, he never has those things on the table. No, nor fruit either—though in a delightful passage he represents it as never failing throughout the year, "pear upon pear". Nor yet does he exhibit his people as wearing garlands or using unguents. The minstrel and the tumblers are the only diversions of the banquet.[1] The heavy meat-eater, filling himself with proteid, must, I am told, be some sort of a hero, hunter, warrior or athlete, or he will pay for his ill-balanced diet. So when they have put from them desire for eating and drinking, they will be off to their athletics, the disc and the spear.

The modern scholar[2] supplements this comment of Athenaeus, but has little or nothing to change. He too emphasizes the simplicity of the diet—and of the service of it; no plates, no forks, and knives only incidentally—

οἱ δ' ἐπ' ὀνείαθ' ἑτοῖμα προκείμενα χεῖρας ἴαλλον.

They ate, like Charles II, with their fingers, and got themselves in as much of a mess, and water poured on the hands was very necessary. Professor Seymour adds to the menu of Athenaeus bread, which is obvious, or at least baked cakes of wheaten flour or meal, not loaves, and not leavened; onions and salt; in lieu of butter or fats, pork fat, suet and marrow; honey; cheese—sometimes grated over the wine. Penelope kept geese—obviously to be eaten, but we only hear of an eagle actually doing it. The nameless bird that we call fowl

1 Athenaeus, I, pp. 8E–10D.
2 T. D. Seymour, *Life in the Homeric Age*, chapter VII.

is never mentioned in Greek literature before Theognis; Aristophanes says in jest or earnest that it is a Persian bird;[1] but chanticleer is pictured on pottery said to be Minoan, so we must not draw too hard an argument from silence. On Circe's island Odysseus kills a stag for his men; and in sore need Menelaus and his men eat fish. Athenaeus remarks that they must have had fish-hooks with them. One allusion to an oyster-diver in the *Iliad*, and masses of cockle shells found at Troy and of oysters at Mycene, perhaps imply further variety; but there may be differences of race. There are British subjects who will not eat whelks or shrimps if they can help it. The Phaeacians dried their grapes to make raisins as Robinson Crusoe did. Simple as this Homeric diet may seem, there is no suggestion of hardship or shortage about it: Ithaca and Phaeacia are both pictures of plenty.

When we turn to historical Athens, we are in another environment. It is city life—the life of small people who do small marketings, as we see in one and another description of Aristophanes; people who live in small rooms, and have no country demesnes, no common fields, urban as cockneys, and as dependent on the country people or others who will bring them food-stuffs to market. And the outstanding change is that instead of being, like the Homeric Achaeans, meat-eaters, they live more upon fish, or at any rate they talk more about fish and make more jokes about it; and their fish is chiefly dried fish from the Black Sea. Country life is not extinct; there never was an author more typical of country life than Xenophon—"the most English of the Athenians", as Andrew Lang called him, and, you might add, the most Homeric. The charcoal burners and country folk who throng Aristophanes' comedy will not be forgotten either; but, all the same, Athenian life is urban. How has the change come?

It is quite possible that there really was no change; that the Athenians were no Achaeans, but "Pelasgians" (whatever that means), and that they preserved in diet, as in religious usage and other things, the ways of an older day before ever the Achaeans came from inland Europe. The Achaeans seem

1 Aristophanes, *Birds*, 707; 833.

to be of another race, to judge from their early use of iron, their lavish burning of the dead (which would seem to imply forest); and their aversion from fish may be the prejudice of an inland race rejecting the unfamiliar. Other considerations come in, however. We have no statistics, and, if we had, they would be probably wrong—inaccurately recorded and worse transmitted; we can only guess at the growth of population in the centuries between Homer and Solon, but it must have been very great. There were centuries for it to grow in, and endless unoccupied lands round the Mediterranean shores for it to expand over. The colonies are evidence enough of the main fact; and they imply that Greek populations constantly outgrew the home food-supply. Even if Mr Tozer is right in saying that early Greece was well wooded, which is very likely, that deforestation, which has been one of the curses of Greece, probably began very early to be a factor.[1] In historical times shipping timber had to be imported. The charcoal-burner and the goat were for centuries the enemy of the trees; and deforestation must have meant then what it means now—change in climate and temperature;[2] floods when there is rain, drought if rain fails; and denudation as the soil is washed out of the hillsides. The farming was eminently unscientific and remained so in general; and under such treatment the land is exhausted, and recuperation is impossible. At all events, we have to note great changes in Greek life and new attempts to fit life to its conditions, if the conditions cannot be changed.

Let us leave this Greek problem, for a while, and turn overleaf to another phase of our subject—to a story where the problem is not altogether the same nor indeed quite parallel, and where the solutions are different. Our subject is Diet in History, and we have to see how it works change and development. The experience of one race or nation may illustrate

1 Glotz, *Ancient Greece at Work*, p. 256, quotes Plato for this, but gives no references. Professor F. M. Cornford suggests it may be *Critias*, 111 C.

2 See a very interesting essay by W. Warde Fowler, in his *Year with the Birds*, on the Birds of Virgil. His problem is that Virgil speaks of birds nesting in his country which do not nest there. His solution is the steady destruction of forest (in which business Virgil's father was engaged), the resulting change of climate and the retreat of the birds to a cooler region.

that of another, even if it is not wholly or even in general parallel.

There was some years ago a Scot at Cambridge who had a grievance against the teachers of English history and their textbooks; one of the greatest names of the eighteenth century they never mentioned, the name of the man, he used to say, who had changed the face of England. It was Jethro Tull who had done this and the common histories and historians never spoke of him. A great historian of art once asked me if I knew what was the real foundation of the work of Reynolds and Romney and Gainsborough and the great painters of their day; and when I preferred that he should answer his own question, he told me "The turnip". The two men had the same thing in mind.

Medieval England was very largely unreclaimed or uncultivated, and what was under cultivation was worked upon the open-field system. There was much division and subdivision of property, and in places much communal property; and the whole village worked on the same lines, doing the same things at the same seasons, with the very minimum of individual enterprise or reflection. Indeed Lord Ernle says that the country as a whole made no general advance in agriculture between the thirteenth century and the eighteenth.[1] Each village was isolated and self-sufficing, he tells us; roads were bad and farmers ill educated. Every man had to keep step with his neighbours, and the stupid man of the village could frustrate every attempt at improvement. The farmers formed a body like Wordsworth's cloud that "moveth all together if it move at all". The farming was in general bad. Communal ownership or operation was against new ideas, and it was ideas that were wanted. The land was not producing anything like what it might have, as afterwards appeared. A system, which may have been reasonable in its way, in a newly settled country with a small population, was really outgrown. Grain was raised; and so were cattle, but poor beasts, ill bred and ill fed. There was not enough meadow land to raise the hay needed to keep them alive through the winter, and they had

1 Lord Ernle, *English Farming*, p. 194.

to be slaughtered in November. The meat was salted down, and whether it were kept at home or sold, those who ate it lived on preserved meat. It is significant that those who fancied their food—like the Ménagier de Paris who wrote the cookery book (with much else) for his fifteen year old wife—insisted on meat dishes being very heavily seasoned and spiced. The ribald critic of the monks, whose verses are printed under Walter Map's name, says

> Crocum, caryophyllum, piper et cuminum
> Cocus terit, conficit, onerat catinum;
> Perfundit diluvio gustum hunc divinum
> Medus mera sicera moretum et vinum.[1]

A modern layman may be allowed to shirk exact translation in detail; but it is a great accumulation of flavours, and the central idea seems to have been to avoid tasting the meat, which you thought it due to your system to swallow somehow. The beasts that were spared, reduced to the lowest possible number, barely survived on straw and tree-loppings, exposed if sheep to scab and rot, if cattle to the murrain.[2] Whatever country people could stand, this was no diet to promote the health of towns, least of all when towns were so full of every kind of filth and smell.

There were of course regions with alternatives. We are told that when the great migration took place from Oxford in 1209, the attraction of Cambridge in the fens was that it actually lay among the fens, on a river that connected it with the sea and brought sea-faring ships to it, and in the midst of abundance, fish and eel and wild-fowl—a place of comparative plenty. Somewhat the same picture emerges of Boeotia in Aristophanes, with its lake or swamp Copais, and its famous eels, and other dainties. Cambridgeshire, however, was at one time a land of ague; and, says Lord Ernle, Bedfordshire in 1794 "still disputed with Cambridgeshire the reputation of being the Boeotia of agriculture", and twenty years later had long lain under the imputation of being the worst cultivated county in England.[3] It is fair to say that another contem-

1 Walter Map, p. 248, *de Mauro et Zoilo*, ll. 165–8.

2 Ernle, *English Farming*, p. 65. 3 Ernle, *op. cit.* pp. 241, 243.

porary critic, Marshall, counts Devonshire the most benighted county.[1]

Throughout the Middle Ages, then, the supreme necessity of diet, if it is to be palatable, is spice—not only in England, as the name Spicer reminds us, but in Germany and France. Pepper, ginger, anything—to get the stuff down! But these things do not grow in Europe; they had to be fetched from the East; no one was quite clear of the exact region, and for long it was supposed to be Arabia. The Venetians and the Genoese were the great middlemen who supplied the North with spice and anything else that the Orient produced. But in the fifteenth century Constantinople fell, and the Turks won a new hold on the Mediterranean, which they did not use very cannily. At the same time in the West new ideas were gaining ground; could not the Orient and the spice lands be reached by sea? Renewed interest in ancient geographers had revived the idea of a spherical earth, and the voyage of Columbus to reach the Indies from the West had unexpected consequences. Under the stimulus of Henry the Navigator the Portuguese meanwhile had crept farther and farther round the West African coast, southward and southward, till at last Vasco da Gama entered the harbour of Calicut on 20 May, 1498. "What in the name of Shaitan are *you* doing here?" shouted a voice in Arabic, as da Gama and his officers passed through the streets.[2] They were soon to know, and so were the Venetians whose envoy at Lisbon saw what it meant and reported it (in Latin) to his government.

It was, says Admiral Ballard, a supreme step in history that had been taken, and, ever since, those seas have been more and more controlled by Western navies. But ours is the humbler task of watching the table. The spices now came by sea and were immensely profitable to those who brought them. But mistakes were made. Portugal and her dominions fell under the Spanish rule, and the prevailing economic theory was that gold is wealth, and that the precious metals must not be allowed to leave the country. Erasmus once suffered from this theory at Dover. The Spanish government prohibited the

1 Ernle, *op. cit.* p. 204. 2 Ballard, *Rulers of the Indian Ocean*, p. 32.

export of gold to the Orient, and the Oriental insisted on it. Then in religious zeal Philip II forbade Lisbon to sell pepper and spices to heretics.[1] This was inviting the heretics to come in and fetch the goods themselves, and they duly accepted the invitation. And here an odd trick of race helped; the Portuguese, whom they had to face, and now and then to fight, in the Orient, were the children of Hindu mothers, for whom the Mediterranean man had not the repugnance of the man of the North, then and now resentful of mixing races. So the Dutch made good their footing, till in an evil hour they put up the price of pepper and spice, and London resented it and formed our own East India Company. The history of that Company is long and curious, and need not be told here; but if ever diet affected History, it was surely when bad English meat and high Dutch prices drove Englishmen to fetch their own pepper.

From about the time of the Commonwealth new ideas of agriculture were aired; and in spite of great opposition, the face of England was changed, as Mr Mackenzie put it, in the eighteenth century. Common farming yielded to enclosures, to experiments with clover[2] and turnips. The common feeding of cattle over the fields had to stop, and our hedge-rows are monuments of a victory for scientific agriculture.[3] It was not all pure gain; villagers had often to go to the towns and work in the new factories; but in any case, with the increase of population, and the appeal of work and wages, that must often have been more or less inevitable. But the gain was fresh meat all the winter and an obvious gain in national health. It meant immense new values in land and profits from farming. "The improvements", says Lord Ernle, "enabled England to meet the strain of the Napoleonic wars, to bear the burdens of additional taxation, and to feed the vast centres of commercial industry, which sprang up as if by magic, at a time when food supplies could not have been

1 Ballard, *Rulers of the Indian Ocean*, p. 144.

2 Lucerne or alfalfa seems to have been originally Persian, πόα Μηδική.

3 Ernle, *English Farming*, p. 28, the hedge bulked big in the new agricultural books.

provided from another country".[1] And the great landlords and farmers had their wives and daughters painted by the great painters, and England was the richer for ever, even if the originals sometimes cross the Ocean.

But the English table, recruited by Oriental spices brought in English ships, by fresh meat fed on Persian clover and Swedish roots, by wheat grown on lands improved by care and science, was further enriched from overseas. The potato is an American plant, even if it is called the Irish potato, and in our own day we have seen it re-inforced by its more delicate cousin, the tomato. But America had a greater gift for us; our subject is diet, so you will not think of tobacco. But here let Charles Lamb speak for me: "This is Christmas day 1815 with us," he writes to Thomas Manning in China, "...if it should be the consecrated season with you, I don't see how you can keep it. You have no turkeys; you would not desecrate the festival by offering up a withered Chinese Bantam, instead of the savoury grand Norfolcian holocaust that smokes all around my nostrils at this moment from a thousand fire-sides....'Tis our rosy-cheeked, home-stalled divines, whose faces shine to the tune of 'Unto us a child is born', faces fragrant with the mincepies of half a century, that alone can authenticate the cheerful mystery"; but he trenches on Theology in the holy tide with bowels refreshed. And he forgets to thank China for his tea.

To finish off our own story, we all know how English population outgrew our own supplies of wheat and meat, how the corn-laws were swept away and free trade brought in and the markets of the world captured by English goods. We see to-day[2] the deadlock in the United States between manufacturing people and farmers—free entry for Canadian wheat, if not stock, and every article of daily life protected. "They may say what they like about eating and drinking", but diet takes and keeps a big place in History.

One last question before we return to Classical Greece. What, I was once asked, and I could not answer, what did Africa eat, before the white man brought from overseas, mainly

1 Ernle, *op. cit.* p. 149. 2 Perhaps by now one should say "yesterday".

from the New World, the banana, the bread fruit, the pea-nut, the cassava, the yam and the maize? I leave that question, with an added problem; there is in West Africa hardly any meat-supply (other than the human) as a result of the tse-tse fly; was it always so, or is the fly an immigrant also?

In Greece, as we saw, the population easily outgrew the food-supply. One-fifth or so of the soil of Greece, we are told, is all that is fitted for cultivation; a still smaller proportion if Boeotia and Thessaly are set aside.[1] The margin between normal life and starvation was always and everywhere much narrower than was pleasant or safe. Mardonius once commented on the absurdity of Greek warfare: "When they have declared war against each other, they come down to the fairest and most level ground that they can find, and there they fight, so that the victors come off not without great harm; and of the vanquished I say not a word, for they are utterly destroyed".[2] He is right in his facts, but his comment is that of a prince from a far more spacious empire. That fair and level ground was obviously the one or the best wheat-field of the community—its very life. If the enemy could hold it long enough to reap or ruin the crop, how were the town people to live? They must go down to that fair and level ground and fight as long as the enemy chose to stand. There was little need there for tactics or strategy; the soldier should be heavily armed—and he was; Greek armour was very heavy, the helmet heavier than the medieval; he must stand his ground and be able to bear the blows of the enemy and deal his own. It was so far war at its very simplest, and it produced the best heavy-armed troops the world saw for centuries—a specialized type of soldier, good, incomparable at his own work, but useless at other kinds of fighting, as Demosthenes learnt and Iphicrates proved. The hoplite grew out of the necessity for the six bushels of wheat that the average man is computed to have consumed per annum in Greece.[3] It is perhaps relevant to interpolate two other estimates; the average American of to-day is supposed to consume the same amount of wheat, but

1 Grundy, *Thucydides*, p. 246. 2 Herodotus, VII, 9. See p. 65.
3 Glotz, *Ancient Greece at Work*, p. 256.

his six bushels are helped out with much else that the ancient Greek never knew—ice cream, for instance; French consumption on the other hand is said to be eight bushels per man per annum.

Greece never moved away from the feeling that the first thing in war must be to destroy the enemy's food supply or to protect your own. It says a great deal for Pericles that he saw that Athens could ignore the destruction of her farms by the Spartans in the Peloponnesian War; and how strong was the conservative opposition to this new form of national suicide, we see in Aristophanes' good Acharnians. Of course it made a difference if you were a farmer. But it was a new and uncomfortable idea that the city within the walls that linked her to the Peiraieus was to be regarded as an island and the rest of Attica sacrificed. Sacrificed it was by the end of the twenty-seven years: even the tiles of the farm houses were sold by the pillaging invaders to Theban dealers. Yet that Athens did in fact hold out for those years is a sign of the triumph of the ideas of Solon, his conviction that Athens need not raise her own food if she could hold the sea. Megara had not that control of the sea, and the devastation of her small territory ruined her.

Elsewhere in Greece, if not everywhere, we find another outcome of this narrow margin in food supply in the bitter spirit that animates Greek politics. Once again we may need the caution that there are more factors than one in any important feature or movement of a national life. But it is hard for people who have never looked starvation in the face to determine the limits to which the starving should go or will go, when they believe, rightly or wrongly, that their traditional opponents have plenty. The wars of religion should warn us, however, how far people will go for ideas; and the Greeks were always far more interested in ideas than Anglo-Saxons have as a rule shown themselves. Political theory could disturb them more quickly than it does us. But the food problem is not to be ignored.

It was very early that this food problem began to be felt and it continued for centuries, though the solution varied from century to century. The first great attempt to meet the need was to send the surplus population where it could hope to find food, if there were not enough at home. Colonization was an amazing success in the long run, whatever unrecorded disasters accompanied its beginnings, as has been the experience of most other colonizing peoples. It relieved the pressure at home; it found food and dwellings for the overflow, and further growth of population and its needs, which in its turn meant increase of activity and production, and expansion of commerce. The new colony called for goods at once—for woollen clothes for the settlers in South Russia—for tools probably and all sorts of immediately needed implements and conveniences, till the craftsmen in the new place found their feet; and all this meant stimulus to employment in the old home town, paid for in raw material and in food supply. Whatever disagreements might arise between *metropolis* and colony—Corinth and Corcyra are the typical instance—none the less one might say that colonization made the Greek world, as later on, after Alexander, a rather different type of expansion made the Hellenistic age. Each outpouring of men, trained by Greek life to think—πόλις ἄνδρα διδάσκει—meant in the long run a new attitude to life, new reactions, fresh movements in art and in philosophy. We need not regret too much the meagre table of the Greek.

In Athens the solution was rather different. Her arrival (so to speak) in the Greek world was late, for various reasons not all of which are explained. Miletus and Corinth were ahead of her in the colonial field; and when Athens did attempt colonization it failed. Thurii has one famous citizen who is reclaimed by Halicarnassus. But when Athens found herself, like the other Greek communities, confronted by the food problem, it was solved for her by a man of genius, the greatest and the first of Greek economists. Solon knew the Mediterranean world; a man of business, a traveller, and something of a poet, he combined the experience, the intelligence and the imagination that a statesman needs. He saw a hungry people and a meagre soil. It was to that meagre soil, as Thucydides recognized, that Attica owed her immunity from invasions in the days of the great migrations. The land would never, Solon saw, raise enough wheat for a considerable people; and meanwhile what it did raise was going over the border to feed the nearest commercial rival. The Megarid was notoriously a hopeless patch of stones, yet Megara was or had been a great colonizing power and remained a great commercial centre. Megara's food supplies came from the Black Sea[1] and from Attica. Solon at once cut off the Attic supplies, prohibiting export of any agricultural produce except olive oil which (he knew) had a ready market in the Black Sea wheat-fields; and he made it plain that Athens' future was to be upon the sea. A modern community cannot easily shift from wheat to garden produce and poultry; and the olive is a plant of slower growth than the lettuce. Time was required; meanwhile came Pisistratus, and the vine[2] was added to Attica's main products, and a fresh assault was made very successfully on Black Sea markets. Solon's main work, however, was to turn his people almost bodily from agriculture to manufacture and to commerce.[3] A country, like our own, which led the modern world in the application of steam to industry and simultaneously secured a large share of the world's carrying trade, and which has long maintained the safety and the freedom of the seas with an efficient navy, is only doing again what Athens did in the ancient world. For generations starvation was no real risk in England or in Athens; persons here and there might starve, classes might have insufficient food or inadequate food; but in neither community was the old dread on the whole more than a memory, hard to realize. German submarines and Aegospotami in the one case and the other might bring it back, did bring it back; but such experience of war was unusual.

Yet the Peloponnesian War was longer than the European, and it unsettled Greek life irrecoverably. Communities did recover; the Peiraieus regained its trade; but Greece, for all the loss of life in the War, found herself again with more

1 On Black Sea products and their control, see Polybius, II, 38.

2 Vines, Mr Tarn says of later Ionia, gave roughly five times the profit of wheat off the same acreage; *Hellenistic Civilization*, p. 205.

3 This point is noted by Plutarch, *Solon*, 22. See also pp. 27, 28.

population than her farmers and traders could feed. Isocrates is the *vox clamantis* that tells of poverty and of homeless men driven by poverty to wander. One cannot be certain, at such a distance of time, how many of these unemployed would have cared to turn back to the employments of peace. Aristophanes lets us see in some of his earlier plays that the munition-workers were against peace, and in the latest of them that socialistic theory was familiar in Athens. But in any case the food problem was solved, temporarily and badly, by the growth of mercenary armies, available retail and wholesale, for mischief or empire, and in fact required by the development of military science. Cyrus called off 13,000 mercenaries, a large part of whom returned to Greece or its neighbourhood; and after that there was always a demand for them in the Persian Empire and in the kingdoms that succeeded Alexander. The new foundations of the great Macedonian kings drew off much population from Greece; and if the individual families still felt the pressure of the food problem, they solved it by infanticide.[1] But till the Roman civil wars Greece was not actually depopulated.[2]

Throughout, it will be noted, apart from Solon's diversion of agriculture from wheat to the olive and vine, no real attempt seems to have been made to improve methods, or to make a science of agriculture. Xenophon in his Ischomachus draws the ideal farmer: but he is a glorified disciple of Hesiod rather than a forerunner of Jethro Tull or Lord Townshend.

So far for the greater issues that depended on the diet; and now a little about the diet itself.[3] Here, not Athenaeus with the appalling menus of princes and plutocrats in the Hellenistic period, the monumental meals of history, but Aristophanes may be our guide. A comic poet, like a satirist, warns us to be on our guard about his statements; but, with care, we may use them; he is bound to touch fact now and then, as Polybius suggests in his remark about Homer; it will not all

1 W. W. Tarn, *Hellenistic Civilization*, pp. 86, 87.

2 Tarn, *op. cit.* p. 88.

3 The modern Greek diet, with its staples of olive oil, milk and wheaten bread, is discussed by D. G. Hogarth, *The Nearer East*, pp. 191, 192, who praises its effect in producing a vigorous and healthy manhood.

be invention. A poet, then, who writes about peace and its blessings, is almost bound to include plenty among them, and Aristophanes had no reluctance. The bread, the main staple of life, as we saw, came from the Black Sea, and continued to do so down to the days of Demosthenes, who says in the Leptines speech that "of all men we use far the most imported wheat".[1] And so it continued. In the second century B.C even the country population had to buy grain,[2] and paid for it by exporting honey, figs, and olives. Barley, too, had its place in the diet, and was grown to some extent in Attica.[3] Ἀγαθὴ καὶ μᾶζα μετ' ἄρτον, said the proverb; barley bread would do, failing wheaten. Dried fish came in quantities from the Black Sea, where it was caught in the Sea of Azov, as cod is caught to-day on the banks of Newfoundland and sent dried to Greece to help the pious through the fast days. "Cheaper than dried fish" is a flout of Aristophanes,[4] who contrasts the luxuries of the peace, which Dikaiopolis is to enjoy, with the soldier's rations. "Boy," cries Lamachus, "bring me my knapsack!" ("my supper-basket", says Dikaiopolis)—"onions!"—("I'm sick of onions")—"rotten dried fish!"[5] No! No! Dikaiopolis doesn't want such things; he wants fat meat, and thrushes and ring-doves, hare and hare soup—the hare plays a large part; even Socrates is set by Xenophon[6] to discourse on hare-hunting—and sweetbread and cheese cakes; and a cask for the casque that Lamachus will have. And there are such things as fried cuttle-fish too, we learn before the play is over; and who forgets the eel, addressed in Aeschylean strains varied with Euripides? "Eldest of Copais' fifty daughters, O loved and lost and longed for! Heaven send that not in death itself may I be without thee—stewed in beetroot!" A pre-Christian *Meum est propositum.* In the *Lysistrata* we have a market scene—the soldiers in their arms crawl among the cabbages bargaining for shrimps, stowing omelettes in their helmets and stealing fruit.[7] In general, it

1 Demosthenes, *c. Lept.* 31.
2 W. S. Ferguson, *Hellenistic Athens*, pp. 313, 248.
3 Aristophanes, *Peace*, 1322. 4 *Wasps*, 491. 5 *Acharnians*, 1097 ff.
6 Xenophon, *Memorabilia*, III, 11, 8; cf. his *Cynegeticos*, 6, 8.
7 *Lysistrata*, 557 ff.

seems a simple diet. The athlete was exceptional among Greeks in the quantity of meat that he ate ("the slave of his jaw and his belly"), and in the stupidity of mind that it induced, and his all-round uselessness for anything but his own form of athletics.[1] The political triumph of the "Sausage-Seller" and his powers of vituperation will be recalled by readers of Aristophanes, who will draw very many inferences from his trade and his manners.

Another comic poet, Hermippos, writing in 429, gives us a custom house inventory of imports—some at least for the table—from the Hellespont mackerel and dried fish; from Italy grain (spelt) and sides of beef; from Syracuse pigs and cheese; from Rhodes raisins, and figs that give you good dreams; from Euboea pears and noble sheep; from the Paphlagonians walnuts and rich almonds, the dainties of the banquet; from Phoenicia dates and fine wheat flour. We need not catalogue the lies imported from King Perdiccas of Macedon, and other indigestible things; but an odd little note in Xenophon's *Anabasis*[2] chronicles an interesting discovery—"As for the dates of the palm, the sort one sees in Greece were put aside for the servants; but those reserved for the masters are selected, marvellous for their beauty and size, and look like amber—a pleasant thing at a banquet, but apt to cause headache".

We are told that this Athenian diet was sound enough, if there was plenty of fresh vegetables. No reader of Aristophanes is likely to forget that the mother of Euripides sold garden stuff; the exact ground that made "the son of the garden quean"[3] discreditable, and the botanical description of the vegetables, are lost to history; but someone, it must be presumed, bought and probably ate them. Small fresh fish were also sold in the market—sprat, anchovy and sardine,[4] etc.; larger ones, too, whose scales might be mistaken for the very small silver coins, three-cent pieces as it were, that people went marketing with—coins which, for want of ticket pockets, they

1 Cf. E. Norman Gardiner, *Greek Athletic Sports*, pp. 126–8.
2 *Anabasis*, II, 3, 15.
3 *Frogs*, 840.
4 *Wasps*, 493 ff.

carried in their mouths.[1] Beans, too, are mentioned—a food forbidden by Pythagoras for some inscrutable reason.

But perhaps the most famous item of all we are forgetting. "O shining old town of the violet crown, O Athens the envied", quotes the chorus in *The Knights* from Pindar. Yes, says the earlier chorus in *The Acharnians*, you always tumble to that quotation, every embassy quoted it; "violet-crowned" and you sat up at once.

> And then, if they added the *shiny*, they got
> whatever they asked for their praises,
> Though apter, I ween, for an oily sardine
> than for you and your City the phrase is.[2]

"The gray-leafed olive, nurturer of children", is the staid phrase of Sophocles,[3] and the epithet is specially fitting, the commentator tells us, as it follows an allusion to Demeter and Korê, who at the Thesmophoria receive prayer addressed to them and to Earth "nurturer of children". A more prosaic and literalist interpretation sees in the epithet the fact, recorded also by Juvenal, that the olive played a large part in the nurture of children.

Further we need not go. The extravagances of the menu devised in the Hellenistic age by absurd monarchs, and copied later on by absurder Romans, have their place in history, no doubt. They wasted labour, they sent gold and silver back to the Orient in exchange for flavours and nonsense, they gave the chronicler and the satirist not exactly new themes but modern instances; and they reveal a certain degree of moral breakdown to be followed by financial failure. But they can hardly be classed under our heading of Diet. They are the freaks of individuals and not the daily round of nations. But that there is a field for historical study in the common dishes and tastes of the people, in their necessities, we may agree—if it was ever really disputable.

1 *Wasps*, 791. 2 *Knights*, 1329; *Acharnians*, 637 ff.

3 Sophocles, *Oed. Col.* 701, and D. G. Hogarth, *The Nearer East*, p. 191, "Olive oil has no superior in its rapid capacity both to satisfy and nourish".

METALLURGY AND DEMOCRACY

πὰρ δ' ἴθι χάλκειον θῶκον καὶ ἐπαλέα λέσχην.

"PASS by the smithy seat", says Hesiod to his brother,[1] "where men gather to idle in the sun in the winter season, when the cold keeps a man from work in the field. For then a diligent man may do much for his house—lest in bitter winter helplessness and poverty overtake thee, and thou must chafe a thick foot with a lean hand." What a picture he gives—the smithy with bellows and anvil, the smith (a mighty man is he with large and sinewy hands), and always some work doing that implies contrivance, something to watch, something to learn—and the drifting life of the village; there is little to be done in these winter days, but he has jobs on hand, and can crack while he makes the bellows roar. Idle fellows! says Hesiod, and goes homeward with some practical purpose. But Perses, of course, doesn't like work—a true Greek, he can spend his time in nothing else but either to tell or to hear some new thing. A wasteful way of living—get on with the job! But there was more at the smithy than Hesiod saw. One of his words was to have a great future in Greek life—λέσχη; leisure, idleness, chat, exchange of ideas, Socrates, Plato, they all hang together. Pass them by, and get to work. No, it was the smithy and the seat in the sun that made Greek life; the exchange of ideas, political discussion, tales of travel, what not? and out of it came Greek industry, Greek art, Greek democracy. Another word is to be noted, though of less significance, a mere link with the past; but such links sometimes have tales to tell; the smith is a *chalkeus*, a worker in bronze, by etymology, but, in fact, by all probability, a blacksmith, a worker in iron. Our old English name, in contrast with whitewright, tells how words survive. The first Greek smiths worked in bronze, and Greek smiths are ever after *chalkeis*. It may hint at a continuity through dark ages of history.

1 *Works and Days*, 493.

For let some centuries pass and we are back in the smithy, this time at Tegea in Arcadia. Once more the smith is busy, and an idle stranger from over the border watches with interest. And when the smith saw him wondering, he stopped his work and said: "I tell you, Laconian, if you had seen what I saw, you would have wondered and no mistake, when you make such a wonder now of the working of iron". And what had the smith seen? To make a short story of it, he had been sinking a well in his yard and had come on a coffin seven cubits long, and the man inside filled it. So that was what he saw; and the stranger fell thinking—and that is what people did in these smithies. Some lines of verse came into his head, a fragment of an oracle—

> Where two winds blow of strong necessity,
> Where shock meets shock, and woe on woe is laid.

It flashed upon him that here it all was, the bellows and the wind, hammer and anvil, both of them iron, and everybody knew that iron meant woe. So he made a shrewd guess as to the giant buried in the yard; and he was right, as Herodotus tells us,[1] and great results followed. What a pity for Sparta, if Lichas the herald had acted on Hesiod's advice! It was an anti-heroic poem, that *Works and Days* of Hesiod, Grote said;[2] it was too practical, too commonsense, good reading as it is and full of human nature. Perhaps Perses was an idler and better away from the smithy; but wonder is the key to Greek achievement,[3] and perhaps Hesiod had lost it or used it too little.

It is a long story, the history of tools, from obsidian to tungsten, and it is not my present purpose to show how imperfectly I know it. Pliny says obsidian was a discovery of a Roman, Obsidius, in Ethiopia—stuff of a glass-like texture, very dark in colour, sometimes transparent, available for gems and wall-mirrors; and he quotes another authority for its being

1 Herodotus, I, 67.

2 *History of Greece*, vol. I, p. 69: "The tendency of the *Works and Days* is anti-heroic....Prudence and probity are his means,—practical comfort and happiness his end".

3 Cf. Aristotle, *Metaphysics*, I, 2.

found in India, Samnium and Spain.[1] In an age long before Homer men went from all the Aegaean world to the island of Melos for it—happy island, with a monopoly and a great trade in it![2] And then in an evil hour someone made experiments with metal; who or where, we do not know, nor did the Melians perhaps; but their prosperity waned, as men found out in one smithy and another what could be done with bronze; and the market for obsidian was gone for ever—except as an Ethiopian curiosity. What is the Greek for obsidian? The very thing seems to have been forgotten. It might repay us to picture the prehistoric politicians of the island, as their market grew more and more desolate, and living became harder and harder, arguing for export duties, or protection, or something anyhow, blaming the folly of the rulers or the impiety of the rising generation, and never realizing that the world had moved clean away from them and their obsidian. *Λιμὸς Μήλιος*, "Melian starvation", was long after a saying of the wags of Athens; it referred to a siege; but it must have fitted those earlier days when human invention set the Melians in a backwater.[3] But the most famous statue in the world reminds us that obsidian is not the only bid one can make for good fortune.[4]

How long a time it was from the first working of bronze to the Homeric age, it would need a bold man to compute; and perhaps to date that age itself would involve us in too many quarrels with archaeologists and philologists. I will only remark how curious it has been to watch opinion move away from the guides of my youth, to see Homer's date recede again to something like his old traditional *floruit*, and to find Homer really taken to be (as Andrew Lang used to urge) a poet and not an archaeologist,

> A man and not a syndicate—
> Not botched and bungled, patch on shred,
> The counterfeit of ancient dead,

1 Pliny, *Nat. Hist.* XXXVI, 196–7; the editors are not even sure of his name; was he really Obsius and the stuff *obsiana*?

2 *Cambridge Ancient History*, vol. I, p. 599.

3 See J. T. Bent's fascinating book, *The Cyclades*, chapter on Melos, with its long note. Cf. Aristophanes, *Birds*, 186, *τοὺς δ' αὖ θεοὺς ἀπολεῖτε λιμῷ Μηλίῳ*. Melos had its share of prosperity again in the fifth century B.C.

4 See (beside Bent) Michaelis, *A Century of Archaeological Discoveries*, pp. 49–51.

A random, loose congeries
Of bards of four vague centuries—
But man and poet, heart and mind,
Awake to all that moves mankind.[1]

But do not let me forget my purpose for the joy of finding an old friend alive again. Homer quite definitely pictures his heroes in bronze armour, with sword and spear of bronze—χαλκοχίτωνες.[2] These are the nobles and princes, they wear "pieces of armour" which "clatter as they fall". But the common man, as Professor Seymour points out, did not carry a bronze shield nor have one carried for him; his affair was a *laisëion*, hardly a shield at all, made of ox-hide, it would appear. At least it is so long afterwards in Herodotus;[3] and Pausanias, drawing perhaps on old tradition, says that in the first Messenian War, a very early war, each man had a corselet or shield, or, lacking these, he wore a garment of goatskin or sheepskin; some were clad in the skins of wild beasts, wolfskins and bearskins being especially worn by the highlanders of Arcadia.[4] Homer does not tell us very much about the common soldier;[5] he had the poet's instinct for a hero rather than a mass movement, and, as Goethe suggests, the poets are apt to be royalists. Homer clearly was. But one is left with the strong impression of a marked contrast between the armoured warrior and the rank and file. Just as the blacksmith in Greek remains a bronze-smith, the common word for helmet is κυνέη, the dogskin cap. We find the κυνέη in Homer made variously of other skins, weasel (*Iliad*, x, 335), goat (*Od.* xxiv, 231) and ox (*Iliad*, x, 257). Whatever view we take of the detail of the prince's armour—and there has been as much dispute over it as over the arms of Achilles—the common soldier is another story. He receives no equipment from any headquarters; he has to look after himself; and he quite frankly counts for much less than the hero in bronze.

1 *Cambridge Review*, 15 November, 1906; a review of Andrew Lang's *Homer and his Age*.

2 Cf. Lang, *Homer and his Age*, chapter IX; T. D. Seymour, *Life in the Homeric Age*, chapter XIX; *Cambridge Ancient History*, vol. II, p. 484.

3 Herodotus, VII, 91.

4 Pausanias, IV, 11, 3.

5 Cf. Lang, *World of Homer*, p. 55.

Long afterwards we read the story in Herodotus[1] how men of bronze appeared in Egypt, and how King Psammetichos recognized the words of the old oracle and engaged them to fight his rivals, with supreme success. The men of bronze were Ionians and Carians in armour; and Egyptians in linen were no match for them. Two centuries later again the battle of Plataea was fought, between Spartans and Persians; and "in spirit and valour the Persians were no worse, but they had no armour";[2] and Herodotus repeats it in the next chapter, "what did them most harm was their manner of dress, without armour, for they had to fight all but naked against hoplites". It is the same story that we meet in Roman history and in English; the Gaul fights stark naked, but for a shield, against the Roman, and, though he belongs to the tallest and most beautiful tribe on earth,[3] he has no chance in the long run, for all his valour; nor had his kinsman the Highlander in attire almost as light, or perhaps like the Gaul, with none at all, against the mail-clad Norman in the Battle of the Standard.[4] So in Homer, even if we allow something for the fact that exact tactics hardly lend themselves to poetic treatment, while single combat readily does, we get the impression of the tribe or clan with chief and nobles in bronze armour, and the commons furnished as best they can manage with ancient and primitive substitutes of much less value or use.

Bronze is the metal of war. Polybius gives us a poor account of the iron sword of the Gallic invader of Italy; the thing would bend, and needed to be beaten straight before it could be used again—a great disadvantage in a battle. Andrew Lang suggests aptly that after all the bronze sword in the days of Troy might have been a good deal more reliable. Iron is found, of course, in Homer; when Odysseus drove the burnt stake into the eye of the Cyclops, it hissed "as when a smith (*chalkeus*) dips a great axe or an adze into cold water, hissing aloud, to temper it, for that is the strength of iron".[5] The

1 Herodotus, II, 152. 2 Herodotus, IX, 62.
3 Polybius, II, 15; and Pausanias, X, 20, 7.
4 R. S. Rait, *Scotland*, p. 39; cf. A. Lang, *History of Scotland*, vol. I, p. 105.
5 *Odyssey*, IX, 391.

smith is making tools, not weapons. When Achilles gives the great lump of iron (σόλος) as a prize at the games upon the death of Patroclus, he says it will last the winner a good five years; "though his fat land be distant from the city, ploughman or shepherd who lacks iron shall not need to go thither, but this shall suffice".[1]

We have only to recall the shield of Achilles to realize the great satisfaction that men of the Homeric period found in metal-work, and the very high standard of skill attained by the craftsmen. Granted that the shield of Achilles is the work of a god, a creation of a poet, and never likely to be found however lucky the excavator, still the Vaphio cups would have been incredible before they were found, and much else. Call him *chalkeus*, worker in bronze, or *chrysochoos*, worker in gold, his craft is metallurgy; he is brother to the blacksmith; and the three together prophesy an age that came.

Where in the earliest days they found their metals, we hardly know,[2] but Asia Minor and its neighbourhood had gold deposits in historical times. Jason is known to Homer for his voyage, and a later day had a simple, perhaps too simple, explanation of the golden fleece. Strabo, speaking of the Eastern end of the Black Sea, tells us that "it is said that in their country gold is carried down by the mountain torrents, and that the barbarians obtain it by means of perforated troughs and fleecy skins, and that this is the origin of the myth of the golden fleece". But other people said other things, and some concluded that the *Argo* was not one ship but many, and sums up many voyages of trade and exploration.[3] Thasos and Thrace in historic times had famous mines, and the isle of Siphnos too, as a sad story reminds us.[4] The Pactolus had a great name later on. Meanwhile a prince comes from Lycia in golden armour, worth a hundred oxen, which, the poet tells us, he changed with Diomed for bronze worth nine;[5] so the Greek got the better of it. Mycene, above all things, is

1 *Iliad*, XXIII, 834.
2 See p. 223 for Strabo and the Chalybes.
3 See p. 5.
4 Herodotus, III, 59; cf. C. T. Seltman, *Athens, History and Coinage*, p. 128.
5 *Iliad*, VI, 236.

famous for being rich in gold; and so it was, but the origin of the metal is unknown. Silver plays a very small part in Homeric society as contrasted with gold and copper.[1]

But now let us pause, and sum up what we have so far. Here is an age of bronze, with a great deal of fine work in the precious metals and at any rate some work in iron—smiths and craftsmen in plenty in the background; and it is an age of princes. There follows a dark period, full, we find, of migrations and colonizations, with no literature beyond Hesiod that survives, and no history beyond what we can gather from legends and pedigrees and deduction. Colonization there was and plenty of it—eighty colonies of Ionian Miletus alone, and Miletus was Carian in Homer. Colonization means exploration, adventure, preparation, traffic and trade between home town and colony in every necessary article for years together, whatever follows; it implies ship-building, and smiths above all other craftsmen, both trades implying a watchful and growing intelligence. The smith is the figure of whom we can be most certain during the dark interval. If less art-work was produced in gold, immense progress was made in metallurgy. Bronze goes out for ever, as obsidian did before, and the reign of iron begins.

The race of bronze was gone, Hesiod tells us—the third race that Zeus made, in no way equal to the silver, but terrible, strong, delighting in Ares and in insolence. Bread they ate not, but great was their might; of bronze was their armour, of bronze their dwellings, with bronze they wrought. Black iron was not. And these by their own hands slain went down to the dank house of chill Hades. The fourth race was better but came to an end at seven-gated Thebes, and Zeus set them to dwell, with soul untouched of sorrow, in the Islands of the Blest by deep-eddying Oceanos. And Hesiod sighs that he should live among the fifth race of men, in a time of labour and sorrow, when right and natural affection and shame are unknown, and there is no help against evil, "for now indeed is a race of iron".[2]

1 Cf. Seltman, *Athens, History and Coinage*, p. 112.

2 Hesiod, *Works and Days*, 176. Grote, *History*, vol. I, p. 66, says he does not place much confidence in the various explanations which critics have offered of the five races of men.

We deduce the smith, and Hesiod assures us of the iron; and from now onward the history is plain enough, though not always in detail, abundant as detail often is. We have an age of iron, an age of hoplites and democracy.

Mr Grundy has done much to explain the significance of the hoplite, the man in heavy armour, the weight of which is very great. The Persian prince Mardonius remarked on the folly of Greek warfare—its one idea the selection of the best level ground, and then steady massacre.[1] The troops were heavy-armed on both sides, with a minimum of drill, manoeuvre, tactics or strategy; and Mardonius' comment does not misrepresent what happened. Mr Grundy gives the clue.[2] The level ground represented the food of the city, the wheatland; and there the fight must be till one party is killed off or driven off. The result was, as he says, that the common Greek army was composed of a type of force which could not possibly have been effective in four-fifths of the area of the country, and that it is very difficult to say what part the light-armed played in the fighting of the period. The Greek was slow to think of fresh possibilities in war—as slow as English soldiers to believe that a navy may serve instead of an army. Dash and movement were hardly to be expected of troops so heavily laden, but they would not have their armour lightened; the Greek soldier was a hoplite, and he was riveted to the hoplite idea. He had plenty of experience, first and last, to confirm him—experience in Egypt under Psammetichos, at Plataea against Mardonius, eighty years later at Cunaxa under the younger Cyrus; given the conditions he was invincible, and in Greece the conditions were given. When it was clear that light-armed troops were needed, they were hired from abroad, often from Thrace, where light-armed fighting was the rule, where men (peltasts) were trained to it and understood it. The Greek, in spite of Iphicrates, remained a hoplite; and the hoplite implies the smith who can do what he likes with iron, the practised hand in metallurgy.

Now let us turn to politics. In the heroic times, says

1 Herodotus, VII, 9. See p. 50.
2 G. B. Grundy, *Thucydides*, pp. 244–8, 262.

Aristotle, the kings were benefactors of the people in arts or arms; they took command in war.[1] We have seen that they did and were the backbone of the fighting. The kings pass; and the rule of nobility or oligarchy succeeds—which name you give it seems to depend on whether you are in the ring or outside it. Aristotle is quite clear that such a group will hold the government only so long as it can defend it. "When the country is adapted for cavalry, then a strong oligarchy is likely to be established. For the security of the inhabitants depends upon a force of this sort, and only rich men can afford to keep horses. The second form of oligarchy prevails when there are heavy infantry; for this service is better suited to the rich than the poor. But the light-armed and the naval element are wholly democratic."[2] He writes in the fourth century, and he probably thinks of Athens when he speaks of the sea-faring people. Wealth is associated with cavalry, and so it remained; and so it always must in urban communities, perhaps in every community except the nomad and the pastoral. Wealth is associated with heavy armour—for a while; in the bronze period, as we saw; in the earlier stages of the iron period, an almost inevitable guess. It is not clear how far or how soon the state supplied troops with armour. The seller of breastplates in Aristophanes' *Peace*[3] appears to be looking for private customers, but that of course may be due to distress brought on by the unfortunate return of Peace; the breastplate is splendidly got up and worth forty minas. The trumpeter follows him with a trumpet now useless, "which I [and he says ἐγώ] bought for sixty drachmas". On the other hand Plato speaks of the aristocrats arming a part of the *demos*.[4]

In any case let us concentrate for the moment on our antithesis; an age of bronze and of princes; an age of iron and of democrats. Metallurgy supplies one key to the explanation; no doubt there are others to be used as well. In History it is seldom that one key opens all the locks; the problems of History, like the best modern safes, open with combinations,

1 Aristotle, *Politics*, III, 14, 11; 1285 b.
2 Aristotle, *Politics*, VI, 7, 1; 1321 a.
3 Aristophanes, *Peace*, 1224.
4 Plato, *Republic*, 551 D.

and the clock sometimes comes into them too. But look in again at the smithy. There are new processes, depending on new supplies of iron, far larger supplies, which imply a wider range of traffic in it. Ἄγω δ' αἴθωνα σίδηρον will be said by a great many more mariners. There are more mines worked, more seas sailed, colonies are planted, life keeps growing more complicated, trades rise and fall (as long ago with the forgotten obsidian); and the men on the smithy seat have a great deal more to talk about, with a vastly greater variety of interest. New processes, in days before modern Ford industries and the employment of men on single items of the car or machine, meant a great deal more intelligence, an all-round development, for the craftsman had a whole job, he made the entire thing, not merely a bit of it.

Meanwhile after generations of democracy, Aristotle, like Plato, feels a reluctance in allowing artisans or mechanics to be citizens in any ideal state. Plato lays it down for his second-best or possibly practicable state that no native citizen shall be engaged in a manufacturing trade; the smith is not to be carpenter; one trade is enough for a man; the citizen has his work cut out for him in learning and understanding how to develope and to save the state.[1] Are we, asks Aristotle,[2] to include the mechanic among the citizens? There is really, he urges, no more absurdity in excluding them than in excluding slaves and freedmen. To be necessary to the state is not sufficient title to citizenship; children are necessary but are not citizens in the full sense. In ancient times, and among some nations, the artisan class were slaves and foreigners; most of them are so still.[3] The best form of state will not admit them to citizenship; for no man can practise virtue who is living the life of a mechanic or labourer.[4] But they have obtained citizenship where extreme democracy prevails.[5] This may all seem doctrinaire. Solon, the great practical states-

1 Plato, *Laws*, VIII, 846D.
2 Aristotle, *Politics*, III, 5, 1; 1277b. Cf. also III, 4, 12.
3 See p. 88.
4 *Politics*, III, 5, 5; 1278a οὐ γὰρ οἷόν τ' ἐπιτηδεῦσαι τὰ τῆς ἀρετῆς. Cf. VI, 4, 12; 1319a.
5 *Politics*, III, 4, 12; 1277b.

man, the greatest economist of the ancient world, took exactly the opposite view; he offered citizenship at Athens to persons who came to practise a handicraft and brought their families.[1] Like Will Crooks, he thought "the missus and the kids" were a stake in the country; and he "put honour" upon crafts.

The cheapening of armour is one aspect of it; and Aristotle more clearly adds another—"many of the mechanics are rich".[2] So we find three outstanding results of developing metallurgy—cheaper production of weapons, with armour for all; a growing and widening intelligence; an increase of national wealth and its accumulation in new hands—hands that have made it. Arms, brains and wealth spell political change. It does not look well, says Plato, for the same man to be busy with money-making and with war in the same state.[3] So many an oligarch must have thought; *e pur si muove*.

But beside armour there was another product of advancing metallurgy, which was even more solvent of society. "The Lydians were the first of men known to us", says Herodotus,[4] "who coined gold and silver money and used it; and they were the first retail shopkeepers." The statement as to coinage is generally accepted as accurate, say the commentators. The history of coinage is not our present concern, but its effect. We are told there was no native coinage in Egypt before the Persian conquest,[5] or even the Macedonian; nor in Southern India in the days of the Roman Empire, Pausanias says,[6] though in Bactria there was gold coinage in imitation of Alexander's. But Greeks quickly saw the advantage of the new invention, adopted it, and then found with surprise what a curious thing money is, and what amazing effects it has. The change from barter to currency seems, at first sight, simple enough; but, like other simple reforms hastily adopted (and this one was inevitable), it carried with it quite unforeseen factors.

To begin, perhaps at a point earlier than we need, with a modern instance. The Dinkas in the Sudan had most of their

1 Plutarch, *Solon*, 24.
2 *Politics* III, 5, 6.
3 Plato, *Republic*, 551 E.
4 Herodotus, I, 94.
5 The silver coins of Aryandes minted in Egypt, Herodotus, IV, 166.
6 Pausanias, III, 12, 4.

wealth in cattle, and it was tribal property. Slave raiding took members of tribes far afield amid distant towns and new ideas; and some escaped, to return with a new form of property, very private indeed, which, unlike cattle, could be carried in the waist-band without attracting attention. Coin meant with them a sudden development of the idea of private property. The Greek had the idea long before coin came in, but even so coin must have individualized wealth. It was possible to hoard it. Virgil notes as a mark of primeval barbarism, that the people "had neither law nor grace of life; they knew not to lay up stores nor to save their gain".[1] Thrift is the first virtue of civilization; but, if you are to lay by for a rainy day, there is nothing that suffers less damage by keeping than coin. The Greek had the option at first of hoarding his coin underground in some hole of his own contriving, or in a temple. The former way has served the modern numismatist best. The latter at times gave the contemporary more sense of national wealth, which was not the owner's first intention. Banks came later, as we know them in fourth century Athens.

Translate the wealth of the iron-workers, created by the demand for tools and for armour, a demand which incessant colonization heightened—translate this wealth into currency. Then remember the dealers, the middlemen who gathered wheat from the farmers and sold it in the cities, or oil from the owners of olive yards and olive presses, and sent it in bulk, in large jars, to the Black Sea, or again wine (or grapes perhaps) for export to Egypt. The farmer once paid rent in kind to the noble; this rent was changed to a fixed sum, with most confusing results; one year the farmer gained; the next the landlord; the third both seemed out; but in all three years the dealer or exporter seemed to make his profit. No doubt he too had bad years, when war or weather worked against him, or competitors in other lands had the luck of the Black Sea. But, broad and long, the dealer made money like the manufacturer. Next comes money-lending, money-changing, banking, with all sorts of perplexities, which to this day one business community and another fails to master. I dismiss the

1 Virgil, *Aeneid*, VIII, 316–17.

moral problems, which were in part due to using the metaphor of "offspring" (τόκος) for interest. In the early days of capital, when it is relatively scarce, when republics and pirates are many, when seas are un-lighted and un-charted, and risks are great, interest is high; and compound interest without Arabic numerals was terrible to calculate or to check. Coinage was a clever invention; once grasped, it was inevitable; but it sent wealth flying about in strange ways to nest and multiply in strange homes. Very few of these homes, one gathers, were those of "ancient wealth", of landowners and nobles, ἀρχαιόπλουτοι; and that fact accentuated all the changes that we have seen begin to follow from improved metallurgical methods with iron.

Currency is so generally in modern times a national affair, that it comes with some surprise upon us to learn how much coinage was done in early Greek days by individuals, magistrates or others. The great man in power would stamp his family device on the currency; thus the coins of Athens between 590 and 570 B.C. show the constant fluctuations of government in those years. The modern numismatist[1] is able to trace the career of Pisistratus in his currency, from the early issue bearing the front half of the horse to the great days when he standardized for two centuries of triumphant commerce the emblems of Athena and the owl—not without a glance at his issues in Thrace, where in his exile he had plenty of silver from the mines but was worse off for artists. Mr Seltman also throws a new light on the expulsion of the family. The Alcmaeonids secured the contract to rebuild the temple at Delphi; this put masses of bullion into their hands; they coined it, hired mercenaries, made their attack on Athens;[2] luck favoured them, all went well, and they were able to fulfil their contract, though there were several days when it looked as if the god would lose his money.

King Archidamus, we read, told the Spartans that war

1 See Mr Seltman's attractive volume, *Athens, its History and Coinage*, p. 24, the changes; pp. 38 ff., Pisistratus; p. 80, Delphi.

2 Isocrates, *Antidosis*, 232, says Cleisthenes persuaded the Amphictyonic Council to lend him some of the god's capital, and so brought back the *Dêmos*. Cf. Demosthenes, *Meidias*, 144.

depends on finance.[1] Somehow, till Mr P. N. Ure wrote about it, no one seemed interested in knowing how the tyrants raised their forces. Aristotle says they generally began by being demagogues; but, as Mr Ure saw, judging from American parallels (and to-day we could add English), a demagogue who is to be solidly successful must have campaign funds. Mr Ure suggested that we must look for the sources of the Greek demagogue-tyrant's funds in the new movements of wealth that followed the spread of currency. Town or tyrant, to have a currency, must have some considerable reserves of precious metal,[2] and in the case of Athens we know a good deal about it. "They have a fountain of silver," says the Persian in Aeschylus' play, "a treasure of the land."[3] Pisistratus appears to have tapped it early. Then came the famous days when the state controlled Laureion, and the mines yielded phenomenally, and with some difficulty Themistocles persuaded the Athenians to build a fleet with their silver instead of frittering it away.[4] We read of Nicias making big money by leasing slaves to work in Laureion—a heartless contract, so much for the pious general *per diem*, and the same *number* of head of human cattle to be returned to him.[5] The mines helped Athens through the Peloponnesian War,[6] and then declined in productiveness.[7] Strabo says they were abandoned in the time of Augustus,[8] but Sir John Mahaffy says they were not really exhausted. Modern processes have made profit out of waste dumps beside old Spanish mines.

To return, we find the device of coinage, a metallurgical device, has altered all the financial relations of Greece; the

1 Thucydides, I, 83, 2.

2 We are told that in 1931 Britain had 100,000,000 ounces of silver in silver currency.

3 *Persae*, 234.

4 Herodotus, VII, 144; Plutarch, *Themistocles*, 4. See an interesting account of Laureion, and its eighty to a hundred miles of galleries, in Zimmern, *Greek Commonwealth*, pp. 398 ff.

5 Plutarch, *Nicias*, 4, 2; and Xenophon, *Mem.* II, 5, 2.

6 Thucydides, II, 55; VI, 91.

7 Xenophon, *Mem.* III, 6, 1: "Now for the silver mines," says Socrates to the young Glaucon, "I am sure you haven't been there, so you can't say why the revenue from them has dropped off".

8 Strabo, c. 399.

old rich are relatively poor; the traders begin to count. Wherever political reform, as in Athens, is graded by financial status, the movements of coin must involve parallel movements in the political body; and the constitution may automatically change its character, as Aristotle points out, from a disproportionate increase in one section of the state. Sometimes, as he says, it is the number of the poor that increases out of measure.[1]

But if bronze made the age of heroes, and iron the age of democracy, with complications from silver, it was gold that brought in the kings again. No great development of metallurgy, perhaps, is involved here, but to round off our story, something must be said of gold and its sources, and the conditions of gold mining. It begins innocently enough with the very cordial relations between Croesus and the god of Delphi, to whom the king made remarkable gifts. He had discovered, we are told, that at Delphi was the most reliable oracle in the world. For a modern reader, with little religious interest in Delphi, it is hard to believe these gifts quite disinterested, when he finds Croesus in the same years busy reducing the Greek ports of the Asian littoral. Suspicion is heightened when we read how the Spartans sent to Sardis to buy gold with intent to use it for the statue of Apollo, which now stands at Thornax in Laconia, and how Croesus refused to sell it to them but made them a free gift of it, and asked to be their friend.[2] There was another story, with some little chronological doubts about it, that told how Croesus invited Alcmaeon to keep as much gold as he could carry from the king's treasury on his person at one time; and how the Athenian got a tunic with a wide fold and huge buskins, which he stuffed with gold, how he filled his mouth with gold, how he plastered his hair with gold dust, and dragged out as best he could, hardly looking like a human being; and how Croesus fell laughing and gave him as much again.[3]

The river Pactolus may have been one of the Lydian king's sources of gold supply. It flows through Sardis, says Herodotus,

1 Aristotle, *Politics*, v, 3, 6 ff.; 1303a.

2 Herodotus, I, 69.

3 Herodotus, VI, 125.

and brings down gold dust from Mt Tmolus.[1] Strabo says that the gold dust was found in large quantities, and gave rise to the fame of the riches of Croesus and his descendants, but that by his day the gold is found no more.[2] This leads to the supposition that the immensely rich Pythios, about whose dealings with Xerxes Herodotus tells two stories, one charming and the other shocking, was of the stock of Croesus.[3] Plutarch makes a moral tale out of his wealth, and the forced labour in his mines, and his wise wife.[4]

But the vividest picture of all deals with other kings. To King Cleomenes of Sparta, of all her kings most interesting, most original and perhaps most mad, came a clever stranger from Asia, with a story of boundless treasure which the king might gain, "and then you need not fear to challenge Zeus for wealth". The frivolous suggestion of king and god matching gold pieces till the god's stock runs out, is not unintentional. All this wealth belongs to the Persian king, and in a series of interesting chapters Herodotus tells how the tribute comes in from everywhere, is cast into ingots, and is stored.[5] It was on the basis of this immense revenue that the Persian king was able to organize the great expedition against Greece, no haphazard affair, but thought out, as Mr Grundy has shown, with everything arranged for commissariat and a sound plan for the co-operation of army and navy. The expedition came to utter grief, and the Greeks looted a great deal of treasure in one way and another. But when Persian movement began again with a new policy after the younger Cyrus came to the Aegaean, the hoards of the king were again effective, or, more probably, without touching them, his revenue sufficed. Agesilaus said that he had been driven out of Asia by ten thousand archers.[6] The bow was the Persian weapon, and the gold daric (weighing about as much as a guinea) bore a bowman stamped upon it. Agesilaus was probably right; the era of Persian subsidies had begun; conquest and war were need-

1 Herodotus, v, 101; I, 93.
2 Strabo, c. 625.
3 Herodotus, VII, 27.
4 Plutarch, *Mulierum Virtutes*, 262 D.
5 Herodotus, III, 89 ff.; 96. Cf. Xenophon, *Agesilaus*, 8, 6, on Persian accumulation of all the gold of the world, and the silver, with a view to empire.
6 Plutarch, *Agesilaus*, 15 (end).

less; control of Greece was as convenient at an immensely smaller cost. A balance of power among the jealous republics was not so difficult to maintain or to upset; a contribution, and the weaker state was hiring mercenary soldiers; and all Greece was in confusion, gambling upon the consequences to follow from the change of *hegemony*, as they called it, the change in leadership. Not that the leading state really led to anything, but its political preferences gave a lead in the smaller states, a lead to fresh faction, perhaps to revolution and massacre. The half century that follows the fall of Athens is dominated by Persian gold; and men began to realize that "thus far and no further" had been said to democracy.

There follows the most startling change in ancient history. Greeks had shown a curious inability to realize that any form of government but the city state could be really natural, or that anything could threaten the city state. The Persian king came from the ends of the earth before *you* were ready, was said to the Spartans;[1] it could practically have been said to them all. Now comes another surprise. Macedon had made several attempts to turn itself into a modern, united and efficient kingdom; and every time an unlucky death, natural or violent, removed the central figure, and all was chaos again. But now one great king consolidates the kingdom, makes Macedon mistress of her own shores and some of her neighbours' shores too; and, when he is murdered in the old Macedonian way, a greater king succeeds him—the greatest, perhaps, that the world has seen. He carried the old war into Asia and threw open the huge hoards of the old Persian kings. The economic effect of this release of gold and silver to the extent of hundreds of millions sterling was incalculable.[2] The poorer tribes of Greece, that supplied the bulk of the mercenaries, were now the richer; Elis and Aetolia began to know refinement and luxury.

But the great change was the dominance for ever of the prince. The old Greek states have still their value; this is a

1 Thucydides, 1, 69.

2 George Finlay computed it at something between seventy and eighty millions sterling; *Greece under the Romans*, chapter 1; see also Beloch, *Gr. Gesch.* 1, 343.

fortress, that has old associations, Athens is a fortress, a university, a legend; and it is important to the ambitious king to control their fortresses and to have their support or neutrality. But they are makeweights, hardly more. Every king, says the caustic Polybius, begins by "liberating" them; so did the Romans. He describes two competing liberators busy with the task that meant anything but the old liberty. Nothing could stand up against the awful wealth of the kings. Their pageants even did not exhaust it. The reader of the old Classics has only to turn to the description of one such pageant, set by Antiochus Epiphanes, to realize that he is in a new age.

It was not only on the old hoards of Persia that the kings depended. There is in Diodorus[1] a passage describing the gold mining carried on for the Ptolemies on the Nubian border—a passage notable for its horrors, but perhaps unique for the information it gives to the student of mining and metallurgy. Until recent times, gold mining was of two kinds. There was alluvial gold in the rivers, such as the Pactolus and the stream that Sutter and Marshall diverted in California;[2] and the age-long plan was to take up the dirt, sluice it well with water, and rock it in a "cradle", till, loosened by the water and the motion, the gold, being heavier than mud or pebble, sank gradually to the bottom. A good deal of gold, recoverable by modern methods of cyanide and bubble, which do not directly concern us in studying antiquity but are of great significance in political history, was lost by this method; but it was the only way possible. If the gold was imbedded in quartz, as it was in these Nubian mines, the only way was (and, I suppose, still is) to reduce it artificially to the same condition as alluvial gold in mud. The quartz was hacked out, and broken up; and then, thirty years ago, it was put into a "stamp", worked by machinery, which reduced it to powder; after which it was put in a "jigger" (the old "cradle") shaken

1 Diodorus Siculus, III, 12–14; the passage is supposed to be derived from Agatharchides. Cf. W. W. Tarn, *Hellenistic Civilization*, p. 204; Mahaffy, *Silver Age of Greece*, p. 77; Glotz, *Ancient Greece at Work*, p. 356. I am indebted to Mr T. A. Rickard of Berkeley, California, for explaining to me the processes described by Diodorus.

2 See the full and interesting account in Strabo, C. 146, on the use of the flume—exactly the device which revealed *accidentally* to Sutter and Marshall the presence of gold in California.

and rocked by machinery, with the same result to the gold. Only in Ptolemy's day there was no machinery, and convicts, prisoners of war, and the victims of false accusation were used instead—they and their wives and children—under the whip of barbarian guards.

The soil was black with layers and veins of quartz, and Diodorus, with a good deal of pathos original or borrowed, describes the quarrying, no matter of art or knack, he says, but of brute force, which we can believe. They had to follow the veins, very naturally, and this meant galleries driven underground and work in the dark, with lamps tied to the naked miner's forehead. The half-grown boys fetched out the broken ore, which had then to be hammered down by men with pestle and mortar in the first instance, and then ground by hand. This latter work falls to the women and old men, two or three to the spar that turns the millstone, working naked and ill-kept, till what they received in lumps the size of peas they have ground to powder. The next stage is one still familiar to the gold miner—the tilted plank with the grain parallel to the ground, over which the powdered quartz is gently dropped with water, which washes away the stone and leaves the fine particles of gold, or still mixed quartz and gold, caught upon the grain of the wood. This has to be repeated a number of times, and an elaborate smelting follows, a five-day job. As the workers were all considered waste lives, there was no sparing of them; food, conditions and treatment were all execrable, and the life had the one advantage of being short. *Proxima morti poena metalli coercitio*, says the Digest.

The conditions and methods of gold extraction hardly bear perhaps upon democracy, but they are not very familiar. Looking Westward for a moment, when we read in Polybius of forty thousand men employed in the silver mines of Spain, producing a daily return of 25,000 drachmae for the Roman government, we are faced with a volume of hardship beyond conceiving.[1] Strabo[2] has a fuller account of the various pro-

1 Polybius, XXXIV, 9, 8–11.

2 Strabo, C. 146–8. Pliny, *Nat. Hist.* XXXIII, 66 ff., has a long section on gold and mining, rather full of technical terms and rhetoric, but very characteristic.

cesses used in Spain, the sluice, the "gold-wash" (*χρυσοπλύσιον*), the smelting (with the use of chaff as in Egypt), the high chimneys of the silver-smelting furnaces. The silver mines, says Strabo, are not state property either at New Carthage or elsewhere, but have passed into private ownership; but most of the gold mines are owned by the government. It is passages like this which make Strabo so interesting and so valuable. Gaul was long associated with wealth of gold; the dying Gaul, in the statue, true to his race and its habits, has fought and died naked, but with a gold torque round his neck.

But to conclude. "The economists, from Finlay onward," says Mahaffy,[1] "who have speculated upon the financial life of the Roman Empire, and its passage from apparent opulence to universal penury or bankruptcy, have noticed as an active cause... the constant exportation of the precious metals to the far East in payment for luxuries such as jewels, unguents, etc., without any parallel production in Europe to induce a return of gold for European industry." Masses of Roman currency are to this day found buried in India. But Pliny was ahead of George Finlay and the economists. "At the least computation," he says, "100,000,000 sesterces (i.e. £1,000,000 sterling) every year is taken from our empire by India, the Chinese and that peninsula. So much our luxuries and our ladies cost us!"[2]

1 *Silver Age of Greece*, p. 313.

2 Pliny, *Nat. Hist.* XII, 84.

THE WANDERING GREEK

οἴκοι ἀβέλτερον εἶναι, ἐπεὶ χαρίεν τὸ θύρηφι.

Misquotation.

SOME years ago an American book appeared with the title *Hawkers and Walkers in Early America.* The America with which it dealt was the new West of 1800 and onwards, and it revealed an interesting society of small settlements and villages, dependent on wandering peddlers and craftsmen of all sorts for many of the commodities of life. The carpenter wandered from job to job, carrying his tools, to repair the wooden houses and their simple furniture; the printer carried his press and types with him; the clock-maker peddled at a high profit clocks that others had made and that would sometimes keep time; the vagrant painter decorated the house, and might add the conscientious family portraits. The medical man, qualified or unqualified, might cover a good deal of territory; and it was long before any but the chief cities could boast a stationary dentist. The preacher, cleric or layman, also went his rounds, sometimes immense rounds. In *The Winning of the West*—a most readable book, and fuller than most of American atmosphere and spirit, as real an interpretation of the country and the people as can be found in print—Theodore Roosevelt tells us that in early days in Kentucky and Tennessee it was the lay-preacher, riding his horse alone through the Cumberland Gap and worse places, armed and in peril of Indians, who brought religion to the new settlements—rough, solid, earnest preaching it was; but after all it remains that "all that's grammar isn't grace", a maxim of rather wide application.

Men seem born to wander. "Over the hills and far away" is one of our oldest tunes. In spite of our prudential proverbs about moss and such things, in spite of the changes that time and so-called civilization bring, the roaming kind have made an immense contribution to human history—literally immense, for it is beyond measuring, and immense in our common sense of the word, for it is widespread and all-pervading. That the wanderers are generally of the lowly and commonly leave no great records, may obscure their influence but does not prove it trivial. Clocks, lightning-rods, the Gospel, those American hawkers and walkers carried out with them—conveniences, knick-knacks, "Yankee notions," ideas; they carried back tales of a great country, prophecies of a great future, everything to excite the imagination, pictures of boundless opportunity, stirring yarns of wild beast and Indian and adventure; they helped to shape a people and to guide it to its "manifest destiny".[1]

But men roam over wider regions, and the travellers' tales are few that lack all reference to the flotsam and jetsam of humanity washed up in the unlikeliest places, "gone native" in South Sea islands, and Moslem in Mecca; and the tales are so far generally true. The sailor does not like his captain or the first mate, and the ship has to sail without him; and, if it is but seldom that a *Typee* results, or that a Pakeha Maori writes of Old New Zealand, it is only because men of letters are so seldom in forecastles and such places. But to this day settled life galls certain types of nature, and men tire of the monotony of civilized society, the pendulum swing between house and college.

> I should like to rise and go
> Where the golden apples grow;—
> Where below another sky
> Parrot islands anchored lie....
> Where in sunshine reaching out
> Eastern cities, miles about,
> Are with mosque and minaret
> Among sandy gardens set,
> And the rich goods from near and far
> Hang for sale in the bazaar.

"I think", wrote Pindar, "that the fame of Odysseus is more than ever were his toils, and all because of sweet-voiced Homer; for over the feigning of his winged craft abideth something of

1 I should like to call the English reader's attention to the charming little *Lakeside Classics*, published Christmas by Christmas, by Mr T. J. Donnelley of Chicago, authentic narratives of pioneers and travellers and captives among Indians.

majesty, and the excellence of his skill persuadeth us to his fables unaware."[1] That is but half the explanation. The ready credence we give to Homer is not all due to his winged craft; there is something in us that craves the tale of wandering and adventure; but he knew it, and appealed to it. And the other great tales are of wanderers—Jason, *Don Quixote*, *Robinson Crusoe*, the *Pilgrim's Progress*, *Lavengro*.

Odysseus is the typical wanderer, who "sees the cities of many men and learns their mind". In that line one of the keynotes of the wandering life is struck at the very beginning of the poem which gives its name to all Odysseys. But it is as a beggar, a mere tramp, that Odysseus reaches his own home; and here, in the oldest of European poems, the tramp is described exactly as we know him. Melantheus, the disloyal goatherd, sees him in his disguise with the divine swineherd, Eumaeus; and he speaks with taunts:[2]

See how God ever like with like doth pair,
And still the worthless doth the worthless lead!
Unenviable swineherd, tell me where
This wretch wouldst thou bestow? Not such we need,
Banes of the banquet, very wolves to feed.
He by the doorposts loitering in the way
Will rub his shoulders, and to sate his greed
Prowl mid the suitors for vile scraps of prey,
Nor sword nor caldron earn by any manly play.

If thou wouldst lend him for a while to me
The stalls to sweep, and for the kids supply
Young leaves for pasture, very soon would he
Swill the rich whey and nourish a stout thigh.
But the ill caitiff of all toil is shy,
And with a hell-deep maw doth cringe about
For victuals. Mark me, for I will not lie!
Once let him set foot mid the suitors' rout,
Soon will his ribs and head the flying stools wear out.

Eurymachus as readily recognizes the type, and makes the tramp another offer of work, which he does not expect to see accepted:[3]

He spake, and turned him to the warlike sire:
"Friend, are you willing on my farm to try

1 Pindar, *Nemeans*, 7.
2 *Odyssey*, XVII, 119; Worsley's translation.
3 *Ib*. XVIII, 359, Worsley.

Work—if I take you at sufficient hire—
Cull stones for fences and plant trees? For I
All the year round will feed you, and supply
Good raiment at your need, and sandals stout.
But thou, I know it, of all work art shy,
And liefer through the town wouldst cringe about
And get the wherewithal thy belly to bulge out".

And Odysseus, true to the type he pretends to be, explains that he really is a first-rate worker, when he has a proper chance. The suitors have already, in Irus, a loafer to go upon their errands. The slave-woman, Melantho, has her taunt for Odysseus; let him go and sleep in the smithy or the common bothy, or he may find some worse opponent than Irus.[1] The smithy, as Hesiod tells us, and as we all know who were small boys in the days of horse-shoes, is a prime place for the loafer,[2] and warm too. So there we have our tramp, drawn to the life; and he is a familiar figure already. There are plenty of him, says Antinous indignantly;[3] why should the swineherd bring another?

Find we not vagabonds enough to feed,
Beggars, the bane of feasts, and very wolves for greed?

But there are other wanderers of a more useful type. "Who", asks Eumaeus, "who would call one from another land, except those who are workers for the people (δημιοεργοί), seer, or healer of ills, a worker in wood, or a god-inspired bard?" Some of these wanderers we have seen already in early Kentucky in the nineteenth century, and we are to see these very types persist all through historical Greece. Dynasties rise and fall, strange tribes come over the mountains, Mycenaean civilization ebbs and another rises; but the wandering men never fail. The human needs never fail, to which they undertake to minister; the sea is always in Greek history, and the shipwrecked sailor is never far to seek, nor the slave in a strange land, kidnapped in peace or the captive of war. The rich and the well born are not always safe, as we see in the *Odyssey*, but it is the lowly who do most of the wandering, who spread and develop the arts, and train the mind of Greece.

1 *Odyssey*, XVIII, 328. 2 See p. 58. 3 *Odyssey*, XVII, 376.

Unlike Odysseus, many of them never see the homeland again; and it is with these chiefly that we have to deal. The prophet in distress is rescued by Telemachus and serves him well—Theoclymenos, by name. Two bards are named in the *Odyssey*, Phemios and Demodocos, neither, it would seem, a wanderer; but if the legends of the Greeks are true, which is like enough, there may be a gentle touch of autobiography in the inclusion of the divine bard among those whom a man is glad to bring in among his own people. We shall see by and by a wandering physician, a historical figure, famous among cities and kings, who can embroil nations as well as heal diseases.

The causes that sent men wandering we can well guess; but guessing is not necessary; authentic glimpses are not denied us. The poet Hesiod, for instance, tells us how it was that his father emigrated[1]—"your father and mine, foolish Perses" (he is addressing an idle brother), "was wont to sail on ship-board because he lacked good livelihood. And one day he came to this very place, across a great stretch of sea; he left Aeolian Cyme in the black ship, and fled not from wealth nor from riches and substance, but from evil penury which Zeus lays upon men; and he settled near Helicon, in a sorry hamlet, Ascra, bad in winter, hard in summer, never good".[2] There is one of the permanent motives—poverty; and the others are there.

Sometimes home, whether it be clan or town, grows too hot to hold the man, and he has to go. Theoclymenos has killed a man at Argos, a man of a powerful clan, and he is going for his life. On the beach at Pylos he finds Telemachus ready to embark and begs him to save him; and Telemachus takes the prophet on board and over the sea to Ithaca.[3] A pier-head jump, as modern sailors have called it, is still sometimes the way to safety. The exact stage at which clan society has arrived in *Iliad* and *Odyssey* may be a difficult question. But

1 Hesiod, *Works and Days*, 633–40.

2 *Ib.* 640; H. F. Tozer, *Geography of Greece*, p. 140, says this account of Ascra "is generally confirmed in modern times".

3 *Odyssey*, 15, 223.

the killing of a man, on purpose or by accident, was still, and long remained, a matter for the clan. The lad, who, like Patroclus, killed a playfellow, had before him a life of exile. Exile or death it will be for the man-slayer, unless some payment soften the avenger of blood. The trial scene on the shield of Achilles tells the story—"the folk were gathered in the assembly place; for there a strife was arisen, two men striving about the blood-price of a man slain; the one claimed to make full atonement, expounding to the people, but the other denied him and would take naught; and both were fain to receive arbitrament at the hand of a daysman. And the folk were cheering both as they took part on either side".[1] It is the same sort of picture that we find in the Icelandic sagas. And, if there is no appeasement, it is

Home no more home to me, whither must I wander?
Hunger my driver, I go where I must.

He will be *ἀφρήτωρ ἀθέμιστος ἀνέστιος*,[2] a man outside clan and law and hearth, with no tribesmen to guard him, no custom to save him, no hearth to shelter at; he must go, and go quickly. And we can believe that there were plenty of these men, too.

Sometimes the clan wanders, and in its wanderings clashes with another and is a clan no more; and those who survive and are not made slaves are like the stray murderer, solitary figures, broken men, wanderers. Kidnapping and slavery scatter men and women over Homer's seas; and, though perhaps we read of no captive breaking away, modern analogies from the nearer East and Africa give us glimpses of the slave, who has regained freedom but never reaches home or clan. These drifting men without anchors must have been everywhere in the Greek world; we have seen them in Homer, and, when first we touch the historic Athens, we find it a haven for men driven from their homes by war or sedition[3]—effective men, Thucydides says, men with trades, Plutarch implies.

1 *Iliad*, XVIII, 497–502.
2 *Iliad*, IX, 63.
3 Thucydides, I, 2, 6; Plutarch, *Solon*, 22. Cf. G. B. Grundy, *Thucydides*, p. 66.

The *Odyssey* again is full of traders, taking gleaming iron overseas, amber necklaces, cattle, stolen children, and Phoenician goods. The trader, the kidnapper and the pirate are not accurately subdivided trades; given the ship, in those days all things were possible. One feigned tale which Odysseus tells of his early adventures sets it all out clearly enough. He was, he alleges,[1] a rich man's son from Crete, but his mother was a bought slave-woman; his father treated him well; but on the father's death the true-begotten brothers gave him only a meagre share, man of arms as he was:

Such was I seen in arms, but held not dear
Thrift in the house and labour of the hand,
Which things are wont a splendid race to rear.
Arrows and bows I loved, and fleets well manned,
Spears, and a noise of fightings in the land.
All that seems hateful and uncouth to men
God taught my eager spirit to understand.
Such wild delight I drank in warfare then!
Thus divers works, I ween, give joy to divers men.

So, he tells Eumaeus, he turned pirate and plunderer. Before the Greek fleet sailed for Troy, he had led ships and men nine times on forays, and taken much spoil. After the Trojan War a month at home sufficed him, and he went off raiding in Egypt and came to grief. Only shipwreck saved him from being sold as a slave by a Phoenician; he lands somewhere in Thesprotia and is given clothes; yet ill-luck dogs him, he is robbed by ship-mates, but he drops off the ship and gets ashore in Ithaca. It may be one of Odysseus' feigned tales, but it is a true picture of Greek life; if it had not been, Odysseus would not have told it. Restlessness—"if a man should say of the Athenians that they were born neither to rest themselves nor to let anybody else rest, it would be the simple truth". So, we are told, said the Corinthians,[2] and many agree that the Athenians only differed from other Greeks in being more Greek; and, if this sentence seem ambiguous, Pericles said something very like it. We have

1 *Odyssey*, XIV, 199 ff.
2 Thucydides, I, 70, end.

Wanderlust then in Homer, and wherever the Greek blood stirs to this day. English is spoken in the Peloponnese with an American accent—"yes! we have no bananas".[1]

The same forces that drove the wandering Greeks of Homer's day afield through the Mediterranean lands were always active. The territory of the Greek city state was rarely large, but the birth-rate must for long have been far higher than we commonly think; the food problem can rarely have been far away. When it was the alternative between bringing food in or getting the eaters out, sheer hunger must have set innumerable wanderers adrift. It was no longer exactly war between clan and clan, but war between city and city was at least as bad. The whole population of a conquered city was sometimes sold into slavery; and, while it is clear that ransoms were effected and that citizens sometimes returned to rebuild and inhabit the old town,[2] there must have been many of the dispersion who lived and died slaves in alien lands, and many who escaped but never returned. *Stasis*, faction-fighting, constantly re-appears in the Greek town; and, though of the three great motives to civil strife, hunger, justice and religion, the last was wanting, sheer need was hardly more effective in dividing men than political theory. The exile, of whom we hear most, lived in the sole hope of return, at any cost to his country.[3] We hear less of those who gave up the idea, naturally much less;[4] their aim was not to make history but to make a living; but they made more than that, for surely it was they more than any others who gave the name Hellen its great and universal content. On his

1 The Greek runs the American fruit-stall very commonly; hence the dreadful chorus which could never have become popular but for the familiarity with the Greek immigrant. Henry Pratt Fairchild's *Greek Immigration to the United States* (1911) has a great deal of information of interest to those who care for Greece, ancient or modern. Chapter XI treats of the effect upon Greece of the great emigration, of the men who return, of the $5,000,000 or so remitted annually (at that time) to the old land.

2 Cf. for example Pausanias, VII, 6, 9; IX, 7, 1; and Strabo, C. 403, on the restoration of Thebes after Alexander's destruction of it.

3 *ἔκητι Συλοσῶντος εὐρυχωρίη*, quoted by Strabo, C. 638.

4 If Marco Polo had not had the misfortune to be captured by the Genoese in 1298, and the good fortune to meet Rustician of Pisa in their prison, would the world ever have had the narrative of his amazing travels?

return from the great Anabasis Xenophon met Greek princes, descendants of the Spartan King Demaratus, a family settled among Persian nobles in Asia Minor for nearly a century but still bearing Greek names, the names of the legendary Spartan twins, and sympathetic with their countrymen, in the larger sense of the word.[1] Far more than we sometimes suspect, it was our wanderers who gave the word that larger sense. Home-keeping youths have too often a John Bull attitude to their cousins. Englishmen scarcely realize how galling is their island blend of ignorance and arrogance. It is the overseas people who have created Greater Britain.

It is interesting to find at times that a general invitation was extended to Greeks to join in founding a colony, a common venture for the wandering spirits. Thus Herodotus tells us:[2] "In the time of the third ruler, that Battus who was called the Fortunate, the Pythian priestess admonished all Greeks by an oracle to cross the sea and dwell in Libya with the Cyrenaeans; for the Cyrenaeans invited them, promising a new division of lands". A great multitude gathered to Cyrene, and it meant, as so often in Western America, immediate encroachment on native lands; and the natives called in the Egyptians to help them. Aristotle says that such mixed colonies did not prosper; "a state is not the growth of a day, neither is it a multitude brought together by accident"; and he gives a string of examples of failure.[3] But, early or late, the love of wandering is in the Greek, and we have to recognize that he would not have been Greek without it.

So far we have not noticed the man who travelled ἱστορίης ἕνεκεν, like Herodotus, to inquire, to learn and to know. At first sight, he may seem far removed in spirit from the ordinary wanderers, but in reality they are probably more akin than we think; the one may have more stirrings of mind than we suppose, and the other more of mere restlessness.

1 *Anabasis*, VII, 8, 18; and *Hellenica*, III, 1, 6.

2 Herodotus, IV, 159.

3 Aristotle, *Politics*, V, 3, 11, 1303a. Cf. Xenophon's notion of turning the Ten Thousand into a new Black Sea colony, *Anabasis*, V, 6, 15; 7, 1–7; VI, 4, 7.

It is not always enough acknowledged that emigrants are very generally the energetic and individual spirits among the class from which they come. Their native land is only too certain to retain the stupid and unenterprising.

We have next to survey, as far as we can in brief, the types that took to wandering. "Doubtless", says Aristotle, "in ancient times and among some nations, the artisan class were slaves or foreigners, and therefore the majority of them are so now. The best form of state (he adds) will not admit them to citizenship."[1] Both statements deserve attention; artisans, he held, lived a mean life which incapacitated the mind, robbed it of the outlook and the training that a citizen should have. That is his theory. The fact he cites is hardly less surprising—that industries in a Greek city were largely in the hands of aliens. A tyrant, he says, will vex his subjects, if he wastes the taxes taken from their pitiful earnings in gifts to women, foreigners and craftsmen.[2] It was to the tyrant's interest to multiply foreigners, dependent on himself and without local traditions, like the Jews about Renaissance princes in Germany. Pindar says explicitly that Hiero, tyrant of Syracuse, was "a wondrous father to foreigners";[3] other people tell us that Syracuse was made up of all sorts and kinds of people and was very factious and disorderly. The foreigners that a tyrant would be favouring would include not only poets and physicians (to whom we shall return) but cooks, actors, dancers, robe-makers, armourers, ship-builders, and men to work in his mint. Hiero's Syracusan coins are famous; and kings, says Polybius,[4] especially hereditary ones, come to think they should be distinguished from their subjects by a special dress, and that there should be a peculiar luxury and variety about their viands. The earliest historical ship-builder, whose name we know, was Ameinocles, a Corinthian, and he built four ships for the Samians—his country's allies, it would seem—about 700 B.C., as Thucydides dates him.[5]

1 Aristotle, *Politics*, III, v, 3, 1278a.

2 *Politics*, v (VII), 11, 19, 1314b.

3 Pindar, *Pythian*, 3, 71.

4 Polybius, VI, 7, 7.

5 Thucydides, I, 13, 3.

Athens affords us a curious amount of evidence as to foreign craftsmen. "We admitted", says a client of Demosthenes,[1] "that we sell ribbons, and live, not as we would, but as we can; and if you conclude from that, Eubulides, that we are foreigners"—the English reader would not have concluded it. It appears, not from literature which ignores them, but from their own works, that the leading potters in Athens had foreign names and presumably were foreigners—sometimes they are race-names rather than personal names; Scythes, Lydos, Colchos, Sicanos, Brygos were obviously not Greeks. Nicknames, such as Mys and Smicros, are less decisive; but we meet definitely Greek names with no indication of a parent. The famous Douris appears to have been a foreigner.[2] Andocides assumes that a man who makes lamps (of clay) will be a foreigner.[3] Among the builders of the Erechtheum are foreigners,[4] and there are foreign sculptors.[5] An inscription of about 403 B.C., decreeing citizenship to foreigners, mostly with Greek names, who had stood loyally by the Demos, mentions their trades, which include, beside some farmers, a cook, a builder, a muleteer, a gardener, a baker, a fuller, and an image-maker.[6] Old Cephalos, the friend of Socrates, and the father of Lysias, was a Syracusan and manufactured shields in the Peiraieus. The shrewd economist, Solon, offered Athenian citizenship to foreign Greeks who would settle with their trades in Athens, provided they were permanently exiled from their own cities, or brought their families with them; both classes, he felt, could be trusted.[7] Cleisthenes did the same by a number of foreigners, when the tyrants were expelled;[8] there they were, brought in by the Pisistratids, and it was as well to make them good democrats. Themistocles also favoured them, but

1 Demosthenes *in Eubulidem*, 31.

2 Cf. Glotz, *Ancient Greece at Work*, p. 182; Edmond Pottier, *Douris*, p. 11; Dugas, *Greek Pottery*, pp. 91, 92.

3 Andocides ap. Scholiast on Aristophanes, *Wasps*, 1007.

4 Glotz, *op. cit.* p. 172.

5 W. S. Ferguson, *Hellenistic Athens*, p. 246.

6 Hicks and Hill, *Greek Inscriptions*, no. 80.

7 Plutarch, *Solon*, 24.

8 Aristotle, *Politics*, III, ii, 3, 1275b.

Pericles made citizenship harder to attain, much harder.[1] The times had perhaps changed; the politician's problem was different; but it has never, I think, been fully recognized what Solon and the statesmen who took his lead really did for Athens in making the wandering Greek welcome. They made the city the focus of the real life of Greece, the centre to which brains and ideas, art and industry, naturally gravitated; and by doing this they created the nidus in which, during the great century that followed, genius flourished as never before or after. At the beginning of the fourth century a writer, whose work is attributed to Xenophon, wrote on Athenian finances, and urged more attention to foreigners—they should be encouraged to settle, allowed to acquire land to build houses, relieved of useless disabilities; exchanges and hotels should be built in the Peiraieus, and better seats reserved in the theatre; and efforts made to get a larger and better class of settler, for he seems not to esteem the Lydians, Phrygians and Syrians.[2] The garrulous man, in Theophrastus, babbles about the number of foreigners in town; and Isocrates growls about their being made citizens.[3] Later on, it is the Athenians who emigrate.[4]

To confuse traders with the mere wanderers we found in the *Odyssey* may seem to abandon our theme; but, as Homer makes clear, the same man may play many parts. We have to remember the immense trade of the great age of Greece, and its sea-captains and sailors, good men and true, and some not so good, like Hegestratos who tried to scuttle the ship and then had to bolt for it and was drowned in his attempt to escape on the ship's boat.[5] Only an occasional lawsuit, or a stray anecdote or reference, tells us of these people. They went everywhere; the wheat dealers, says Socrates, had such a feeling for grain that they would dash off overseas to any place where wheat was most highly

1 Cf. G. B. Grundy, *Thucydides*, pp. 66, 157; Zimmern, *Greek Commonwealth*, p. 353.

2 Πόροι, 2, 1–7; 3, 12 (hotels); 3, 4 (theatre).

3 Isocrates, *de Pace*, 88; *Panath.* 124.

4 W. S. Ferguson, *Hellenistic Athens*, p. 97.

5 [Demosthenes], 32; *Zenothemis*, 5, 6.

valued. The wine trade, too, carried men to Egypt regularly, sometimes further afield, as when the gale swept Kolaios away to Spain.[1] Herodotus[2] has a tale of Sappho's brother Charaxos, who went to Egypt, with a cargo (Strabo adds[3]) of Lesbian wine for the Greek town of Naucratis, and there he fell in with a Thracian girl called Rhodopis. She was the property of a Samian, called Xanthes, who brought her there to practise her calling; and Charaxos fell in love with her, bought her and set her up on her own account; and very popular she became, for she was very lovely, and she made a great deal of money. Sappho wrote a poem bitterly reproaching her brother for his folly.[4] Rhodopis became very famous; all the Greeks knew her name, and some would have it that she built one of the pyramids. But, says Herodotus, the pyramid must have cost thousands of talents beyond reckoning; Rhodopis grew rich—for a Rhodopis, but nothing like so rich as to build a pyramid; in fact, you can calculate her wealth from the tenth she dedicated in Delphi. Strabo tells another tale attached to her memory, a Cinderella tale; how, when she was bathing, an eagle caught away her slipper from her maid, and flew to Memphis; how the king was dispensing justice there in the open air; how the slipper dropped into his lap; and how he was so impressed with its shapeliness and the strangeness of the occurrence, that he made search through all Egypt, till he found her, and she became his queen, and so was buried at last in the pyramid. Some echo of her story survived to Arab days, of a rosy-cheeked woman of the pyramids or a rosy-cheeked sphinx.[5] Other women of beauty we read of under similar conditions—the woman of Cos whom Pharandates brought to Greece on the great Persian expedition;[6] the "clever and beautiful" Phocaean, whom Cyrus took with him on his march against the king, and whom the king captured after the disaster,

1 See p. 19.
2 Herodotus, II, 134, 135.
3 Strabo, c. 808.
4 Athenaeus, XIII, 596b, will have it that Rhodopis and Doricha (whom Sappho denounces) were different women.
5 See *Journal of Hellenic Studies*, vol. XXIV, article by H. R. Hall.
6 Herodotus, IX, 76.

while the younger girl, from Miletus, when caught, broke away and escaped naked to the Greeks;[1] others, too, among the Ten Thousand; and the Athenian Thais who at Persepolis "led the veterans on".[2] But there is some uniformity in the story of these wandering women.

Egypt reminds us of mercenary soldiers, carving their names on the legs of the colossi at Abu Simbel about 590 B.C., of merchants gathering at Naucratis, and, in later generations, the multitude of poets and scholars, soldiers, sailors, and all sorts of people, who came, or were brought, or drifted, to Alexandria. The papyri and the potsherds are full of their family affairs—marriages, divorces, lawsuits, quarrels, friendships, scandals. But many of these people will really be settlers rather than mere wanderers, and others will be country bred. One point, however, should be noted, how in process of time the inevitable took place, and Greeks married native wives and produced Levantines. The mixed marriage and its influence are incalculable, and we meet it from the first. The slave-girl's son by her master in the *Odyssey*; Herodotus and his relatives with Carian names; Thucydides' family tree with its Thracian connections; Xenophon's foreign[3] wife; all these touch literature somehow; but there must have been thousands of persons all over the world with Greek blood, and perhaps Greek brains, whose names were never in story. But Egypt has diverted us from our plan, as it has done many a man; and before we roam further, we had better pause to choose our company, for there were many afoot and afloat beside those we have seen.

We have our choice of athletes and their trainers, going from festival to festival, but perhaps in earlier days not true wanderers, in that they took with them their city's name, that she shared with them in the glory of their victory, and they returned to her. In a later day perhaps it was otherwise, when empire and emigration shook the old loyalties. The mercenaries of the earlier time opened Egypt to their

1 Xenophon, *Anabasis*, I, 10.
2 Q. Curtius, v, 22; Plutarch, *Alexander*, 38.
3 Presumably foreign.

countrymen, as we have seen. One went much further. We know him as we know Charaxos, for he was the brother of a poet. A fragment of Alcaeus survives addressed to Antimenidas who served in Babylon, and, if we take the earlier rather than the later date assigned to Alcaeus, it was in the armies of Nebuchadnezzar himself. Here are the lines of Alcaeus:[1]

Thou hast come from the ends of the earth;
    And the hilt of the sword thou dost hold
Is of ivory wrought, a thing of worth,
    Bound and studded with gold—
Of thy prowess the splendid mead—
    For in Babylon's ranks afar
    Thou didst mightily aid in war,
And didst work a valiant deed,
    Slaying a monstrous man.
And dread was the terror he cast—
Five royal cubits he towered vast,
    Lacking only a span.

Two centuries later the father of Demosthenes manufactured such sumptuous swords in Athens.

After the Peloponnesian War mercenary soldiers abounded. Industries and commerce were disorganized; men lacked work; war had in twenty-seven years become a science, and they had learnt it, and had no other trade. Isocrates[2] laments their case—"men without a city, deserters, the clotted scum of all knavery"; wars and factions and sheer poverty drove them abroad to fight for their enemies against their friends; even Xenophon's Ten Thousand (Isocrates says six thousand) were not picked for their valour, it was the hard times that would not let them live in their own lands. Xenophon denies that poverty was the cause, and Mr W. E. Heitland comes to his aid—"full-blooded men were not content to drag on ill-found stagnant lives in corners of Greece".[3] Not only the rank and file sold their services; we read of would-be generals and instructors in the art of war travelling in search of work at their very specialized trades. One famous general served

1 Preserved by Strabo, c. 617.
2 Isocrates, *de Pace*, 44; *Paneg.* 168; *Paneg.* 146.
3 Xenophon, *Anabasis*, VI, 4, 8; Heitland, *Agricola*, p. 54.

with the Carthaginians some generations later and set their forces in order. Xanthippos, a Spartan, came with a batch of hired troops and shrewdly observed that Carthage had to thank her own generals, not the enemy, for her troubles. He served for one year in command, and then left. "One man and one brain restored the fortunes of a state which in the eyes of all was utterly fallen, and revived the deadened spirit of its soldiers." So says Polybius,[1] whose judgments are to be trusted, and who was not apt to overpraise Spartans.

Our list of travellers includes gentler arts. Actors, dancers, tumblers and conjurors travelled about Greece. At the banquet, which Xenophon describes, a Syracusan was brought in to amuse the company. He had with him a fine flute-girl, a dancing girl who could do acrobatic tricks, and a boy who danced and played on the lyre. The girl danced, whirling hoops into the air and catching them, which set Socrates propounding that woman's nature is not really inferior to man's; and when she turned somersaults through a hoop set round with upright swords, he urged that courage could obviously be taught. Antisthenes suggested that the girl might be hired to teach Athenians courage. But this seems not to have been done. We read of conjurors bringing fire out of their mouths, swallowing knives, and making pebbles pass from one cup to another; and Theophrastus' "Reckless Man" will collect the coppers at the conjuror's show.[2] Travelling actors were even engaged to act as temporary diplomats; their art was their safe-conduct. Terpander, the musician from Lesbos, we recall, performed in Sparta, where extreme conservatism had not yet developed. The rhapsodes also wandered, reciting Homer's poems; and the Greeks told of Homer's wanderings from city to city, the greatest of all rhapsodes. "Beggar is envious of beggar, bard of bard", says Hesiod in his abrupt and revealing way.[3] The poet of the Homeric hymn to Apollo bids the women who hear him to remember him, and, if any ask hereafter who was the

1 Polybius, I, 35, 5.
2 Theophrastus, *Characters*, 16, with Jebb's note.
3 Hesiod, *Works and Days*, 26.

sweetest of singers, to answer "A blind man and he dwells in Chios' rocky isle".[1]

We saw how men in Homer's day would bring a prophet, a seer, a *mantis*, to their home, and do it gladly. That tribe never ceased to wander. Plato[2] indignantly describes how priests (ἀγύρται) and prophets go to rich men's doors, with a host of books written by Musaeus and Orpheus, who were the sons of the Moon and the Muses, and try to persuade the rich that they have power from the gods to make atonement for their sins, or those of their fathers, by means of sacrifices and charms, and very enjoyably too; and, for a small charge, they can injure an enemy for you, good man or bad, whichever he be, with their spells; yes! and bind the gods to their will by their enchantments. The two most famous picaresque novels of antiquity, the *Golden Ass* of Apuleius, and the less golden *Ass* attributed to Lucian, alike describe the inglorious adventures of strolling priests of Cybele. These last were at first not Greeks.

Physicians, too, are among the wanderers. Democedes is the most famous, if we except the great Hippocrates of Cos, who practised in Athens a generation or so later. Democedes[3] was born at Croton in Italy, but he found his father ill to live with, and went Eastward to Aegina. There, "though he had no equipment nor any implements of his calling", he excelled all other physicians, and in his second year the men of Aegina paid him a talent to be their public physician. In the next year the Athenians hired him for one talent forty minae—a substantial rise—to have him lured away by Polycrates the tyrant of Samos for two talents. And among the staff of Polycrates he found himself a prisoner at Susa, and healed King Darius' foot when the Egyptian surgeons failed. The king gave him golden fetters—"doubling my pains for mending you", said the Greek and greatly pleased the king. He saved the lives of the hapless Egyptian doctors, healed Queen Atossa's breast, and had terrible trouble in ever getting away back to Italy. Another famous physician at the Persian

1 *h. Apollo*, 166–72.
2 Plato, *Republic*, 364B ff.
3 Herodotus, III, 129 ff.

court was Ctesias of Cnidos, who was for seventeen years medical attendant of King Artaxerxes and wrote books about the Assyrians and Persians which had more circulation than credit.[1] We learn that he accompanied King Artaxerxes on the campaign which saw the end of Cyrus.[2] There were eight physicians, we are told, with Xenophon's Ten Thousand. Meanwhile there was not a doctor left in all Athens, in the hard times after the war, who might give sight to the blind god Plutus;

> "There are no fees and so there is no art."
> "Let's think awhile." "There's none!" "No more there is."[3]

Poets of course travelled, as the dolphin of Arion and the cranes of Ibycus remind us. Pindar went to Hiero, Euripides himself to Archelaus of Macedon. In Athens in the fourth century, some of the most famous poets of the New Comedy were foreigners—Antiphanes, for example, Alexis and Philemon.[4] Plato[5] would not have ordinary poets in his ideal state; but then they would go to other cities and readily find acceptance, and no doubt forgive the idealists who crowned them, and most politely put them over the frontier. The travelling philosophers of ancient Greece and even of the Roman Empire—with their students who thronged to Athens[6]—surely belong to a tribe more august than our common wanderers; more like, we might say, to the professors, who in America rise from altitude to altitude till they reach Harvard, than which only Heaven is thought to be higher.

But to return to the range of the wanderers. How soon, for instance, ought we to look for Greek influence at Rome? Rome was founded, they say, in 754 B.C.; Syracuse in 734 B.C. and Marseilles about 600 B.C.—far more reliable dates.[7] How soon, then, did ships and sailors from Syracuse and Marseilles come up the Tiber? How soon did restless sailors desert a Greek ship, to lie hid in the small streets of Rome, perhaps

1 Strabo, c. 656.

2 Xenophon, *Anabasis*, I, 8, 27; Plutarch, *Artaxerxes*, 13, says that Ctesias was ambitious and always allowed space for himself in his narrative.

3 Aristophanes, *Plutus*, 407–9.

4 Glotz, *Ancient Greece at Work*, p. 190.

5 Plato, *Republic*, VIII, 568B.

6 Isocrates, *Antidosis*, 224.

7 See p. 24.

to settle there and marry more or less, as far as laws allowed it to be called marriage, and add to the mass of the Plebs, plebeians with Latin names but Greek brains and Greek ideas? Is it all guess-work? Strabo, Livy and Dionysius all tell us of the Corinthian exile, Demaratus, who took a company of Greek artisans to Etruria, and became the ancestor of the Tarquins.[1] Legend it may be, but the archaeologists assure us of Greek masons and builders early at work in Rome, which after all is what we ought to have expected.[2] The alphabet and its dissemination should tell a tale. One Greek writer of Aristotle's time, Heracleides of Pontus, is quoted by Plutarch[3] as authority for a tale (in his book on the Soul) of a Hyperborean host taking Rome, a Greek city, somewhere on the Great Sea; "I would not wonder", adds Plutarch, "if Heracleides, who loved a myth and a fiction, touched up the true story of the capture of Rome [by the Gauls] by bringing in the Hyperboreans and the Great Sea". A Greek city? We must not touch up our story, nor engage in the quarrels of archaeologists, but the wandering Greek who drifts to Rome is far from incredible. And we must not forget our Horace—

Caelum non animum mutant qui trans mare currunt.

The Greek is still Greek, wherever he drifts, argumentative, challenging, and politically-minded.

But he went to stranger lands than Egypt and Latium. The gold ornaments of the Scythians—twenty thousand objects in Russian museums[4]—and the vases speak of Greek goldsmiths and painters, Attic and Ionian, wandering for generations in South Russia, from the Greek settlements on the Black Sea.[5] Who were the countless interpreters who made life so interesting in Asia for Herodotus and all his readers, but wandering Greeks? He tells us as much of some of them, and other Greek stories of war and travel imply

1 Strabo, c. 220, 378; Livy, I, 34; Dionys. Halic. *Antt. Rom.* III, 47.
2 Grenier, *Roman Spirit*, p. 51.
3 Plutarch, *Camillus*, 22. Cf. Pais, *Ancient Legends*, p. 27.
4 Now being sold by the Russian government outside the country.
5 See Michaelis, *A Century of Archaeological Discoveries*, pp. 107–9.

their presence in lands further afield.[1] Or the actors, who played Euripides at the Parthian court?[2] Greek sailors, from about the time of the Christian era, used the monsoons to go to Malabar and return; and there is concrete proof in the hoards of Roman coin found in Southern India. The *Acts of Thomas* describe the apostle being sold as a carpenter or builder to go to India.[3] North Indian architecture, Bactrian coinage, the Buddhas of the Swat valley, all show Greek influence; and we know that Greeks ranged into those lands. The hungry Greek did not confine himself to Italy—*in caelum jusseris ibit*—and nobody ranged the world with more zest.

The effects of all this movement, the influences exerted and received, are beyond our computation. As we have followed our wanderers, we have speculated upon what they were, and what they did; can we sum up our evidence, our impressions, our guesses—recognizing that such things are hard to add together, and that there may be inaccuracy in our result? Let it be said at once that any conclusions we draw are more likely to fall short of the reality than to exceed it. We have suggested that there might well be Greek blood in plebeian veins here and there in early Rome; can we say with the Roman poet *Fortes creantur fortibus et bonis*, and deny abruptly that aptitude for political life (for instance) may be transmitted, and may be nourished in a boyhood spent with the father who transmits it? What does the double tradition mean in a family—the memories and longings and old tales brought from two countries far apart instead of all coming from one village, the clash of instincts and ideas? It has been suggested that genius is often helped by parents whose minds and tastes conflict, that the best combination for a man (in our islands) is a Lowland father and a Highland mother. It is common experience among ourselves in the British Empire, that a man from the old country who has lived long in one

1 Cf. Polyaenus, III, 9, 59, ἄνδρας ἐμπείρους τῆς Περσίδος γλώσσης. Cf. also Pigres the interpreter, Xenophon, *Anabasis*, I, 2, 17; and Timesitheos of Trapezus who can interpret the Mossynoeci, *Anabasis*, V, 4, 4.

2 Plutarch, *Crassus*, 33; Jason was the singer who played the horrid part of Agave with the Roman's head.

3 See p. 32.

of the Dominions comes back changed; the old country is not the same; he has two loyalties, which may be contributive or confusing. Let it be both, in the long run it is all gain to have men whose experience makes them interpreters and mediators. And so it was with our wanderers of the ancient world.

The influence of these wanderers, of these homes with two traditions, modifies religious outlooks. Among polytheists there will not be the stark clash involved where one parent is monotheist and the other not. We are told that when mixed marriages, or their equivalents, occur in Burma, where the immigrant parent is Hindu, the child is Buddhist (the caste system secures that; he is born out of caste); but where the immigrant parent is Moslem, the child is Moslem.[1] Ancient polytheism had no such divisions, and outside Egypt no castes. But, if there was little quarrel about polytheistic rites, when there was every reason to keep both kinds, and none against it, none the less one thing must result, and did in fact result. The gods and heroes of Greece could be very local. A man of Sicyon will be loyal to Adrastus, of course, while he is at Sicyon. You cannot blend (as was quickly found[2]) the gods any more than the traditions of Argos and Corinth. But transport your men from Sicyon, Argos and Corinth a thousand miles away; and where is the local god? This was a question raised for all time by Alexander's expedition; it involved fresh thoughts upon the unity of the godhead. But these thoughts were not official, exactly; officials do not think effectively on such matters; such thoughts come from the situation. Then must they not have risen in a thousand instances before ever Philip heard of his horse's victory and his son's birth?[3] The way is opened for the syncretism of the Macedonian and the Roman Empires. With it comes inevitably—or even precedes it—a sense of the real unity of the Greek race. In the Armenian mountains even the most locally-minded of the Ten Thousand must realize that Greeks were Greeks and not Kurds. It is all preparation for a new view of the world, and thoughts more

1 Cf. Ameen Rihani, *Around the Coasts of Arabia*, pp. 136 ff., on mixtures in Islam. 2 Xenophon, *Hell.* IV, 4, 3–6. 3 Plutarch, *Alex.* 3.

fertile, in that Hellenistic period, which English scholars are in general so strangely reluctant to study.

But there are earlier results. Greeks talked wherever they went, a nation of talkers, as the Roman wearily noted, fond of questions, lovers of theory, quick-eyed, with the traveller's zest for travellers' tales *in excelsis*. So they saw the hippopotamus and the crocodile in Egypt, and the river more wonderful than its creatures—the mysterious stream, that like its creatures contradicted all Greek experience of nature. And the gods, too, they noted—queer gods, very interesting and immeasurably old. By the way, asked Xenophanes, are gods black or white? How could they be black? Well, you see black gods in Africa. "To whom then will ye liken Me?" They brought home fresh questions, fresh wonder; and wonder, as Aristotle says, is the mother of philosophy.[1] So it is the wanderer who sets Greece on the road to Thought. There can be no connection in etymology between *wander* and *wonder*, but there surely is in History, and above all in the history of Religion and Philosophy. And here again our wanderers are the true pioneers of the Hellenistic age, the great monarchies and the Roman Empire with its common Greek speech, its common citizenship and its universal religions.

Nor must we forget the part of the wanderer in propagating the Christian religion along with the cults of Isis and of Mithras. The names of those who spread the faith are not known; legend sent St Mark to Alexandria, St Thomas to India; but we have only to read the *Acts of the Apostles* and St Paul's Epistles to see how obscure were the wandering preachers, mere laymen of the road with a new faith. How effective they were, three centuries revealed; for the Christian church was not made by organization but by men.

But is not the element of conjecture in these judgments rather large? Then what is the significance of Plato's dislike of the sea? "The sea", he says,[2] "is pleasant enough as a daily companion, but it has also a bitter and brackish quality; filling the streets with merchants and shopkeepers, and be-

1 Aristotle, *Metaphysics*, I, 2, 982 b, διὰ γὰρ τὸ θαυμάζειν οἱ ἄνθρωποι καὶ νῦν καὶ τὸ πρῶτον ἤρξαντο φιλοσοφεῖν.

2 *Laws*, 705 A; cf. Cicero, *de Rep.* II, 4, 7.

getting in the souls of men uncertain and unfaithful ways—making the state unfriendly and unfaithful both to her own citizens and also to other nations. There is a consolation, therefore, in the country producing all things at home." This is a theory held by Mr Gandhi, too. Plato would therefore plant his ideal city in the centre of the country.[1] "The intercourse of cities with one another is apt to create a confusion of manners; strangers are always suggesting novelties to strangers." So he says,[2] and dwells on "the confusion which arises from the reception of strangers, and from the citizens themselves rushing off into other cities, whenever anyone young or old desires to travel abroad at any time or to go anywhere". Of course, to exclude *all* strangers would be impossible, and other nations would think it ruthless and uncivilized, and foreign opinion counts too. But he would suggest that none have leave to go abroad at all till forty years of age, and then not in any private capacity, but only on some state errand. And "when they come home they shall teach the young that the institutions of other states are inferior to their own".[3] But if the man who goes abroad appear on his return home to have been corrupted, pretending to be wise when he is not, he must not be allowed to talk to people, and, if he will not keep quiet, and shall be convicted in a court of law of interfering about religion and the laws, let him die.[4]

Could there be more emphatic testimony to the significance of the wandering Greek?

Most stories end in the long run with an epitaph; so let us end with one: "I am an Athenian woman (Ἀτθὶς ἐγώ), for that was my city; but from Athens the wasting War-god of the Italians took me for a spoil long ago, and made me a citizen of Rome; and, now that I am dead, sea-girt Cyzicus wraps my bones. Fare thou well, O land that didst nurture me; thou, too, that thereafter didst hold me; and thou, that at the last hast taken me to thy bosom".[5]

1 *Laws*, 745 B. 2 *Laws*, 949, 950. 3 *Laws*, 951 A.
4 See also the discussion of this whole question in Aristotle, *Politics*, VII, 6, 1327 a.
5 *Anthol. Palat.* VII, 366; cf. 376, a man of Lesbos, buried in Spain.

THE BOY AND THE THEORIST

God sends us meat and the deil sends cooks.
Scottish Proverb.

PROBABLY most human beings would by now regard it as a truism, or even an axiom, that to be tedious it is only necessary to discuss education. There are people —they are called educationists by way of distinction from teachers—who find it interesting to debate about essential subjects, school certificates, mark-standards and such topics; but no one else does. Some sardonic observer has made a collection of subjects "absolutely essential" and finds they number (I think) sixty-seven, all to be assimilated by the unhappy child. No wonder race-suicide prevails; it is only humanity.

But, every now and then, the question of education forces itself upon a people. Some anxiety is felt, some need for protection against a church in the midst, against an efficient enemy without, or against some insidious propaganda that saps national life. The nation must bestir itself and exert some control. At such a time, as everybody is either educated or uneducated, especially in a democracy, everybody has an opinion of importance; even the mothers join in, quoting the opinions of their children at school. The trouble, however, is that, when we get to the facts, nobody is quite educated or quite uneducated, and we all of us generalize from our own tastes and from our own schooldays. In some cases our schooldays were forty years ago, in others ten years ago; in either case they appear to have a special value, even though the world has greatly changed since we were educated, or though our own education was perhaps obsolete, or scientific, or premature—sterility has many forms. But it is easy to make fun of our own outlooks, or other people's. Perhaps, as Harry Vane said, nearly three centuries ago, no man is wise enough to govern us all. Let us hope no man ever will, nor woman neither.

In Athens, about the time of the Peloponnesian War, a great discussion blew up about education. Not only the experts (then known as sophists) discussed it, but it became a matter of general concern and common talk. So much so, that a rising young poet wrote a comedy about it for the Great Dionysia in March 423 B.C. He was somewhat disconcerted to find it awarded only the third prize; but he revised it carefully; and, whether he again presented it or not—he says he has never served up the same thing twice, but has always fresh ideas[1]—the play was preserved in the revised form. Genius does not save a man from making the strangest mistakes about popular tastes and interests and intelligence. But it should be significant that such a man, with such variety of topics to choose from, and such gifts of wild and brilliant invention, chose to write a play on Education. No doubt the central figure was a man much in the public eye, in many ways the oddest and most interesting figure (apart from mere politicians) in Athens; but that does not explain all. Some eighteen years or so later Aristophanes wrote a comedy all about literary criticism, and was awarded the first prize, and the play was called for again. It all suggests that he had to deal with a remarkable people. How long did it take the British public to grasp the central idea of Darwin—something about our descent from monkeys, or Einstein's queer notions? Of course, a city state occupies less ground, and a man may more easily become a figure in a city of half a million than in a modern nation; but in how many modern cities of that size could a visiting philosopher get a nickname which represented his central idea or even be generally recognized on the streets? Yet Anaxagoras was called *Nous* in Athens.[2] No doubt by the end of the century Socrates was a conspicuous figure, an obvious Silenus whom you could not mistake; but when Aristophanes attacked him in *The Clouds*, Socrates was only about forty-six. There is

1 Aristophanes, *Clouds*, 546.

2 So it is commonly said. Plutarch, *Pericles*, 4, 4, says merely that the men of that time so called him; but Anaxagoras was also the centre of public attack in Athens, Plutarch, *Nicias*, 23, 3.

something surely remarkable about the thinker or the community or both, when a philosopher in middle life is singled out for the central figure in a popular comedy, on a subject so impossible with us as Education.

If the comedy failed of the prize, it did not miss its mark. When Plato wrote his *Apology of Socrates*, he represented Socrates in his last great speech, his one public speech, referring to the comedy of Aristophanes, which you have yourselves seen—we should note it was more than twenty years since they had seen it—"in which he has introduced a man whom he calls Socrates, Σωκράτη τινὰ, going about and saying that he can walk in the air, and talking a deal of nonsense about matters of which I do not pretend either much or little".[1]

The Athenian public perhaps took note of intellectual movements more quickly than a modern community might, with all its supposed advance in education and its undoubted journalism. But the movement was not wholly new when *The Clouds* was produced. We have seen the effect of a great war in a new challenge to education. The battle of Salamis, in 480 B.C., marks, as Eduard Meyer says, a line crossed in national experience; it is a date like 11 November, 1918; the end of an age and the beginning of an age. Strictly it brought nothing new into the world, but it made everything new in a whole series of new realizations. Men thought in a new way about foreign peril, inter-state unity, navies, policy; in a wholly new way Greece rose to a new sense of power—realized her strength in war, in exploration and commerce, and in thought. A new confidence in the power of his mind alters all a man's thinking; he will think more—perhaps more deeply, certainly about more things—and he will come to ask more questions. In spite of the numbers of men and women who "think in compartments", the thinking tends to break through the compartments, and all life becomes a unity; and as a unity, the whole of it, it is subjected to inquiry and speculation; and, as Plato makes Socrates say, "the unexamined life" becomes "un-live-able for a human

1 Plato, *Apology*, 19c.

being". Not for all human beings, as we know very well; but even stupid people catch themselves uneasily wondering, and there is no telling what clever people will get into their heads. The Germans give to this period of Greek history the name that belongs to their own eighteenth century; it is the *Aufklärung*, the "Illumination".

It is associated with the sophists and the Sicilians. Sometimes a branch of a race, planted in a new land overseas, will give the old country new ideas. A Hiero and a Gelo strike out new conceptions of government and empire; a Rockefeller will suggest new methods of business or a fresh start in handling disease and its causes; new forms of preciosity, or slovenliness, in speech, new slang, come overseas —names need not be given here. Sicilians came to Athens to make a new language for Greece; others came to make men wise. The range of their activity can be seen, when we recall that Socrates' address to Polus, ὦ λῷστε Πῶλε, with its careful balance of syllables and studied recurrence of vowel and consonant is a playful parody of sophist style, and when we also remember the gravamen of the charge against the whole sophist breed that they teach how to make the worse appear the better reason. Between trivial niceties in sentence building and the overthrow of elementary morality there is a wide span of possible evil.

We are told to think of Herodotus and Thucydides, and the chasm that separates them—the one simple, old-fashioned, discursive and credulous, the other hard, modern and intellectual. The difference between them is indeed great; but closer reading with leisure and sympathy leaves us with another view of a Herodotus not at all so simple nor so credulous, but an artist of the highest order with a range of interests, a recognition of real factors in life and history, far beyond most of the ancients, often beyond his clever successor. Ancient criticism calls our attention to another side of Thucydides often obscured by modern insistence on his cold intellectualism, his "exclusively political point of view", his refusal to consider moral standards or to take justice or morality into account, his habit in characterizing a man to refer only to his intellectual powers. The ancients emphasize his mastery in pathos; but, apparently, because he will not unpack his heart with words, he must have been incapable of feeling; to such naïveté does criticism come. Yet there is an ocean of difference between the two historians, not all to be accounted for by diversity of temperament. If they could have changed periods, it would not have meant exchanging minds. But a new education has indeed come between them. Thucydides, however, had the good fortune to escape Aristophanes; it is impossible to think of him as the central comic figure in a play, even if with a modern novelist we picture him as a rather deaf old gentleman.

But what was it that made the difference between Aeschylus and Euripides? Here again we have to go carefully. "Aeschylus", boomed the resounding Dr Kennedy, "may well be called a pessimist, nay, the very patriarch and first preacher of pessimism."[1] "Aeschylus", says the Oxford scholar, the Scot Lewis Campbell,[2] more quietly, "is no pessimist." There is after all no sense in calling a man a pessimist who believes in an intelligible universe ruled by law; *δράσαντι παθεῖν* is an explanation of the ways of the universe, and it runs through all the thinking of Aeschylus. You can never be pessimistic where you see intelligence dominant. The same recognition of some order in times out of joint, in the shattering of human life and character, is to be read in Euripides. The great cry of Hecuba to Zeus in *The Trojan Women* is not altogether the chance utterance of a single character; it is very like a confession of faith by the poet and it is supported, not by the *dénouement*, but by the value of other plays of great significance.

> O stay of earth, who hast thy seat on earth,
> Who e'er thou art, ill guessed and hard to know,
> Zeus, whether Nature's law, or mind of man,
> I pray to thee; for, on a noiseless path,
> All mortal things by justice thou dost guide.[3]

1 Introduction to his edition of the *Agamemnon*.
2 L. Campbell, *Guide to Greek Tragedy*, p. 113.
3 *Troades*, 884–8.

But, again, Euripides is different from Aeschylus; his language lacks grandeur; his characters quibble and bandy verbal points; his women don't care what they say or do; and Hippolytus declares that the swearing of his tongue does not bind his mind. We owe these discoveries, and others, to Aristophanes. The German critic, Nestle, tells us that "in the last line passionate sensibility is the source of Euripides' criticism". Others remark what a vast amount of philosophy comes out in stray observations by his characters.

But, allowing our deductions, we feel the change of atmosphere; less care for the traditional belief, more open appeal to emotion (which is always apt to be individual and isolating), verbal technique, a fearless, even a careless, raising of questions, which common people will never stop to answer and will therefore suppose unanswerable. How many an emancipated lady of to-day supposes that, because a thing may be questioned, it ceases to be of importance or indeed to be verifiable! The emancipated woman is one of the figures of the sophistic period; Euripides and Aristophanes both knew her, and neither liked her; but neither gives us any statistics as to the exact numbers of emancipated women. No one ever does; the "girl of the period" is always an abstraction, but she implies something—change of outlooks beginning to be felt. The common view, put forward by Decharme in his book on Euripides, which sometimes discovers the obvious and misses the real, is that in Athens the courtesan had what virtuous women lacked—grace, education, *esprit*.[1] Mr A. A. Bryant, whom I shall have to quote again, takes a lower view of the *hetaira's* intellectual development; intellect was not her strong suit, nor perhaps stupidity the wife's. The feminine, in one form or another, has often a charm which the academic cannot much enhance.

The Peloponnesian War had the effect that all great wars produce. On neither side, says Thucydides, was anything small designed; both were full of enthusiasm; "men always take hold of a thing with more spirit at the beginning"; and all Greece was keyed up, "was in the air"; rage, terror,

1 Paul Decharme, *Euripides* (tr. J. Loeb), p. 97.

omens, hopes and fears, carried everybody out of themselves.[1] Even, as the war goes on, the Athenians have "larger ambitions"[2]—*orexis*, an appetite fed by Cleon and war-demagogues; they batten on hopes,[3] and on hatreds, of course, as we also did. Hope, hatred, hysteria—we know the combination too well. Men comment on the tone even of Euripides in referring to Sparta; and in home politics we have the oligarch's tract on Athenian Democracy, with its emphasis on the thorough consistency of the national plan of government of the worst, by the worst and for the worst. Yet even so the contrasts are strange—the ruthless cleverness of Aristophanes devoted to producing hatred of a Cleon and of a Socratēs, and the contentment of Demos at seeing his favourite leader made ludicrous and hateful.

In this atmosphere *The Clouds* is produced. We need not here analyse a familiar and favourite play; but the elaborated contrast of the old and new in education concerns us. The poet, in his youth and fury and cleverness, reminds one of the bright conservative undergraduate long ago in Union debates—except that no undergraduate was ever so clever, not even George Otto Trevelyan. But, in spite of good commentators, one cannot help wondering whether the wicked panegyrist of the Good Old Ways is not laughing a little at them too, in his graceless way. It is not very easy to translate the names of his two characters—Right Logic and Wrong Logic, B. B. Rogers calls them, not very satisfactorily; the Fair Word and the Unfair Word, the Right and the Wrong, have connotations of their own and miss some suggested by the Greek; Righteousness and Unrighteousness sound far too like the Old Testament; nor are the Right Way and the Wrong Way adequate. But the *Dikaios Logos*, however you translate him, gives a vigorous account of the great old days of the grand old discipline, "when I flourished, and self-control, σωφροσύνη, was the way".

Then it was understood that boys should be seen and not heard; *then* they went to the music school, the harpist's,

1 Thucydides, II, 8. 2 Thucydides, IV, 41.

3 See F. M. Cornford, *Thucydides Mythistoricus*, p. 122; and Thucydides, III, 45.

naked, you might say, though it snowed hard; *then* they learnt the old songs to the tunes the fathers handed down; *then* they did real gymnastics, without the modern indecencies; *then* the fare was plain and wholesome, and so were the manners. (Very old-fashioned, smells of Noah's Ark, interjects the *Adikos.*) Thus grew the heroes of old to be hardy and bold, the men who at Marathon fought.[1] They would rise from their chair if an elder were there, with love and with fear their parents revere, and deep in the breast was the image imprest of Modesty simple and true (*Aidos*); and there was no going to the devil in the modern way. Athletics flourished, and the gymnasium; there was not the preference (as phrased by K. J. Freeman[2]) for conversation rather than exercise. And look at the physique it produced!

The modern advocate next has his say, in clever parody. For Aristophanes is a good controversialist. He mistrusts the democratic movement of the day, the sophistic teaching, the spirit of criticism altogether, as it is turned on morals, religion, art and politics; he recognizes in Socrates and Euripides the leaders of this intellectual movement; he identifies them with their opponents—most unjustly, say his critics. "Not at all," he might rejoin, "sophist and Socrates meet on one plane, and off that plane I am going to keep, and I mean to head everybody else off it; it is only the difference of Tweedledum and Tweedledee". He will not meet them on their own ground, for that would be to concede their general attitude, their right to question; he attacks from another level; he tries to laugh them out of a hearing. He might urge that he is only doing what Socrates does with Callicles;[3] he is trying to enlist instinct against rationalism.

I have sometimes wondered, in thinking of Euripides' *Cyclops*, whether it is after all a mere case of conforming to the traditional type of satyric drama, or whether Euripides meant what he was doing when he contrasted Odysseus, as representative of the really Greek spirit, with the Cyclops,

1 Phrases from B. B. Rogers. The idyllic picture seems to need verse.
2 *Schools of Hellas*, p. 75, perhaps anticipated by Aristophanes, *Frogs*, 1069.
3 Plato, *Gorgias*, 494.

with Silenus and the satyrs. The whole pack of them are alike —sensual, gluttonous, superstitious and cowardly—"I know a charm of Orpheus, a right good charm, to send the stake marching on its own account into the skull of the one-eyed son of Earth".[1] The attentive reader or spectator may remark that, in language and instinct and taste, they closely match the regular hero of Aristophanes, the average good citizen, as the comic poet draws him. We are not well supplied with satyric dramas; but it is remarked what freedom in spite of traditional myths, and a conventional theatre, chorus and so forth, Euripides achieved for the expression of a very individual and original mind. Before we pass on, it is to be remarked that, long before *The Clouds* was ever staged, Pindar in one of his *Odes*[2] had a somewhat similar debate between two views of life—one that of monkey and fox, clever, adroit, nimble as a cork afloat; the other his own. "Best for every form of polity is a man of direct speech, whether under a despotism, or whether the wild multitude, or the wisest, have the state in their keeping. Against God it is not meet to strive."

So we have the different schools and their ideas in rough outline before us; the new school with its emphasis on training tongue and brain, the old still valuing what the English call character; and the last sentence from Pindar bringing in a conception of which we had lost sight, but which Plato will make central.

Meantime what are we to suppose to be the object of education? What is it that we seek to produce? Meno asks Socrates if virtue can be taught—a question much considered then and for long after. Of course he plays into the old man's hands.

That native trick "What is it that you mean?"[3]

the mark of the true-bred Athenian, is not wanting in

1 Euripides, *Cyclops*.

2 Pindar, *Pythian*, 2, 72–96; see Gildersleeve's note. It may be added that King Archidamus (in Thucydides, 1, 84) speaks in much the same vein as the *Dikaios Logos*; "our habits of discipline make us both brave and wise"; "one man is much the same as another, and he is best who is trained in the severest school".

3 Aristophanes, *Clouds*, 1173.

Socrates; it is the keynote of his teaching; was it not his business to bring thought to birth, to get it shaped? So he asks Meno what Meno means by virtue. No trouble at all, says Meno; first, there is the virtue of a man, "to be competent to manage the affairs of the city (state), and so to manage them as to serve his friends well and his enemies ill, and escape harm himself".[1] For a woman, and for others, children and the old, it would be something different. We need not now follow the discussion, but Meno has of course to try again and quotes "the poet", *χαίρειν τε καλοῖσι καὶ δύνασθαι*[2]—"to rejoice in things honourable and to be able"—which raises fresh questions. But we, like many who discussed with him, will refuse to be led by Socrates into disputing of virtue in the abstract. For, as Aristotle says,[3] "people with different ideas about virtue naturally disagree about the practice of it", and that affects education—"should the useful in life, or should virtue, or should the higher knowledge, be the aim of our training? All three opinions have been entertained".

Citizenship, the useful, virtue, knowledge—perhaps other things may emerge as aims, or different aspects of the four we have. But let us get useful education out of the way first; that will be a help. The three R's are admittedly useful—"in money-making, in the management of a household, in the acquisition of knowledge, and in political life".[4] So children should be taught to read and write; and they may also be taught to draw, for it may be useful, but chiefly because it makes them alive to the beauty of the human form.[5] Not all useful things should be taught to children, only those that will be useful without vulgarizing them.[6] For to be always seeking after the useful does not become free and exalted souls.[7] The question that a modern may ask about the usefulness of natural sciences is answered by Plato;[8] numbers, for instance, must not be studied as they

1 Plato, *Meno*, 71 E.
2 Plato, *Meno*, 77 B.
3 Aristotle, *Politics*, VIII, 2, 2.
4 Aristotle, *Politics*, VIII, 3, 7.
5 Aristotle, *Politics*, VIII, 3, 11; W. L. Newman compares Plato, *Symp.* 210.
6 Aristotle, *Politics*, VIII, 2, 3; *βάναυσον* is the word.
7 Aristotle, *Politics*, VIII, 3, 12.
8 Plato, *Rep.* VII, 525 C.

are by merchants or retailers for the sake of buying or selling, but for the sake of the soul itself. There was really very little of what is sometimes called scientific education in the ancient world. The ancients had to do without automobiles and wireless and sanitation and things of the kind; they had no business colleges, such as America boasts by the score and England (we are told) should copy; but he would be an ignorant or paradoxical person who would say that their minds were worse as a rule than ours, for all our changes in aim and method and locomotion.[1]

But now citizenship, which again raises questions. How wide a view of the world should a citizen take? The question becomes growingly urgent since the great war, and even in the middle west states of America there are signs of a feeling that mankind is not bounded by the Rockies and the Alleghanies. Men in old days commended Lycurgus, or whoever invented the Spartan constitution, for making war and conquest his sole aim. But, as Aristotle says,[2] surely the Spartans are not a happy people now that their empire has passed away, nor was their legislator right. One mistake in particular the Spartans made, for which many have commended them—"they brutalize the children with their laborious exercises in order to make them manly";[3] they make them just like the beasts (θηριώδεις), physically fit at the cost of everything else. There are other conceptions of the ideal citizen. There was the "gentleman", "the beautiful and good"—"that great name, τὸ σεμνὸν ὄνομα, *kalos kagathos*" is Xenophon's phrase, and very like Tennyson's; not quite idly did Andrew Lang call Xenophon "the most English of the Athenians". A generation earlier we read a speech in Thucydides where the word is apologized for—"the so-called *kaloi kagathoi*"; the allies of Athens will say that they were "the persons who suggested crimes to the popular mind, who provided the means for their execution, and who reaped the fruits them-

1 Herodotus makes mistakes in Arithmetic; but even his enemies, like Plutarch, admit he is delightful.

2 Aristotle, *Politics*, VII, 14, 16–18.

3 Aristotle, *Politics*, VIII, 4, 1.

selves".[1] But the name was already coming into friendly use. We read elsewhere how a pleasant lad was stopped in an Athenian lane by an ugly old man, who asked him where one thing and another was to be had; and the boy told him. Then came a harder question: Where do men become *kaloi kagathoi*? The boy hesitated. "Then come with me and learn", said the old man.[2] And after that Xenophon was the pupil of Socrates. But the oligarch who writes of the democracy makes it clear that a good many people doubted whether a gentleman would be a good citizen at all.[3]

As for the educational ideal of knowledge for its own sake, long before this period Heraclitus had said that polymathy does not teach sense;[4] and, later again, Alexandria was to prove that learning does not make a poet. Pindar had said so, Pindar whose soul (his best translator said[5]) rejoiced in splendour—splendour of palaces, splendour of temples, splendour of Pan-hellenic Games, of chariots and horses and naked athletes and the great sons of gods. "The true poet", said Pindar, "is he who by nature hath knowledge; they who have merely learnt, strong in the multitude of words, are but as crows that chatter [the pair of them; a dual verb] vain things in strife against the divine bird of Zeus."[6] "That which cometh of nature is ever best; yet many men by virtues learnt have essayed to achieve fame. The thing done without God is better kept in silence."[7] When a poet like Pindar speaks of God in the singular, it is even harder to be sure of his meaning than when Meno or ourselves speak of virtue. He does not mean Nature in Wordsworth's sense or the Stoic's; he thinks of the poet born a poet. "The cant of his class", says his American editor, rather suddenly.[8] Still, even a democrat may believe that poets are born, not made. There

1 Thucydides, VII, 48, 6.
2 Diogenes Laertius, II, 6, 48.
3 [Xenophon], *Ath. Rep.* 1, 7; 2, 19.
4 Bywater, *Heraclitus*, fr. 16, *πολυμαθίη νόον ἔχειν οὐ διδάσκει*, or else, he adds, Hesiod, Xenophanes and others would have been different.
5 Ernest Myers, *Pindar*, Intr. p. 14.
6 Pindar, *Ol.* 2, 86.
7 Pindar, *Ol.* 9, 100.
8 Gildersleeve on *Pyth.* 10.

is only too much evidence that there are things which education cannot do.[1]

There are also things that educators hardly propose to do. So careful of the type they seem! Every one of them dreams of some ideal manhood, and sets himself to devise a system for producing that type for ever. A great type it may be. Of all varieties of young man that I have met I know none to match the English public schoolboy, for beauty of feature and build, for charm of manner, for sheer manhood, for the ruling of men and the ruling of himself, *ingenui voltus puer ingenuique pudoris*. I echo the praise of Pindar for his athletes, of Xenophon for his young Spartans, and I think with better right than they. Yet I feel the English public school takes from its boys something God-given. "You Greeks are always children," says the old Egyptian priest in Plato's tale, "you are always young in your souls."[2] But when once Plato and Isocrates and Dr Arnold take to educating youth, that divine ἄωτος is somehow rubbed off; the type triumphs, splendid but stereotyped; the unexamined life, the tradition of Rugby, of the "Old Worrelian", claims them. No scheme of education appears to hold the door open for the new type, for the next generation's man. Pindar seems to be right; it is God, or Nature, butting into our systems, breaking a hole here or there, that gives us the best. The public school chapel-door is too narrow somehow for God. Or, to speak in prose, is it this? Is it not true that genius does best in an oldish but not too old community, where things are set and established, but not so set that the young mind cannot revolt, where he is controlled by tradition but inspired by Nature, where, like the best Greeks, he can make a blend of law and liberty, obey and revolt in the same moment, use and transcend the great tradition? God educates mankind, it has been said, in the breakdown of our ideals. Would it be too violent to say that the greatest of idealists for youth was the greatest

1 A mere detail on this point, but a significant one, may be added from Aristotle, *Poetics*, 22, 9, 1459a: "The greatest thing by far is to be a master of metaphor. It is the one thing that cannot be learnt from others, and a sign of genius, εὐφυΐας σημεῖον".

2 Plato, *Timaeus*, 22B.

sinner—not actually, of course, but in his dreams of perfection? To Plato we shall return.

Let us leave ideals for a little, and look at the real Athenian world. It is always difficult to find the real young man. "You dons", said a pleasant undergraduate to me, "always talk of 'THE undergraduate'; there's no such person." Perhaps he too was generalizing about THE don. So difficult is it to be accurate. The most satisfactorily average man I ever knew was quite unique; nobody was ever so supremely average. Who was THE young Athenian? Pheidippides, the mother's darling in the play, wasteful, horsey, degenerate?[1] or the young Theaetetus whom Plato describes—no beauty; for he has a snub nose and projecting eyes like Socrates, only not quite so marked; but there is hardly any one his equal in natural gifts, in quickness of apprehension, in quietness of manner and in courage. Quick wits generally mean quick tempers, like ships without ballast, darting about, rash rather than brave; and the steadier sort you might almost call stupid (νωθροί πως). But Theaetetus is better balanced. "He must be a fine fellow", says Socrates.[2]

How were the lads bred, then? There was no one system. "Most states", says Xenophon,[3] "let every one train his children as he likes, and let the older people live as they please, and then they make laws", which they expect to be observed, about theft and assault and adultery and so on; not so the Persians, he says; but the Persians can wait. *Laissez-faire* is the rule; and if Theaetetus is possible under it, perhaps it is defensible. Education, says Plato,[4] begins with earliest childhood and goes on for ever; mother and nurse and father and tutor are quarrelling about the improvement of the child as soon as he can understand them: he cannot say or do anything without their setting forth to him that this is just and that is unjust, this or that honourable, holy or the opposite; "do this and don't do that". Like a piece of warped wood, he has to be hammered straight. After this come teachers who have to teach him his letters and his

1 In *The Clouds*.

2 Plato, *Theaetetus*, 144 A, B.

3 Xenophon, *Cyropaedeia*, I, 2, I.

4 Plato, *Protagoras*, 325, 326.

music, and his manners above all. Then the poets, to be read at school; the lyrists and the gymnasts, to train him—if the parents can afford it all. And then the city and its laws.

All this can be illustrated at large. There is the famous nurse in Aeschylus' play, and other nurses; and the quarrelsome mother of good family and large tastes in *The Clouds*; there are bogey tales[1] and fairy tales and legends; and the manners, "little points", are spoken of by Plato,[2]—"when the young are to be silent before their elders; how they are to show them respect by sitting down and rising up; what honour is due to parents; and hair-cutting, and brooches, and footgear; and how to hold your body; and behaviour in general".[3] School is described, luridly. There were fairly big schools, for we read of the roof falling in on a school in Chios, and crushing all but one of the hundred and twenty boys,[4] and of a worse disaster at Mycalessos where Thracian mercenaries burst into a school and butchered the boys—"no greater calamity than this ever affected a whole city", adds Thucydides, who does not often comment so.[5] Schoolmasters were not greatly esteemed. "Shall I tell," cries Demosthenes, attacking Aeschines, "how your father Tromes was a slave in the house of Elpias, who kept an elementary school near the Theseum, a slave with shackles on his legs and a timber collar on his neck?...And you, when you were a boy, helped your father drudging in that school, grinding the ink, sponging the benches, sweeping the schoolroom—a slave's job, not a free-born boy's."[6] It is quite a modern thing for boys or fathers to respect the schoolmaster; in Rome it appears that he might be bought in the slave market. As for the Greek usher—the soldiers felt towards Clearchus, says Xenophon, like boys to a schoolmaster; he had no graciousness, he was difficult and rough.[7]

There were toys for little children, and games for them as

1 Plato, *Crito*, 46C; *Phaedo*, 77D.

2 Plato, *Republic*, 425.

3 On all this, see a later essay, page 161.

4 Herodotus, VI, 27.

5 Thucydides, VII, 29; Theophrastus, *Characters*, 25, says the Mean Man will not send his children to school, when there is a festival of the Muses, in order that they may not contribute.

6 Demosthenes, *de Corona*, 129; and 258.

7 *Anabasis*, II, 6, 12.

they grew—the names of some of them are mentioned, *phaininda* (ball games),[1] *posinda* (finger flashing), *ostrakinda* (heads and tails and chasing), *kynetinda* (kissing); and perhaps these also were educative. Aristotle at all events stands up for leisure; Nature herself, he says,[2] would have us *μὴ μόνον ἀσχολεῖν ὀρθῶς ἀλλὰ καὶ σχολάζειν καλῶς*—a sentence that should be carved up in our schools: "to be busy with sense and to be idle with honour". One does not quite know whether Plato was altogether martinet, or was perhaps touched with sentiment—*haec olim meminisse juvabit*—when he laid it down that in the ideal republic the children would not be allowed to alter their games or to dance any but the old dances;[3] his excuse that you must not start them innovating may not be his only reason.

Sleep, drink and music men reckoned as the three main kinds of leisure, and some added dancing.[4] Of music I cannot well speak, but Aristotle goes on to ask why we should *learn* it—"if music should be used to promote cheerfulness and refined intellectual enjoyment, the objection still remains—why should we learn ourselves instead of enjoying the performances of others? We may illustrate what we are saying by our conception of the gods; for in the poets Zeus does not himself sing or play on the lyre. Nay, we call professional performers vulgar". Very vulgar they were too. Why, indeed, should you learn music, or, as the Rajah asked, play cricket, when somebody else can do it for you? There is divergence on the arts. Polybius is proud of his Arcadians; unlike other Greeks, when they feast they do not hire musicians but do their own singing; from earliest childhood their boys are trained to sing hymns and paeans in the ancestral way to the old gods; music, in short, is beneficial to all men, to Arcadians it is a necessity.[5] As for the other great arts, "no

1 On *phaininda* see Athenaeus, 14, 15.

2 Aristotle, *Politics*, VIII, 3, 2.

3 Plato, *Laws*, 798; 800.

4 Aristotle, *Politics*, VIII, 5, 3. Cf. Plutarch, *Alcib.* 2, Alcibiades would not learn music; "let the sons of the Thebans play the flute", he said; "they cannot converse". Cf. Athenaeus, 337 F. (on the flute player).

5 Polybius, IV, 20.

youth of good natural parts", says Plutarch,[1] "from seeing the Zeus at Olympia would wish to be Pheidias, nor would the sight of the Hera at Argos make him wish to be Polycleitos".

Gymnastics, as we saw, completed the education of every boy whose parents could afford it. But here three remarks may suffice. Aristotle notes that training could be, and was often, overdone; very few boy-victors at Olympia ever won victories as men.[2] There was a great contrast between the ancient boy's athletic work and school games to-day; the modern boy's play is pre-eminently team-work, of old it was boxing, wrestling, running, jumping, all individual work and glory. Lastly, there was too much looking-on, and it opened the door to more vice than is pleasant to remember.

But there was yet another phase to the ordinary boy's training. His father might take him to religious ceremonies, to the great plays in the theatre, even (it would appear) sometimes to the ecclesia itself. A boy may be a man too soon, but it is also possible to be an old schoolboy too long. Simonides left one famous sentence of three words—*πόλις ἄνδρα διδάσκει.* The city teaches the man; and Athens began to give her lessons early in life; the boy realizes early that he is to be a citizen and is trained, unconsciously, without quite realizing that he is being trained, to understand the life of a great city, the problems of an empire. The great speech of Pericles, without his knowing it, without its being quoted to him, is being written in his heart; he grows up to understand Athens and to love her.

Here is the true defence of Anytos. That unhappy citizen, branded for ever as one of the prosecutors of Socrates, is introduced as a speaker in the *Meno*.[3] By Herakles! no! he exclaims, he would not have anybody he cared for exposed to the corrupting influence of the sophists; not he! Well, what would he prefer? Why, any Athenian gentleman (*kalos kagathos*) will do the boy more good than the sophists—if the boy will do as he is told. And how and where do Athenian

1 Plutarch, *Pericles*, 2; cf. Lucian, *Somn.* 14.

2 Aristotle, *Politics*, VIII, 4, 8.

3 Plato, *Meno*, 94.

gentlemen learn all this? Oh! I should think, from the older generation; don't you think we've had a great many fine men in this city of ours? But Socrates wants to pin him down to this or that famous democrat leader, whose own sons came to nothing much—could ride perhaps and knew some music, like Pericles' sons. No, friend Anytos, it looks as if virtue could not be taught. And Anytos gets a little hot and warns Socrates to be careful what he says of other men; it is so easy to injure people in a city like ours.

This is exactly Socrates' method; and Anytos, as so many who argue with Socrates complain, is made to look ridiculous. The city is more than the man, as Plato himself brings out when he frames an ideal republic. Anytos is not talking nonsense, not at all; British tradition is with him. He is supported by a great many good citizens, Aristophanes, for instance, and Cleon, and the Spartan King Archidamus. A city can have too many clever people, Cleon urges; what it wants is good sound dull men, average men—"dulness and sense are a more useful combination than cleverness and licence. The more simple sort generally make better citizens than the intellectuals. These are always wanting to look wiser than the laws, while the others mistrust their intelligence and allow the laws to be wiser than they are; and as their judgment is not crossed by ambition, they are more often right".[1] The late Dr J. R. Tanner, the Pepysian scholar, once told a college society that he was planning a Wordsworthian Ode to Stupidity; one line he quoted to us—

For me the meanest alderman that blows—

and all else was lost in the laughter of the audience. J. A. Froude in his *Erasmus*[2] has much the same idea; "John Stuart Mill called English conservatives the stupid party. Well, stupidity in its place is not always a bad thing. Conservatism, at least, represents ideas which have proved themselves capable of being practically worked".

Anytos was not all wrong; the community counts. This

1 Thucydides, III, 37; and King Archidamus, Thucydides, I, 84.
2 Froude, *Erasmus*, lecture 8, p. 17.

happy-go-lucky unsystematic way of training boys had made Athenian empire, Athenian art, Athenian literature, Athenian philosophy; it had given the nidus and the impulse, and made all these things possible and actual. It had produced Aeschylus, Sophocles, Euripides, Pericles as well as Cleon—and Pericles' speech is always evidence for its value—and finally where else had Plato grown but in Athens, and where else could he or Socrates have been possible? Assuredly not in Plato's own republic. What does the world owe to Sparta or to any race, country, or system of one idea? Even the most established churches need dissenters or Turks or Voltaires, if they are to keep the mind alive. The only dangerous heresy is orthodoxy.

But, after all, we all have our children taught the three R's, and once all the girls did music; and, if they do not do it now, they do gymnastics and athletics instead like their brothers—and, more or less, like the Spartan girls.[1] Every father has the feeling of Anytos that he wants his son to be like the substantial men of the city, and has his faith that environment will do it. Demos is still, as Plato said, the chief corrupter of youth[2]—not the sophist but the honest old Athenian public; not the woman novelist, nor the Bolshevik, nor the American, but John Bull himself. "Living under a popular government, how could we avoid in a great degree conforming to our environment?" So Alcibiades asks of the Spartans.[3] America, for all its boasts of freedom, is the land of standardization; Demos will tolerate no man falling out of step or out of line. So far we are not so very different from the Athenians.

Where we differ chiefly is that our modern education centres above all in the study of fugitive scientists, and theirs centred in the study of eternal poets; and, what is more, Demos would have it so. In the delightful *Banquet* of Xenophon, the guests pass round the question, "What is the most

1 Cf. Pausanias, v, 16, 3. See Zimmern, *Home Life of Ancient Greeks*, pp. 131, 132.

2 Plato, *Rep.* 492.

3 Thucydides, VI, 89.

valuable knowledge you possess?" and the turn comes to Niceratus. "My father", says he, "was anxious that I should grow up a good man; so he made me learn all Homer's poems by heart; and I could here and now recite the whole *Iliad* and *Odyssey* from memory." (Well done! father of Niceratus!) "Just a point", says Antisthenes the Cynic, who is in a critical vein this evening; "have you failed to observe that the rhapsodes, too, all of them, know these poems?" "How could I, when I listen to them reciting nearly every day?" "Well," snarls Antisthenes, "do you know any breed of men sillier than the rhapsodes?" And the poor lad doesn't, but Socrates comes to his aid; the rhapsodes don't understand the inner meaning of Homer.[1] The question is raised, however, by some modern readers whether Niceratus was or was not exceptionally full of Homer.

So there we have evidence, corroborated on every hand. Homer is recited in public, is read in private, is learnt by heart, and is the secret spring of character.[2] Nobody perhaps in England to-day is asked to learn anything by heart. In Canada years ago children had to learn stuff, "compared with which", said a colleague of mine, "'Mary had a little lamb' is positively virile". I have met, however, young Finns who learnt the whole *Kalevala* at school in Finland—20,000 lines in three years. Finland means to have a national consciousness, as Greece did; and Homer gave it to the Greeks. If literature is any education at all, and I think it is, where, before Queen Elizabeth's reign, was there greater literature? and it may be only national pride, surrender to Demos, that shapes my question so.

But the Greeks are quite explicit, against our literary critics, on the solid and practical didactic value of their great poets. "Well does the poet Hesiod speak of such men as Demosthenes," says Aeschines,[3] "for he says somewhere, by way of teaching the people and advising the cities to have

1 Xenophon, *Symp.* 3. 5.

2 Plutarch, *Alcib.* 7; Alcibiades is said to have struck a teacher who did not own a Homer.

3 *Against Ctesiphon*, 134.

nothing to do with corrupt demagogues,—but I will quote the lines; for I think that as children we learn the thoughts of the poets to be able to use them when we are grown up." The proper work of poets, says Aeschylus in the *Frogs* of Aristophanes, is to teach; it always was from the beginning; the good poets have always been useful.

First, Orpheus taught you religious rites and from bloody murder to stay your hands;
Musaeus healing and oracle lore; and Hesiod all the culture of lands,
The time to gather, the time to plough. And gat not Homer his glory divine
By singing of valour, and honour, and right, and the sheen of the battle-extended line
The ranging of troops and the arming of men?...
And thence my spirit the impress took, and many a lion-heart chief I drew...
The tale may be true, but the tale of vice the sacred poet should hide from view,
Nor ever exhibit and blazon forth on the public stage to the public ken.
For boys a teacher at school is found; but we, the poets, are teachers of men.[1]

It is the naïvest of criticism to suppose that Aristophanes will not let his humour play upon people and things he really admires. A great deal of the current criticism of ancient authors is amazingly naïve—the grammarian commenting on the poet. But Aristophanes is like Plato; each of them has unfortunately a sense of humour, with the lamentable result that sometimes they will be serious and nonsensical at once to the great confusion of matter-of-fact persons, Athenian and English. But Aeschines is above suspicion, and is confirmed by the indignant Plato. People did suppose the poets existed to teach, even to preach; they did propose to draw from them by detached quotation lessons for practical life. M. Paul Girard, in his book on Athenian education,[2] suggests the reason. Greek religion had nothing, or next to nothing, to do with morals or the forming of character; it was concerned with ritual and formula, with accommodation

1 Aristophanes, *Frogs*, 1030 ff. (Rogers; but the seventh line adjusted to cover the omission).

2 Girard, *l'Educ. Athén.* pp. 139–141; Plato's revolt in the following pages.

between men and gods—gods already in Homer on a lower moral plane than the heroes. The highest thoughts upon life were not to be found about the temples—far from it. It is from Plato and the philosophers, not from the priests, that the impulse to moral progress comes after 400 B.C. Before that, all that was best in Greek life was in the poets. There was no Bible, and a man who wanted to know the highest levels of the human heart and mind must go to the poets. The father of Niceratus had more insight than a modern at first glance might allow him. "The ancients", says Strabo,[1] "assert that poetry is a kind of elementary philosophy, which takes us in our boyhood and introduces us to life and teaches us of character, feeling, action, and does it to our enjoyment. ...That is why the states of the Greeks begin the education of the young with poetry, not merely to stir their souls but to train them (*οὐ ψυχαγωγίας χάριν δήπουθεν ψιλῆς ἀλλὰ σωφρονισμοῦ*)."

When this is realized, we have a clue to Plato's attack on poets and poetry. He owns to "a certain love of Homer from boyhood, an awe",[2] which would check speech; but he speaks in no uncertain tone. His first great principle is that we must always speak of God as He is; and the poets are full of outrageous legends about the gods. As Xenophanes said in his conscientious verse,

> Homer and Hesiod charged upon the gods
> All that is shame and blame among mankind.

As for moral training, it is nonsense; gods and heroes do all sorts of things—those very heroes, who are held up as examples to youth. The moral sense is confused; "the noble Hesiod" promises you, if you are virtuous, fine crops and good calving seasons; spiritual rewards, in fact, to be paid in material currency, which is all wrong,—wrong in observ-

1 Strabo, c. 15; against the opinion of Eratosthenes and his very word quoted in c. 7.

2 Plato, *Rep.* 595B, *φιλία* and *αἰδώς*. It may be of interest to add that Aristotle, according to Walter Leaf, "quotes Homer habitually with the most slovenly inaccuracy"; while the Stoics had a high admiration for Homer, enhanced by their method of allegorical interpretation.

able fact, wrong in outlook. In the *Ion* Plato sketches the artistic temperament; the little dialogue is a masterpiece of humour, kindly but merciless. He draws an unstable personality, swayed by emotions, fond of contemplating itself, anchorless. There is the effect of undiluted Homer—wave upon wave of sheer sentiment. What can such utter surrender to emotion do to brace the soul, to quicken the mind? There is something fundamentally wrong with poetry; its effect is no mere accident. "The poet is a light and winged and holy thing, and there is no invention in him until he has been inspired and is out of his senses, and the mind is no longer in him."[1] The man is not responsible for his poetry; look at Tynnichos the Chalcidian, who wrote "the paean which everybody sings, perhaps the finest we have"—the invention of the Muses, he called it, as if God meant to show that the poet is only the interpreter and nothing in himself, when the best of songs comes from the worst of poets. Elsewhere Plato says the same thing with added emphasis, speaking of the "*madness* of those possessed by the Muses, which enters into a delicate and virgin soul, and there, inspiring frenzy, awakens lyrical and all other numbers.... But he who, with no touch of the Muses' madness in his soul, comes to the doors of Poetry and thinks that he will be a sufficient poet by art—he, I say, and his poetry are not admitted; the sane man is nowhere at all when he enters into rivalry with the madman".[2] It is very much what Pindar said in his pride. "Aeschylus, you do the right thing, but you have no idea what you are doing" is a saying attributed to Sophocles.[3] But perhaps Plato's greatest saying on this matter is the assertion that "there is an ancient quarrel between Philosophy and Poetry".[4] Himself, it is pointed out, he knew from experience the appeal of Poetry and had to make a determined effort to resist it. He is not referring to degenerate poets of a later date, but to the greatest. Homer is no diet for a philosopher. Reason and

1 Plato, *Ion*, 534B.
2 Plato, *Phaedrus*, 245. Cf. S. H. Butcher, *Harvard Lectures*, pp. 138ff.
3 Athenaeus, 22A.
4 Plato, *Rep.* 607B.

intuition cannot occupy the same mind; inspiration is unreason. So he will not have the inspired poets in his republic; but hymns and paeans shall be written to order by responsible persons, under supervision, to convey warrantable ideas.[1] Arthur Benson might have suggested Christopher Wordsworth to him as quite reliable for this purpose.[2] The laws might be in verse, for the children to learn.

Yes, there is indeed an ancient quarrel between Poetry and Philosophy, and it still goes on; and it is ill for the man in whose soul that warfare is not waged.

So Pindar and his kind won't do as educators in Utopia, nor, it would seem, in Athens; and Plato is not better satisfied with the sophists who for half a century made a strong appeal to the Athenian mind. Sophist and sophistry have much the same connotation as Jesuit and jesuitry in modern speech, and in each case the people concerned have only themselves to thank. Education had become in Athens, as we saw, a popular question; there was a new demand for culture, for training in public speech, for development of the mind—for sheer cleverness, if you meant to have a political career; and the sophists undertook to give you what you wanted. We shall cease to be surprised at their vogue, when we reflect how in our own day in England education has been subordinated to Economics and in America to Psychology. Everybody must have the popular nostrum—Psychology in the American university, Rhetoric in Athens; and probably Athens chose more wisely. Neither line of study, as popularly pursued, seems to make for moral development, but the Athenian way did more to develop the individual's faculties and made a real contribution to Greece. Perhaps the simplest and most illuminative illustration is the discussion, recorded or invented by Xenophon (always readable) between the young Alcibiades and his elderly relative, Pericles.[3] The young man is very clever and copies Socrates to the life in cross-examining the great statesman, who makes no great show for himself;

1 Plato, *Laws*, 801.
2 A. C. Benson, *The Leaves of the Tree*, p. 278.
3 Xenophon, *Mem.* 1, 2, 40ff.

it might have been Anytos a generation later. At last the old gentleman gets a little tired of it—"Well, yes! when I was your age, that was the way we talked ourselves—tried our wits in just that clever way". "How I wish," the indomitable youth rejoins in a superb "Alcibiadism", "how I wish I had known you at your best, Pericles!" That the cleverness taught by the sophists obscured the difference between right and wrong; that "they made the worse appear the better reason"; that Rhetoric was on a level with cookery, a mere adroitness in catching the popular taste of the moment;—we have all read in Plato; and Greece in the long run accepted his estimate. Adroitness and rationalism do not make an endearing combination; there is nothing fundamental in either; and it is natural to man to want something solider, something to prepare him for "the whole tragedy and comedy of life"[1]—all men by nature desire to *know*, says Aristotle.[2] So the sophist movement died down, and we hear little of sophists after about 380 B.C.

But the sophists made a real contribution to Greek life—like other men, by their demerits as well as their merits. There is only one line of reply to rationalism, and that is reason. The sophistic movement challenged everything; and in Socrates and Plato—one may add Euripides—reason rejoins to rationalism. So the foundations are shaken, are they? Then reason will show that they are not, or will lay them again so as not to be shaken. Meantime education of a new kind has become a popular demand. Greece is forcibly driven into thinking, into philosophy. Literature is studied anew; style becomes a living issue. How to speak, how to write—the questions take you back to another, how to think.[3] All education is correlated, is lifted to a new plane, where it still is—a plane, where idea, notion, controversy keep men's interest in it alive. The sophists are succeeded by better men; and, when they are gone, we find a new thing in Athens. It is not quite the University in our sense, nor in the medieval sense. A minimum of building or endowment, no examina-

1 Plato, *Philebus*, 50 B.
2 Aristotle, *Metaphysics*, I, I.
3 Plato, *Phaedrus*, 259 E ff.

tions or diplomas, but real schools, real study, the living intercourse of teacher and learner, which is the real thing in any university, however organized or disorganized. Garfield's old dictum about the liberal education hits it off—a log with a boy on one end of it and Mark Hopkins on the other.

But we must go back to the Peloponnesian War. It gives us another landmark in its dreadful ending. The shattering effect of it is seen in the new speculation about the ideal state and the ideal education. The happy race of amateurs, described in the inimitable speech of Pericles, has come to grief. The speech has been called its epitaph, written by the historian in full view of disaster. Whoever was the author, the statesman or Thucydides, all that is over. The highly organized state, in which efficiency for war and conquest was the one goal of education, has overborne all. The democrat, living as he chooses, a whole "bazaar" in himself of impulses and fancies, inconsequent, incoherent, unstable—the reader will recognize the borrowed phrases—the democrat has failed, utterly. A way of life more profoundly thought out is needed. Athens tried two or three political changes, and swung quickly back to the old democracy—swore amnesty and peace, "and Demos abides by his oaths", says Xenophon. So Demos did, but there was one outstanding account to settle, and he made Socrates drink the hemlock—a fatal triumph of the average man. The whole thinking world revolted; and, though Demos probably never repented of his blunder and even forgot it, the thinkers and the writers never forgave it, and they had the ear of posterity; for centuries nobody wrote like Plato and Xenophon. For a generation, however, the Spartan idea was dominant, till at Leuctra Spartan power came to an end. But not the Spartan legend; that lived in the pages of Xenophon, it was revived by the Kings Agis and Cleomenes in the third century, and written up again by Plutarch about 100 A.D. It became immortal. Even in the French Revolution we meet Lycurgus.

Yet one wonders. For now we reach the great educators, and a brief survey, perhaps too abrupt and casual, of three of them shall end our present study. Xenophon wrote a great many books, which have had their ups and downs, have been in fashion and out of fashion. They are out of fashion now, for the moment, in education; but they will be read again and again, and always be loved by humanists and historians. He wrote, then, a *Republic of Sparta* and *The Education of Cyrus*. Posterity very quickly made up its mind that the latter was not exactly history, but it seems generally assumed that the former was. "They do these things better in France" is a tune we know, the tune to which Matthew Arnold wrote his book *A French Eton*, pleading for state meddling with education—a strange book to read after fifty years. After France came Germany; she was so efficient. And so was Sparta; everybody knew that, from 404 to 371 B.C. So Xenophon draws you the picture of an efficient state, a thought-out way of life, a good practical education that produced the manliest of lads, brave, obedient and hardy, and modest as girls—no Pheidippides there, nothing like the "democratic man" familiar to us in Plato and Aristophanes, and not unknown in the modern world. Xenophon is always good with boys, and good for boys. The key lies in the house at Scillus; he had twin sons, and he liked living with them, and telling them stories (he was a master at that) and taking them with him when he went hunting. But he did not accept a proposal to make them Spartan citizens, much as he admired Sparta and certain of the Spartans. It is the common guess, an easy one and a pleasant one, that, when he drew the boy Cyrus, it was not quite a fancy picture. The young prince is the most genuine boy in Greek literature—"a bit of a talker", interested in everything, wants to wear armour, longs to learn to ride, loves the prospect of a horse of his own, uses his fists, has his first knife, makes friends as he goes, and is punished at school for being unjust and sees where he was wrong—

καὶ πάϊς οἷόν πού τις ἐέλδεται ἔμμεναι υἷα.[1]

The story perhaps had its origin in the saying of Herodotus that the Persian teaches his son three things—to ride the

1 *Odyssey*, XX, 35.

horse, to shoot with the bow, to tell the truth. To these Mahaffy added a fourth from Herodotus' pages—loyalty to his king. Xenophon, like Herodotus and Alexander the Great, knew the Persian at first hand, and, like them, thoroughly liked and admired him. So his second Utopia is not at Sparta but in Persia; and a delightful tale he makes of it, including, though this may not be education, the best love story in Greek prose. It is remarked that Xenophon's women, Pantheia and the little wife of Ischomachus, are real women and charming. It is something for a historian and a writer of Utopias to be able to draw a real boy and a real woman.

The second of our three educators is the most ambiguous figure. "That old man eloquent" was supposed "killed with report" of Chaeronea,[1] but he really favoured Philip. Isocrates taught the Greek world the prose style they kept; yet one and another Greek critic will have it that he was tepid, a slave to rhythm, monotonous, commonplace. The moderns echo them; insipid, mannered, monotonous, more rhythm than reason, no creative imagination—so Jowett piles up the indictment. He lived in Athens all his very long life, and Niebuhr calls him a bad citizen and an old fool. To this an English historian, Mr G. B. Grundy, rejoins that in all his period Isocrates is the only writer who took a statesmanlike view as to the greater needs of his race.[2] Plato and Aristotle disliked him, and he was himself no admirer of Plato. Yet he forecast the future of Greece; he had the sense to see that Persia was the enemy of Greek inter-state peace; to see that Greece must be united and once more expand over the world; to see at last that only a monarch could do all this for Greece. This was not Demosthenic patriotism; but it was the plan of Providence, the actual course of Greek history, and it brought back, on the whole, a happier age. So much for the old fool. A quieter German critic calls him the forerunner of Hellenism, a humanist, the creator of the *Koinê*, the Greek speech of all the world. He foresaw too the future of Athens; nationality was to go, Greek culture was to be

1 Pausanias, I, 18, 8.

2 Cf. G. B. Grundy, *Thucydides*, p. 95.

the new bond that held mankind together; and so it was, and Athens was once more the world's centre. Odd as it may seem, he forged the mould in which the Gospels were cast; he devised the short biography that brings out character, and was eclipsed at once by Xenophon, and immeasurably surpassed later on by Plutarch and St Luke. The arrogant Master of Trinity dismisses him as liked "where learning is still in a backward state", and on the same page allows his popularity at the Renaissance and his appeal to Cicero. He certainly trained the taste of later Greece. So perhaps he, too, was a creative man after all. Mahaffy calls him the father of the periodic or oratorical style in all the languages of Europe—not popular, perhaps, at present; but, in one age after another, Mahaffy sees his influence in the great orators, in Demosthenes himself, in Cicero, Chrysostom, Massillon, Burke. Probably even to-day, and outside Oxford, it would be conceded that there are few better ways of education than *Litterae Humaniores*; and that too is the conception of Isocrates, some philosophy, a good deal of literature, and the essay. And yet how dull a great deal of his writing is, and how tiresome he grew when he passed eighty! There is no comparison between him and Plato, between his influence and Plato's, but he too is one of the formative and prophetic figures of Greece.

But if there is paradox in the story of Isocrates, Plato's is more surprising. The ruthless critic of democracy, of Athens, of contemporary taste, rationalism, literature and everything, he devised—perhaps was the first to devise—an imaginary republic of his own. It should out-Sparta Sparta. No man in antiquity did more to liberate the human soul—that is plain fact; and he designed a soul-less community without a vestige of liberty, worse than Paraguay with a Jesuit and a Spanish soldier at every corner, as bad as emancipated Russia. Plato is all for control and safeguards. No one was even to think independently, let alone speak. The great type of soul is to be made by machinery, by Act of Parliament as we used to say. Contact with other ways of life was to be shut off as much as possible; persons, who were allowed to go abroad, "shall, on their return home, inform the young that the political institutions of foreigners are inferior to our own".[1] Even in America that is not enforced by law nor secured by a death penalty. We have seen how even the children's games and songs were to be fixed.

We have to remember that Plato and Aristotle were pioneers—mere theorists, men would have said—in this matter of popular and controlled education. How little, too, they knew of state control, to have such faith in civil servants! The guardians of the ideal republic could have been nothing else. What university teacher to-day would say that the best minds among his pupils ever went into the civil service, or, once entered, continued to be best? It is something to be without one illusion of the old idealists, but it is a sad lucidity of soul we have gained. It is, of course, arguable that Plato understood what he was doing, and wished a government of civil servants without new ideas.

The Greek boy, whom Xenophon took hunting, is a strange figure in Plato; he is alternatively "a wild beast, of all animals hardest to manage, since he has within him a fount of reason as yet unregulated; so he is a creature of devices, shrewd, and outrageous"[2]—all this, and withal "not an earthly but a heavenly plant".[3] One is reminded of the Cambridge humourist, Barry Pain, who said that the English schoolboy is a blend of the pig, the pirate and the poet. The object of man's life is to prepare for death (*μελέτη θανάτου*); and the purpose of all training is to become like God (*ὁμοίωσις τῷ θεῷ*).[4] So the Jesuit might have said, and endorsed Plato's leaning to science and numbers and geometry as the means of education. Xenophon here had the advantage, which Plato and the Jesuit had not, of living with real boys, his own sons.

No one, it would seem, has ever wished to become a

1 Plato, *Laws*, XII, 951 A.

2 Plato, *Laws*, VII, 808 D. Cf. Dionysius Halic. *Antt. Rom.* II, 26, mild punishments for the young do not answer; hence the ill-behaviour of Greeks to their parents.

3 Plato, *Timaeus*, 90 A, *φυτὸν οὐκ ἔγγειον ἀλλ' οὐράνιον*.

4 Plato, *Theaetetus*, 176 B.

naturalized citizen in Plato's republic; no one has had the chance, though the modern world edges uneasily toward it with its inspectors and scientists, and its government control of education and of everything else. Nobody would adopt his republic, but everybody read his books. His system they dismissed; his soul, his charm, his genius, set them free, and did more to bring about that "growing like God" than any factor in the ancient world. If this seems over-bold, then read Clement of Alexandria, and he will confirm it. "The Law was the *paidagogos* of the Jews to bring them to Christ, and Philosophy of the Gentiles." He loved Plato, and so did thousands of his readers; right or wrong, genius is the thing; and Cicero hit the nail on the head when he said: "I had rather be wrong with Plato than right with the others".[1]

So Athens had plenty of advisers, and followed none of them all the way. Elementary education went on as before; Isocrates standardized culture; Plato and Aristotle left schools; Stoics and others followed; and eclecticism ensued. From Xenophon or others Athens borrowed the Spartan idea of the cadet corps and developed the ephebate. Athens became, as I said, the centre of culture for all the world; and her own sons were trained and drilled, stereotyped and standardized; they were admirable people, but not creative. Flattery and fustian is Milton's summary of the work of a controlled Italy; Polybius would have said it of Athens.[2]

> And the end men looked for cometh not,
> And a path is there where no man thought;
> So hath it fallen here.[3]

1 Cicero, *Tusculans*, I, 17, 39.

2 He did say it, substantially; XVI, 25.

3 The end lines of several plays of Euripides, and of a good deal else of man's contriving.

CURIOSITIES OF NATURAL HISTORY[1]

Magna ludentis Naturae varietas.
Pliny, *Nat. Hist.* IX, 102.

THE other day I was turning over the leaves of a translation of the Greek romancers. Long ago I had read all I wanted of Achilles Tatius; his heroine, like so many of her kind, was a doll, and his invention, plot and incidents sterile and improbable. But this time I lit on something that went to my heart. Cicero tells us that there was a kind of belief in the minds of the Roman populace that the elephant really has some sort of kinship or affinity with man.[2] Did I not myself, when Pershing, "weapon of destiny", as the posters of the day called him, in 1919 marched in triumph through New York—did I not let the legions thunder past and turn in the evening to the quiet pachyderms of Central Park?

"Have you ever seen an elephant?" asks Menelaus,[3] when Charmides winds up a full description of the hippopotamus by saying you might call him the Egyptian elephant. Charmides has seen the real thing, from India; and as the hero, the *ego* of the story, has not, here is a chance to fill the page and thrill the reader. The period of gestation—ancient naturalists always inform us of this, if possible[4]—is ten years, so that the elephant is born old already, "invincible in fight, long to live, slow to die", apt to live as long as Hesiod's crow, nine generations of men, to wit, or 270 years. Charmides says he appears to have two horns, but they really are tusks. It was a much debated point. Pausanias, the great guide of all tourists in Greece, in Greek art and Greek history, says they are horns—horns like the Celtic elk's horns or the Ethiopian

1 Readers, who loved as boys Frank Buckland's books with this title, will know why I use it again.

2 Cicero, *ad Fam.* VII, 1, on the destruction of 18 elephants in Pompey's show; with further horrid detail in Pliny's *Natural History*, VIII, 21, where the one redeeming fact is that the spectators rose and cursed Pompey, and their curses, adds Pliny, were fulfilled. It is very curious to find such feeling in so insensitive a people.

3 Achilles Tatius, IV, 4.

4 Contrast Job XXXIX, 1–3.

bull's; and he clinches his assertion by adding that horns fall off annually and grow again, in both stag and elephant, while no full-grown animal renews its teeth.[1] Pliny adds that the elephant knows man has a fancy for ivory, and so takes care to bury it out of reach.[2] Charmides, if a little more rhetorical, stands here with the modern naturalist. Between the tusks, of course, comes the proboscis, like a trumpet in shape and size, and highly useful to the creature in various ways. He feeds with it, picks things up with it and hands them to his master, the Ethiopian, his new cavalier, who sits on high and controls him with an iron axe. (Polybius and the author of *Maccabees* call the mahout an Indian; even Hannibal's mahouts are called Indians.[3]) Charmides once saw a Greek put his head into an elephant's mouth, and the elephant kept it open and breathed on him—a marvellous exhibition of courage in the one and of good humour in the other. The Greek said he did it to cure a headache with the fragrance of the breath, and the elephant, like an advertising doctor, wants his fee first. Then he will keep his mouth open as long as you like; he knows he has sold his breath.

"And whence has so shapeless a beast such delightful fragrance of breath?" Well, India is neighbour to the sun, and in India a wondrous flower grows, or perhaps a leaf rather, which will not waste its sweetness on the desert air, but, if transported, will change from leaf to flower to endue itself with odour. "'Tis the black rose of the Indians"—food for the elephant there as grass for the cow here; and years of such diet make him too all fragrant, a fountain of sweetness. The subject is dropped, the characters part, and the commentator decides that the black rose is the clove.[4] So there we start, with the wonders of Nature and of Greek eloquence, observation reinforced by theory and exquisite phrasing.

1 Pausanias, v, 12, 1.

2 Pliny, *Nat. Hist.* VIII, 7. See Emerson Tennent, *Ceylon*, II, 274, on the legend of the tusk shedding. The elephant of Ceylon rarely has tusks to shed. The epigrammatist Philippus of Thessalonica (*Anth. Pal.* IX, 285) stands for teeth; the elephant is μυριόδους—a magnificent adjective not to be taken too literally.

3 Polybius, I, 40, 15; XI, 1 (Hannibal); 1 *Maccabees* vi, 37.

4 Pliny, *Nat. Hist.* XII, 30, describes the Indian *caryophyllon*, which, some say, is the clove, but he does not tell this story. For *caryophyllum*, see p. 46.

"O Father Zeus!" cries the poet Oppian,[1] in his charming poem, lately given to us with an attractive rendering in the Loeb Library—"O Father Zeus, how many things hast thou devised, how many forms hast thou created for us, how many hast thou given to mortal creatures, how many to the finny things of the sea!" The ejaculation is called forth by the description of the giraffe, clad in the shameless hide of a pard, but itself splendid, lovely and gentle to men. Long is his neck, spotted his frame, his ears small, bare the head above, long the legs, broad the soles, the fore-legs far longer than the hinder, two little horns (yet not horny horns) on his brow, and a tail like the swift gazelle's. Oppian seems to have written in the early third century A.D.; and if his book is described as a didactic work on Hunting, it is really Natural History and very delightful in its variety and enthusiasm. I cannot say that I have found so much enjoyment in the companion poem on Fish; but I am on the side of the mammals, with a dubious tolerance for birds and a considerable hesitation about fish, reptiles, insects, and germs generally. A poem like Nicander's *Theriaca*, on snakes and the remedies for snake-bite, full of lexicographical pedantries and no other sign of genius,[2] I find simply unreadable—not even mediocre, as the kind French critic calls it. It is a sad defect no doubt not to be a man of science, but it allows one to ramble with more sympathy among old beast-lovers, who wondered and observed, and forgot and misrepresented and guessed, and enjoyed themselves at every stage. The people, with whom I deal, represent a middle period between the close observation of the primitive man who lived by hunting—observation attested by his marvellous drawings—and the elaborate research of the modern biologist, who sometimes forgets that Aristotle preceded him, as shrewd and careful an observer as himself and often a stronger thinker of a wider range.

Three or four books, definitely given to Natural History,

1 Oppian, *Cyneg.* III, 464.

2 Cicero says that Nicander, who had least of all men any connection with the country, wrote *Georgics* "with a capacity poetic, not rustic, and admirably". See Conington, *Virgil*, vol. I, 127 ff.

will supply much of our material, but by no means all of it. First we must set Aristotle, though our subject implies some wandering from him. His *History of Animals*[1] is a most remarkable book; the veriest duffer can see that; but listen to Darwin:[2] "Linnaeus and Cuvier have been my two gods, though in very different ways, but they were mere schoolboys to old Aristotle". It is aside from our present purpose to pursue him to the dissecting room with the modern man of science. Yet he tells with care and accuracy the life-history of the common gnat, from the larva stage onward; he traces the common fly to its dung-hill; the butterfly and its earlier stages he knows, of course, but he does not linger over it; he has not the poet's affection for it, nor the collector's. A much larger space is given by him than by most modern writers of Natural History to the phenomena of reproduction in animals. Herdsmen, hunters, bird-catchers, apothecaries, and above all the Mediterranean fishermen give him his facts, and sometimes add fictions or fancies—about goats breathing through their ears, vultures impregnated by the wind (as other men tell us of other creatures) and stags caught by music. He refers to the Indian *martichoras* with some caution—"if we are to believe Ctesias" (501 a). Very few people did believe Ctesias—at any rate among authors. But Aristotle goes far beyond hunters and fishermen. "My dear sir," says one of the gastronomers in the scandalous Athenaeus,[3] "I have wondered about that Aristotle of yours, whom the wise talk about so much; how on earth he learnt it all? Did somebody come up from the bottom of the sea, Proteus perhaps or Nereus, and tell him what the fishes do, and how they sleep, and how they live?"

Next we may put Pliny's famous *Natural History*. "Scientifically the work is contemptible", says Charles Singer in *The Legacy of Greece*. Very likely; but, as he says, everybody read it, in the darkest as in the more enlightened ages; everybody transcribed it and borrowed from it, "so that through its

1 See W. D. Ross, *Aristotle*, chapter IV; and, in *The Legacy of Greece*, Prof. D'Arcy Thompson's brilliant article on Greek science.

2 *Life and Letters*, III, 252.

3 Athenaeus, VIII, 352 D.

agency the gipsy fortune-teller of to-day may still be reciting garbled versions of the formulae of Aristotle and Hippocrates". There are other possible views of the book. "Judged solely by its information, that is to say its facts and anecdotes, apart from manner of telling, which is variable, the *Natural History*", says Wight Duff,[1] "is one of the half-dozen most interesting books in the world." He is surely right. Pliny is indomitable in pursuit of fact and of phrase, a born collector with a passion for epigram, readable wherever you open him, with a Latin you would sometimes rather read than construe.[2] He reckoned that he was giving us 20,000 facts—one would have guessed a larger figure; and he got them, he says, from one hundred authors and two thousand volumes; a modern count gives a list of over five hundred writers; so, of course, much of his matter is not original. But he himself is, as people say, an original, and there is nobody like him. If he drew all he could from books, he represents the better the current beliefs of the ancient world.[3] If he had been a modern, he would have been called a martyr of science, for he lost his life in the great eruption of Vesuvius in 79 A.D., which he went out to study; but, being what he was, a dilettante and a humourist, we give him no martyr's honours, but treat him as a brother, and read his book in happy snatches.

Aelian's book on Natural History is a mass of anecdote, handled rhetorically. It cannot pretend to be scientific; facts or stories are jotted down without any obvious arrangement; it is pleasant enough reading, if you wish to read it; but there is little trace of a great mind or a singular personality. Yet such a book represents one aspect of the general interest of the ancient world in animals, and, only too faithfully, the kind of very miscellaneous reading popular in the Roman

1 *Literary History of Rome in the Silver Age*, p. 369.

2 W. C. Summers, *Silver Age of Latin Literature*, p. 306, "His Latinity is perhaps the worst that has reached us from any man with pretensions to culture before the fourth and fifth centuries".

3 Cf. Pliny, *Nat. Hist.* II, 85, *incomperta haec et inextricabilia sed prodenda quia sunt prodita*. The book, says J. W. Mackail (*Latin Literature*, p. 196), is "a priceless storehouse of information on every branch of science as known to the ancient world".

Empire. It would be difficult to compute the number of authors who compiled book after book of oddments, curious, useful, informing, trivial, in this style. Even so serious a writer as Clement of Alexandria used the method in his *Stromateis* (*Counterpanes*, or *Patchwork*, which it is indeed).[1]

It is not always realized what opportunities the Western world had, from the latter days of the Republic onward, of seeing wild beasts, or what enormous expenditure was incurred in procuring them. The quickest way to remedy this will be to turn to Claudian's poem on the Consulship of Stilicho (409 A.D.).[2] There the poet, in a hundred and thirty lines of rhetorical verse, describes Diana assembling her huntress nymphs, their shoulders and arms naked, their hands armed with javelins, quiver and arrows on their backs, untrimmed maidens but lovely. She tells the need; they must capture wild animals for Rome's delight; and away they go. Gaul, Germany, Spain, the Apennines, Africa are scoured; boars, lions, pards, are fetched overseas—"whatever is terrible with teeth, splendid of mane, noble of horn, shaggy with bristles". "Deep wonder falls on Indian streams, the elephant wanders inglorious, bereft of his tusks." Translate this into earthly terms, and you have (as we learn from other and more prosaic sources)[3] an infinite variety of strange beasts assembled, butchered to make a Roman holiday, and paid for in a stream of precious metals flowing Eastward, and leaving the Empire poorer for every show.[4] There was little study of the animals; they sometimes died for want of proper care, like Symmachus' crocodiles which would not eat.[5]

Scientific interest in Nature as a whole, particularly in Physics or Geo-Physics, is another thing, and very old. Xenophanes and Herodotus are both at home in geological speculation. But it is one mark of the difference between

1 See p. 175.

2 Claudian, *de Consulatu Stilichonis*, III, 237–369.

3 E.g. the letters of Symmachus; cf. *Life and Letters in the Fourth Century*, p. 161.

4 There is an admirable chapter on Indian animals in E. H. Warmington's *Commerce between the Roman Empire and India*.

5 Symmachus, *Epistles*, VI, 42.

Aristotle and these men of an older day that he was, as the modern critic tells us, stronger as biologist than as physicist. The savage lives by watching wild animals and learning their habits; agriculture wipes out the necessity and often the opportunity for such knowledge; the wild animals are fewer and keep out of the way except when hunger drives them into field and village.[1] But the old interest survives in some degree, and there is always the instinct of wonder. From wonder comes philosophy, Aristotle said;[2] so indeed it does, though not always. Men like the tale that is new. Travellers' tales are a proverb, but men would think little of travellers who brought home no tales, nothing incredible.[3] They might as well never have gone abroad. Genuine interest in Nature, dreamy wonder, love of the strange, sheer fancy, work together; and men tell and re-tell the tale of the strange things overseas; and the telling sends others over the hills and far away; many pass to and fro, and knowledge is increased. Yes, says the caustic Lucian,[4] and there are people who prefer falsehood to truth, who take a real pleasure in lying, who have a disinterested love of falsehood for its own sake. Perhaps we may add this motive here and there to the others.

But, in spite of the good precedent for the artless and orderless presentment of our material, let us try to classify what we find—roughly of course, "in outline", as Aristotle says, "rather than exactly". We may group what we collect under three main heads, and gather illustrations of all three kinds. First we may set the motive of sheer wonder, the love of the marvellous and the unexpected, the museum instinct as we used to know it. Next, though our term may be misunderstood, we may put the practical instinct—not the commercial instinct that grows sheep for wool and crocodiles for

1 How much did Homer know of wild animals, and was it personal observation? It would be an interesting piece of research for one not intimidated by the tale of Homer's blindness. No one who has watched a baby act like Hector's child will believe that Homer had *not* seen a baby do it.

2 Aristotle, *Metaphysics*, I, 2.

3 Let us misquote Lucan, and apply *quorum quidquid non creditur ars est* to travellers.

4 Lucian, *Philopseudes*, I.

leather—far from it, but the feeling, almost universal, that beasts and men are somehow related, and that, if you study your birds and beasts aright, they will tell you what to do. Divination comes under this head, and the interpretation of dreams; medicine, too, on its magical side, with food taboos and questions of diet. On the borderline between this section and the third I should like to refer to the Orphic poem on the semi-precious stones; though they are not strictly animals perhaps, they might be classed as Natural History. And, finally, we come to the philosophic or theological instinct, which will see the universe steadily and whole, and will relate this to that in the hope of explaining life better. The rationalist, the theologian, the sacerdotalist may all have something to say here.

"There's nought so queer as folk", says the Yorkshire proverb, "and yet they put wild beasts in menageries." Sophocles was before the Yorkshireman—"many are the wondrous things", he sang, "and none more wondrous than man". Pliny re-inforces them; his *Natural History* shall begin with man, who has a natural right to come first in the narrative, since Nature seems to have created all the other creatures for him; she balances her gifts, however, by making man pay so dear for them that it is difficult to decide whether we should count her kindly mother or harsh stepmother. Everything else comes equipped and protected into the world —with bristles and scales and what not; even the trees have their bark; but man is born naked, born to cries and tears; it will be forty days before he laughs, "the weeping animal that is to rule the rest".[1] And look at his peculiar gifts—to him alone are given sorrow, luxury, ambition, and avarice; to him alone boundless love of life, superstition, anxiety about burial and what will come when he is gone. Other beasts have their enemies outside their kind; man's worst evils come from man.[2] Elsewhere he notes physical peculiarities. Man alone has ears that will not move—the English schoolboy practises to overcome this defect. Man alone has a face; the rest have

1 Pliny, *Nat. Hist.* VII, 1–3, *flens animal ceteris imperaturum.*
2 Pliny, *Nat. Hist.* VII, 5.

mouths, beaks, brows perhaps, but the face that is the index of emotion is man's alone. Other animals have eyes of standard colours; the eyes of men vary immensely. Man alone has cheeks to show shame, and no other animal has a chin.[1] Aristotle adds that no other animal has buttocks.[2]

Beginning with men, the ancients spoke of various kinds quite unfamiliar to modern anthropologists. There had been, they were certain, giants in olden days; huge bones were found which proved it—in Arcadia, for instance, as Pausanias says,[3] but he indignantly maintains, against many believers, that giants have not serpents for feet; for, when the river Orontes was diverted, a huge coffin, eleven ells long, was found, and the feet within were human feet; and the oracle at Clarus said the dead giant was Orontes, an Indian. And "if it be true that the first men were produced by the sun warming the earth, what land is likely to have produced men earlier or bigger than India, which to this day rears beasts of extraordinary size and strange appearance?" Pausanias quotes the Arcadian tale that a man may turn into a wolf, but not for life; if for nine years he will abstain from eating human flesh, he may be a man again. He saw a Triton at Rome, which he describes—a human nose; gills under the ears; hands, fingers and nails like the shell of a mussel; and a tail like a dolphin.[4] There was a headless image of one at Tanagra, commemorating one that used to attack women bathing and carry off cattle; and one story was that wine was set out for him; he drank too much and was beheaded as he lay.[5] Some say that Tritons speak with a human voice, he adds, while others say that they blow through a pierced shell. But, he continues, "lovers of the marvellous are too prone to heighten the marvels they hear tell of by adding touches of their own; and thus they debase truth by alloying it with fiction".[6] As to satyrs he made many inquiries, and a Carian told him of islands in the outer

1 Pliny, *Nat. Hist.* XI, 136; 138; 141; 157; 159.
2 Aristotle, *Hist. Anim.* 491.
3 Pausanias, VIII, 32, 5; VIII, 29, 3; the giants.
4 Pausanias, IX, 21, 1.
5 Pausanias, IX, 20, 4.
6 Pausanias, VIII, 2, 4–7, lycanthropy and Tritons.

Ocean inhabited by them; they have red hair, and tails, and such disgusting habits that sailors are reluctant to land.[1] We must not too abruptly conclude that he means Ireland, which was known to geographers;[2] and Sir James Frazer warns us against supposing the West African "gorillas" of an early Carthaginian mariner to be meant—whether these hairy creatures were women or great apes.[3] For dog-headed men Ctesias vouches—a whole nation of them, tens of thousands; naturally they cannot very well speak, but they can yelp or yell, and wear skins of animals; but you believe Ctesias at your peril. One wonders whether it is an Oriental legend borrowed. But the dog-headed constantly recur, and they die hard. And the sciapods, whose feet are so large that they use them for sun-shades, share the dubious immortality of the dog-headed, and men whose heads do grow below their shoulders.[4] The Libyans in the days of Herodotus said that two of these tribes were to be found in their country among the elephants and horned asses; the historian tells us they *said* so, and leaves it at that.[5] Sir John Mandeville, our splendid fellow-countryman, and Othello tell later ages of these joyful creatures with more assurance. Pliny says that magicians (or Magi) bind up the hairs of *cynocephali* (men or apes?) with swallows' feathers and amethysts (inscribed with the name of moon and sun) as a protection against drunkenness;[6] but this is anticipating another division of our subject. Let us return to the animals, varying with region and climate, wildest as a rule in Asia, boldest in Europe, most diverse in Africa,[7] for man is not the only creature affected by climate and country.[8]

1 Pausanias, I, 23, 5; 6.

2 Cf. Strabo, c. 72. Ierne lies beyond Britain, and is a wretched place to live in because of the cold, so that the regions beyond it are considered uninhabitable, and the people, some said, were cannibals. See p. 253.

3 See H. F. Tozer's very interesting *History of Ancient Geography*, p. 108; and Hanno's *Periplus*, § 18.

4 Other strange tribes who sleep in their own ears, or have no mouth, or only one eye, or back-bending fingers were reported from India, with animals as wonderful; but "most people who write about India are liars", Strabo says (c. 70). History repeats itself.

5 Herodotus, IV, 191.

6 Pliny, *Nat. Hist.* XXXVII, 124.

7 Aristotle, *Hist. Anim.* 606b. Strabo, c. 127, thinks wild animals scarce in Europe.

8 Pausanias, IX, 21, 6.

Not every naturalist has the same classification, but, if size is to count, there is a great deal to be said for beginning, like Pliny, with the biggest of animals, particularly when he comes next to man in sense and even ahead of him sometimes in moral virtues—in probity, prudence and justice, in a religious feeling for the stars and veneration for sun and moon.[1] Some tell us that in Mauretania, when the new moon shines, the elephants leave the forests and go to a certain river, and there solemnly purify themselves, sprinkling the water; they salute the moon, and return, carrying the weary calves. Strange tales are told of their intelligence; one was even taught to write a Greek sentence.[2] They understand the religion of others, too, and it is said an elephant will not embark on a ship unless the captain takes an oath about the return passage. They know they are hunted for their ivory, and (as we saw) they will bury it. The elephant who meets a man fairly and squarely in the desert, where there is no fear of treachery, will be quite courteous[3] and will show him the way—which is more than a Jew will, according to Juvenal. They are by nature modest, to an almost mid-Victorian degree; they know nothing of adultery, and do not fight for their partners.[4] The Indian elephant is larger than the African. So far Pliny.[5] Polybius says the same about the comparative sizes, a matter that told in the famous battle of Raphia in 217 B.C.[6] Aelian says that the Ceylon elephant is larger even than the Indian.[7] Modern naturalists maintain that the African is largest, and the guess has been made that

1 "The only harmless great thing", says Donne.

2 Yes, says Aelian, *Var. Hist.* II, 11, I saw it do this; but the hand of its teacher was on it. He has a description of elephants trained to dance,—odd, he says, for an animal without joints.

3 See Emerson Tennent, *Ceylon*, II, 283, for a true story of a tame elephant voluntarily making way for Tennent on horseback.

4 "From the beasts", writes Cervantes in *Don Quixote*, part ii, ch. 12, and he draws from Pliny, "have men received many lessons and learnt many things of value, as from storks the clyster, from dogs the vomit and gratitude, from the crane vigilance, from the ants thrift, from the elephants chastity, and from the horse loyalty."

5 Pliny, *Nat. Hist.* VIII, 1–32.

6 Polybius, v, 84.

7 Aelian, *Var. Hist.* XVI, 8; Emerson Tennent, *Ceylon*, II, 291, says the Ceylon elephant is rarely more than nine feet high, generally eight or so, and has not the African's height.

there was once a smaller North African type. Aristotle dismisses the hard-dying fable that the elephant has to sleep standing because he has no joints[1]. Aelian discusses the tusk or horn question, emphasizes the elephant's chastity and love of marshes—he is a regular fen-man—and his dislike of the noise of a grunting pig.[2] He is not a river-animal, says Aristotle; he is a poor swimmer, but as long as the tip of his trunk is above water he can get on very well.[3] To the Roman of the Empire the elephant must have been very familiar; Juvenal, supported by an ancient inscription, tells us that the emperors kept a herd of elephants at Laurentum in Latium.[4] How Aristotle came to be so well informed as to elephants, we may wonder. No doubt Greeks returned from the East, who had seen them and asked questions about them. We are told, too, that Alexander sent him strange animals; dare one dream of an elephant among them? What a present for a sage from a king! Haroun al Raschid sent one to Charlemagne.

After so much prose, we turn again to the poet. Oppian,[5] however, begins with an argument to prove that the tusks of the elephant are really horns, and he adds the surprising contention that the teeth of wild beasts do not yield to art and appeals to the skill of the ivory-cutter. Here one may recall that ivory was known to the Greeks long before they ever saw the elephant; there is plenty of ivory in the Homeric poems, but Homer is silent about the elephant.[6] But one must not interrupt a poet. "Seeing an elephant thou wouldst say that a huge mountain-peak or a dread cloud, fraught with storm for hapless mortals, was travelling on the land.

1 Tennent says the elephant can sleep standing, though it has joints.

2 Aelian, *V.H.* IV, 31; VIII, 17; IV, 24; VIII, 28.

3 Aristotle, *Hist. Anim.* 630b; cf. Emerson Tennent, *Ceylon*, II, 310.

4 Juvenal, 12, 102–110, *arboribus Rutulis et Turni pascitur agro Caesaris armentum.*

5 Oppian, *Cyn.* II, 489ff.

6 Pausanias, I, 12, 4, notes the abundance of ivory and the absence of the elephant in Homer, who would surely, if he had known, have mentioned elephants rather than pygmies. Herodotus, IV, 191, barely mentions elephants in Libya, along with the huge snakes, bears, horned asses, and dog-headed men, not very convincing company. One is tempted to apply the remark of Pausanias to him; if he had known ——. He appears to be the first western writer to use the word of the animal.

The head is strong, with ears that are small, hollow and polished. The eyes are small for such a frame, great as they are. Between them reaches forth a mighty nose, thin and crooked, which men call his proboscis. That is the creature's hand; with that they do full easily what they will. The legs are not equal in measure, for the fore-legs rise to a far greater height. The hide that covers the body is rugged, impenetrable and strong, which not even iron, hard, sharp and all-subduing, could pierce. Wild without limit is his spirit in the bosky wood,[1] but among men he is gentle and kind. In the green glens of many cliffs he uproots and lays on the ground beeches and hazels and towering palms, assailing them with his mighty and sharp tusks. But in the strong hands of men, he forgets his spirit; his fierce heart leaves him; he endures the yoke, the bit in his lips, and bears on his back boys to set him his tasks. The tale is told that elephants speak one with another, muttering from their mouths the speech of mortal men. But not of all is their speech heard; only the tamers hear it. Yea, and this marvel have I heard, that the mighty elephants have in their breasts a prophetic soul and know in their hearts when doom inevitable is near." So the swans are not quite unique, and the poet passes to the rhinoceros. Pliny tells us that the hippopotamus bleeds itself to cure its obesity.[2] But enough of pachyderms for the moment, with one backward glance for Horace's white elephant, which he couples with the giraffe.[3]

I do not know who first proclaimed the lion king of beasts; he reigns unchallenged in *Reynard the Fox*. Perhaps Aesop gave the first hints of coming royalty. The lioness, one well recalls, was taunted by the vixen with bearing but one cub in her lifetime.[4] The vixen would seem to have read this in Herodotus, who explains that the cub with his claws destroys the uterus for good and all.[5] It is a good thing to

1 Emerson Tennent, *Ceylon*, II, 287, on the elephant's love for the thicket depths of the forest.

2 Pliny, *Nat. Hist.* VIII, 96.

3 Horace, *Epp.* II, 1, 194–6, *seu | diversum confusa genus panthera camelo | sive elephans albus vulgi converteret ora.*

4 Aesop, *Fables*, 240.

5 Herodotus, III, 108.

read Herodotus, but the vixen was only too like some of our ancient naturalists who neither went to Nature, nor read Aristotle, nor even Homer; for, as Gellius remarks, Homer uses the plural of the lion's cubs.[1] The philosopher says that the tale and explanation of Herodotus are pure fable invented to account for the rarity of lions, which in Europe are only to be found between the rivers Achelous and Nessus. In Syria, he adds, the lioness has five cubs in her first litter, and one less every time she bears.[2] At the Bristol Zoo they tell a different story, but their lionesses are African. However, there was the vixen inaccurately taunting the lioness. Observe her aplomb in reply; she does not argue, nor quote Aristotle or the Bristol Zoo; she lets the vixen put it as she pleases—"But that *one* is a LION", she says. The fabulist surely need not tell us that the fable teaches us that it is quality not quantity that counts. The same feeling for quality is perhaps in Xenophon's remark that no gentleman would wish to keep camels to ride, nor to practise fighting on camel-back.[3]

With the bear it is another story—"a deadly race" (I am quoting Oppian[4]), "crafty in counsel, clad in a shaggy coat of fur, unkindly in shape, with all-unsmiling eyes". In rapid rhetorical short clauses he describes the beast, and gives it a character unfamiliar to us. A bear robbed of her whelps is King Solomon's famous phrase,[5] and the Hebrews claimed for him a wide knowledge of the beasts.[6] The Greek poet maintains that the she-bear is far more interested in her mate; she is in such a hurry for Aphrodite that she gives Eileithuia too little attention; and that is why her cubs come to the light half-formed, unjointed, mysterious to behold, and she has to lick them into shape. They all seem convinced, Pliny, Ovid, Aelian, that the bear has a lot to do for her queer unshaped offspring; and Aristotle in some degree supports them. The bear's gestation, he says, is thirty days, and the cub when born is of all animals smallest in

1 Gellius, *Noctes Atticae*, XIII, 7.
2 Aristotle, *Hist. Anim.* VI, 579b.
3 Xenophon, *Cyrop.* VII, 1, 49.
4 Oppian, *Cyn.* III, 149ff.
5 Proverbs xvii, 12.
6 1 Kings iv, 33.

proportion to the dam, larger than a mouse but smaller than a weasel, smooth and blind.[1] So the bear gives us two familiar proverbs while still a cub, and others later in life.

Wolves next—*triste lupus stabulis*, as we remember; but there is another danger. If the wolf sees you before you see him, you lose your voice. So Moeris found in Virgil's Idyll, and the great commentator Servius tells us the *physici* say so too; and Pliny says it is believed in Italy.[2]

To be fair to the rest of creation, let us pass to the birds. The swallow teaches us to be just by the pains she takes to be fair to each of her children and to teach them justice.[3] The legs of the ibis, with her beak, will form an equilateral triangle, which suggests the same lesson.[4] The migration of the cranes is familiar to readers of Euripides and Virgil; Aelian adds that they carry ballast, each swallowing a stone for the purpose, and that the eldest crane marshals them, inspects them three times, and then falls dead; they bury him carefully, and then fly straight to Egypt with never a rest nor an anchorage.[5] Pliny, unlike White of Selborne, tells us that the swallows migrate.[6] Hardly any of the wonder tales is to be matched with the strange fact that swallows ringed in England have been caught again in South Africa.[7] Robin and redstart change into one another, season about.[8]

The lower kinds, too, have their marvels. The crocodile watches his young as they creep out of the egg, and, if they do not instantly try to catch something, a fly or some insect, he kills them as bastards; if the new-hatched instantly snaps at something, he is a true crocodile and counts as one of the tribe.[9] The crocodile, Plutarch says,[10] has no tongue and is thus the symbol of the silence of God; its sixty eggs, hatched

1 Pliny, *Nat. Hist.* VIII, 126; Ovid, *Met.* XV, 379; Aelian, *V.H.* VI, 3; Aristotle, *Hist. Anim.* VI, 579a.

2 Virgil, *Eclogues*, IX, 53 (cf. Theocritus, 14, 22); Pliny, *Nat. Hist.* VIII, 80. Cf. Plato, *Rep.* I, 336D.

3 Aelian, *V.H.* III, 25.

4 Plutarch, *de Iside*, 75, 381D.

5 Aelian, *V.H.* II, 1.

6 Pliny, *Nat. Hist.* X, 70, 73.

7 See the map of the swallow, A. Landsborough Thomson, *Problems of Bird Migration*, p. 159.

8 Aristotle, *Hist. Anim.* 632b.

9 Aelian, *V.H.* IX, 3.

10 Plutarch, *de Iside*, 75, 381B.

in sixty days, and the sixty years of its life, suggest the measures of heaven—the old Babylonian system of sixty degrees and minutes. If you cut a lizard in two, each half keeps going on its two legs; and, if you let them alone, they will join up again.[1] People said that spotted fish in a certain Arcadian stream sang like a thrush, especially at sunset, but they would not sing for Pausanias.[2]

It will be observed that so far I have said nothing of two obvious sections of my subject, but I propose to neglect them. But why pass over the phœnix,[3] the *martichoras*,[4] the griffin?[5] Do they not deserve mention, and the gold-digging ant as big as a fox in Herodotus? Herodotus only saw the phœnix in a picture, and the ants seem to come from some Oriental tale, framed to explain the Sanskrit term *Paippīlika*, "ant-gold".[6] The *martichoras* is supposed to derive from the man-eating tiger, and I cannot help thinking that Oriental art supplied him with his strangely mixed features; and the same may be true of the griffin. Of the strange sea-beasts and the mermaids, to be seen in the Ocean about Ceylon, of which Aelian writes,[7] I say nothing. One mythical creature I have pursued with care and hope through the Classical books; but he did not, I fear, interest the ancients. The *floruit* of the unicorn is mostly medieval, and his existence is justified by medieval and later reference to the Old Testament. The Christian apologists contrived to find in him a type of the Cross.[8] But Pliny barely mentions a one-horned creature, and Strabo a horned horse with the head of a stag.[9] I am sorry, for one of my proudest possessions is the horn of a unicorn, nearly eight feet long, with the correct spiral markings. Modern naturalists, in defiance of apology, scrip-

1 Aelian, *V.H.* II, 23.
2 Pausanias, VIII, 21, 2.
3 Herodotus, II, 73.
4 Aristotle, *Hist. Anim.* 501 a; Pliny, *Nat. Hist.* VIII, 75.
5 Aelian, *V.H.* IV, 26.
6 See H. G. Rawlinson, *India and the Western World*, p. 23.
7 Aelian, *V.H.* XVI, 18.
8 See Justin Martyr, *Dialogue with Trypho the Jew*, 91 (318B, C), who quotes Deuteronomy xxxiii, 17.
9 Strabo, C. 710.

ture, medicine, legend and romance, say it is merely the tusk of a narwhal.[1]

With the same cavalier neglect I have omitted the legends of transformation, and all connected with them. Are they not written *ad infinitum*, and even greater length, in the fifteen books of Ovid's *Metamorphoses*, which, if he had not happily had other things to distract him, he could and would so easily have made thirty?[2] These are all tales of the past; Actaeon has nothing to do with Natural History, even if Ovid tells the name of each of his thirty-two irrelevant dogs.[3] Even Pausanias cannot believe that a man should be turned into a bird.[4] Another line of inquiry in this same general direction I have avoided. The reader will recall Andrew Lang's assault on the anthropologists who would have it that Persephone was once a pig.[5] I do not even raise the question; no one would, who enjoyed the Homeric Hymn or Claudian's Latin poem on the goddess and her daughter. The aboriginal relations of gods and beasts were more than half forgotten in the Classical period; and we can leave them alone. *Non scire fas est omnia.* Furthermore in those wide fields of conjecture, haunted by the adepts of pre-primitive religion, knowledge is the last thing to be discovered. I also pass over proverb and fable, for there too often it is not the real animal but a human being, not a sheep that speaks, but a philosopher in sheep's clothing.

We may now pass to the second division of our subject, the bearing of Natural History upon life, its practical uses for man's guidance, quite apart from any commercial value. And first of all we have to deal very briefly with Divination.

1 Professor Adcock calls my attention to Mr Cyril Bunt's article in *Antiquity* (Dec. 1930) entitled "The Lion and the Unicorn". He traces their fight over fifty-five centuries—the constant motif in art of the fight between the lion and the bull, gazelle or unicorn. In Assyrian art the beasts are in profile, so one horn only is seen, which he suggests led early travellers to vouch for the creature with one horn. On the narwhal see Harry C. Whitney, *Hunting with the Eskimos*, p. 359.

2 It is suggested to me that the curate's egg—"parts of it, my Lord, are excellent"—is anticipated by Quintilian's comment on Ovid, *laudandus in partibus* (x, 1, 88).

3 Ovid, *Metam.* III, 220ff.

4 Pausanias, I, 30, 3.

5 A. Lang, *Homeric Hymns*, Intr. p. 63.

A good many strains are blended here. That certain birds and animals are weather-wise is common belief—is common knowledge, one might say. Quite apart from annual migrations, which imply instinct for climate and seasons, birds respond to atmospheric pressure, or the insects they hunt do. Harry C. Whitney, the American hunter, who spent a winter marooned among the northernmost Eskimos, was sure that the relieving steamer was a fortnight late the next August; the Eskimos were as sure it was not; and they were right. He went by his watch and what he took to be nights and days in the Arctic winter; they went by the plumage of the little auk and the colour of the hare.[1] Dim memories, legends, sacred tales, associated birds and beasts with gods, to whom they belonged. All the world believed in divination; therefore it must be right, or at least partly right, on Stoic principles. The gods signified their will, or shared their knowledge of the future, through the flight and notes of birds, the spotted liver of the sacrificial beast, and all sorts of things.

Not to go into detail, and sternly repressing the desire to quote Horace's *Impios parrae*, let me cite a story told by Plutarch, and his comment upon it.[2] A ram's head with a single horn was brought to Pericles from his farm; and Lampon the prophet predicted from it that the political party of Thucydides would come to grief, and all the guidance of Athenian affairs would come into the hands of Pericles. Anaxagoras was there, and had the skull cut open and showed how the one horn was atrophied and the other developed in conjunction with some malformation within; and he captured the admiration of all. But the laugh was with Lampon a little later, when his prophecy came true. "There was nothing, I think," says Plutarch, "to hinder them both being right, the man of science hitting the cause and the prophet the purpose. The business of the one was to study the causes and the natural development; of the

1 Harry C. Whitney, *Hunting with the Eskimos*, pp. 421, 429; a splendid adventure book.

2 Plutarch, *Pericles*, 6.

other, to predict the object of the occurrence and its significance. Those who say that the discovery of the cause is the annulment of the sign do not notice that along with supernatural symbols they abolish those contrived by man—such as the clanking of quoits,[1] the light of beacons, the shadows on the sundial; every one of these things has been devised, by some cause and contrivance, to be the sign of something else. But", he concludes, "perhaps this belongs to another discussion."

He omits to notice that there is commonly agreement in a household as to the significance of bells and gongs, with lucid explanation, and that there is always something arbitrary in the interpretation of omens,—a double assumption that they are signals and that the code is known on both sides. But Plutarch was all for the maintenance of traditional religion without too many questions. Widely read as he was in philosophic literature, he was no great thinker. Still it is something to be a writer of charm.

Alongside of divination, we may set the interpretation of dreams. Under the inspiration of Apollo Mystes of Daldia, a book on the subject was written by Artemidorus of that town. Very proud of it he was, too, and of the scientific principles on which he classified his dreams, collected over a period of many years at the festivals and in the cities of Greece, Asia, Italy and the islands. The twelfth chapter of his second book deals with dreams about animals. Sheep seen in a dream are good, whether white or black; the ancients were dubious about black sheep, but Artemidorus' own observation warranted him in saying they are good, though white are better. They are, in particular, good for magistrates entering on office, for lecturers (*σοφισταῖς*) and teachers. A ram suggests a master or ruler or emperor, a leader of the flock; to ride on a ram, safely and over level ground, is a good dream for a scholar (*φιλολόγοις*). All goats are bad dreams; asses are all right—their name suggests *ass*istance (*ὄνοι* and *ὄνασθαι*); mules vary; oxen are good. A lion

1 Used as gongs; as in India a piece of rail hangs in every small railway station and is hit with a stick to signal to the engine-driver to start the train.

in a friendly mood means for a soldier profit from his king, for an athlete, profit from his good condition; an angry lion is a bad dream and prophesies illness; a lion's cub means a new little son; but a lioness can be unlucky for a rich man. A bear means a woman; you see, Callisto in the myth was a woman who turned into a bear; but the star called the Bear suggests change, so the bear may mean sickness or travel. A monkey means a scoundrel of some sort; and a hyaena is unpleasant—perhaps a woman who deals in poisons. An elephant, outside of Italy or India, means danger because of its colour and size, and because it terrifies those not used to elephants. In Italy it means the Emperor or your master; and to ride safely on an elephant means luck from one or other of them. He has often noted that to be chased by an elephant prophesies sickness, to be caught by him death. But he is a bad dream for a woman any way; "I know of a woman in Italy, rich and not sick, who dreamed she was riding on an elephant; and, not long after, she died". Snakes and reptiles you would not wish to dream about.

Health and food may be grouped together. The whole world has been, and very largely still is, full of food taboos. The Israelite must not eat an animal unless it chewed the cud and had cloven feet. This excluded the pig, about which Plutarch's father thought that it was good eating and in no way contrary to religion;[1] and many Christians agree with him. "Bacon," drawled Mark Twain, "bacon would improve the flavour of an angel." Whatever the date of the Mosaic rule, as it stands, it looks like a late classification, an attempt at some sort of principle. Behind all the food taboos lay the belief that something quite different from what moderns might call carbon compounds may pass into you from your food—something of the animal, which may not be desirable, still less if the animal is sacred to some god; it may kill or madden you.[2] From some similar fancy, or for some reason based on symbolism, Pythagoras forbade beans to his followers. On the other hand, to eat some part

1 Plutarch, *Sympos.* IV, 4, 4. The opposite view stated in Plutarch, *de Iside*, 8, 353F–354B. 2 Cf. Sir Andrew Aguecheek, *Twelfth Night*, Act I, Sc. 3, 81.

of some animal may give you strength; I heard in Burma of a hunter's servant wanting to eat part of an elephant in the hope of securing strong sons. Even external application may be of use. Every American of the Southern States knows the value of a rabbit's foot; it is not only negroes who carry them. Perhaps it is due to a feeling that Brer Rabbit has the brains and comes out successful. Lucian gives us a prescription in derision.[1] "Pick off the ground with your left hand the tooth of a field-mouse just killed; wrap it in the skin of a lion newly stripped from him; tie it round your legs; and the pain will go." The experts differed; one urged not a lion's skin but a deer's—courage was the lion's virtue; swiftness the deer's; and that was what you wanted. No, says the other authority, though he had thought so himself till lately, when an African pointed out that the lion runs down the deer. And when Lucian asked if they thought an amulet hung outside you can cure a mischief rooted within, they laughed at him as a fool of no common order.

But amulets (περαρτήματα) bring me back to Pliny and the *Lithica*. *Amuletum* is Pliny's word, and from him about the year 1600 it passed into English; but where it came from, is unknown. Whatever the origin of the word or the variety of name, the thing and the idea are very old. "All races", writes Sir William Ridgeway, "ascribe magical powers to crystals and other stones of striking form or colour, and employ them as potent amulets. In fact all jewellery has its origin in magic rather than in aesthetic."[2] The *Lithica* is a strange book of verse, setting forth the magical values of the semi-precious stones.[3] "If a man bring jasper, with spring in its hue, and so do sacrifice, the heart of the gods takes delight therein, and they will full soon satisfy his fields from the clouds." "All the Orient", says Pliny, "is said to wear jasper as amulets"—

There's plenty jasper somewhere in the world—

1 Lucian, *Philopseudes*, 7.

2 *Companion to Greek Studies*, §302, p. 286 (Cambridge).

3 Jasper, in *Lithica*, 264; Pliny, *Nat. Hist.* XXXVII, 118; Opal, *Lith.* 279; magnet, *Lith.* 301.

but hear one more sentence of Pliny: "it is pleasant in passing to note here also the folly of the Magi, for they say jasper is useful to the Orator". In the opal, too, the denizens of heaven take delight, the opal with the delicate skin of a lovely child, a helper of sore eyes. Ares loves the magnet that draws the iron to it, as a maid the lad she loves. All these stones affect the gods, it is to be noted. There are affinities in Nature; Sympathy is the philosophic word; and the gods have revealed their kinships; and by theurgy, with the right formula in the right speech, with the right jewel in your hand, and the right offering, you can *compel* the god you will to grant your prayer. Iamblichus[1] explains that sacred formulas cannot be translated; there are peculiar turns that no other tongue can convey. Mrs Besant defends the same belief in Hinduism; the words in another tongue would set up different vibrations or wave-lengths in the air or the aether. Strange to have philology and physics shutting heaven against meaning! But we stray from Natural History perhaps. Still let the reader turn to Pliny on amber, and he will find an immense wealth of ancient theory leading up to the true explanation of amber; and he will learn something of the travels of Pytheas in amber-bearing regions, and, to swing back to our birds, he may enjoy the naturalist's scorn for the poet. Why should Sophocles, the tragic poet, tell us that amber comes from the annual weeping of Guinea hens (*meleagrides*) in India, for Meleager done to death in Greece? how did the hens hear of it, and why such big tears?[2]

So far we have dealt in detail. But the ancient world had thoughts of wider range suggested by the animals. Herodotus finds a witness to the wisdom of divine Providence—his *divine* is neuter, τὸ θεῖον—in the structure and habits of the creatures. The whole of Arabia, say the Arabs, would be full of the horrible little winged snakes but for the ordinance that

1 See Iamblichus, *De mysteriis*, v, 23 (stones); vi, 3 (sacrifices); vii, 5 (translation ruins the formula).

2 Amber, *sucinum*, in Pliny, *Nat. Hist.* xxxvii, 30–51. For the quotation of Sophocles, see Pearson, *Soph. Fragments*, vol. ii, p. 66. Strabo, c. 215, gets the guinea fowl nearer the Po, but does not believe in them. It is curious that amber should have so many unrelated names.

makes the female eat her mate and be consumed by her young within her. The lion's rarity we have noted; but he adds that the hare can go with two litters at once. The animals that are timid and good to eat are prolific, and the others are not; so a balance is kept. Oppian has the same thought—"of wild creatures some are wise and cunning, but small of body; others again are valiant in might, but weak in the counsel of their breasts; others are craven of heart and feeble of body, but swift of foot; to others God has given all things, cunning, counsel, strong frame, swift limbs. But they know each one of them the bright gifts of his own nature".[1]

Even the more disgusting beasts have a sort of value. The rather dull epistle attributed to Barnabas bids "the children of gladness" (his one good phrase) recognize moral law in the food taboos of Moses.[2] "It is not a commandment of God that they should not bite with their teeth, but Moses spake it in the spirit." The pig is banned to warn us away from men like swine; the hare, because its structure suggests sin; the hyaena because it changes its sex year by year; the weasel—and so on. Mere fancy, all untrue to Anthropology, all aside from all we know of taboos; but an endeavour to reach something beyond the physical, something akin to moral order.

If Virgil astonishes some of his readers by repeating the old fable of the bees issuing from the dead carcase of an animal, it is an Alexandrine passage—perhaps taken from earlier work requisitioned to fill a gap made by external circumstances in his poem. He has a nobler thought, suggested by the bees,[3] *Deum namque ire per omnes....* Here is

1 Herodotus, III, 108; Oppian, *Cyn.* IV, 25; and compare Lucretius, V, 862, and Cicero, *de Natura Deorum*, II, 50, 127; and Pliny, *Nat. Hist.* VIII, 217, on rabbit and hare.

2 Barnabas, chapter x. Cf. Plutarch, *de Iside*, 353 F; 376 A; 381 A; for similar zoology and symbolism; and Clement of Alexandria, *Strom.* II, 67; V, 51.

3 Virgil, *Georgic*, IV, 219–227. I am tempted to note the contrast between the traditional explanation of silk as of vegetable origin given by Virgil, *Georgic*, II, 121, with the accounts in Aristotle, *Hist. Anim.* V, 551 b and in Pausanias, VI, 266–8, which describe, with differing degrees of accuracy, the silkworm and its history. But see G. F. Hudson, *Europe and China*, p. 59, n. 3.

Lord Burghclere's rendering—though the fourth line goes far beyond Virgil's simplicity—

By such high samples and exemplars swayed,
Some hold the bees, like mortals, have their part
In the divine and universal mind,
Lipping the chalice of ethereal fire.
For God, they say, is everywhere alike,
Or in the utmost corners of the earth,
Or in the waste of ocean, or above
In the illimitable depths of heaven.
And from His spirit creatures of this world,
Mankind, and flocks, and herds, and beasts of the field,
Draw at their birth the subtle breath of life.
So likewise in their end to Him return,
And at their dissolution find a home.
Death hath no habitation in their midst,
But, deathless, to the starry host they soar,
And claim their lofty heritage of heaven.

With two further quotations from men of very different calibre and environment, let me close this rambling survey of ancient error, fancy and knowledge. Here is Aristotle, the man of science, the master of those who know. "The glory of the heavenly bodies fills us with more delight than the contemplation of these lowly things....But the heavens are high and far-off, and the living creatures are at our own door, and, if we so desire it, we may gain ample and certain knowledge of each and all. We take pleasure in the beauty of a statue; shall not then the living fill us with delight? and all the more, if in the spirit of philosophy, we search for causes and recognize the evidences of design. Then will nature's purpose and her deep-seated laws be everywhere revealed, all tending in her multitudinous work to one form or another of the Beautiful."[1]

Four hundred years later Seneca, an author far more sincere than the wealth of his language or his moral discursiveness suggests, wrote toward the end of his book of *Natural Questions*: "The day will yet come, when the progress of research through long ages will reveal to sight the mysteries of nature that now are concealed. A single lifetime, though

1 Quoted by D'Arcy W. Thompson in *The Legacy of Greece*, p. 156.

it were wholly devoted to the study of the sky, does not suffice for the investigation of problems of such complexity. It must take long successive ages to unfold all. The day will yet come when our descendants will be amazed that we remained ignorant of things that will to them seem so plain". *Veniet tempus quo posteri nostri tam aperta nos nescisse mirentur.*[1]

A great conclusion in the true spirit of Science. Let us look back over our course. We have seen error, fancy and knowledge strangely intermingled, but through all two factors that make for progress, the two factors that make us men—wonder, for one thing, and the other, sheer disinterested love of creature and creation.

1 Seneca, *Nat. Quaest.* VII, 25, 2.

THE MANNERS OF A GENTLEMAN

τῶν νόμων...ὅσοι ἄγραφοι ὄντες αἰσχύνην ὁμολογουμένην φέρουσιν.

Pericles, in Thucydides, II, 57.

Et mehercule est quam facile diligas αὐτόχθων in homine urbanitas.

Cicero, *ad Atticum*, VII, 2, 3.

IT is curious how often a race that is admired in the type fails to please in the individual. The Englishman in the abstract, England—yes! but in the great Dominions the actual Englishman who comes in as an immigrant, or as a visitor, too often annoys the very people who have idealized the type. The great qualities of the race he may in some degree possess, but he may be awkward in his use of them. He does not make advances to his new neighbours, he is slow in accepting them, he does not propose to reveal himself, and his clumsiness exhibits him in his weaknesses; he is suspected of contempt; his better quality may not be so readily recognized; he is strange and uneasy, and takes long to make himself at home. Yet in one Dominion at least it is possible to make oneself at home too plausibly; a cheap intimacy in the Jewish immigrant or the American drummer does not immediately or securely endear them in Canada.

In the ancient world there was a good deal of the same feeling. The Roman was stiff and stupid; the Greek was clever and supple; the *gravitas* of the one became a tiresome pose, and the *levitas* of the other revealed a cheap character. Greeks like Polybius and Plutarch did not fail to understand the greatness of Roman character in spite of the promoted peasants, who posed and tyrannized over their intellectual superiors. The influence of Greek literature and Greek philosophy upon laws and letters in Rome, and upon life and thought generally throughout the Empire, was one thing; that influence any thoughtful man would feel and would welcome; the casual Greek of commerce or of the lecture theatre was another story.

What the vulgar Roman felt about the common Greek is

to be read in Juvenal. No one can deny the cleverness of Juvenal—his journalistic smartness in turning sentences and knocking off epigrams. He comes nearer to the modern journalist than any Classical writer of Rome. "He always writes at the top of his voice", as some one said of a certain royalist in contemporary France; and he always writes what will be instantly recognized as clever and applauded. One of his butts is the little Greek, and the epithet "hungry" heightened the contempt. "The hungry Hamiltons" was not a phrase of pity in Scotland. The hungry little Greek, with his repulsive suppleness, vexed the conventional Roman—his quick wit, his reckless audacity, his headlong chatter, his profession of all the arts from rhetoric to rope-dancing. *Non possum ferre, Quirites, Graecam urbem.* Then let him go back to Aquinum and repress his own flow of headlong declamation; he is not even Aquinum's greatest son.

But more serious Romans than Juvenal felt a certain distaste for the run of Greeks whom they met. The cheap compliments which a miserable ecclesia would vote to the visiting Roman,[1] the perjuries and dishonesties (which Polybius admitted[2]), the manners, the gesticulation, the vulgar and too expressive use of rolling eye and shrugging shoulder, are remarked by Cicero. He admits that he knew many Greeks who were men of character and culture. Yes, but Sir John Mahaffy asked,[3] even if Cicero says he lived with this Greek or that *familiariter*, did he ever really regard any Greek as a friend on the same level with himself? They were busy in trade, or at best in medicine and education; you had to use them for both purposes if you had a family; but would a Roman gentleman wish to associate with a medical man or a schoolmaster? Would an English gentleman, of a county family? "Professions", says Cicero,[4] "in which a greater degree of intelligence is involved, or from which some real utility is expected, such as medicine, architecture, or

1 Cf. Cicero, *ad Quintum fratrem*, I, I, 9, 26.
2 Polybius, VI, 56.
3 J. P. Mahaffy, *Silver Age of Greece*, pp. 166–9.
4 Cicero, *de Officiis*, I, 42, 151, which with the preceding section contains an interesting discussion of vulgar professions.

higher education, are quite reputable for persons whose social status they become (*iis, quorum ordini conveniunt, honestae*)." So if the medical man is above the perfumer and the dancer, he is obviously not in society. As for the general run of Greeks, "I am sick and tired", Cicero writes to his brother, "of their want of character, their obsequiousness, their attention not to principle but to the moment".[1] It may be rejoined that war and faction had gone far to kill off most Greeks who could have been described as nobles or gentlemen. Alexander the Great evidently found something in the Persian nobles that he did not in the Greeks he commonly met, something congenial, a natural dignity that impressed him.[2] It may also be urged that Greek gentlemen, if they still existed, might not be seeking the acquaintance of Romans, either to do their banking, to educate their sons, to give them popular lectures, or to doctor them.

For the type was not unfamiliar to the Greeks. The reserve of Pericles is commented upon by Thucydides; he is not unlike the great peer of the Victorian epoch,—a more popular-minded Salisbury, a quicker-witted Devonshire, a great orator indeed but quite unlike the Greek rhetorician of later days. He was not afraid of his people, nor of ideas. Xenophon draws us an Athenian gentleman in Ischomachus, grave, good and didactic, with more passion, however, for tidiness than for humour. But he had a dear little impulsive wife to train, whose mother perhaps had not enough emphasized order among the domestic virtues. "What a beautiful sight it is (ὡς καλόν), to see the boots of all sorts and kinds arranged in a row....The wit (ὁ κομψός) might laugh, but no serious person, when I say that there is a rhythm (εὔρυθμον) even in pots marshalled in order."[3] Ischomachus is something akin to John Bull, and his illustration drawn from the order of a ship, his instinct to have things at home "shipshape and Bristol fashion", completes the parallel of a big kindly gentle-

1 *ad Quint. Fratr.* 1, 2, 2, 4, *pertaesum est levitatis, adsentationis, animorum non officiis sed temporibus servientium.*

2 Pharnabazos, in Xenophon's *Hellenica*, remains in the mind as the type of the Persian noble, a great figure and a man.

3 Xenophon, *Oeconomicus*, 8, 19.

man, well qualified, in Xenophon's famous phrase, *ἄρχειν καὶ ἄρχεσθαι*, to recognize authority and to exercise it.

From the very beginning the Greek knew the difference between good and bad manners. Good manners prevail in the house of King Alcinous; Nausicaa is one of the most charming girls in literature, or out of it. One young man, Euryalos, lapses into very bad manners, and suggests to Odysseus that he will be no athlete but a seafaring man, whose thought is of ships and sailors, of freight and gain. He receives a swift and well-deserved rebuke. "Stranger, thou hast not spoken well; thou art like unto one ill-bred. So true is it that the gods give not all gracious gifts to all, neither shapeliness, nor wisdom, nor speech....A man may be like the deathless gods in beauty, and yet his words have no crown of grace upon them."[1] And with this word Odysseus catches up the weight and hurls it far beyond all of them. Euryalos later on, at a word from the king,[2] makes amends and gives Odysseus a sword. It is far otherwise among the Suitors in the house of Odysseus. If, like the men of their day, they set their hands to the viands laid ready before them, and ate with their fingers, they need not have thrown bones about nor insulted the stranger. Antinous is perhaps worst-bred among them, as bad as the goatherd Melanthius and the goatherd's sister; and the reader, like the listener of old, has a certain sense of satisfaction when the arrow-head passes clean out through his delicate neck;

ὡς ἀπόλοιτο καὶ ἄλλος ὅτις τοιαῦτά γε βάζοι,

if we may so far misquote.

Hesiod, at the end of his *Works and Days*, puts in some maxims on manners and morals, curiously mixed and curiously phrased, some with sacred reasons behind them, some with social. You must never taunt a man with his poverty—the gods send it; nor slander good men; nor be boorish at a meal where all contribute; "nor, at a feast of the gods, cut the withered from the quick from the five-branched with gleaming iron"—in prose, don't trim your

1 *Odyssey*, VIII, 158.　　2 *Odyssey*, VIII, 396.

nails in public. Along with these rules are others against pouring a libation to the gods with unwashed hands (they will spit back your prayers if you do), and laying the ladle on the mixing bowl (a most uncanny action); and others again, which I know but do not mention.[1]

In historical Athens there was a keen feeling for the difference between good and bad manners, between the gentleman and the *βάναυσος*; and, because there as among us it was possible for a man to be well-born without being well-bred, there were all the grades that separate the best from the worst, including the cad, the snob, and the "quite the gentleman". In the ideal state, Plato says that education will begin when the children begin to play—"the spirit of law", as Jowett paraphrases it aptly, "must be imparted to them in music, and the spirit of order will make them grow"; and so they may rediscover what those before them have spoiled, "the little things, it may be, that seem to be good customs". What sort of things? Why, these; the silences that befit the younger when the older are there; etiquette about sitting down (literally, lying down, the posture for meals, which must have been more of an art), and rising up (which also must have needed grace); and about courtesy toward parents—yes, and about the cutting of the hair, about brooches and shoes, and how to hold one's body,[2] and a good deal else of the kind.[3] The Socrates of Xenophon notes the same sort of thing—"is it not the usage everywhere that the younger should make way for the older when they meet, should rise from his seat for him, should let him have the comfortable couch and the first word?...Courtesy is the way to win a gentleman".[4] "I was trained", says the aged Cyrus, in the other great book,[5] "by my country, which is your country too, to yield place to my elders—not merely to elder brothers, but to citizens also—whether it were on the road, or whether

1 Hesiod, *Works and Days*, 706–764.
2 "Bear your body more seeming, Audrey"; *As You Like It*, v, 4.
3 Plato, *Republic*, 425.
4 Xenophon, *Mem.* II, 3, 16, τοὺς καλοὺς κἀγαθούς.
5 Xenophon, *Cyropaedeia*, VIII, 7, 10.

seats were concerned, or speech."[1] So it was in Sparta too,—Utopian Sparta or actual. Lycurgus, says Xenophon, knew that, when a boy ceases to be a child and becomes a lad, then is the period of maximum self-will, of the tendency to break laws and to seek pleasure; so he put his mind to discipline for youth, and he succeeded. The Spartan lad walks with his eyes on the ground, his hands under his cloak. Lycurgus has proved that, even where modesty is concerned, the boy outdoes the girl. You would expect to hear a stone image talk sooner than a Spartan boy, or a bronze statue to turn its eyes upon you; yes, the Spartan boy, you would say, is more modest than a maid on her wedding night.[2] Aristophanes[3] has the same story of the manners of old—

To rise from your chair if an elder be there, and respectfully give him your place,
And with love and with fear your parents revere, and shrink from the brand of disgrace.

But here must come a digression, the first of two or three, upon the social customs of the time. Equipment, furniture, implements, lighting, outlooks, all affect manners. What would seem bad manners now, would not be bad under quite different conditions. To the modern taste there must have remained some elements of roughness at table in the absence of spoons and forks; but we are told that King Charles II had to eat without a fork, and would get himself in the same mess as the ancients. Water for the hands was a necessary accompaniment of a meal, as it is still in many parts of the world for the same reason. The Athenian cleaned his fingers on lumps of bread; instead of a spoon a bit of bread was used, sometimes shaped like a scoop; and when he was done, he threw the bread to the dogs, for those unclean parasites of man were still there. In the *Knights* of Aristophanes the sausage-seller, who is to oust Cleon from the leadership of the Demos, says these bits of bread were *his* food in boyhood—

I think in shamelessness I'll win; else vainly in the slums
Have I to such a bulk been reared on finger-cleaning crumbs.

1 Dr Johnson "hoped he knew his rank better than to presume to take place of a Doctor in Divinity". Birkbeck Hill's *Boswell*, II, p. 162.

2 Xenophon, *Lac. Rep.* 3, 1–5.

3 Aristophanes, *Clouds*, 993.

His enemy rejoins—

On finger-pellets like a dog? And, reared on these, you seek
To fight a dog-faced fierce baboon! I marvel at your cheek.

This use of bread for spoon is alluded to in the same play; Demos is to be fed—and here, says the sausage-seller,

And here I'm bringing splendid scoops of bread,
Scooped by the Goddess with her ivory hand.[1]

A purpose never dreamed by Pheidias when he made his great Athene of gold and ivory.

After the meal, if a symposium was to follow, the tables were changed for smaller ones. There were three libations to the gods, and tradition would have them accompanied by the flute. This opened the door to the flute-girl. "I move", says Eryximachus[2] "that the flute-girl, who has just made her appearance, be told to go away and play to herself, or, if she likes, to the women who are within." So things begin in Plato's *Symposium*; but by and by[3] "there was a great knocking at the door of the house as of revellers, and the sound of a flute-girl was heard. Agathon told the attendants to go and see who were the intruders. 'If they are friends of ours', he said, 'invite them in; but if not, say that the drinking is over.' A little while afterwards they heard the voice of Alcibiades resounding in the court; he was in a great state of intoxication, and kept roaring and shouting, 'Where is Agathon? lead me to Agathon!' and at length, supported by the flute-girl and some of his companions, he found his way to them. 'Hail, friends', he said, appearing at the door crowned with a massive garland of ivy and flowers, his head flowing with ribands. 'Will you have a very drunken man as a companion of your revels? Or shall I crown Agathon, which was my intention in coming, and go away?'" They invite him to stay, and he catches sight of Socrates, and he asks for some of his ribands back to crown "the marvellous head of this man who conquers all mankind in his discourse"; and he crowns Socrates, and very

1 Aristophanes, *Knights*, 413–416; and 1168 (Rogers).
2 Plato, *Symposium*, 176E.
3 What follows comes from *Symposium*, 212–216.

shortly makes a speech about him. It is the famous speech in which he compares Socrates to the figures of Silenus that people see in the shops of the statuaries,—there sits Silenus, with pipe or flute at his mouth; but open him, and there is a god inside. And the effect of Socrates' voice! Other speakers, even good ones, how little influence they have! He has heard Pericles, who was eloquent enough; but the very fragments of Socrates and his words, even at second hand and imperfectly repeated, astound and entrance—he is the only person who has ever made me ashamed, who has made me feel I ought not to live as I do. That's why I run away from him; that's why I have often wished him out of this world, and it's sorry I should be if he were gone; I don't know what to make of the man. Men have been more drunk than Alcibiades.

In the *Symposium* of Xenophon, quite a different one but with its own charm, we find another entertainment. There is Philip "the laughter-maker", a jester by trade, self-invited. When the tables are changed, a rather vulgar Syracusan brings in a skilled flute-girl, a dancing boy, and a dancing girl who does clever tumbling tricks and turns head over heels into a stand set round with knives and out of it. Which shows, says Socrates, that courage can be taught. Couldn't we get her to teach the Athenians? says some one. The tumblers were traditional at banquets from Homer's days. It can well be believed that, where there was no Socrates, such entertainments were less philosophic, and had a bad effect upon morals. If it be urged, and it can be, that morals and manners are different things, it must be allowed that they react on one another.

Democracy, according to Plato,—the sophists and Socrates, according to Aristophanes,—made havoc at once of the old manners and morals of Athens. The city is full of freedom and frankness[1]—a man may do what he likes, a supremely delightful way of life. Democracy does not care about trifles, such as principles in education, traditional morality and the like. Why should you distinguish between pleasures necessary

1 The rest of the paragraph is taken from Plato, *Republic*, VIII, 559–563.

and unnecessary, between desires honourable and dishonourable? Reverence, *αἰδώς*, is driven out of the young man's soul, and old and new desires wanton there; and he returns to the land of the Lotus-eaters. If older men have anything to say, he will not listen; reverence is silliness, temperance is unmanliness; and his heart becomes the home of insolence and anarchy and waste and impudence, in bright array with garlands on their heads. Insolence, *ὕβρις*, becomes good breeding, anarchy is the new liberty, shamelessness is manliness. The master is afraid of his scholars, and they despise him; the young man is as good as the old, ready to match him in deed and word; and the old men—they don't like to be thought unpleasant or domineering, so down they come to the level of the young, all pleasant and gay together. And slaves, of course, and women—oh! they are all free and equal; and the bitch is as good as her mistress, and the horses and asses on the street no more think of yielding place than the young men. Nobody wants laws written or unwritten; everything is bursting with liberty.

Isocrates has the same lamentable tale to tell. In the good old days they trained the young men—drilled them in riding, gymnastics, hunting and philosophy; and the Areopagus saw to it that they behaved. Perhaps the exact date is a little vague, but we all know well enough when the good old times were, every *laudator temporis acti se puero*, though some of us, like Isocrates, prefer the age of George III to the Victorian. But now, we all say, and Isocrates says it—but now—well, look at the contrast. In those days "to contradict older men or to speak abusively to them was counted worse than it is to-day to sin against parents. To eat or drink in an inn—nobody would have dared to do it, not even a decent slave. They studied dignity not buffoonery (*βωμολοχεύεσθαι*); and the wits (*τοὺς εὐτραπέλους*) and the people with a gift for scoffing, whom nowadays we credit with good natural parts (*εὐφυεῖς*), they considered unfortunate".[1] We may waive the decline in morals, for we are at present only dealing with manners.

1 Isocrates, *Areopag*. 49.

It will be noted in all this that so far, apart from general complaints about degenerate ways, the one constant particular is a declining respect for older men; in the old days the young always courteously *rose* from their seats on the approach of their elders, a laudable custom indeed.

But we must have more detail, and Athenaeus gives it. Of course he is not contemporary, but he knew our period and its literature and traditions, and in his amazing cyclopaedia of dinners, menus and manners, *The Gastronomers*, he constantly gives us material gathered from a very wide reading, even if large part of it were in other men's handbooks. Here is a paragraph from him, about dress and public appearances.[1]

"Men of the old time were careful to gather up their garments decently and ridiculed those who were careless about it. Thus Plato in the *Theaetetus* speaks of men who can do certain services smartly and quickly, but do not know how to throw their cloaks from left to right as a gentleman should, nor ever acquired the music of discourse to hymn aright the life of the gods and of men blessed of heaven."[2] Sappho mocks at Andromeda—

What country wench beguiles thee, one that knows not
To cover up her ankles with her frock?

Then Philetaerus:

Cover your ankles! let your cloak down, fool!
Don't bunch it like a boor above your knees!

Callistratus, the pupil of Aristophanes, has abused Aristarchus[3] in a book for his want of rhythm in his dress, for even a detail of this sort reveals something of a man's culture. Thus it is that Alexis says:

One thing will stamp a man no gentleman—
To walk unrhythmically down the street,
When he quite well could move with dignity...
Such gait brings credit to the man who has it,
Gives pleasure to beholders, grace to life.
What man of sense would fail of such reward?

1 Athenaeus, 21 B.

2 Plato, *Theaetetus*, 175 E; compare the scorn of Poseidon in Aristophanes (*Birds*, 1567) for the Triballian god who wears his cloak ἐπ' ἀρίστερα.

3 A queer echo of professors' controversies in Alexandria.

The Greek was very sensitive to a man's gait and movements. Here are a pair of Demosthenes' contemporaries, people in the business world—the old banker sneaking about the streets, hugging the wall, with a sour look on his face—the spendthrift stepson "with quick walk and loud voice" (as he admits) swaggering round in a *chlamys*, a woollen cloak, a sure sign of extravagance, three attendants at his heels, and a look of dissipation on his face. We owe the description of each of them to the other. Phormion engaged Demosthenes to describe Apollodorus.[1] Plato drew much the same picture of the men of business, stooping as they walk and pretending not to see the people they have ruined.[2] Aristotle has a similar distaste for the visible effects (and the spiritual effects) of trades and crafts upon men.

Trousers, *ἀναξυρίδες*, were to the Greek the Oriental's garb, perhaps later the Gaul's, the wear of men who rode more than Greeks or Romans as a rule did. The long linen *chiton*, and later the short woollen one, sleeveless, loose-hung but girdled, fastened on the shoulders with brooches of some sort, with a cloak, *himation*, of some pattern above it, was the man's dress. The *chlamys* came in during the fifth century, a big loose thing secured by a brooch at Adam's apple. It was etiquette to wear both *chiton* and *himation*, though the poor and the Cynic philosopher might discard the *chiton*;[3] and so did those who affected Spartan style—"affectation" indeed, says Aristotle (*ἀλαζονεία*),[4] and therefore bad manners.

With Athenaeus' passages in mind, and this note on dress, the picture of Cleon has new meaning. "He robbed the *bema*, the platform, of its dignity (*κόσμον*)", says Plutarch, "and was the first man to bellow when he harangued the people; he would pull back his *himation*, slap his thigh, and race up and down the platform as he spoke." His manners were as bad as his policies and his character, and "induced in other politicians the slapdashery and contempt for decency

1 See *From Pericles to Philip*, p. 325 (The House of Pasion).
2 Plato, *Rep.* VIII, 555 E.
3 See Alice Zimmern, *Home Life of the Ancient Greeks*, pp. 11–20.
4 Aristotle, *Ethics*, IV, 7, 15.

that ruined Athens".[1] The Oligarch who wrote the tract on the Athenian Republic explains that in Athens you cannot safely punch a slave on the street; he may, quite probably, prove to be a free man and an Athenian citizen; they dress just as badly and behave exactly alike. The three outstanding Greek words for *vulgar* picture to us the ways and manners of artisans, porters and slaves—*βάναυσος*, *φορτικός*, *ἀνελεύθερος*. The gentleman is *καλὸς κἀγαθός*, beautiful and good, and *ἐλευθέριος*, a product of freedom.

The vulgar had their own language; they did not talk literature; their speech was homely and commonplace. At the cost of another short digression, we may recall how the critics note it when a great man of letters drops the literary language for the popular. The perfection of style, says Aristotle, is to be clear without being commonplace (*σαφῆ καὶ μὴ ταπεινήν*);[2] but he allows such use of common words as will prove right. "A successful illusion is wrought, when the composer picks his words from the language of daily life; this is what Euripides does and first hinted the way to do."[3] Long afterwards Longinus made the same comment on the great poets using "common and plebeian words with nothing particular about them" and achieving dignity without seeming commonplace (*ταπεινοί*); and he instances the saying of Herakles in Euripides

> *γέμω κακῶν δὴ κοὐκέτ' ἔσθ' ὅπου τεθῇ*
> I am packed full of trouble, and can hold no more.[4]

Longinus, however, is less pleased with Herodotus, when he says that, after the great storm, which wrecked the Persian fleet, the wind *ἐκόπασε*, flagged, or grew fagged, and that men on a wreck had an unpleasant end (*ἀχάριστον*).[5] The critic Dionysius went still further back for an illustration; he quotes the fine scene where Telemachus appears to his father in the swineherd's hut. Every one, he says, would bear witness to the enchantment of the passage, but look at the words!

1 Plutarch, *Nicias*, 8.
2 Aristotle, *Poetics*, 22, 1; 1458a.
3 Aristotle, *Rhetoric*, III, 2, 5; 1404b.
4 Longinus, 40, 2, 3; and Euripides, *Herc. Furens*, 1245.
5 Longinus, 43, 1; Herodotus, VII, 191; VIII, 13, *ἄχαρι*.

It is all woven of the cheapest and most commonplace words, which a peasant, or a seafaring man, or an artisan, might employ, anybody in short who took no thought of fine language but used any that came along.[1] One more illustration that genius may break rules, and an indication that people of good manners will stick to the rules and not use vulgarisms or words of everyday life.

Let us pass on to a very famous person, Aristotle's Magnificent Man, who stands removed alike from meanness and vulgarity.[2] His virtue concerns the right use of wealth, proper expenditure for proper ends; he is liberal, though the liberal are not always magnificent. He will expend money freely, but well, upon the gods and the temples, votive offerings and sacrifices, on the trireme for his city's navy, on the chorus for its theatre, on the entertainment; but preferably on such works as are permanent. The vulgar man (*βάναυσος*) overdoes things, squanders big sums on trifles; he will entertain his club at a breakfast as sumptuous as a marriage feast, or bring a comic chorus on to the stage in purple, like the Megarians; and all to show how rich he is, and in the belief that he will be admired for doing such things. Such vulgarity is a vice, Aristotle says, but it does not exactly bring disgrace; it does not injure one's neighbour, and there are things more unseemly. We will dismiss it as bad manners, but we will remember that vulgarity is the outcome of bad motive.

The High-Minded Man[3] follows who regards himself as worthy of high things, and is worthy of them; for high-mindedness can only exist on a large scale, as beauty can only exist in a big frame, *ἐν μεγάλῳ σώματι*; short people may be neat and well proportioned, but not beautiful. His character has to be compact of virtue; high-mindedness is, as it were, a cosmos of the virtues; it makes them greater and cannot exist without them; you cannot be high-minded if you are not a gentleman (*ἄνευ καλοκἀγαθίας*). Such a man

1 Dionysius Halic., *de Compositione*, 3.
2 Aristotle, *Ethics*, IV, 4–6; 1122a–1123a.
3 Aristotle, *Ethics*, IV, 7, 8, 1123b–1125a.

will accept honours, as his due or even less than his due, and as the best that others can give. Trivial compliments from trivial people he will not regard. He may even seem to be a little supercilious, not ready with admiration; but he is essentially truthful and never harbours a grudge; he takes a moderate view of wealth; he is no gossip; and he speaks ill of no one, not even his enemies—unless it is purposely to insult them (*εἰ μὴ δι' ὕβριν*). This seems to square with the modern English definition that a gentleman is one who will never hurt another person's feelings *un*-intentionally. The High-Minded Man will be slow in his movements; his voice will be deep, his manner of speaking sedate; a man of his instincts and feelings is not the sort that will hurry or be emphatic. Shrill speech and bustle come from small desires and lack of proportion. Conceit, which is high-mindedness erring in excess, makes people ignorant of themselves—conspicuously so. They try dress and pose, and talk about themselves, as if that were the road to honour.

Passing by some other contrasts, we come to a subtler matter. Aristotle is always clear that relaxation is a part of life; and playfulness and good taste in speech will contribute to it, the gift for knowing the right things to say and the right way to say them, and the right company in which to say them. Those who exceed are of course buffoons and vulgar (*βωμολόχοι καὶ φορτικοί*); their aim is ridicule at any cost, laughter whoever suffers; laughing at themselves or others, using language that the man of taste (*ὁ χαρίεις*) would not use nor sometimes want to hear. The man without humour, who never says a thing you can laugh at, seems a boor, a useless, uncontributive creature; and he takes offence at everything. Between them is the man of humour (*εὐτράπελος*). Humour never needs to look far for subjects, and most people like fun, so sometimes the mere buffoon gets the better name. The real humourist has tact (*ἐπιδεξιότης*); the humour of a gentleman (*ἐλευθέριος*), of an educated man, is quite different from that of the uneducated and the working classes (*τοῦ ἀνδραποδώδους*). It is seen in the difference between the Old Comedy with its coarseness and the New more apt with suggestion. But recreation and amusement are necessary, he repeats; and the man of taste, the gentleman, is as it were a law in himself. With which we can probably agree.

Few books left to us by antiquity are more amusing than the *Characters* of Theophrastus; few perhaps have evoked more imitators. The author, we read, would appear at the Peripatos (the school of Aristotle), at the regular hour, bright and well groomed; he would sit down, and, as he talked, he would give free play to every motion and gesture; and once, when he was mimicking a glutton, he put out his tongue and licked his lips.[1] Not all philosophers of his powers and repute are so lively. Liveliness is the note of the *Characters*. Thirty pictures of types are drawn for us, quickly and deftly, every one of them full of life; and types are at once easier to draw than individual figures, and, therefore, harder to succeed with. The difficulty in dealing with them is to omit, but let us practise a stern relevancy, and concentrate on manners, beginning outdoors and then looking into the house.

Here is the market full of people, and by the stall, where nuts and myrtleberries and fruits are sold, stands a man with his mouth full, busily munching.[2] Some one passes, and is accosted by name, though a stranger. Another comes, and he shows him his purchases and invites him to his house, and then, standing at the barber's door or the perfumer's, he explains that he means to get drunk. Such is the Gross Man. Here is another, clumping along in roughly patched shoes—"strong as horn, these patches", he says; and inside his cloak you can see the meat and vegetables the Mean Man is carrying home himself. "When I was campaigning with Alexander", begins a loud voice, and it goes on to talk at large of gemmed cups brought home—and the artists of Asia are better than the European—and in the famine, why, he couldn't say No to anybody, and it cost him five talents.

1 Athenaeus, 21 A.

2 There were Americans who did not like to see W. J. Bryan, when Secretary of State, eating radishes from a bag on the street.

Just count, he says to the strangers near him, and brings the total up to ten. Nobody needs to be told he is the Boastful Man.

We meet a succession of ill-mannered people, as we come away. First there is the Offensive Man in a very thick *chiton* and a very light cloak (and very dirty); and his finger nails—but they're hereditary, he says. Then another of the loud-voiced kind, shuffling along in shoes too big for him, and a cloak too short; he halts to gaze—at what? Oh! some goat or donkey—the Boor! But the next man steps along the Odeum Street with hair daintily trimmed, his nails accurately pared, and his cloak in exquisite order; and his political opinions are quite frankly given: "It's dreadful what we have to suffer in the courts from the juries!" "A graceless thing the mob! always at the disposal of those who will bribe!" He is the Oligarchic Man.

Indoors now, and the talk is freer, and the manners. The Gross Man spits across the table. The Unpleasant Man declaims on his house being made an inn; his friends are like a cask with a hole in it, never to be satisfied. The Garrulous will tell you his dream. The Surly won't answer, or only says "Don't bother me!" He won't wait for anybody, sing, recite or dance when asked to, and a courtesy at table—catch him touching what is offered him! The Flatterer brings apples and pears for the children, and kisses them—"Chicks of a good father", he says, and a great deal else that is too kind. The Complaisant Man asks to see the children—"As like their father as figs!" Then there is the Unseasonable Man who never can hit the right moment; at a wedding he must declaim against women; he tells his stories to people who know them, and at immense length; "and, when he is minded to dance, he will seize on somebody not yet drunk". The Loquacious Man knows all about it; listen to him and then you'll know; on a jury he will hinder his fellows from coming to a verdict, at a theatre the people near him from seeing the play, at a dinner the guests from eating, apologizing the while, "it's so hard for a talker to keep quiet, and his tongue is so well oiled—couldn't hold it, not if you called him a bigger chatterer than the swallows". The Gross Man who was hiring a flute player when we saw him outside, beats time with his hands as she plays, and hums an accompaniment. The Boor answers the door himself.[1] The Evil Speaker tells you the scandals about Sosias and his family and his aliases, but above all abuses his friends and of course the dead, and calls it all "plain speaking" and "republican candour". Last we may look at the Man of Petty Ambition, with his hair kept very short and his teeth very white, and constantly new clothes; he has a negro slave and a monkey; and he puts up a little tombstone to his pet dog inscribed A SCION OF MELITA.[2]

The reflection rises that, if Greek manners did not please the Roman, there were Greeks and Greeks; and it is followed by the sad thought how many people, of manners not much better, we meet in America and England, and perhaps elsewhere. "Mankind advances", said Goethe, "but man remains the same"; and the *Characters* of Theophrastus will help us to believe it. Set them beside Aristotle's pictures and the various comments of Plato and the rest, and we shall be asking Cicero to limit his statements; and that great genial nature will.

If he does not, we will appeal against him to two Stoic philosophers. Epictetus has a great discourse on cleanliness, which he would allow to be very near godliness; for, as men approach the gods by reason, they crave to be clean. Nature has given men hands and nostrils; so, if a man does not use his handkerchief properly, "I say, he is not fulfilling the function of a man". Nature has provided water; "so wash your teeth, she says. Why? in order that you may be a man and not a beast—a pig". If a man will not bathe and use the strigil and have his clothes washed—think of the people near you, and "either go into the desert where you deserve to go, or live alone and smell yourself". He prefers a young man to have his hair carefully trimmed, than rough and dirty; it means "some conception of the beautiful"

1 This was the complaint brought against Abraham Lincoln by his wife.
2 See page 255; but Jebb will not allow it to be Malta.

which needs only to be directed to things of the mind; "but if a man comes to me filthy and dirty, with a moustache down to his knees—what can I say to him?" "But whence am I to get a fine cloak? Man! you have water; wash it!"

He uses table manners as an illustration. "Remember that in life you ought to behave as at a banquet. Suppose that something is carried round and is opposite you. Reach out your hand and take it with decency. Suppose that it passes by you. Do not detain it. Suppose that it is not yet come to you. Do not send your desire forward to it; wait."[1] And for actual banquets he gives rules[2]—to lead the conversation naturally to what is fitting, or to be silent; not to laugh too much; nor boast of our morals, nor be disagreeable to people whose morals do not suit us; think how Socrates or Zeno would have behaved in the company you are to meet; take care not to try to provoke laughter—it is a slippery path to vulgarity (*ἰδιωτισμός*); as for obscene talk, stop it if you can, by silence, if no other way.

Marcus Aurelius, in the first book of his diary, sums up his indebtedness to teachers and kindred. Rusticus taught him not to pose as the moral athlete, to avoid fine language, not to agree too readily with the voluble. In Sextus he found an example of tact, and learnt from him to praise quietly, to have learning without parading it. From Alexander the Platonist he learnt one of the finest of all lessons in courtesy, "not to say often nor write in letters that 'I am busy'" and make this an excuse for neglecting the claims of others. An Emperor, charged with all the responsibilities of an Empire, with supervision of the normal administration of the civil servants, with the protection of the frontier against the invading Germans, he is grateful for having been taught to avoid the trick of saying he is busy, the lesson that leisure for others is part of courtesy, part of a man's duty to his fellows.

Among the Emperor's contemporaries, in an age when literature flourished, and learning, humour and religion,

1 Epictetus, *Manual*, 15. 2 Epictetus, *Manual*, 33.

everything almost except history, found expression in books that posterity took the trouble to copy and re-copy and that are still full of life, perhaps there is no more graceful or charming figure than Clement of Alexandria. At a time when Celsus dismissed the Christian church as an association of the baker, the fuller and the slave on the verandah, Clement stands out as a scholar and a thinker, and not at all the only one whose works survive in volume to suggest modification of the taunt. His longest work is a strange blend—a medley as he admitted when he called it *Stromateis* (patchwork quilts)—full of Bible and Plato, chronology, fancy and charm. Medleys were the fashion of the day, as Gellius tells us in the preface to his *Attic Nights*. But Clement has left two other books with more recognizable construction about them, and one of them claims our attention. The *Paidagogos* was a familiar figure in the Greek world; the faithful slave, often elderly, who had charge of the boy, who had to take him to and from school and to train him in good manners. St Paul said that the Law was the *Paidagogos* whose business it was to bring Israel to Christ; yes, adds Clement, and Philosophy was the *Paidagogos* of the Greeks to lead them in the same direction. He makes a very good case, too, for his claim, and he takes the name as the title of a very interesting work.

In spite of Celsus—or, perhaps, his irritation is itself evidence to the fact—the Christian church was not limited to bakers and fullers, slaves and freedmen. Clement's *Paidagogos* shows us that he saw there was a place for a book of instruction in conduct, morals and manners, for what we might call a Christian gentleman. Families of the upper classes were beginning to come over to the church, and it is conceivable that, as England saw in the case of the Wesleyans, the redeemed soul shed its vices and the wastefulness that vices involve, and developed intelligence, with unexpected results, economic and social. The heathen had their standards in morals and manners—in all the apparatus of social life, dress, deportment, entertainment, expenditure. The Christian standard in morals was obviously set by Christ; He was the norm. But the application of a rule, quite apart from observance of it, involves problems; how does it bear on the case before us? If a man of wealth became a Christian, what followed? Of course, all paganism was to be eliminated from the daily round—no easy thing, as we see in Tertullian's tract *On Idolatry*. The social meal began with a libation, it was served by slaves, it might be served on silver plate, there was perhaps a toast (as we should say) to the Emperor. What was implied by the last? To-day the same problem rises in Japan; is it Emperor-worship, the admission that the Emperor is a god—or only something like a European courtesy, the bowing to the portrait required in every school? The picture of Confucius raises a similar question in China. The libation to the heathen gods, of course, must go. The slaves—there was no Abolition campaign against slavery; it was an unchallenged economic fact; but the Master had "taken upon him the form of a slave (δοῦλος)", the slave might be a brother in Christ, and from both facts inferences of duty and kindness were drawn. But the silver ware?

"Follow God", says Clement,[1] "without ἀλαζονεία"—the foible or vice of the Boastful Man in Theophrastus, who "shows off"—and Clement cites Plato against the accumulation of useless gear which serves no necessary purpose. And another old Greek word comes in—ἀπειροκαλία, want of sense for the beautiful and fitting. Who would wish a spade of silver? If the table knife has not an ivory handle studded with silver, can't you cut bread with it? Can't you wash in an earthenware basin? or sleep on something less than an ivory bed with purple coverings? "The Lord ate from a cheap bowl; he made his disciples lie on the grass; he put a towel about him and washed their feet, he, the lowly-minded God and Lord of the Universe; he carried about with him no silver footbath from heaven. Use, not display, was his canon." And he concludes aptly that as regards food, clothes, furniture and so forth, the proper standard must be set by the station, the age, the profession, of the man concerned, and by the time; and we have not got much further. The

1 Clement, *Paedag.* II, 2, §§36–38; cf. III, 11, 56, appropriate dress.

wearing of gold is not banned;[1] a Christian, who has anything of value in a household of slaves (to say no more)[2] must lock it up; and in those days the locking up was sealing up. So a signet ring was as essential as a Yale key. The ring was gold; but what of the device, which is essential? Not an idol's face, a sword, a bow, or a drinking-cup, he says; but, he suggests, a dove, a fish, a ship in full sail, or an anchor—or a man fishing to remind you of the children drawn out of the water.[3] A man should keep his hair short, unless it is naturally curly, wear his beard ("it gives no trouble, and lends dignity to the face and paternal discipline"), but a moustache is apt to be dirtied in eating and should be trimmed, not with a razor but with scissors.[4] Gait—once more we are reminded of the unrhythmic swing of the vulgar—posture in standing, every movement, like dress, must be that of the gentleman, and we have the old word, in the superlative, *ἐλευθεριώτατον*; and he warns against loitering.

In social life Clement stands firm for the old tradition. Perhaps vulgarity is most commonly shown in "tricks", in mannerisms that call attention (let us say) to the part or the particular. The Romans disliked to see Pompey scratch his head with one finger.[5] Clement warns the Christian gentleman against all such things as the loud sneeze and the hiccough—to try to make them louder is a mark of bad breeding; and people who scrape their teeth, make their sores bleed, scratch their ears, he roundly calls unpleasant (*ἀηδεῖς*);[6] and few will disagree. Fidgetting, to be forever changing one's position, when in company, is the mark of light-mindedness; and a well-conducted man will take a small helping, and neither grab nor gobble.[7] The ancients noted

1 *Paedag.* III, 11, §53.

2 *Paedag.* III, 11, §57: "if all were well trained, seals would not be needed".

3 Cf. the well-known significance of ΙΧΘΥΣ and Tertullian's phrase, *et nos pisciculi in aqua nascimur.*

4 *Paedag.* III, 11, 60, 61.

5 Plutarch, *Pompey*, 48, *τίς ἑνὶ δακτύλῳ κνᾶται τὴν κεφαλήν;*

6 *Paedag.* II, 7, §60.

7 *Paedag.* II, 7, §55.

the fidgetting of the Emperors Tiberius and Julian.[1] In some parts of the Orient (it is familiar in *The Arabian Nights*) it is the custom to clap the hands to call a servant. Clement does not want the Christian gentleman to call the attendant by snapping his fingers, whistling or chirruping. And, further, *hoi polloi* will wipe their noses and spit while at table, unrestrained by respect for their company; a gentleman will not do these things, nor noisily clear his throat. He adds a too explicit reference to the indifference of the ox and the ass for such courtesy to their company.

Clement is true again to tradition, when it comes to laughing and joking. A gentleman is known by the way in which he laughs, we all know; "great wits laugh least", said George Herbert. Man, says Clement,[2] is a laughing animal (γελαστικὸν ζῶον); but that does not mean that he should laugh all the time, any more than the horse hinnies all the time. The smile is the seemly relaxation of the face; the unseemly ones are the giggle in women and the guffaw in men. "A fool in laughter raises his voice", he quotes from *Ecclesiasticus*. Even smiling needs thought, sometimes we ought to blush, not smile. We don't want professional buffoons (γελωτοποιοί again) in our society; so we need not imitate them ourselves. Pleasantry is the thing, not waggery (χαριεντιστέον οὐ γελωτοποιητέον). Jibes lead to quarrelling,[3] and there are jests that the apostle forbids. The Greeks of old sang *skolia* at their banquets; but we must not have erotic songs, nor revelry; we have to put off the works of darkness, as St Paul said, walking honestly as in the day, not in rioting and drunkenness (κώμοις καὶ μέθαις).[4] Scythians and Celts and Spaniards indulge in drunkenness; but we, a people of peace, drink sober cups of friendship; and he swings back abruptly to his centre, to the example that gives him all his principles of manners, behaviour and courtesy—"how

1 Suetonius, *Tiberius*, 68, 3, *molli quadam digitorum gesticulatione*, which Augustus remarked; and Gregory of Nazianzus, quoted by Socrates, *Hist. Eccles.* III, 23, 18, on Julian's loose neck, twitching shoulders, uncontrollable laughter, spluttering speech and fidgetting feet—all nervousness.

2 *Paedag.* II, 5, §§45, 46.

3 *Paedag.* II, 7, §53.

4 *Paedag.* II, 4, §40.

do you think the Lord drank, when for us he became man?"[1]

Once more, as in all our long story, manners rest upon principle; if they are traditional, the tradition rests upon something real; the courtesies that make life pleasant are not accidents, even when they are associated with conventions; they come from within and represent a philosophy of life; and the deeper and truer it is, the more gracious will be the manners.

1 *Paedag.* II, 2, §32.

THE ANTIQUARIES

A mere antiquarian is a rugged being.
DR JOHNSON, Letter of 23 April, 1778.

He lived till ninety, an' this deein' wiss
He whispered, jist afore his spirit flew—
"Gweed grant that even in the land o' bliss
I'll get a bield whaur some things arena new".
CHARLES MURRAY, *Hamewith* (The Antiquary).

"WE study the past", said an antiquary of a former generation, "because we don't believe in the future." It is only pedants, of course, who look for mathematical accuracy in epigram and epitaph—the innocent devotees of record office and epigraphy. It is safer to answer Augustus Jessopp with Cicero: *Est istuc quidem, Laeli, aliquid; sed nequaquam in isto sunt omnia.*[1] There is something in it. The love of the past is at least a disinterested passion; and three fair arguments can be advanced for it—you know much more about the past than about either present or future; they were much nicer people; and you have no responsibility for them. More seriously, it is above all the memory of the past that distinguishes man from beast, that gives a foundation for morals as well as for arts. Memory, according to Aeschylus, is the mother of the Muses;[2] the difference between barbarism and civilization is that the barbarian lives from hand to mouth, spiritually and economically.[3] If some of us tend to idealize the past, others undervalue it. The doctrine of irresistible human progress is, as Bury showed, a very modern thing, chiefly based on nineteenth-century America's gift for mechanical contrivance and on the wealth that America in the same period drew from a quick and relentless exploitation of natural resources in forest, mine and oil-well. It is a local doctrine. History shows periods of decline and cataclysm, which are not more tolerable, not less menacing, because of the whooping satisfaction of short-

1 Cicero, *de Senectute*, 3, 8.
2 Aeschylus, *Pr. V.* 461.
3 Cf. Virgil, *Aen.* VIII, 316–317.

sighted plutocrats, politicians and pleasure-lovers. "Hannibal withdrew at last from Italy"; wrote Warde Fowler, "in the next two centuries Rome gained the world and lost her own soul." Such things happen to nations, and optimists read them as progress.

In Rome's case there was soon evidence that unbounded prosperity, limitless wealth and world-wide empire, with a hedonistic philosophy, no more meant national health or safety than it does in modern America. It is not my purpose here to trace the decline and fall of the Roman republic, but to study, for a little, one instinct that it quickened into new life.

> We live by Admiration, Hope, and Love;
> And even as these are well and widely fixed,
> In dignity of being we ascend.

So Wordsworth,[1] and he speaks truly. But as the republic declined, there was less and less of hope for the Roman, educated or partly educated, less hope of the republic, less hope of any real all-round life for himself; and the instinct of admiration turned to the past. There at least there was much to admire, much to love. What Tacitus wrote of his father-in-law was true of the old Rome that was gone—*quidquid amavimus, quidquid mirati sumus, manet mansurumque est.* All was not lost, and the heart of man turned back and lived in an admiration and a love full of a new consciousness, a new sense of values, a new feeling for beauty and moral grandeur. *Antiquitas* becomes the term that stands for the true old Roman character, a summary of Ennius' famous line

> *Moribus antiquis stat res Romana virisque.*

With this heightened appeal of the old goes a new feeling for the native. Foreign fashions, foreign language, foreign persons invade Rome; the Orontes becomes a tributary of the Tiber. So much the more men turned back to the Italian, to the race

> *Proles Sabellis docta ligonibus*
> *Versare glaebas et severae*
> *Matris ad arbitrium recisos*
> *Portare fustes. . . .*
> *Damnosa quid non imminuit dies?*

1 *Excursion*, IV, 763.

—to the scenes, the hill-top towns, the quiet waters, to the legends and usages, to the very words used by the sturdy race in its better days.

Of course, like all human passions, this also had its humorous side. It was Walter Scott who wrote the *Antiquary*, and drew Mr Oldbuck of Monkbarns from his own looking-glass. Where the antiquary has not the humour to do this himself, there is often some one else to undertake the task. Parody, protest and practice tell the tale, and give us our evidence, and in plenty. For the most part we shall stick to the Roman half of the world, but once or twice we shall cross the Adriatic; for there, too, lay remains of a great past consecrated in glorious literature. Don Quixote is by now as truly an English citizen as Falstaff, or Christian, or Dr Johnson, or any other great figure in our books; he has been, since Thomas Shelton gave him to us in 1612, three years before Cervantes finished his story. Achilles was no foreigner to the educated Roman; for generations Troy was nearer Rome than Mantua; and, after all, did not the greatest Roman families come from Troy?

Let us begin with words—*nedum verborum stet honos et gratia vivax?* It is a pity but they should. *Dignitatem dat antiquitas*, says Quintilian[1]—"words, that not anybody will use, make speech more venerable, more admirable; they are an adornment that Virgil—and none has a keener judgment—has used in his own way, inimitably". *Olli*, *quianam*, *miis* and *pone* he quotes. But it can be overdone; it can become an affectation, *odiosa cura*, and lead to the perverted taste that fits theme to word, and not language to subject. Sallust overdid the trick, culling his phrase from writers of the past, as the epigram upon him reminds us—

Sallust, who dost Jugurtha's story teach,
And crib the words from ancient Cato's speech.

No, he says elsewhere,[2] some words won't do, words from distant and obliterated ages; who would wish to use such words as *antegerio*, or *exanclare*, or *topper*—an obsolete word by now in every tongue—or the phrase of the Songs of the

1 Quintilian, VIII, 3, 24.

2 Quintilian, I, 6, 39.

Salii, which even the priests, the Salii themselves, do not understand? Old ladies of good family, says Cicero, keep the old language, pure and undefiled, which they learnt as girls, and he speaks of one whose talk reminded you of Plautus and Naevius.[1] (After Naevius was gone, we remember, the Muses lamented that no one was left who could speak Latin.[2]) But gentlewomen are never "precious" in their speech; that they leave to the blue-stocking, the *antiquaria* of Juvenal.[3]

"I hate a woman", says that downright poet, who in truth hates a good many types, women and men, "I hate a woman who is for ever consulting and poring over Palaemon's *Art* (*of Grammar*), who observes all the rules and laws of language, the she-antiquary who quotes lines I never heard, who corrects the slips of her countryfied lady friend. Surely a husband may be allowed a solecism." It is Remmius Palaemon, the famous grammarian of the early Empire, to whom he refers. There were many grammarians, whose simple biographies are given in short compass by Suetonius, and are worth reading once. Perhaps Verrius Flaccus most concerns us, who compiled a dictionary *de Verborum Significatu*, an immense glossary in alphabetic order, embodying the work of predecessors, known to us only "in ruins" and abridgements.[4] Unlike Varro, he had a fancy for deriving Latin words from Greek, as others of his day and of later days would do. Not merely words did he assemble; his work was "a treasury of old Roman literature, custom and myth—an encyclopaedia of language, of grammar, but also of antiquities, religious, legal and political".[5] Varro had the same encyclopaedic knowledge[6]—"he read so much", says St Augustine,[7] "that we wonder he had time to write anything, and wrote so much that we can hardly believe anybody could ever have

1 Cicero, *de Oratore*, III, 12, 45.

2 The epitaph quoted by Gellius, *Noct. Att.* I, 24.

3 Juvenal, VI, 454.

4 H. Nettleship, *Essays in Latin Literature*, two essays; see especially pp. 205–210.

5 Wight Duff, *Latin Literature*, p. 630.

6 See Wight Duff, *Latin Literature*, pp. 330–346.

7 Augustine, *de Civitate Dei*, VI, 2.

read so much". Varro, so Gellius tells us, admitted that by his seventy-seventh birthday he had written seventy times seven books; and he lived some more years and wrote a good many more. "My eightieth year hints to me to pack up my trunks for my last journey." Twenty-five of his books dealt with the Latin language, of which six survive. His books are, of course, not scientific as moderns count science; they are reproached for want of plan or perspective; his etymologies are sometimes fanciful and were smiled at by the ancients; he is a polymath, with a polymath's discursive love of curiosities. Yet he interested such men as Cicero, Caesar and Pollio in grammar; and his quotations from old Latin poets preserve rare words and usages.

The fancy for the archaic language did not die. Far from it; in the reaction from Seneca it triumphed over Latin style. Fronto,[1] the tutor of Marcus Aurelius, did not spare to inculcate his own ideas of writing; his main headings are summed up as vocabulary, arrangement, archaism (*colorem vetusculum*). He desiderates the full and rich Latin vocabulary, the *insperata atque inopinata verba*, of the old Republican days before Cicero had invented that prose which Mr Mackail calls the prose of the human race.[2] And Gellius[3] was with him in his love of good old Latin words. Gellius, we are told, used to buy ancient books to hunt for old words in them. The French critic classes him with the honest and industrious pupils who repeat throughout life with exactitude the lessons they have learnt—"cet excellent Aulu-Gelle". Yes, and like others of the day, it is essentially his notebooks that he gives us in his *Attic Nights*, no constructive work, but an accumulation of miscellaneous bits of knowledge. It won, however, the praise of St Augustine and Erasmus by the grace of its style. He despised Verrius Flaccus, ignored Tacitus and Quintilian, attacked Seneca. Seneca, he tells us, is a foolish and

1 On Fronto see M. Dorothy Brock's attractive book *Studies in Fronto and his Age*. Some phrases here are borrowed from her, pp. 30, 31, 103. Also Comparetti, *Virgil in Middle Ages*, p. 39.

2 J. W. Mackail, *Latin Literature*, p. 63.

3 See Wight Duff, *Latin Literature of the Silver Age*, p. 651; Boissier, *La Fin du Paganisme*, I, 178.

tasteless person (*ineptus atque insubidus homo*), who has compared the dignity and colour of early Latin with the sofas of Sotericus, as if they had no charm and were already obsolete and despised; and his own style is atrocious.[1]

And yet Gellius gives us one of the happiest pieces of sense in the whole controversy, bigot and dilettante as he is—"live with the manners of the past, speak with the words of the present" (*vive ergo moribus praeteritis, loquere verbis praesentibus*); and he follows it up with Julius Caesar's caution to avoid an unheard-of word like a rock.[2] For, quite apart from Cicero and "the prose of the human race", the archaists did not have it all their own way. Augustus had an equal contempt for innovators and archaizers, sinners in opposite directions; he criticized Tiberius for his occasional fancy for obsolete and out-of-the-way phrases; and he called Mark Antony a madman for writing to be admired rather than understood.[3] Dare one quote Seneca, after hearing Gellius upon him? His quip was directed against those who "talk the Twelve Tables".[4] Quintilian's dictum on Cicero shall end this part of our subject; it illustrates his point of view and lays down a great principle: the man who enjoys Cicero may be sure he has made progress on the right road.[5] It is to be noted in passing that a similar movement back to Atticism prevailed among the Greeks of the period, and any one who has had to read Polybius at any length must rejoice in it, even if it were a little artificial.

The same passion for the archaic shows itself in the period in the growing appeal of "association pieces". Horace describes a conversation with Damasippus—a real person in his day and one of half-a-dozen mentioned both by Cicero and Horace; he seems to have offered to take some purchases off Cicero's hands, apparently statues.[6] Here is what

1 Gellius, *N.A.* XII, 2, 11; Sotericus appears to be known only from this passage—a mid-Victorian sort of person.
2 Gellius, I, 10, 4.
3 Suetonius, *Augustus*, 86.
4 Seneca, *Ep.* 114, 13, *Duodecim tabulas loquuntur.*
5 Quintilian, XII, 1, 112, *Ille se profecisse sciat cui Cicero valde placebit.*
6 Cicero, *ad Fam.* VII, 23, 2.

he says to Horace in the slightly expanded version of Mr Howes:[1]

Of late my sole ambition was to amass
Not current gold, but rare Corinthian brass;
Proud if I chanced with some old vase to meet,
In which sly Sisyphus had bathed his feet.
Oft I pronounced in all the pride of taste
This rudely sculptured and that coarsely cast;
Would name the price with connoisseur-like air
To here a *busto*, a *relievo* there.
The auction-hunters, when they met me, smiled
And pointing cried—See Mercury's favour'd child.

Now Sisyphus was very ancient history even in the days of Homer, to say nothing of Aeschylus who seems to have described the very basin that Damasippus bought, though, to be sure, his question leaves one uneasy.

Λεοντοβάμων ποῦ σκάφη χαλκήλατος;
Where is the brazen bowl on lions poised?[2]

So Damasippus was very lucky, if Mr Howes is right; but Prof. Palmer suggests that forgeries are implied by the connoisseur's Latin, and Conington seems dubious; perhaps Damasippus only hoped to find the real thing. This brings up another doubt.[3]

A chalice of a curious mould
That graced Evander's royal hands of old—
Some ware
Evander's once, inestimably rare—

So Howes and Conington; but the scholiast, with his prosaic mind, speaks of a modern Evander, a chaser of silver and statuary.[4] But it must be the king who is meant. For Juvenal speaks of a cup from which Philip of Macedon drank;[5] and Martial and Statius both speak of a statuette of Hercules by Lysippus, the property of Novius Vindex, but formerly owned in succession by Philip, Hannibal and Sulla—only a foot high, seated on the Nemean lion's skin; but "that is the breast that crushed the ravager of Nemea; those the arms that

1 Horace, *Satires*, II, 3, 20.
2 Aeschylus, fragment 229 (Dindorf), from the satyric drama *Sisyphus*.
3 See *Satires*, I, 3, 90, *catillum Evandri manibus tritum*.
4 Horace, *Satires*, I, 3, 90.
5 Juvenal, XII, 47.

swung the fatal club!" Such was the skill of the artist's hand—and the luck of Vindex.[1] Auctus enrages Martial with "the furious pedigrees of his silver" from Laomedon to Dido.[2] After this, so simple and so possibly authentic a thing as the clay lamp of Epictetus, bought for three thousand *drachmae*—let us say dollars to-day for a rough equivalent—seems very matter-of-fact.[3] A plank of the *Argo* would have little artistic value, but, if you could believe it genuine, what a treasure![4]

Other objects of art had associations, local associations, but were collected none the less by the Romans. It is needless here to transcribe the speech of Cicero in which he sets out Verres' "art-purchases"—statues (of Praxiteles), pictures, cups, works of art, looted (it was nothing else) all over the Greek world. Polybius speaks of such proceedings, common enough long before Verres, with restrained indignation. Specie it was natural for them to take; aiming at universal empire, they must cripple the rest of the world and possess themselves of the means for their end—"but they might have left in their original sites things that had nothing to do with material wealth; and thus at the same time have avoided exciting jealousy and raised the reputation of their country". Suppose, he says, a people to accumulate into their own hands all the possessions of the rest of the world, even if (in a way) it calls the plundered to come and see them, it makes things twice as bad; it ends in hatred of those who do such things.[5] Polybius has no ill-will against Rome for her conquest of Greece; as things were, it was a stroke of luck.[6] But the spoliation of the works of art was an old story. Rome sacked Volsinii in Etruria in 280 B.C. and took away two thousand bronze statues; the Greek Metrodorus of Scepsis said he supposed Rome made war for love of art.[7] In the end Rome became, in Mrs Eugenie Strong's phrase,[8] what

1 Martial, IX, 43; Statius, *Silvae*, IV, 6.
2 Martial, VIII, 6.
3 Lucian, *adv. Indoct.* 13.
4 Martial, VII, 19.
5 Polybius, IX, 10. Cf. p. 72, n. 5.
6 Polybius, XXXVIII, 18, 8–12.
7 Pliny, *Nat. Hist.* XXXIV, 34; Tenney Frank, *Econ. Hist. Rome*, p. 76, who quotes this, suggests that many of the statues would be melted down to be coined.
8 Mrs Strong, *Art in Ancient Rome*, I, 73.

she still is after centuries of plunder by other barbarians (and Barberini), the greatest museum of the world. Strabo tells us, no doubt quoting it from a lost section of the History, that Polybius himself saw Roman soldiers, after the siege and fall of Corinth (in 146 B.C.), playing draughts on famous pictures, looted and thrown on the ground.[1]

Quite apart from all plunder and outrage, we learn from other quarters of the taste for an older art. The Hellenistic period shows already a return to older models, even a preference for the archaic, and in the second century B.C. a movement is observable in Greece and Asia Minor toward the simplicity of the art of Pheidias.[2] The Venus di Milo, as she is generally called—or the Aphrodite of Melos, if you prefer—belongs to that century; and the severer critics note something of Praxiteles in her body, while "the face has been cut with a fifth-century severity". It is allowed that she is "one of the few statues of all times which is not only intelligible but beautiful from all sides".[3] The Roman, if he could not acquire the original masterpiece, was apt to like a copy of it.[4] "Roman copies" are not always esteemed by the experts, but without them we should know much less than we do of Greek art. One point remains; the difference between a reproduction and a forgery is sometimes a psychological one, dependent in some degree on the knowledge and judgment of the purchaser. It is believed that the Roman sometimes was the victim of the forger. Julius Caesar was himself an enthusiastic collector—*animosissime*, says his biographer—of gems, carvings, statues and pictures by early artists; and there were those who said that he was led to invade Britain *spe margaritarum*,[5] though these might not be antiques and might be ruled irrelevant to our subject.

But Julius Caesar is relevant, for it was an infirmity of that noble mind to claim a pedigree of the most ancient and

1 Strabo, VIII, 6, 23; c. 381.

2 A. W. Lawrence, *Classical Sculpture*, p. 303.

3 A. W. Lawrence, *Classical Sculpture*, pp. 307; 317.

4 A. W. Lawrence, *Classical Sculpture*, ch. v, pp. 64–71; and Eugenie Strong, *Art in Ancient Rome*, I, pp. 101 f.

5 Suetonius, *Julius*, 47.

exalted. When his famous aunt, the widow of Marius, died, he spoke, in the formal laudation at her burial, of her long descent, which implied his own—on her mother's side from the ancient king, Ancus Marcius[1] (Marcius Rex was the family name), and on her father's side from the goddess Venus. And he drew the inference (we are told explicitly): "our stock therefore has at once the sanctity of kings, chief rulers among men, and the reverence due to gods who hold sway over the kings themselves". It may be noted how Horace seems to echo this phrase in an ode he wrote for Augustus—*reges in ipsos*.[2] Half a century before this speech the head of Venus appears on the coins of the Julii, to mark their descent from Iulus, Aeneas, and the divine mother, *Aeneadum genetrix*. And how many other noble families of Rome do we learn in the *Aeneid* (to go no further, though we might) to have been descended from Trojan exiles? *Stemmata quid faciunt?* asks Juvenal—a foolish question fit for a declaimer. Horace had answered it long before—*fortes creantur fortibus et bonis*. A pedigree requires an antiquary, and there were plenty of both in the last centuries before Christ. It is perhaps to be regretted, though perhaps it is natural, that their statements did not always agree.

Everybody to-day who knows anything knows that Romulus and Remus founded Rome; it has the authority of Lord Macaulay, Virgil, Livy and others. But it is an index of the wide devotion to antiquarian studies that the claim of Romulus was challenged. Some said the Pelasgians, after wandering over most of the earth, settled on the Tiber and called the town Rome because of their strength (*rôme*) in war. The Pelasgians have always been a most useful people for historians in doubt. Of course, again, there were the Trojans, and one of their heroic women, eminent for birth and brains, was Roma. Or Roma was a daughter of Italus, or perhaps

1 It is sad indeed that Dionysius of Halicarnassus, III, 36, should have to record that most people believed Ancus Marcius murdered King Tullus Hostilius and his family and burnt his house over him. He gives grave reason for doubting such a scandal, so likely to be detected, "but let every one judge as he pleases". Livy ignores the story, I, 31.

2 Suetonius, *Julius*, 6; and Horace, *Odes*, III, 1, 5.

of Telephus the son of Herakles; and she married either Aeneas or his son Ascanius. Odysseus comes into the story, for a son of his by Circe, Romanus by name, perhaps founded Rome; or perhaps it was Romus, a Trojan sent for the purpose by Diomed; or Romis a champion of Latins against Lydians; and even if it was Romulus, of how many various parents he was born! But the most widely accepted story, says Plutarch (whom I have been summarizing[1]), comes from Diocles of Peparethos and was adopted in general by Fabius Pictor, and Lord Macaulay and the rest. Still his mother raises a question or two; was she Ilia, or Rhea, or Silvia? All three names have authority. As to Diocles, he is quoted three or four times and is otherwise unknown; Fabius Pictor was a Roman of Hannibal's time who wrote Roman history in Greek and was used by Livy, Dionysius and Polybius—by the last with some reluctance. "Philinos", says he, "will have it that the Carthaginians invariably acted wisely, honourably, courageously, and the Romans exactly the reverse; and Fabius transposes their rôles".[2]

There are authors more widely read to-day than "the good Dionysius", who spent years in Rome, learnt Latin, associated with learned men, and read the works of such esteemed authors as Cato and Fabius Pictor, Valerius Antias and many more of no little distinction, and so attempted his task in gratitude to the city that did so much for him.[3] In a work of such learning much was bound to be preserved that is of value, even if we reject the speeches of the national heroes in Dionysius as in Livy. Reporting was an art hardly even in its infancy in the days of Romulus. But oratory was inevitable in ancient histories, and it is one of the signal merits of Polybius to have hardly any speeches in his pages. But Livy is full of them, and Plutarch does not resist the temptation. Livy's history, the twenty books of Dionysius, Plutarch's lives of Romulus, Numa and the rest of the old Roman worthies, all bear witness to the wide interest felt in the ancient days of Rome. One rationalizes, the other enjoys

1 Plutarch, *Life of Romulus*, cc. 1, 2.
2 Polybius, 1, 14.
3 Dionysius, *Ant. Rom.* 1, 7; and last clause of 6.

portents and marvels, but they are all intent on the remote past. There is no lack of detail, but its very abundance makes it suspicious. Livy's first book tells the stories of the kings magnificently; it could not be done better,—if it can be done at all; but who can believe in the strategies, the political manoeuvres, the phrases, of six hundred years ago,—who is intended to believe in them? When one has spent years in the study of the four great Greek historians, it is difficult to think of Livy as a historian in the same sense of the word. But history is a word of wide scope, and a historian writing the story of another age may be revealing the mind of his own.

Others beside the professed historians undertook the study of the antiquities of Rome. To Varro we shall return later. Propertius turns from his Cynthia to "sing of sacred things, and days, and ancient names of places";[1] but the subject did not greatly inspire him. "Best of nurses for our state, she-wolf of Mars, what walls have grown from thy milk!"[2] No, Ovid did better in his *Fasti*, though he is surely right in saying that no age could suit him better than his own.[3] A cruel critic has said that Latin poetry would not have been much the poorer, if Ovid had destroyed the whole twelve books of the *Fasti* instead of merely six. It is a harsh judgment; with all their rhetoric, their amazing technique, their inevitable cleverness, the books contain a great deal of archaeology and a number of tales admirably told. No one who reads Ovid's *Metamorphoses*, another exercise in modernizing legend, can fail to see that the Elegiac is his metre; his hexameters are often only elegiac couplets in disguise.[4] Even Horace felt the appeal of the ancient Rome, felt it enough to withstand it and to play with it—

Ire tamen restat Numa quo devenit et Ancus

and again

Nos ubi decidimus,
Quo pius Aeneas, quo Tullus dives et Ancus,
Pulvis et umbra sumus.[5]

1 Propertius, v, 1, 69.
2 Propertius, v, 1, 55.
3 Ovid, *A.A.* III, 121, *prisca iuvent alios; ego me nunc denique natum gratulor; haec aetas moribus apta meis.*
4 Cf. Ovid, *Metam.* IV, 306–309; 581; 610.
5 Horace, *Epp.* I, 6, 27; *Odes*, IV, 7, 24.

The ancestor of Julius Caesar's aunt never served mankind so well.

But the *pius Aeneas* reminds us of the greatest of all the antiquaries. All the Latin writers who deal with him are impressed with Virgil's wide reading, his minute learning, his exact knowledge of ancient times; and as one reads and re-reads the *Aeneid*, one sees how right they are. But there are moods in which one misses the learning altogether in the triumph of the poetry. Yet as substructure it is there, and the poetry would not be the same thing without it. The critics are right who call our attention to the invocation of the Muse in the seventh book; Italy is the heart of the poem. To the foreigner, no doubt, the second, the fourth, the sixth, —I will say, the whole first six books—appeal more directly; but without the motive, without the passion for the great past of Italy, they might have been no more than a *Thebaid* or a *Herakleid*. But here a great poet, one of mankind's very greatest, handles the dim past; and it is no *Fasti*, no interlude in Cynthia's story, no brilliant "history" of seven mythical kings; it is, as they called it, the *Gesta Populi Romani*, the national epic that interprets the nation to itself and to mankind. It is more still; it is, as truly as Homer's poetry (though less obviously), the story of mankind. Antiquarianism never served so high a purpose.

It is not only the story of the past that appeals to Virgil; he loves the scene—the great mother of harvests, Saturn's land, great mother of men. Point by point as Aeneas sails up the coast of Italy, the poet sees the headlands and tells the story. Here on Italian soil, sheltered by dark lake and the gloom of the forests, guarded by the vapour that keeps even birds away, lies the awful opening into the world of the dead. Here the pleasant Tiber stream breaks to the sea, in swirling eddies, laden with yellow sand—Tiber, it has lost its ancient name of Albula. Here and there are the old towns on their hilltops, and the rivers gliding under ancient walls:

praeruptis oppida saxis
Fluminaque antiquos subterlabentia muros.

One by one in the "catalogues", which the example of

Homer justified, he surveys the ancient homes of his people. No one, I will wager, had ever thought Italy so beautiful before. Steep Praeneste, the Hernican rocks dewy with streams, rich Anagnia—the men in the old garb[1]—the apple orchards through which Abellae looks down—Mantua rich in ancestry, threefold her race, under each race four cantons, and her strength is of the Tuscan blood. The men too—

patiens operum parvoque adsueta iuventus—

and their legends, the prophet, the leech, the hero. Centre of all is Rome herself—the Rome of Evander, which is also the Rome of Augustus. Aeneas is brought up the Tiber to Rome,[2] to land exactly where, almost at a glance, he could see every spot most hallowed by antiquity in the mind of the Roman. Evander speaks to him of the ancient history of the site, and of Latium; and then from his mother's altar the view is opened up between the Palatine and the Capitoline to the hollow which became the *forum*; and then the Capitol, "golden now, of old rough with forest and brake", but even then awful with the presence of a god, felt but not known. Here dwells Evander—"Me, driven from my native land, wandering to the uttermost bounds of the sea, all powerful Fortune, and avoidless Fate, set in this place; the dread warnings of my Nymph-mother Carmentis led me, and Apollo gave the word". The scene is full of heaven, and then comes the moral note—"dare thou, too, my guest, to despise riches; mould thyself like him (Hercules) to the dignity of godhead; and with grace come where poverty calls".

For men of culture all literature was one, as all history moved to one great unity, as Polybius saw. The scenes, whence Aeneas and Evander came, had their appeal, the Troad and Arcadia; and Romans would visit both. The charm of the old world and the old poetry called. Caesar, in Lucan's poem,[3] is described as he visits the sands of Sigeum, the waters of Simois, the shades that owe so much to the bards.

1 Tenney Frank, *Vergil*, p. 172, holds that Virgil examined the old armour, in temple and tomb, beside reading Cato and Varro.

2 What follows is borrowed from Warde Fowler, *Aeneas at the Site of Rome*, pp. 71, 72.

3 Lucan, IX, 961–986.

He surveys the burnt remains of Troy, a name and a memory, seeks the traces of the wall that Phoebus built. Barren wood and crumbling trunks overspread the palace of Assaracus and the temple of the gods; thickets hide Pergama, even the ruins are lost—an impressive picture of desolation, but drawn in Lucan's way from fancy. Caesar goes on, through the country round, the woods of Anchises, the cave of Paris, the hill of Oenone; *nullum est sine nomine saxum.* Every stone has its name; and, as a wicked young Cambridge man pointed out, the sentence is double-edged; for the traveller even in antiquity would scratch his name upon the famous stone, as the Greeks did at Abu Simbel, six centuries before Christ, and after, too, and give the date. "I heard Memnon speak", writes one and adds the day, the 25th of Asyr in the 15th year of Hadrian.[1] So modern could the ancients be.

But of all the travellers the most thorough and painstaking is Pausanias who describes Greece in the age of the Antonines.[2] Before Richard Ford's handbook to Spain there was no such guide ever written. Of no other part have we so minute and trustworthy an account; of no other could we so much have desired it. Place after place he visits, and describes them—"I shall now add a notice of the most remarkable sights", or the notable objects, temples, statues, not all of them but those of interest for their artistic merit or their associations; and he will also add "the most valuable traditions". A lucid order, careful statements of distances, show that he means travellers to use his book; and they well might. If ever a man was equal to his task and not above it, it was he. His antiquarian knowledge impresses you by its sheer mass; he knows all the legends, the pedigrees, the heroes; and he knows the history too, and will break off to give you in short outline the historical associations of the place; and, as luck will have it, sometimes he is our only authority, or very

1 *C.I.G.* 4727; cf. Merivale, *History of Romans*, VIII, 241. Strabo also heard Memnon, but does not name the day of the month, c. 816.

2 In what follows, I have freely availed myself of the introduction to Sir James Frazer's fine edition of Pausanias. "Take Herodotus", wrote H. F. Tozer (*Geography of Greece*, p. 26), "and eliminate all his wit (using that term in its widest sense), and you will have Pausanias."

nearly. He is always at leisure for the local ritual, the strange things of this and that shrine, quaint customs, strange beliefs. How many ways have come down from olden times of learning the future! How much magic! What folk-tales, of Epimenides asleep, of King Nisus with his purple lock of hair, of the finding of the babe Asclepios by the shepherd. But there are countless other things—white blackbirds (albinism, as we call it), a black Demeter, the lump of clay out of which Prometheus fashioned the first man (and the lump has a curious human sort of smell). Above all he is interested in the actual monuments of the past, and like so many critics of this period he prefers the older to the later art, and temples to secular buildings. Images and idols fascinate him—queer old relics like the three-eyed wooden Zeus at Argos, Demeter with a horse's head, the war-god at Sparta fettered to keep him from running away, the pyramidal stone that represents Apollo at Megara, Athena with a purple bandage on her thigh. And again votive offerings, garlands, myrtle boughs, and women's hair. And wonderful relics—the eggshell from which Leda hatched Castor and Pollux, the hide of the boar of Calydon, the sceptre of Agamemnon, the very sceptre that Hephaestus made and Homer described—and a daily sacrifice was paid to it. Things more historic, too, he saw and noted—the statues of Polybius in Arcadia, the trophies and the graves of Marathon and Plataea, the ruins of the house of Pindarus which by now like temple and tower had gone to the ground. And as for Olympia and Delphi——But as Servius says (and he adds that Virgil knew it), it is part of the poet's art not to tell everything.[1] The book is one of those lucky ones where you can read as much or as little as you like, and where you are sure, wherever you stick in your finger, to find it touching something of interest. He was no great thinker, no great stylist, but he knew a good thing when he saw it, an honest traveller and an honest writer.[2]

1 Servius on *Aen.* 1, 683, *artis poeticae est non omnia dicere.*

2 H. F. Tozer, *Geography of Greece*, p. 30, emphasizes his diligence equalled by his accuracy, and his freedom from "sentimental enthusiasm or dilettante criticism", his strongest exclamation being that the great statues of antiquity are "worth seeing", *θέας ἄξια.*

But now let us hear the critic. "You take a journey", cried Epictetus, "a journey to Olympia to see the work of Pheidias". Yes, men did, and Pausanias gives a famous description of it, in fuller detail than anyone else; but one after another the ancients speak of its majesty, its deep impressiveness. Dio Chrysostom says that a man heavy laden, deeply versed in misfortune or sorrow, if he were to stand and look on this image, might well forget the griefs and troubles that come with human life. "You take a journey", says Epictetus, "to Olympia to see the work of Pheidias, and every man of you thinks it a misfortune to die without having seen such things. But in cases where no travel is needed, where you have the things at hand, will you have no desire to look, and to understand?—Oh! but there are bothers and troubles in life!—And aren't there at Olympia, heat, crowding, want of water? noise, clamour, and so on? But you put up with it, for the sight compensates for all." And the moral lesson follows.

One feature of Rome's life was that the Roman let nothing die; if some usage accompanied or expressed some aspect of national religion or government (and the two ran into each other), that usage would be kept, would be annually repeated, though all value or meaning had long left it. The standard instance concerns the consulate. The *comitia curiata* did not elect the consuls; but, for them to have the consular *imperium*, a *law* must be voted by the *curiata* to give it to them; and it duly was. There is no record of any attempt at chicane here; whatever irregular practices were notorious at the election, the "thirty lictors" duly met and duly passed the required law. To the student of politics such survivals may be of the utmost significance; they need examination, of course, and it is not always easy to guess their origin, or the circumstances that gave rise to them. But Roman life abounded in survivals, old formulae, old customs—a constant study and delight to the antiquary for centuries.

An hour spent on Plutarch's *Roman Questions* will suffice most readers; a gateway will be opened into a vast field of problems where they can guess to their hearts' content with as much probability of being right as Plutarch or Varro himself—with even more consciousness of success if they know a little about "comparative religion" or have dabbled in folklore. Here are some of the questions in the order (or disorder) of the book. Why do they light five torches (*cerei*), neither more nor less, at a wedding? Why alone among Diana's shrines is that in the Vicus Patricius barred against men? Why in worship of the gods do they cover the head, and uncover it in compliment to men? Excepting Saturn, of course; but why except Saturn, and worship him with uncovered head? Why, if Terminus is a god and celebrated in the Terminalia, has he no sacrifices? Why is the temple of Matuta forbidden to female slaves, and then one slave-girl is brought in and slapped on the face? Why is January now the beginning of the year? Why has Janus two faces? Why is the second of the month an unlucky day for starting a journey? Why do women wear white for mourning? Why must children not swear by Hercules under a roof, but only out of doors? What does the cry *Talassio*, in vogue at weddings, mean? Why at the full moon in May do they throw figures of men (*argei*) into the river? Why may not the *flamen Dialis* take an oath? Why does a candidate for office, in canvassing, wear a toga without a tunic (roughly, without a shirt), as Cato tells us? Why are some of the Senators *patres conscripti* and some simply *patres*? Why do the Luperci sacrifice a dog? (There are endless speculations about the Luperci.) Why do people of noble origin wear crescents on their shoes? Why do they not marry in May? Why are boy babies named on the ninth day, and girls on the eighth? Why must the *flamen Dialis* never touch meal nor pulse, nor raw flesh, nor even mention the words *dog* or *goat*?

More than this the reader will hardly need for the moment; but he will see the range covered, and from the very varied and conjectural answers he will realize what constant occupation an antiquary might enjoy. Let us at least be glad that so much was preserved by their curiosity to illustrate one of the most fascinating of our modern studies.

It is familiar how a passion for Alexandrinism swept over

the men of letters in Rome in the first century B.C. "*Flavit ab Epiro lenissimus Onchesmites*—there! take that with its double spondee finish and palm it off as your own on some of your up-to-date young friends."[1] So writes Cicero to Atticus, in genial mockery. The mode was overdone, and the fashion set in for antiquity. So a generation later we have Horace writing to Augustus—at least, at the Emperor's urgent request, he prefixes the Emperor's name and fame to a discussion of literary criticism, abruptly enough. All Rome agrees, he says, in veneration for the Emperor, unique as he is in all history; a very right and proper judgment, too, he says, but they are not nearly so reliable as critics of literature; far from it.

Each loathes with scorn whatever wears the bloom
Of novelty and smells not of the tomb;
Each of departed worth the praises rings:
Name the Decemv'ral code—some league our kings
With Gabii or rude Sabines seal'd of yore—
The Pontiffs' books—the Sibyl's musty lore—
Their rapture knows no bound: The sacred Nine
On Alba's hill, say they, inspired each line!...
In balancing their worth, if questions rise
Which yields to which, Pacuvius bears the prize
Of studious art—Accius of loftiness;
Afranius well, it seems, in Roman dress
Hits off Menander; Plautus more, they say,
In Epicharmus the Sicilian's way
Pours with bold negligence his rapid lines;
Terence in skill, in force Caecilius shines.[2]

The taste continued. Persius a hundred years later makes fun of it[3]—"I know a man", he writes, "who hangs over that shrivelled volume of the old Bacchanal Attius (another spelling of Accius). Nay, I know more than one who cannot tear themselves from Pacuvius and his Antiope, the lady with the warts, whose dolorific heart is stayed on tribulation."

While fashion swung to and fro, and the up-to-date as ever took the fancy of the hour for eternal gospel, three men read the old poets with affection and discernment. Lucretius,

1 Cicero, *ad Atticum*, VII, 2, 1.
2 Horace, *Epp.* II, 1, 22–27; 55–59 (translation of Francis Howes).
3 Persius, *Sat.* I, 76–78.

Cicero and Virgil are all, in their way, to be credited with some real feeling for literature, and every one of them was an admirer of Ennius. The dolorific lady is lost for ever; Ennius survives in fragments of his own—and in the Roman grandeur of his three great readers. Of course all three had their hour of being out of fashion, and they survived it. *Antibucolica* and *Aeneidomastix* were duly written, perhaps read; but there are more to-day, says Tacitus, to carp at the glory of Cicero than of Virgil—people who find the Ciceronian style "turgid and puffy, wanting in conciseness, exuberant, redundant, in a word, not Attic enough".[1] You must blame it upon the malignity of human nature, says Tacitus, that the old is always praised, the modern always disdained.[2]

The temper of the controversy is shown by an anecdote of Gellius, which may be a little abridged.[3] "A very learned man, a friend of mine", says Gellius, "happened in the course of conversation to drop the word *pluria*—not in the least to show off; far from it! he was a man of serious learning, which he devoted to the duties of life, no pedant at all". He was snapped up by an audacious young critic with a certain amount of education of a sort. [Do I catch the suggestion of his diminutives, *audaculus*, *inauditiunculas*?] The young man said *pluria* was wrong; it ought to be *plura*. The old gentleman smiled, and requested him to explain why *pluria* was approved by Cato, Q. Claudius, Valerius Antias, L. Aelius, P. Nigidius, and the great Varro, to say nothing of a great many of the early poets and orators. "O keep", cried the impudent fellow, "keep—and be welcome to them—those authorities of yours, fetched from the age of the Fauns and the Aborigines." It was very rude, very regrettable; *nec plura locutus* let me with Virgil[4] turn to something deeper.

There was in the last years of the republic, and perhaps still more in the decade of Antony, a growing feeling that something had been lost that was essentially Roman, something that, as we saw, could be summed up as *antiquitas*, the *antiqui mores* on which Ennius a hundred and fifty years before

1 Tacitus, *Dial.* 12; 18.

2 Tacitus, *Dial.* 18.

3 Gellius, *Noct. Att.* v, 21.

4 Virgil, *Aen.* VII, 599.

had said that Rome stood. How had it disappeared, and could it be recaptured? Polybius, in a famous chapter,[1] remarked on the excessive attention (as it might seem to Greeks) paid by Roman religion to things beyond the grave; there was a smack of tragedy about it, it was almost stagey. It was because of the common people, he said; in a community of philosophers you could perhaps dispense with it; but the terrors of hell were needed to control the senseless impulses of the vulgar. A great pity, he goes on, that people are letting them go to-day; our ancestors were right; and that is why the Roman administrator is so uniformly honest, and why the Greek public man has so frequently his hand in the public chest. Later on Polybius laments a decline in Roman honesty, and by Verres' day the great chapter must have been read with ridicule or with deep emotion.

The central idea was as old as Critias the friend of Plato. Critias wrote a poem explaining the whole thing; some shrewd legislator invented the gods as a sort of invisible police, a lie and unreason, but a lie that worked very well. A great many speculative Greeks leant to this opinion, but it is something of a surprise to find the pious Plutarch, in his life of King Numa,[2] attributing the idea to that virtuous prince. He had a lawless people, reckless and presumptuous; so "he called in the gods to his assistance". He devised rituals to capture them, sacrifices, processions, sacred dances, "which mingled with their solemnity diversion, charm and a kindly pleasurableness";[3] he reported to them vague alarms from the god, strange apparitions, and menacing voices; and so "he began to enslave and reduce their minds by superstition". Hence his alleged intimacy with Pythagoras was spoken of, and his intercourse with the nymph Egeria, which he did not fail to emphasize.

Expedit esse deos; et, ut expedit, esse putemus;

is the famous line, strange as it is to find Ovid in his *Art of*

1 Polybius, VI, 56. Plato, *Rep.* III, 386, 387, will not say that these tales of Hades "may not have a use of some kind", but he would not have them taught to men who have really to face death.

2 Plutarch, *Numa*, 8.

3 See the views of Strabo, page 234.

Love reaffirming King Numa, and summing up in two sentences the policy of Augustus.[1] They make a queer pair of colleagues—the one for poetic purposes recalling old usages and rituals, the other for political purposes reviving them. The Emperor had, however, in him a dash of the Italian peasant, a superstitious streak, of which the poet had no trace. So he turned to temple-building, and Horace wrote the ode *Delicta majorum* for him. He says on the Monument of Ancyra that he restored eighty-two temples; and Suetonius tells us of obsolete ceremonies that he revived. Varro had claimed credit before him for great services to the gods of much the same kind; he had been afraid they would perish not by the incursion of enemies but by the inattention of the citizens, and he himself by writing his books about them had done them the same service as Aeneas, when he rescued the *penates* from the flames of Troy.[2] It was expedient for states that people should be deceived in religion, he said.[3]

So thought, and so acted Augustus, the greatest and subtlest archaizer of them all. Religion was restored, temples repaired, rituals revived; but Rome somehow did not quite return to the age of Numa. Great administrators and cool philosophers can see the use of religion,—can exploit it at times, as we all know. But there are things about religion that they do not understand—truth and belief, to begin; and the human heart has to be enlisted. The services of Horace and Ovid to religion are not very evident, nor those of Augustus very far reaching. But there were, among those who looked back to the past, some who saw deeper, who divined the need of man more instinctively, and rose to the intuition that History after all does teach the truth of an affinity between God and man, a reality given to life by relating it with Heaven, and does affirm that without this nothing great is possible, and with it more than this world dreams. That, I take it, is the thought underlying the *Aeneid*.

1 Ovid, *A.A.* I, 635.

2 Augustine, *Civ. Dei*, VI, 2.

3 Augustine, *Civ. Dei*, IV, 4; 27.

FOREIGN GODS

NOT so long ago the Mahatma Gandhi made a sudden outburst about Christian missions in India; he resented the attempt to convert Hindus to a foreign religion. Of course, it was not long before he qualified his utterance, as politicians do; he meant——But, taken with others of his declarations—an earlier one rather complimentary to Christ, followed by another on the sufficiency of Hinduism,—taken with similar surrenders by Indian reformers of the nineteenth century, Keshab Chandra Sen and Dayananda, there can be little mystery as to what he meant. Whatever the promptings of his vaguely genial nature, he was speaking for his Hindu people; they do not want a foreign religion in India; and the Moslems know it. Whatever may be said at conferences, or contributed to the American press, the Moslems have lived for centuries alongside of actual Hindus; they know Hinduism at first hand, not in theory perhaps, but on the streets, in the law-courts and in palaces. Islam is a foreign religion in India.

It is a curious matter, this question of foreign religions, when you look into it,—not new at all. Very little that matters in human society is new; new combinations of old factors we meet sometimes, but perhaps as often as not it is a new generation surprised by an old issue. If we turn back, as we in the West may, to our Western history, we find the same complaint made against the same religion by people who were not leading political campaigns, and some deductions may be possible.

Somewhere about the year 178 A.D.—that is the date which has commended itself to scholars, but for our purposes a decade or so does not matter—an educated Greek launched an attack on Christianity in a famous book, *The True Word*. A generation later the great scholar Origen thought that it still needed an answer, and the Christian church carefully preserved his defence. The bare facts, thus baldly stated, show the significance of the book of Celsus. It can be, and has been, reconstructed from the long quotations of Origen, and much of it might be congenial reading to-day;[1] for Celsus was a man of education and culture, with a good deal of insight and a real gift for phrase. He saw and emphasized the improbable elements in the Gospel, and used the *a priori* method against it with great skill. Irony, incisive and remorseless, plays on the doctrine of the Incarnation; and the positive appeal is steadily to the best that the ancient world knew, to Plato and to love of country, to love of the Empire, which the barbarians from Germany were beginning to threaten. Love of country, love of one's own people, can always be heightened by hatred of the foreigner and his ideas—or so patriots in controversy have always thought. How many innocent colonels in the late war had the notion that without hatred a man would hardly be led by reason to fight for his country!

Celsus starts with an old idea, creditable for its Platonic ancestry,[2] and not without some support in Jewish belief and the Hebrew scriptures, though he does not cite them. He does not indeed admire the Jews, but they serve his purpose too. "The Jews, then, are a race by themselves; they have laid down laws in their native way, and they keep them; and they keep a religion of a sort (ὁποίαν δή); at any rate it is an ancestral religion; and in all this action they are like other men. Because every group of men keeps its established ancestral customs, whatever they may be. And it seems to be advantageous so, not merely because various groups have devised various customs and because it is necessary to maintain what has been in common established, but also because the various parts of the earth (it would seem) were from the beginning assigned to various guardian spirits (ἐπόπταις) and distributed in different administrations (ἐπικρατείας), and so are governed. Thus in each section of mankind things will be well done if done as best pleases those guardian spirits. To

1 Unless, of course, the reflection that so much sense and so much ability were expended in vain, should raise uneasiness.

2 See Plato, *Politicus*, 271 D, all the parts of the universe divided by regions among gods who ruled them. Cf. Daniel xii, 1, Michael's position.

overthrow the local usages that have been from the beginning is not holy."[1] Οὐχ ὅσιον—it is not the adjective that might have been expected, but it belongs to the period, a period of revived religion. Again, more explicitly: "I will begin by asking, why should we *not* worship daemons? Are not all things governed according to the will of God? Is not all providence his? Whatever there is in the world, the work of God or of angels, of other daemons or of heroes, everything is ruled by law from the greatest God; and to each several department there is appointed, with power over it, one who has been thought worthy of it—is not that so? Then will not the worshipper of God be entirely right in serving him who has received authority from God?"[2] It is rebellion (στάσις), he says, for any group to "wall themselves off", and break away from the rest of mankind—rebellion against God, and God's order and universe;[3] it is to disrupt the Kingdom of God.[4] To suppose God to resent service of his appointed ministers is to attribute human feelings, human jealousy, to God.[5] There is no blame to be attached to the Jews for holding to their own law; but blame does fall on those who desert their own traditions and play at Judaism; for, anticipating Alexander Pope, he continues, "I do not think it makes any difference whether you call Zeus Most High or Zeus, or Adonaios, or Sabaoth, or Amun (like the Egyptians), or Papaios (like the Scythians)".[6] The Christians are thus wrong in leaving their ancestral ways to follow the teaching of Jesus; they are not a national unity like the Jews.[7] "If it were possible" (it sounds like a prayer of a sort, says Origen) "for those who inhabit Asia, Europe and Libya, Greeks and barbarians, to the ends of the earth, to have one mind and one law",—but Celsus says it is impossible, and "he who thinks it possible knows nothing".[8] As a young Hindu once said to me, standing near Kalighat, "one can travel to Calcutta by river, or by road, or by railway". Perhaps; but

1 Origen, *c. Celsum*, v, 25.
2 *c. Celsum*, vii, 68. Cf. page 265.
3 *c. Celsum*, viii, 2.
4 *c. Celsum*, viii, 11.
5 *c. Celsum*, viii, 2.
6 *c. Celsum*, v, 41.
7 *c. Celsum*, v, 35.
8 *c. Celsum*, viii, 72.

it is not always equally possible or equally good travelling; nor is there always a uniform prospect of reaching Calcutta; but similes often assume what they are intended to prove.

Epictetus, two generations earlier, addressing people who affected to be Stoics, appears to speak of proselytes—"why do you pretend to be a Jew, when you are a Greek? Don't you see how every individual is called Jew, Syrian or Egyptian? and when we see a man trimming between the two, we say commonly 'He isn't a Jew but he is acting the part'. It is only when he has adopted the real feeling of the man who has been chosen (? has chosen) and has been baptized (?? or imbued), that he is in fact a Jew and is so called".[1] The passage is obscure; George Long suggests that Epictetus may be referring to Christians—a name not yet established even as much as "Jew" in decent literature. Nor is it clear, whether Epictetus believes the change in feeling (πάθος) possible. He does not, at all events, like people *playing* at Judaism or any similar affectation. It is not quite the same position as that of Celsus, but it indicates the strong feeling of racial cleavage. Jews were one race (ἔθνος), Gentiles another; and men said (and Christians accepted it) that Christians were a third *ethnos*.

But, not to pursue the natural or unnatural grouping of men as *ethne* and to stick to the central issue, the new religion had nothing to do with Greeks; it was foreign. To accept it meant repudiation of a man's traditions, denaturing himself; for among the ancients, as in India to-day, custom meant race, nature, national character.[2] It was a flat contradiction of the divine order, *stasis* and disruption in God's universe. No! no! to each race its gods! The modern reader may ask what authority or evidence there was for the government of the universe by daemon pashas, apart from Plato's fancy. The scheme of things, which we have quoted from Celsus, is for us a mere guess, a bit of loose thinking, without much interest; but, for men of that day, it was central in the philosophic defence of religion. It only disappeared with paganism.

1 Epictetus, *D.* II, 9, 20.
2 Cf. Herodotus, III, 80, the tyrant changes ancestral customs.

With Hebrew traditions of angels and a strong belief in daemons, the Christian was wiser in driving for historical facts. Waiving the origin of Jupiter, whether he was a deified man, as Euhemerus had urged in his famous romance[1]—and few romances have so successfully launched an idea—or whether Jupiter really was one of the fallen angels, a daemon, and Tertullian and others have much to say about daemons and quite changed the meaning of the word—here is the central question: Then what is Jupiter doing at Rome when he belongs to Crete (and is buried in Crete, Tertullian rejoices to add)? Then why has Pallas surrendered Greece to Rome? Then why has Juno betrayed Carthage? Cybele, too? No, neither gods, nor men, have ever paid any attention to the great scheme of guardian spirits; gods have poached on one another's preserves and abandoned their own; and as for men—just imagine the Roman Senate taking on itself to decide who were and who were not gods! God or not god—turning on votes cast by men in the Senate House! Finally, Providence, on whom the precious scheme is thrown back, has never shown the least interest in it. The historians are with the Christians here against the pietists. Whatever Polybius, when he began, may have meant by *Tyche* (Fortune), his *Tyche* grows more and more like Reason or even Providence, as the historian comes to know the world and the great world-movements. Celsus for all his shrewdness was a traditionalist, and the Christians were not.

Now as I turn over in my mind this matter of foreign gods, weighing up the ancient Christian reply to Celsus, and certain unconscious reproductions of Celsus that are propounded as new to-day and philosophic at that, the question rises whether there is, or ever was, anything at all in this claim for national, racial or local religions; whether it is not true on the other hand that there never were frontiers in religion at all, any more than in natural science, or Truth generally. So far as

1 Sextus Empiricus, *adv. mathem.* IX, 50, Εὐήμερος μὲν ἔλεγε τοὺς νομιζομένους θεοὺς δυνατούς τινας γεγονέναι ἀνθρώπους καὶ διὰ τοῦτο ὑπὸ τῶν ἄλλων θεοποιηθέντας δόξαι θεούς. Cicero, *de Nat. Deorum*, I, 42, 119, *ab Euhemero autem et mortes et sepulturae demonstrantur deorum.* Add Plutarch, *de Iside*, §23, 360A, in protest against the atheism of Euhemerus.

the story of Greek religion bears on the issue, the dogma of Celsus and Mr Gandhi will not hold water. Mr Gandhi at one time preached, in my hearing, the self-sufficiency of the village as an Indian ideal,—the naïvest stuff I ever heard. But all these fancies contradict history and human experience; Terence is a great deal nearer the mark—nothing human is alien, nothing human is irrelevant. The Stoic doctrine of one republic of the universe is a nobler thing than this hierarchy of daemonic civil servants, this scheme of regional gods, that appeals to Celsus. Platonic it may have been; Plato had many dreams; but it is arguable that Celsus was more influenced than he knew by the conceptions of the civil service of the Roman Empire—and how strong their influence was, we know from the transformation of the church. But let us leave Celsus and his day and its government, and see, if we can, what Greeks really did.

To begin with our earliest evidence, he would be a bold man who claimed to know the origins of the Homeric gods, the gods we call Olympian. Before we have read fifty lines of the *Iliad* we meet the double name of Phoebus Apollo, and we quickly remember Pallas Athene. Why does a god have two names, we are asked, when a great many gods, perhaps the majority, and these the most ancient gods, have no names at all? For a god to have a name, is, considering the immense age of mankind, a modern idea; why has Apollo two names?[1] One answer is that the age-long process of identification of gods began long before Homer. Herodotus said that Homer and Hesiod framed the theogony—you might almost say the theology—of the Greeks;[2] modern scholars have denied this flatly; but I have argued it elsewhere,[3] and will only say that, while I uphold Herodotus here, I think Homer was unaware of what he was doing. I doubt if he first combined Phoebus and Apollo; he gave the combination, however, a bright personality that it never lost. The same instinct that identified Greek gods with

1 Cf. F. B. Jevons, *Introduction to History of Religion*, p. 238.
2 Herodotus, II, 53.
3 Cf. *Progress in Religion*, ch. III.

Egyptian, Greek gods with Roman, Roman gods with Gallic, German and Syrian, was at work from the first, from days before Homer down to the twilight, the Neo-Platonic sunset, of paganism, when Macrobius explains to us that all the gods are one god. A similar account may be given of Indian religion. Syncretism, from the first; and the central axiom of syncretism is the frank assumption that there are no foreign gods, that no gods are foreign, that, ludicrous as Lucian meant his parody of Homer's council of the gods to be, crowded with barbaric and half-bestial figures, it was seriously true, and susceptible of a real and valuable interpretation.

Fifty years ago we used to be told that Jupiter and *Zeus pater* were one and the same in origin, known to the Far East as *Dyāuspitar*, the father in the sky; that the gods of the Greeks were part of their ancient Aryan inheritance, with some additions to the pantheon from more modern neighbours. Aphrodite perhaps owed more to Syria than to the Aryan ancestors. Perhaps some of these identifications were right; but it was a long time since the Greeks had talked Sanskrit or the original language from which Sanskrit at last came; and there was no universal and orthodox church, no creed, no dogma, no revealed books, no Dominicans. Hither and thither we must suppose the ancestors of the historical Greeks to have drifted and scattered, taking their gods with them, "only concepts, exceedingly confused cloudy and changing concepts", says Mr Gilbert Murray;[1] and wherever they settled for longer or shorter periods they were apt to find holy places. *Quis deus, incertum est; habitat deus.* There are Moslem shrines in Asia Minor, known to have been Christian once and pagan before that. Small wonder if syncretism began so early; man cannot help noting, comparing, reflecting, explaining; and Father Zeus might acquire strange traits as he travelled. Strange wives, too, perhaps, here and there; and when, at last, some consciousness comes of larger lands, of a broader racial unity, and with it the need for a more intelligible family tree of the gods, Zeus here and Zeus

1 Cf. Gilbert Murray, *Five Stages of Greek Religion*, p. 68.

there, with all their strange ways and wives picked up perhaps in centuries, become one Zeus; and the wives, goddesses, women, or half-divine creatures, nymphs, Nereids, or whatever they were, have to be fitted in somehow. The Western preference for monogamy has to be met; but the local hero is unquestionably the son of Zeus, or of Poseidon, or Apollo, and his mother is the local nymph;[1] still it can be explained. Every explanation tends to take the form of a myth, and a myth is nothing without a personal figure. However many of the gods and goddesses began as vegetation-powers, corn-spirits, or year-daimons, let Miss Jane Harrison be as right as she thought, every time a tale was told about any one of them, he or she grew a little more like a person or a human being, different from men in size, shape, function perhaps, but like in being intelligible; and that implied will, mind, passions.

What state of things Homer found, we can partly see in his treatment of the gods. The anthropologist, with his knowledge of other races beside the Greeks and of many and many a strange survival revealed by such writers as Pausanias, realizes what masses of contemporary religion Homer simply ignored. Fetiches, witches, worship of the dead, gods of the dead, taboos, magical cults, all sorts of things that make folk-lore interesting, did not interest Homer at all. He was for daylight and gods you could see and name and understand; he put the stamp of his genius on them and they became the Olympians. The pre-historic Father Zeus, his daughter Aphrodite, Hittite, Syrian or what you please, Phoebus Apollo, Hephaistos,—they become the universal figures of pan-Hellenic religion, centres round which art and literature so gathered that the gods survive the religion. For the man of genius gives something of his own vitality to everything he creates. That the gods were not in Homer's poems a moral community, was very early remarked by Greek critics, like Xenophanes and Heraclitus; but Homer was perhaps not aiming at a reformation of Greek morals. It would be foolish to say he did not contribute immensely to the moral

1 G. Murray, *Five Stages of Greek Religion*, p. 91.

growth of Greece; his heroes lifted the race,—they lift any reader who has imagination. But Greek views of sex did not allow enough personality to the woman. Homer's gods and goddesses are not much worse than the brilliant Trygaios or Dikaiopolis of Aristophanes, whose heroes are jolly clothes-horses hung all over with wit and nonsense, common passions, sound politics and commonsense, while to the Thratta or the flute-girl is never vouchsafed any characterization at all; like slaves, they are animated tools. As Mr Murray says, "to make the elements of a nature religion human is inevitably to make them vicious". There is little reason to suppose that Homer did this; it was probably done already; but he made his Olympians much more human than ever before, and permanently fixed their characters. He ruined for ever any chance Zeus had of becoming the god of monotheists. The Stoics tried to make a One God out of Zeus, and were wrecked (so to put it) on Ovid.[1] It is a long way from Homer to Ovid, but it is a much longer way from the Zeus of Homer to the Zeus of Cleanthes; and nobody really wanted to read Cleanthes, while the other two poets have never lacked readers by the thousand. The real crux comes when you decide that Homer's Zeus ought to be the Zeus of Cleanthes. What are you going to do then? To anticipate what I have to say later on, you have either to develop your own god or to borrow some one else's; you cannot invent a new god altogether. Even Serapis is not quite new; if he was an artificial combination, as Greeks have maintained or implied, he linked, as is shown by his very name Osiris-Apis, gods who were real enough for the Egyptians. But Zeus did not take to being reformed.

The crux came early. "Dear Zeus!" cried Theognis, "I marvel at thee. Thou art king of all; thou hast honour and great power; thou knowest well the mind and thought of every man; thy power is supreme over all, O king! How then, Son of Cronos, doth thy mind endure to have wicked

1 I find myself anticipated by Mr Warde Fowler, *Roman Ideas of Deity*, p. 141, "any chance Jupiter had of becoming the centre of a real religious system such as that of the Stoics, was destroyed by the *Aeneid*".

men and the just under one fate (μοίρῃ), whether a man's mind be turned to self-control or to insolence?" There are hints of a similar problem having crossed the mind of Homer; he, too (to put it fancifully), had glimpses of the Zeus of Cleanthes, a Zeus almighty, conscious (more or less, but not for long) of moral issues. But the *Iliad* and the *Odyssey* were too absorbing to the poet to wait for Zeus to be moralized. Virgil waited for Jupiter to moralize in the *Aeneid*; and, except when the god talks about Rome, some would say he was not worth waiting for.

These gods, says Mr Murray, "never existed. They change every time they are thought of". These local legends and myths,—like the Stoics, you can interpret them as philosophy; "a myth is a rainbow to the sun of truth", says Plutarch impressively but vaguely.[1] But there is no reason for anybody else accepting your interpretation; and you may be sure the common people do not. It is a question to this day whether the thinkers or the common people are the better exponents of a religion. Some things are revealed to babes, but not all; and you cannot recapture Truth by being babyish in religion any more than in mathematics. One great religion invites its followers to be men in understanding. But Greek religion, in spite of the materialists turning Demeter into grain, in spite of the philosophers making Zeus into the dogma of Monotheism, persisted very much as it began, in confusion; as soon as you left Homer for the shrines and cults and mysteries, no one could guess what odd survival of incompatible belief you might have to accept for the time being. It is a religion without Theology—a desideratum with modern emotionalists, but not possible for thinking people.

But now came a problem for common people, priests and thinkers alike—something really to explain, something you could see happening. Zeus, of course, hurled thunderbolts, it was said; but he aimed very badly,[2] or they "just happened"; the thunderbolts were no doubt real, but you had to take Zeus on faith, as you did a great deal else. But here

1 Plutarch, *de Iside*, 20, 358F.
2 So Aristophanes, *Clouds*, 399–402; Lucretius, VI, 416–419.

came new phenomena. From Thrace, people said, from the North at any rate, came a strange movement. Something would fall upon a community, a village or little town, and men and women went mad or something like it. By night, the scene lit by torches, with deerskins on their shoulders and cone-topped wands in their hands, they danced; they seized upon animals, and, with a miraculous strength, tore the creatures to pieces, and ate them raw; and then came ecstasy, possession by a strange spirit, trance; and then sleep. What possessed them? There was no other word. Where did they get the strength of muscle to rip the poor beasts asunder?[1] Ecstasy—they were not themselves; a god was in them and spoke in strange words and tones from their lips. What is ecstasy or trance? Were the things they said true, the things they saw real? All this we read in the poems of the ancients and it seems not to be invention.

Here is a parallel tale, which I abridge. There came a man, with a name for having occult power, and he went about the town prophesying a great disturbance to come on a certain day, when the people were to have an assembly for an important ceremony. When all the people were gathered, one of the girls began to laugh and cry hysterically; the infection spread, till between twenty and thirty women were affected. They fought the men who tried to hold them; some rushed off into the bush, some into the forest, some threw themselves down in convulsions. The man, it would seem, had brought certain leaves with him (they were found in his house); those who trod on them or, later on, even looked at them, were bewitched and went mad. Very oddly, the women who had come from other towns were cured of their madness as soon as they crossed the local stream; so true is it (as we know from Tam O'Shanter) that evil spirits cannot cross water. Then came Europeans with Scrubb's cloudy ammonia for those still hysterical, and quinine for those who had worked themselves into fever, and also purgative pills—and sense, and Christianity. For this took place on the Congo, some

1 There is plenty of evidence for this, ancient and modern, Arabian and British Columbia Indian.

hours from San Salvador, in 1929.[1] But Pentheus at Thebes had no ammonia, no quinine, no acquaintance with any religion but the local one, no books about psychopathic phenomena.

There has been endless talk about the *Bacchae* of Euripides; but I cannot think that any one who *saw* it produced in Cambridge in 1930, who watched Agave with her son's head in her hands, any one with any feeling, that is, or imagination, could maintain that in that play Euripides was making his peace with religion. There was that smiling white devil posing as a god—and Euripides once more, as in the *Troades*, throwing up the contrast between the gods of tradition and the real sorrows of men and women. But in eighth-century Greece, as on the Congo in 1929, the only available explanation was the supernatural, and the "religion" swept over the land like an epidemic. Even Apollo had to make a place for his "brother" at Delphi.[2] In the long run the cult was harnessed more or less; the festival of Dionysus became part of state religion at Athens, and for it were written some of the great tragedies of the world—a curious development! As Euripides says at the end of several of his plays, many things are unexpected and turn out the opposite of what you looked to see.

But to get back to our main theme, here was a new god come from somewhere. It might be Thrace—or Lydia—or India; was there not a place called Nysa in India? Alexander's conquests made a new map for Dionysus' travels. And Dionysus turns out to be one with Sabazios (who hardly sounds very Greek), with Zagreus and Iacchos. So whatever was true of Zeus, made anew of many Zeuses, of Apollo linked with Phoebus, of Aphrodite foam-born from across the sea or coming in land-travel with the Hittites; whatever lay behind Homer's Olympus, which was by his day as Greek as Alcibiades; here was a very foreign god, with foreign identifications, domiciled in Greece and honoured with a

1 See *Baptist Missionary Herald*, August 1929, an article by Miss Jessie Lambourne.

2 Cf. *Cambridge Ancient History*, III, p. 627.

Greek citizenship that none questioned; and everybody knew he came from foreign parts.

After Dionysus comes Orpheus—a Thracian, legend said. "From the standpoint of history", writes Professor Cornford, "the figure of Orpheus is lost in complete obscurity. He is variously regarded by modern students as a god or as a man, as the fox-totem of a Thracian tribe, as a missionary martyred by the savage votaries of Dionysus, or as the personified ideal of his own followers."[1] There we can leave Orpheus and turn our attention to Orphism—a very vague term, summing up many spiritual needs, the craving for religion, for something personal, emotional and real, for ritual and symbol, for something to give scope to faith, imagination and ceremony,—no hierarchy, not very much of a theology, but a movement that reveals human instinct in a way little to be expected of the Greek as conventionally pictured to us. The state had laid hold of Dionysus; Pisistratus had recognized the value of the new and universal god who worked visible miracles, and notably his value to a dynasty faced with old clan cults and private priesthoods. A genuinely popular religion, free of aristocratic traditions, supported by the tyrant might do much. Orphism remained independent of the state, an affair of private groups, which a man might join or not join, as he saw fit.[2] It is not the traditional and inevitable religion of the tribe; the shift has been made for all time to private judgment. Draco saw a difference in intention between deliberate murder and accidental homicide, and made clan vengeance obsolete and no less obsolete the theory that man's blood, however shed, pollutes and angers an earth-goddess. He brought mind and thought in as factors in law. So with this change in religion; it is no longer What were you born? but What do you think? The emphasis falls on the individual thinking a good deal about himself, assuming himself as an individual, conscious of personality, conscious in a new way of sin (or something like it), and uneasy about an eternal life which former generations

1 *Cambridge Ancient History*, IV, p. 533.

2 Cf. F. B. Jevons, *Introduction to History of Religion*, p. 328.

had never put in the centre of things. Sin, salvation, a soul of divine origin, immortality—we seem to be a long way from the bright Homeric world, to be drawing nearer to Plato with his other-worldliness, his doctrine of life as a preparation for death, to be asking with Euripides

τίς οἶδεν εἰ τὸ ζῆν μὲν ἐστὶ κατθανεῖν;
Who knows if life be not more truly death?

Such in rough outline is Orphism; and Orpheus, according to the legends, had something to do with Thrace; so a Thracian colony at the Peiraieus, if there was one, might perhaps have introduced his rites—but Gomperz is surely right when he says that much of Orphism is quite beyond any Thracians we actually meet in this period of history. The king's banquet in Thrace described by Xenophon recurs to the mind, but it may of course be no more an index to Thracian religion than certain Aristophanic celebrations to Orphism in Athens. But where, then, did all these new ideas come from? Some of them are in the Homeric Hymn to Demeter, which suggests that Homer did not write it. No one now thinks he did;[1] but the Hymn is evidence that the old gods are changing, are being associated with new ideas. And the best explanation offered by the average Greek of those days is that it all came from Thrace; it was foreign. Another dim figure in the story is Pythagoras with his transmigration of souls, which, we are ardently told, he must have borrowed from India. One explanation of his name confirms it; *-goras*, I have read somewhere, represents *guru*, a very Indian word for teacher; I forget what the first two syllables meant; but, as some eighty Greek names end in *-agoras*, and some begin with it, we need not perhaps delve much further into Tamil. Herodotus, who knew still less Tamil, believed transmigration was borrowed from a source nearer Greece, though foreign.[2] So here in the centre of Greek history we find a foreign god, a foreign religion, foreign doctrines, a native goddess transformed, and new seats assigned in the pantheon. As we saw before, it is hard

1 See page 93.

2 Herodotus, II, 123.

to invent new gods; even the French failed at the Revolution; if new forms of godhead are needed, you must either furbish up old gods with new ideas or borrow foreign gods. All through antiquity the process is to be seen, and reflection shows how inevitable it was. Progressively human contacts widen with travel, with geographical knowledge, with intellectual (as well as manufacturing) commerce among one kind of foreigner and another. Nothing can stop the process. You find men everywhere, and they turn out to be more like you than you supposed; human beings are surprisingly human, and the strangest ideas may prove on examination to fit your own mind. Foreign gods? Who or what really is foreign? If the thing will stand thinking, it is Greek.

Celsus quoted against the Christians the passage in which Herodotus discusses national usages and ends by citing Pindar's phrase that "Custom is king of all".[1] But Herodotus is a witness who tells heavily against Celsus. His long discussion of Egyptian religion is to establish the fact of wholesale borrowing by the Greeks. There was no question which was the older people, the more ancient civilization. Egypt was as she had been hundreds of generations ago. That was certain. The weak link in his chain is his acceptance of the identity of the Egyptian gods with their Greek counterparts. For Herakles, Dionysus and Pan he gives dates. The Egyptian Dionysus lived 15,000 years before King Amasis, the Greek Dionysus about 1500 years before Herodotus, and the interval between king and historian was roughly a century. The Greeks' dates for these gods, he holds, are the dates of their borrowing them. Along three lines Greek religion had been reinforced from outside—ritual practices, ideas, and actual gods. The daughters of Danaus taught Greek women, or Pelasgian, to celebrate the Thesmophoria;[2] captive priestesses, "black doves", founded the oracle at Dodona;[3] pomps and processions in honour of Dionysus were introduced by Melampus;[4] all of these things came from Egypt. Even

1 Origen, *c. Celsum*, v, 34; and Herodotus, III, 38.
2 Herodotus, II, 171. 3 Herodotus, II, 54–57.
4 Herodotus, II, 49.

Libya contributed the god Poseidon.[1] "Moreover", he says, "the Egyptians were the first to teach this word that the soul of man is immortal, and that, on the death of the body, it enters some other living thing then coming to birth, and when it has gone round all creatures of land and sea and air, it again enters a man's body then approaching birth; and the cycle takes it, they say, three thousand years. This word some of the Greeks used, some earlier and some later, as if it were their own; I know their names, but I do not write them."[2] From the tone of his comments on Persian religion, it is easy to divine a certain sympathy with it; but it was long before the Western world borrowed much from Persian religion.

In the fourth century two men made imperishable contributions to the religious thinking of mankind, by raising in a new form and with a new emphasis questions that had always been present but so far had not greatly disturbed the Greek world. Xenophanes had criticized the morality of Homer's gods; but the Greeks preferred Homer's poetry to the very conscientious verse of his critic. But now arose Plato who could write as well as think, and by both gifts captured the attention of his people, and has never ceased to be read. Here at least he was a match for Homer. When he framed his ideal Republic, he swept Homer headlong out of it, genius or no genius. When a man talks about the gods, the first question, and the only one, is, Does he tell the truth about the gods?[3] Homer did not; so out he goes. But how can you know? Plato's test is morality, righteousness.[4] All human society is founded on it; all human well-being and progress depends upon it; and it is impossible to think of the Creator on other lines. Hard as the Creator is to know, and hard the task to tell another of Him,[5] intuition realizes that He is just and righteous, and the universe backs the intuition. Plato's work could not be undone. Gods and rituals of every kind had to face his test; Homer's Olympians,

1 Herodotus, II, 50.
2 Herodotus, II, 123.
3 Plato, *Rep.* II, 379A.
4 Plato, *Rep.* II, 382E.
5 Plato, *Timaeus*, 28C, a much quoted sentence in antiquity.

gods of the mysteries, doctrines of Orphics, were subjected to moral scrutiny, and collapsed one and all. This is not to say they had not a long life supported by the lavishness of the unthinking or the timid—the emotional souls who in every age want a quick and cheap certainty, right or wrong. "It is better to be certain than to be right"—is it? The cults and mysteries throve on that belief, as they do still. In an age of scientific doubt, magic comes in again; and it did of course in the Hellenistic period. But for thinking people Olympus was left empty, swept and orderly; Plato's tenant for it was so very hard to know.

A generation or so after Plato, Alexander had his short reign and spent most of it in Asia, in incredible places at impossible distances from Macedon. The Greeks had long known there was a region called India, far far away; but now it was linked by sea and land to Greece. The world (let us ignore the half-barbaric West, and the unknown China) had been forcibly made one. New races and new religions met; and, all a world away, old local cults of Sicyon and Tegea must look very queer and trivial. Adrastus, the old hero of Sicyon, whose choruses the tyrant had once transferred to Dionysus—what range or scope had he on the Sutlej? When you have found out the geographical limitations of your god, you may want a new one. What began in the great period of Orphism Alexander carries to a further point. It is a wide wide world to be alone in; the huge political unity of that empire, the new unity of world and cosmos, left the individual a small and solitary creature,—with nothing to do, moreover, for all the major activities of man were taken out of his hands. He had time to think, to feel lonely and to grow afraid. The city state was gone, and for practical purposes men wanted something more practicable than Plato and Aristotle; and they found it in Stoicism and Epicureanism, in goddesses of universal range and private mysteries. It has been urged that the city coin types prove the survival of local cults; yes, but how significant are they? *La belle* Stewart has been on our own pennies for two and a half centuries, and long may she stay! The point is that the universal religions swamped the old local gods and rituals, and withdrew from them the living interest of men.

It is not necessary here to expatiate on the religions of Cybele and Isis, who first captured the field. They failed to meet the tests of Plato. Astrology, with the planet week, swept over the world about the Christian era, as Orphism had over Greece in the earlier day. Even outside the Empire the planet week was naturalized in the Teutonic North long before Christianity—a further illustration of the unity of the world, and the ready adoption of religious ideas; for the names of the seven days need not be supposed merely picturesque like Nivôse and the other revolutionary months. Mithras came, too, by and by. We are sometimes told that it was a toss-up whether Mithras or Christ should give the modern world its religion; but such epigrams often omit factors of importance. One thing worth noting on this point is that Zoroastrianism, the faith that gave Mithras to the West, went to pieces at the touch of Islam; Christianity did not; the East is full of ancient Christian churches.

But our concern is with the borrowing of gods, and one point already made has to be repeated. Neither Plato nor Zeno had a god who would meet the requirements now asked of a god—I put it in the language of shopkeepers to make it clear. Mankind wanted a god universal, righteous, personal, and, above all things, kind and good to poor souls of men. Monotheism—yes! but monotheism is a word, or an idea, it has no personality, no heart. Men and women had to look outside Greece, and they did; and for a while Cybele, Isis and Mithras supplied or seemed to supply what was needed. Some looked at the God of the Jews; but the Jew was a dogmatist; his monotheism was too much for the world of the Mediterranean at that stage, supreme as monotheism has since shown itself in appeal to men and in development of character.

Now some reflections to conclude our story. But first a *caveat*. It looks as if at no time it was more than a small minority of the people who really make religion their supreme care. What is truth? said jesting Pilate; and Varro had the answer, given a century before: "it is in the public interest for people to be deceived in religion".[1] So thought Critias,[2] Polybius[3] and a host more,[4] some serious, some flippant, some practical. Much is talked nowadays of the mystery religions; but it is arguable that the mass of mankind in the Hellenistic world and the Roman Empire did not supremely care about sacraments and their imagined raptures any more than about truth. The established routine was good enough for them. The real mind of the ancient world on these matters is to be read in the Christian apologists, who were practical men, deeply in earnest, and knew where the centre of the enemies' position was. None the less, though the common man cared little for any of these things, and left personal religion and philosophy to his betters (though he did not so name them), the story from Homer to Celsus is one of movement and development, the slow growth of mankind, due as always to the people who have both minds and hearts. Let us sum up, as far as we can, what moved them.

Dionysus moved the Greek world—so shook it, that Bury thought it was in danger of a premature[5] Catholic church, forgetting how loose-hung the movement was, how utterly it lacked what has been fundamental with the Catholic church and with Islam, a thought-out theology. So Dionysus shook the world once, and it was like his earthquake at Thebes, in Euripides' play; it left a question whether anything was shaken at all. He fell into his place in the Olympian pantheon; his ritual was controlled; there was no more movement. That god is chiefly of interest because certain poets wrote for his festivals plays which owe nothing to him but the date in the preface. Let him be—a foreign god adopted, nationalized, neutralized.

Superstition, of course, was always on the look-out for suggestive usages. The founders of Virginia carried no "rabbit's foot" in their pockets, so far as I know; Mr Pepys

1 Cf. Augustine, *de Civitate Dei*, IV, 27, *expedire falli in religione civitates; quod dicere etiam in libris rerum divinarum ipse Varro non dubitat.* See page 183.

2 See Sextus Empiricus, *adv. Math.* IX, 54, for the verses of Critias.

3 Polybius, VI, 56.

4 Including King Numa, according to the reverent Plutarch, *Numa*, 8.

5 I borrow the word from another sentence of Professor Bury.

had a hare's foot[1]; but the modern South adopted the rabbit's foot, it would seem from the negro.[2] We have repeated pictures of the superstitious man drawn by humourists and philosophers—spitting and doing all sorts of odd things to avert omens, and daemons, and evil eyes, everything but crossing himself. He of course is on the look-out for new gods; for, in spite of Celsus and his territorial theories, you never can be quite sure that an evil daemon will respect frontiers; other evil things do not; and you cannot be too careful. With him, not perhaps unjustly, we may group the lover of ceremony. One has only to read the last book of the *Golden Ass* of Apuleius to see how people could enjoy laborious and unusual ritual —especially, added the Christian, if (unlike our rites) it was expensive. People without any moral character would be chaste for a holy week for Isis.[3] It was Isis, the Egyptian goddess, who rescued Apuleius or his hero after his sad adventures with the priests of Cybele and others. I do not recall that Celsus has any protest against Isis and Cybele adding province to province, like Mehemet Ali or Napoleon. It will be noted that the mysteries were all foreign, and the philosophies (even if Zeno was by birth a Phoenician[4]) were all Greek.

But the real breaking-down of the frontiers came not so much from the superstitious and the ritualist as from the thinkers. Syncretism we have seen at work before Homer, freely accepted by Herodotus in Egypt, adopted by travellers and rulers all over the world. Every supreme god is Jupiter in the long run, with one exception, because the Jews would have no Zeus-Jehovah. Finally, as we saw, in Macrobius all the gods are manifestations of one divine being, or divine something—a happy device to enable you to have monotheism and polytheism at once, to be a monotheist in mind and a polytheist in practice. It is worth asking why so convenient a device failed in the long run, supported as it was by famous philosophers and beautiful characters, and whether

1 Cf. *Diary*, 20 January, 1664–5; and 26 March, 1665.

2 See that delightful book, by N. N. Puckett, *Folk Beliefs of the Southern Negro*, p. 474.

3 Cf. Tibullus, I, 3, 26.

4 Cf. Diogenes Laertius, VII, 25; VII, 1, 2, the picture of the lean, long, dusky philosopher, once a trader in purple from Phoenicia.

Hinduism, which attempts the same feat, is destined to satisfy the people of India for ever. Beautiful characters and impossible ideas have an odd way of going in company for considerable distances, but in the end in a rational universe straight thinking prevails.

This huge Neo-Platonist system recognized the universe as one vast and co-ordinated unity; it left nothing out, all came under the scheme; it left room for the pietist and his dog-headed god and his obscene image, carefully explained as symbolic; it recognized the soul and its need of improvement (perhaps even of redemption), its craving for divine or half-divine contacts, and its right to some kind of progressively less personal immortality.

But there it broke down. The immortality it promised was not real immortality; it was not quite as bad as the Stoic resolution into eternal atoms, but it was to be, at the last, absorption into something of which you could not even predicate being. It broke down also, because, when all was argued, there was no means of verifying a word of it. Plato had killed it long before, when he insisted on truth about God. Even the Socrates of Xenophon, about whom the modern scholars are so dubious, gives us a canon to dispose of Neo-Platonism—"well", he says to the young man, "when we are no longer *guessing*, but when we really *know*, shall we talk about it then?"[1] It broke down, lastly, because it did not satisfy the moral sense of mankind, trained through the centuries by Plato and by Christ. It did not handle sin with enough depth and earnestness; it had, as Augustine says,[2] nothing for the broken heart, no dynamic, no real rebirth (despite its much talked-of *taurobolia*), no redemption, no love of God, no Christ calling the heavy-laden.

The canon of Celsus will not do, and Mr Gandhi cannot have India to himself. Alexander invaded India and brought it into mankind, and there it stays. Nationalism may be picturesque and sometimes patriotic; but there are greater things, and Truth, for one, laughs at nationalists.

1 Xenophon, *Mem.* III, 6, 11, *οὐκοῦν, ἔφη, καὶ περὶ τούτων, ὅταν μηκέτι εἰκάζωμεν ἀλλ' ἤδη εἰδῶμεν, τότε συμβουλεύσομεν;*

2 Augustine, *Confessions*, VII, 21, 27.

STRABO

THE GREEK IN THE WORLD OF CAESAR

His book is the swan-song of Hellenism.

W. W. Tarn.

AMASEIA was a city of Asia Minor, in the kingdom of Pontus, a very strong city (c. 547).[1] It stood in a deep broad gulley through which flowed the river Iris. A high precipitous rock, with the river at the foot of the precipice, on the one side, and twin cliffs rising sheer above it on the other "towering magnificently"—the site seemed designed by Nature and by Providence[2] for a fortress and a city; and it was both. Walls linked the river to the peaks, there was an abundant natural water-supply, and the city was adorned with the palaces and monuments of kings (c. 561).[3] The country was fertile (c. 547) and not quite without fame in literature. Xenophon with his Ten Thousand had made his way along the shore and had described the native savages, the Mossynoeci; and utterly savage the mountaineers remained after three and a half centuries, a danger to travellers. Pompey himself had lost troops there, drugged with the poison-honey (of which Xenophon spoke[4]) and, while unconscious, attacked and killed (c. 549). Another tribe was more famous still; the Chaldaeans, as men now called them, were the Chalybes of the poets, the inventors of iron and swords and other forms of trouble for mankind—

Juppiter ut Chalybon omne genus pereat!

and there was a thrilling question whether, if Chalybes could be altered in modern days, they might not really be the Alybes of Homer. The Halizones came "from afar from Alybe

1 The references in brackets, thus (c. 547), are to the pages of Strabo. The description of Amaseia is his.

2 The translators want to render πρόνοια "art" here; they may be right; but cf. page 235.

3 The tombs are still to be seen; H. F. Tozer, *Geography of Greece*, p. 23.

4 Xenophon, *Anabasis*, IV, 8, 20; the plant which produces the honey is said to be a rose-laurel, *Nerium oleander*, of the family Apocynaceae.

where is the birthplace of silver";[1] and, says the geographer, there were silver mines there in early days. Names undergo many changes, especially among barbarians, he adds (c. 549) —and the story of North America confirms him, where whole tribes were duplicated by the vagaries of spelling; who would guess the Chippewas and Ojibways to be one and the same? What need then to alter Homer's text, as so many do—Ephorus for instance making the Halizones into Amazons with an unusually long ō, and changing Alybe into Alope, to get them into the neighbourhood of Cyme, his own native place? Not that Alope is so easily found after all. And Apollodorus, who wrote a book on the forces at Troy, is as bad; he will allow no allies to cross the Halys to help Priam. Altogether these emendators take a lot of refutation; but as the iron-founders do not concern us at present, we will leave them, only echoing the geographer's bitter cry that it is rather superfluous (*περιττόν*) to alter a text accepted for so many years (c. 296). The great ports of the country were Amisus and the more famous Trebizond on the Black Sea; inland was a holy city, to which we must return.

Our geographer does not give the account of the climate which we find in Tertullian. Marcion the heretic came from that country in the second century A.D., and his early environment helps to explain him. To the South the country is full of high mountains, sloping Northward to the sea; and across the sea[2] are the huge plains of Russia reaching to the Arctic; so "the day is never open, the sun is never glad, all the air is fog, every breath of wind comes from the North Pole;[3] all is torpid, all is rigid, nothing is ever hot there, except savagery". Tertullian is not altogether wrong here, but human life was sustained with some variety and some culture in spite of Aquilo and Alybes.

About the famous year of Cicero's consulship there lived at Amaseia a family of some distinction. A hundred years

1 *Iliad*, II, 857.
2 *Euxinus natura negatur nomine illuditur; adv. Marcionem*, I, I.
3 *Dies nunquam patens, sol nunquam libens, omnis aer nebula, omne quod flaverit Aquilo est.*

before two boys had been born into it, Dorylaos and Philetairos. Dorylaos became a notable general (τακτικός), and, wandering as such people did in that age, he was employed, on behalf of his King Mithridates Euergetes, in gathering mercenary soldiers (ξενολογεῖν) through Thrace and Greece as far as Crete. That island was full of Greeks, glad to serve as mercenaries or pirates, for Rome was not yet mistress of the Eastern Mediterranean. On one of his visits to Crete, war broke out between the two cities of Cnossos and Gortyn. Cnossos enlisted Dorylaos with the happiest results; for Cnossos won the war, and the general found a home. To any one who has seen Cnossos among its lonely hills and carries away in his mind a picture of excavations, with thoughts of a strange city of pre-historic times, it comes oddly to think of Cnossos engaging in a war in the days of the Gracchi and hiring a general. King Mithridates was very shortly afterwards murdered by his friends at Sinope. So Dorylaos' occupation was gone; he married a Macedonian, called Sterope, and begot two sons, with names as soldier-like as his own, Lagetas and Stratarches.

We need not follow Pontic politics too closely, but every schoolboy used to know how Mithridates Eupator, the Mithridates of history, became king at the age when normal boys may be in the fourth form, founded an empire, lived largely on antidotes (we used to think), and fought the Romans off and on for a generation, taxing their best—Sulla, Lucullus and Pompey. The great Mithridates, then, had a foster-brother, the son of Philetairos, a second Dorylaos (c. 477). Growing up with him, he was very fond of him, and when the chance came, he made him High Priest of the Pontic Comana (c. 557). The High Priests of these Asian holy cities were "almost dynasts" (c. 567), Prince-Bishops we might say, lords of temple lands and revenues, and of temple serfs innumerable (whom, however, they might not sell (c. 558)); they ranked next to the king (c. 535, 557), if they did not actually belong to the royal family (c. 535). So Dorylaos, the foster-brother, wore a diadem (c. 557), and enjoyed the greatest honours (c. 478). He remembered his cousins in

Crete, and sent for them; and the king included them also in his patronage and care (c. 478).

But they were not a very lucky family; perhaps few families were very lucky for long in those days, or in any days among Eastern dynasties. Mithridates' ambition overleaped itself, and he became embroiled with the Romans, who were stronger than he thought in spite of their civil wars. Lagetas had lived in Crete, a good deal nearer the sphere of Roman influence and the province of Achaia, and he made the opposite mistake; he over-estimated the immediate prospects of Roman success. "He was caught in the attempt to make the kingdom revolt to the Romans, on the understanding that he should rule it himself"; and he came to grief and (naturally) his kindred with him. In the meantime Cnossos had fallen on evil days, "ten thousand changes"; so that retreat was cut off, and they were brought very low (*ἐταπεινώθησαν*) (c. 478). Dorylaos was in the plot and shared the disaster (c. 557).

Then somehow fortune smiled again. The daughter of Lagetas was married, probably before this, to an unnamed man, who was brother to a friend of the king. Moaphernes (his name hardly suggests pure Greek descent, nor does his nephew's[1]) was a satrap (*ὕπαρχος*) of Mithridates in the region of Colchis, from which the king drew most of the supplies for his navy (c. 499)—timber,[2] linen, hemp, wax and pitch (c. 498). But once again trouble came. The king put a nephew and great-nephew of his satrap to death. Moaphernes saw his chance of revenge. The king was again at war with Rome, and Lucullus was making a successful campaign. So Moaphernes revolted and brought over fifteen garrisons to the Romans. Lucullus made him large promises; and then disaster came yet again. The Manilian Law (66 B.C.) transferred the control of the war from Lucullus to Pompey; the

1 Strabo, c. 304, says that Athenians call their slaves by the names of their races, Gela and Daos for example, Lydus and Syrus, while a Phrygian will be called Manes or Midas, and a Cappadocian Tibius. Tibius was the name of the murdered cousin, and his son was Theophilus.

2 See Robert Curzon, *Armenia*, p. 3, on the forests of the shore-lands east of Sinope.

two generals hated each other, and Pompey had a mean streak in him. He would have nothing to say to the friends of Lucullus, and meantime he was all-powerful from the Bosporus to Jerusalem.

In the year 63, then, in Cicero's consulship—or it might have been in 64, the year when Augustus was born—the niece of Moaphernes gave birth to a son, whom we know as Strabo. The name implies Roman citizenship, but we are not told how, or when, or by whom the citizenship was acquired. The family, as we have seen, and as Strabo makes quite clear, owed most of its misfortunes to its adhesion to Rome. It is a little odd, however, to find the name Strabo, more often associated with Pompeys, in a group related so closely to Lucullus. If guessing is legitimate, one wonders whether Pompey relented, or found an adherent in the father of Strabo; but by now it is not of much importance. The question has also been raised as to whether once again the family rejoiced in royal goodwill, and whether the Geographer in later life was attached in some capacity to Queen Pythodoris, whom he praises as a woman of prudence and well fitted to rule, as she did in part at least of Pontus, including (it would seem) Amaseia (c. 555, 649). It is a modern conjecture of an Italian scholar,[1] certainly pleasing in its way. What does signify in this story of five generations is the view it gives us of Hellenized Asia—half Greek, with settlers and mercenaries in its towns; savages in its mountains; dubiously Hellenized barbarians on its thrones; and more or less Greek High Priests in its very oriental temple princedoms. "More or less", as Strabo says in one of his half-humorous asides, is a trick of speech much found in kings and geographers (c. 9); neither class can be quite certain of everything, he says, nor can we. In all these researches we have

> The mingled charm of not too much,
> Part seen, imagined part.

The education of Strabo, no reader will fail to see, was very much along the ordinary lines of Greek culture. No really

1 Ettore Pais. J. G. C. Anderson in *Anatolian Studies*, p. 12, finds the theory "at first sight attractive", but far from proven, and at last unlikely.

readable writer of his period has less rhetoric, though he must have studied it in due course. His writing is generally simple and direct, and equal to its purpose. Once or twice, when he has to speak of masters of rhetoric, a slight inflection of tone shows his mind on the matter. Thus, when he writes of the outstanding men of Pergamum, he lumps in with a dubiously royal pretender another who "has been thought worthy of a great name", to wit, "Apollodorus the rhetorician, who wrote the treatise on *Rhetoric* and was the founder of the Apollodorean school, whatever it may be; for there were many fashions, some of them beyond my power of judgment, and among them was the Apollodorean school and the Theodorean. What chiefly exalted Apollodorus was the friendship of Caesar Augustus". Still the man had a capable pupil, a real man of note, Strabo adds with his usual fairness (c. 625). Again, he touches off Hegesias of Magnesia, "who above all started the so-called 'Asian' affectation (ζήλου) and corrupted the standard Attic style" (c. 648); and he quizzes the Tarsians for their universal readiness to improvise oratory and never stop (c. 674).[1] There are no speeches in Strabo's book. Modern readers might not expect them in a Geography; but they know little of ancient rhetoric who think anything impossible for its true addicts. Strabo also wrote a History, where speeches might have been more in keeping, but one remembers his admiration for Polybius, and will not assume that a lost work might have glittered with irrelevance. Strabo is never irrelevant unless Homer gives him an excuse; and Homer was not irrelevant to a Greek geographer or to a Stoic.

Homer was in fact still a large part of a liberal education. What is more, Homer was the chosen author of the Stoics, their Bible, one might almost say, whose virtual infallibility they upheld against the world, by means of a lavish use of allegory, the traditional weapon of the orthodox. The editors of the Homeric Hymns remark that in one respect Strabo's orthodoxy is more than scholastic; he never refers to

1 The aim of History is truth, he says; that of rhetoric is vigour, ἐνέργεια (c. 25).

those Hymns at all—a silence which implies that they are outside the canon.[1] Of course this might be accident, but those who know Strabo well will not think so. Once he pauses for a half apology, which every human heart will surely accept—"I might perhaps not be examining the old stories at such length; it might suffice perhaps to tell in each case how things are now; if one had not grown up from boyhood with the tradition. Amid so many differing voices, a man must make his own choice" (c. 348). If his taste for legend began in boyhood, there will be the less wonder at the wealth of legend that he knows. He does not believe it all, as we shall see, but he rescues a good deal for us. He has a Herodotean instinct for a story, old or new, though he rations himself severely in telling them. Still he lets us see that he knew them and liked them, and often gives us a good outline. "All these are names of places, deserted or scantily peopled, or of winter torrents; but they are often mentioned because of their ancient history" (c. 614). And they were in this instance, in Northern Asia Minor. When he starts upon the Troad, he hopes his readers will forgive him; the country is in ruins and desolation, but its fame! That prompts a writer to "no ordinary prolixity" (πολυλογίαν). Let his readers put the blame not all on him but some of it on those who have a passion for antiquity, a glorious antiquity (c. 581). Had not Demetrius of Skepsis in the Troy region written a commentary of thirty books on sixty lines of Homer? (c. 603). It is remarked to-day that, great as his interest was in Homer and the Homeric scene, his investigations were made in books and commentaries; he does not appear to have visited the Troad himself; it was not nearly as ruinous as he supposed.[2]

Growing up in Pontus and coming of a family connected with holy places, it is not surprising that he is interested in religion. Here is his picture of the Pontic Comana, where his kinsman Dorylaos had been Prince-Bishop. He does not in so many words say he had been there, as he does about the

1 Sikes and Allen, *Homeric Hymns*, Intr. p. liv.

2 See Walter Leaf, *Strabo on the Troad*, Intr. pp. xxviii–xxxi

Cappadocian Comana; but he says the Pontic temple was founded from the other in honour of the same goddess, and that in the rituals, the dignity of the priests and the divine possession (or inspiration or frenzy, as one may prefer to translate *θεοφορίαι*), the places are much alike. Comana, then, is a populous town, and a notable centre of trade for Armenia,[1] and when the processions of the goddess are held, people throng from every quarter, town and country, men and women alike, for the festival. Others permanently reside in the place, bound by vows, and doing continual sacrifices to the goddess. There is a great deal of luxury, the estates are covered with vines, and the town is thronged by women who live by their persons, most of them sacred to the goddess. In a way, the city is a little Corinth; for there too, on account of the swarms of courtesans sacred to Aphrodite, outsiders resorted in great numbers for holidays; merchants and soldiers would waste their money to the last coin, so that the proverb arose regarding them: "Not every man to Corinth may set sail". Such then is Comana. He names four other similar holy places, beside Corinth and the Sicilian Eryx.[2] Only a Hindu could to-day think of such a scene and such a profession as religion; but it was then an act of piety to dedicate slaves and slave-girls to the goddess (c. 532). Pindar—at least it is attributed to him by Athenaeus[3]—wrote a poem for a man who dedicated a hundred slave-girls to Aphrodite at Corinth. But to a thinking man, bred on literature and philosophy, and moving toward the Stoics, it must have raised questions about religion.

Questions were raised by other aspects of popular religion. Θεοφορίαι, god-possession, "enthusiasm", for instance—it interests him very much, and in a long passage (c. 466–473) he discusses it with its adjuncts and varieties. The varieties are many, but there are common features about the god-possessed (*ἐνθουσιαστικούς*), whether it be Bacchic frenzy or

1 Mahaffy, *Silver Age of Greek World*, p. 264, sums it up—these sanctuaries "promoted trade and injured morals".

2 Alexandria had its popular and disorderly religious centre at Canopus (c. 801).

3 Athenaeus, XIII, 573e.

Samothracian; they are ministrants, and the rites are sacred; terror is roused by war-dance, cymbal, drum, flute, arms and shouting. Yes, he says, any discussion of this sort might be said to belong to theology, but it is not alien to the speculations of philosophy; and with great wealth of tradition he discusses it. Ἥκιστα φιλομυθοῦντες, he says—a very small affection for myth he has; others have less. But "every discussion about the gods must examine ancient opinions and myths; for the men of old would speak their thoughts of nature and reality in riddles, and would ever add myth to their arguments. All these riddles it is not easy to solve with precision; but, if the great mass of what is told as myth be set out, some of it harmonizing and some not, one might be able more easily to guess the truth" (c. 474).

Greeks and barbarians alike perform their sacred rites with the relaxation of a festival; in some cases there is "enthusiasm", god-possession, but not in all; music is used in some, but not in other rituals. Some of the ceremonies are done in the mystic way, others openly. And so Nature bids. (Here we catch a Stoic accent.) For the relaxation draws the mind away from human cares, and turns the true mind to the divine (τὸ θεῖον). The "enthusiasm" appears to imply some sort of divine inspiration and to approach in kind the prophetic spirit.[1] The mystic concealment of the holy things (or rites) induces reverence for the divine; it copies the nature of the divine which seeks to avoid our perception. "Music, involving dance, rhythm and song, by the pleasure it gives and by its artistic beauty links us to the divine; and this is the reason. For it has been well said that men best imitate the gods, when they are doing good to others—better still it would be, when they are happy; and joy and festival, philosophy and music, are of that nature....For this reason Plato, and, still earlier, the Pythagoreans, called philosophy music, and tell us that the universe is constituted in harmony, assuming every kind of music to be the work of gods" (c. 468).

Daemons and gods in his age are becoming two classes,[2] but, though he alludes to the daemons a little below, he draws

1 See page 267. 2 See page 263.

no sharp distinction; both groups are called gods (c. 471); here he just touches on the main dogma with which Plutarch defends polytheism—the distinction is vital for Plutarch who traces it to Hesiod. Elsewhere he quotes Polybius to the effect that each of the gods is honoured as the discoverer of something useful (c. 24); Aeolus, for instance, for having taught men the art of steering in the Straits of Messina with their changing currents (c. 23). Here again is a line of thought used a good deal by pagans who reflected on polytheism, used still more and with more drastic effect against the gods by Tertullian and the Christians. Once more he anticipates what we find in Plutarch. "Great Pan is dead", says the mystic voice in Plutarch's story,[1] and the good man writes a tract to explain why the oracles are failing. Strabo, a hundred years before him, chronicles so much; "Dodona like others is in eclipse, has failed" (c. 327); Delphi, in earlier times held in extraordinary honour, has fallen into much neglect (c. 419); and, "after saying much of Ammon, so much I must add that among the ancients prophecy generally and oracles were more in honour, but nowadays there is much disregard for them. The Romans are content with the utterances of the Sibyl, and the divinations of the Etruscans from entrails and birds and signs in the sky. So the oracle of Ammon also has been abandoned" (c. 813).

But old rituals are kept up. The goddess Feronia is still honoured in the town of that name under Soracte, and a remarkable ceremony is performed in her honour; "for those who are possessed by this goddess (δαίμονος) walk with bare feet over a great heap of embers and ash unscathed; and crowds of people come both on account of the annual festival and to see the sight I have mentioned" (c. 226). Virgil also speaks of the fire-walking at this place.[2] At Castabala, not far from Tyana in Asia Minor, in the temple of Artemis, "they say the priestesses walk with bare feet over hot embers unscathed" (c. 537). It is still to be seen done in Japan, as a friend told me who saw it. People still sleep in

1 Plutarch, *de defectu oraculorum*, 17, 419c.
2 *Aeneid*, xi, 785–8.

temples on their own account, and for others, to learn the cure of diseases; sometimes it is better that an experienced priest should do the sleeping for you in the sacred cave.[1] He appears to imply that it is also a regular part of Judaism (c. 761).

Strabo gives a curiously interesting account of Judaism (c. 760). The Jews, as they are now called, are, according to the best accounts obtainable at the Jerusalem temple, of Egyptian descent. For one Moses, from among the Egyptian priests, vexed with things in Egypt, migrated, and took with him a great many people "honouring the divine" (τὸ θεῖον again); "for Moses said, and taught, that the Egyptians had a wrong idea in making the divine like to beasts and cattle,[2] and the Greeks too were wrong in modelling gods in human form. For, he urged, God would be this one thing only, this thing that encompasses us all and land and sea as well, the thing we call sky and Cosmos and Nature. Who with any sense would dare to fashion a likeness of this, like to any thing among us? No, men ought to drop all making of images, and, setting apart a precinct and a grove (σηκόν) worthy of the purpose, worship without [and here a word fails us in the text]"; and then he ascribes the practice mentioned of ἐγκοίμησις to Moses—men who are good at dreams (εὐονείρους) should sleep in the sanctuary for themselves and for others; and, finally, Moses taught that those who live soberly and with righteousness should always expect some gift or sign from God, but others should not.

Judaism has become amazingly Stoic. This identification of God with Nature and the universe meets us in one of the most spirited and eloquent passages of Seneca;[3] but it is not quite Jewish. God as the first author of beauty is the doctrine of the hellenized Jew who wrote *The Wisdom of Solomon*;[4] but that is very far from the sheer Stoicism which Strabo finds in Moses—or attributes to Moses. But the passage is an interesting one, in striking contrast with the story of the ass's

1 c. 649; cf. also c. 801, the temple of Serapis at Canopus. For the same practice in Islam, see Snouck Hurgronje, *Mekka* (trn), p. 37.

2 Cf. Strabo, c. 805.

3 Seneca, *Nat. Quaest.* II, 45.

4 *Wisdom*, xiii, 3.

head which even Tacitus thought worth telling a century later.[1]

It has been made more and more clear as we have gone on that Strabo leant to Stoicism, that he identified himself with the school. The first person in his sentence "which we call sky, etc." implies that the Stoic position is his own; and he makes no secret of it. But his teachers, whom he names, were not Stoics. One of them, Tyrannion (c. 548), taught in Rome—whether Strabo heard him there or in Asia—and was, as we learn from Cicero, one of the unfortunate instructors of the young Marcus and the young Quintus; and he was interested in Geography. Aristodemos would lecture on Rhetoric in the morning and Grammar in the evening (c. 650). Xenarchus was a Peripatetic (c. 670). Strabo does not definitely say that he went to lectures of the Stoic Athenodorus, but he says "he was a companion of mine", and we learn from other sources that he was also the friend of Augustus.

As for popular religion, Strabo makes his position quite clear; it is very much the view of Polybius[2]—"let it alone". We have to look, says Strabo (c. 19), at the emotional nature of the reasoning animal, man. Man is a creature that loves knowledge, and the prelude to knowledge is love of story (*φιλειδήμων*, and *τὸ φιλόμυθον*). It is that love of story that prompts children to listen and learn, and to inquire. Novelty is the thing; but add to it the marvel and the portent, and you increase the pleasure and the appeal. (It sounds like the story of his own boyhood.) Now the illiterate (*ἰδιώτης*) and uneducated are in a sense still children, and like stories; and so with the half-educated (*ὁ πεπαιδευμένος μετρίως*)—a class not often so directly named. The tale of portent can be terrible as well as pleasing; witness the bogeys children are told about, Lamia, Gorgo, Ephialtes, Mormolyce. In the same way, grown persons of the types described can be scared from evil ways when they are told—or are given to understand—that punishments, terrors and threats are used by the gods. "For in dealing with a crowd of women, for instance, or any

1 Tacitus, *Hist.* v, 4. 2 Polybius, vi, 56. See page 200.

promiscuous multitude, a philosopher cannot lead them by reason and so exhort them to reverence, piety and faith. No, there is need of superstition, too (δεισιδαιμονίας); and that requires tales and marvels. Thunderbolt, aegis, trident, torches, snakes or thyrsus, the weapons of the gods are all myths; and so is all ancient theology (καὶ πᾶσα θεολογία ἀρχαϊκή)." The founders of states knew all about this—Numa, for instance, in Plutarch.[1] History and philosophy are later growths, but "philosophy is for the few, while poetry is more serviceable for the people and can fill the theatres". And of course he touches on Homer—he generally does; for Homer gave much thought to truth, but "therein he set" (like Hephaistos making the armour) falsehood also—the one he accepted, the other he used as a demagogue might to outmanoeuvre the masses (δημαγωγῶν καὶ στρατηγῶν). Let us quote here once for all the great sentence of Polybius which is ever in Strabo's mind, and say Goodbye, if we can, to the Homeric question—"to invent everything is neither convincing nor Homeric" (c. 25).[2]

But now for his own belief, which he sets out in a very curious passage (c. 809, 810). Nature and Providence both contribute to the world we see. Nature provides the spheric earth, solid and central, with a spherical covering of water all over it. Then Providence takes a hand, "being herself all full of cunning devices and artificer of ten thousand things" (ποικιλτρία τις οὖσα καὶ μυρίων ἔργων δημιουργός). It is her will to beget (γεννᾶν) living creatures, and, chief among them, gods and men, for whom really the rest exist. But the earth is covered with water, and man is not a water creature but a being of dry land and air and light; so she devises sea and mountain, thus varying the surface of the globe, and providing for further variety in earth hard or crumbling or full of iron ore, and water sweet and salt, medicinal and deadly, cold and hot; and, still further, for future changes of level and surface. (We shall hear of this

1 Plutarch, *Numa*, 8.

2 On Strabo's views of Homer and of poetry, see E. E. Sikes, *The Greek View of Poetry*, p. 171.

again.[1]) Thus the configuration of Southern France moves him to reflect on the harmonious arrangement (ὁμολογία) of the country with river and sea, Mediterranean and Atlantic; that is its virtue (ἀρετή)—so wonderfully adapted to ideal human life—especially nowadays, when, under the influence of Rome, they have taken in earnest to farming, and live civilized. "In such cases, one must believe there is evidence confirming the view that it is the doing of Providence, since the regions are laid out not in a fortuitous way but, as it were, with reflexion, or reason" (C. 188, 189). Perhaps he wavers a little, as a man may, when, in arguing against Posidonius, he maintains that the distribution of animals, plants and climates is *not* the work of Providence, nor the differences of race and dialect; arts and institutions do not depend on latitude, but some on nature and some on training—contrast the Athenians and the Boeotians (C. 102, 103).

Thus with a background of history—the family fortunes visibly linked to the fates of kings—of popular religion, of Greek education and Stoic philosophy, Strabo steps out into the world. So far his literature has only been hinted at, but his book is full of it—not obtrusively at all, when he is not arguing about Homer; but for a well-read man places have associations. Halicarnassus means Herodotus for every human being; and Strabo adds Heraclitus, who has come into English literature in a beautiful epitaph exquisitely rendered; and he does not forget to conclude "and in our own times Dionysius the historian". And here a personal digression may be forgiven. Let a man read Strabo and Dionysius in one long vacation, and he will realize how men of learning may differ, and, without an unkind thought for *ce bon Denys*, as Sainte-Beuve calls him, prefer Strabo.

For, letting the kings and captains pass, and the Prince-Bishops and professors with them, one finds Strabo very good company when once he is done with latitudes and equators, which, interesting and valuable as they are, still are not things of joy but must come into Geography. He is a human being and lets you know on his first page, quite quietly, that

1 See page 250.

he is interested in the animals, plants and fruits of land and sea; they are a part of any real knowledge of the world; and we shall return to them. Timaeus, we read in another author,[1] fancied that, from the number of meals mentioned in the *Iliad* and the *Odyssey*, Homer must have been a good trencher-man—a view very properly denounced. But, even so, it is at least a human trait, and a pleasant one, that the Geographer pauses to tell us whence the best fish-sauce (*γάρον*) comes (c. 159), that the hams cured in the glens of the Pyrenees are excellent, and rival those of Cantabria (c. 162), that Lyons sends the best bacon to Rome (c. 192), that one and another place is *εὔοινος*—Cyprus, for instance (c. 684), and Chios (c. 637); that Caecuban and Falernian are exceedingly good, too (c. 234), as we learn from others; but Samian wine is *not* good, he warns us (c. 637). When he tells of Indian ascetics, "it all tends to sobriety", he admits, "but those other habits of theirs nobody could approve of—solitary feeding on all occasions and no common hour for all to have dinner and breakfast, but each as he pleases. The opposite way is the thing for social life and civilized people" (c. 709); and we can agree with him, and reprobate "the bestial practice of solitary feeding".[2] In one of the many discussions of Homer's tribes, this time about the Abioi, he quotes Posidonius as saying they may well be called so, a race of celibates —Homer obviously thinking life without women only half-life (c. 296).[3] He drifts on into quoting Menander, however, on woman's way of wasting substance in sacrifices—

> Five times a day we had to sacrifice,
> Seven slave-girls with their cymbals in a ring,
> Others a-shrieking to the gods.

Irrelevant to scientific Geography, perhaps, and a digression? But some digressions help the reader, and illustrate the writer's mind. Iasos is an island of poor soil, and depends on fishing; and people, says Strabo, invent stories about it, thus:

1 Polybius, XII, 24; see page 41.
2 R. L. Stevenson, *St Ives*, chapter 25.
3 The Abioi, whom Homer praised, send envoys to Alexander (Arrian, *Anabasis*, IV, 1, 1).

A musician was giving a recital there, singing to his own accompaniment on the lyre. But a bell rang, and everybody at once got up and went out, except one man. The lyrist thanked him for his courtesy, and for his love of music; everybody else had gone when the bell rang. "What's that?" says the man, a little deaf, "the fish-bell rang? Goodbye" (c. 568). He pauses to allude to the wicked slander against Cyme that the people there did not know enough to come in out of the rain (c. 622), and how Magnesia's repute suffers for the omission of an *iota* in a prominent inscription, like Selwyn College (c. 648). A good quotation (c. 670), a happy misquotation (c. 655), will light up the page from time to time, or a proverb about a place—"he put the Colophon on it" (c. 643), as we might say "as sure as God's in Gloucestershire", or "all ship-shape and Bristol fashion". Dealing with Spanish tribes, he writes "I shrink from overflowing with names—they are so unpleasant to write, unless anybody can really enjoy hearing Pleutauroi and Bardyetai and Allotriges, and others still worse and more insignificant" (c. 155). Later on he omits some Arab names for the same reason—they are "so odd to pronounce" (c. 777). When he tells how he and his friends were ferried over the Nile from Syene to the island of Philae[1] in the most terribly primitive contrivances, "we crossed easily", he says, "and all our fears were in vain (δεδιότες μάτηv); for there is no danger—if they don't overload the boat" (c. 818). Why does he tell us of Posidonius' discovery that crows are black in Spain? (c. 163).

This brings us to his travels, of which he was rather proud; few geographers have been much farther; if they have seen more of the West, they have not been so far in the East; for Strabo has travelled from Armenia to Etruria, and from the Black Sea to the frontiers of Ethiopia (c. 117). Polybius and Posidonius appear to have ranged much farther afield; and there are critics who think that Strabo travelled generally in a straight line to his terminus. He tells us he stood on

1 The reader may be glad to be reminded of Robert Curzon's visit to this island, described in his delightful *Monasteries of the Levant*.

Acrocorinthos[1] and saw "Parnassus and Helicon, lofty mountains and snow-clad", and the gulf of Corinth (as we call it) below (c. 379); and he describes the city shortly after its restoration by the Romans (c. 379), when Caesar had Corinth and Carthage both rebuilt (c. 833). But he did not visit Mycene, or he could hardly have said there was not a trace of it left (c. 372);[2] and critics think he did not leave his route so far as to go to Athens.[3] If that is right, it was his loss, not ours; for others have described Athens to us, and there are a hundred places, of which all we know we owe to Strabo. It is, however, characteristic that he notices the view from the citadel of Corinth; he seems to have been sensitive to scenery. He pauses to speak of the waterfall at Tibur[4] "plunging from a great height into a deep gorge" (c. 238); *φάραγξ* is the appealing word; there was a *φάραγξ* at Amaseia. The region we know as Venetia, with its lagoons, where alone "our sea" has tides like the Ocean, reminds him of Lower Egypt with its dikes and canals; and it is a wonderful voyage up the Po (c. 212). Sinope, like Amaseia, is "beautifully equipped by Nature and Providence", set on its peninsula, guarded by shoals, and splendidly adorned by its inhabitants (c. 545). Vesuvius, save for its summit, is covered with farms of great beauty (*παγκάλοις*); the summit is a flat plain, sterile and ash-coloured, with great cracks in the scorched rock, as if eaten by fire—"one might conjecture that in former days it was on fire, and had had craters of fire, quenched for want of anything to burn" (c. 247). There is later evidence that this conjecture was only too sound. Then he discusses the relation of the fruitfulness of the country round, comparing it with the vineyards that flourish under

1 William Mure, *Journal of a Tour in Greece*, II, p. 137, says that neither the Athenian Acropolis, nor Gibraltar, can enter into the remotest competition with this gigantic citadel; but time forbade his ascending it. Mahaffy, *Rambles in Greece*, p. 324, supposes the view to be the finest in Greece. So W. Macneile Dixon, *Hellas Revisited*, p. 69.

2 Pausanias, II, 16, 5, speaks of the walls, the lion-gate, and other remains, familiar to modern travellers.

3 He is very brief on the Parthenon (c. 395). Note in passing that Polybius seems not to have visited Athens. J. P. Mahaffy, *Silver Age of the Greek World*, p. 225, believes most of Strabo's account of Greece is borrowed material.

4 Cf. Horace, *Odes*, I, 7, 14; III, 29, 6; IV, 2, 31.

Etna (c. 247, 273). One of his most interesting pages describes an ascent of Etna given to him by some acquaintances who had recently made it, with some difficulty and courage (c. 274).

Strabo went to Rome, they tell us, in 44 B.C., deducing the date from his statement that he saw Publius Servilius Isauricus (c. 568), who died there in that year. But the most dreadful event of the century, that fell on the Ides of March, he does not mention as within the period of any visit of his. He records the ends of two of the murderers (c. 331, 646). He made other visits to Rome, which readers have tried to date, not always convincingly. Rome he evidently studied with the attention of a geographer, an historian and a lover of art. The site, he thinks, was not so much suitable as inevitable; it was not a strong position to defend and it had not at first much land (c. 230). He gives in outline "the most generally believed" account of early Rome—the coming of Aeneas (not precisely as Virgil does, quite apart from Virgil's art), the older and mythical Arcadian foundation of Evander, the twins (some myth in the narrative here, he thinks), the kings, and the incorporation of Aikouoi and Ouolskoi and other familiar people (c. 231). All Latium is fertile (c. 231)—here pause to note this recurrent term, *εὐδαίμων*, which brings the shore of Arabia quite out of the class of the islands of the Blessed into the category of ordinary fertility, which indeed is something. The Sabines, again, are a very ancient race, with fine old-fashioned ways—if *ἀρχαιότης* represents *antiquitas*—courage, at any rate, and a quality that has kept them to this day (c. 228). One phrase might tempt the reader, but for the variant tale of Aeneas, to think that Strabo knew something of Virgil—"all Italy most excellent nurse of herds and crops" (c. 228)[1]—but one dare not say so. Greeks did not read Latin poetry, and it is with surprise that we find one allusion to it in Strabo—no Horace at Tibur, no Virgil at Mantua, but at Rudiae Ennius (c. 281).

Italy has changed a good deal since the days of Romulus. The Samnites were all but wiped out by Sulla, who had said

1 Virgil, *Georgic*, II, 173, *salve magna parens frugum, Saturnia tellus*.

that "he had realized from experience that no Roman at all could have any peace as long as the Samnites existed as a nation" (c. 249); their towns are reduced to mere villages. The Oscans are a people no longer, though their dialect still lingers and is used on the stage in mimes (c. 233). Romans are intermingled with Umbrians and Etruscans; these old names are kept but the people are all Romans—and so are the Gauls and Ligurians of the North (c. 216). Even the people of Naples, the resort of retired teachers, are Romans now, though much of the Greek way of life (ἀγωγή) survives (c. 246). The old *Magna Graecia* has been "barbarized"; Campanians have occupied some of it, and all is Roman (c. 253).

The city of Rome, capital of Italy, as we should say, and capital of the world, obviously impressed Strabo, and called forth one of his significant comments. The Greeks, he said, had the repute of being happy in the foundation of cities, largely in this that they aimed at beauty and strength of position, and thought of harbours and fruitful soil. The Roman mind turned to what the Greeks neglected—the paving of the streets, the water-supply and sewers that could wash the filth of the city into the Tiber. They levelled their roads through the land with cuttings and embankments. The sewers were vaulted with close-fitting stone, and some of them were big enough to let a cartload of hay through. The aqueducts brought such a supply of water to Rome, that "rivers" flow through the city and the sewers; and every house, you might say, has cisterns and pipes and fountains in plenty. This was largely the work of Marcus Agrippa, though he had also adorned the city with many fine structures. The early Romans made little account of beauty; they had other things to do; but to-day everything is done to make Rome beautiful. The Campus Martius, with its wonderful space and its grass, its chariots and its games, and the works of art all round it, appeals to him; and he lifts up his eyes to the hills whose crowns he sees surrounding the city—it is such a sight that it is hard to turn from it. And much more. Such is Rome, he concludes (c. 235, 236).

But Strabo looks at the place not solely as a tourist. Rome is being ceaselessly rebuilt—like modern New York. Houses fall, are burnt, are sold and torn down; and the rivers of Western Italy, and chiefly the Tiber, are constantly bringing from the forests and quarries of Italy the stone and lumber to rebuild it all (c. 235). From Luna comes marble, white and bluish grey, the best of marbles and quarried close to the sea (c. 222); Pisa has quarries and timber for ship-building (c. 223); Tibur and Gabii send a fine stone for the better work (c. 238). Augustus has laid down new laws, regulating the height of buildings (70 ft.) and establishing a fire brigade of freedmen. And merchandise of all sorts[1] pours in—from the countryside down the Anio, the Nar, the Teneas (c. 235), and up the great roads that span the land, the Appian Way that goes as far as Brindisi (c. 233), the Latin Way and the Valerian (c. 237). The harbourage is poor; with all those tributary streams the Tiber carries a lot of silt, *multa flavus arena*—how much of all this Virgil has told us!—and the merchantmen of the world cannot come in to Ostia unless it is light ship, when the efficient tender system has brought the goods ashore (c. 231, 232). The ships had been bringing things for a long time.

For, as this Greek walked Rome, he noted—and it goes down in his Geography—how many famous masterpieces of ancient Greek art had come to Rome. Lucullus had brought the Apollo of Calamis (c. 319), Agrippa the Fallen Lion of Lysippus (c. 590), and Mummius endless art from Corinth; and he pauses to speak more kindly of Mummius than one would expect—a man "more generous than skilled in art" (c. 381). There is a bitter tone in Polybius[2] when he speaks of all this pillage; easy, he might say, to be generous with other people's treasures; for it was bitterly resented. Strabo quotes Polybius' account of what he saw with his own eyes at the sack of Corinth—the Roman soldiers dicing on the Dionysos of Aristides, one of the most famous of Greek pictures. Strabo saw the picture hanging in honour in the

1 He mentions Patavium as making clothing for the Roman market (c. 213).
2 Polybius, IX, 10, 8.

temple of Ceres in Rome, and tells us that it perished when the temple was burnt not very long ago. This happened in 31 B.C., we are told, which may help us to the dating of his visit or visits, and of the earlier parts of his book.[1] Pillage of Antony's Augustus restored to Samos (c. 637) and to Egypt (c. 595); but he took from Cos the statue of Venus Anadyomene, and dedicated it as the foundress of their family to "the deified Caesar", Julius; and it is said he remitted a hundred talents of tribute to the Coans in exchange (c. 657). Rome has thus another likeness to New York in being adorned with the art of another world and another age.

So Strabo saw the world's centre, and we have a hint as to the beginning of his work; and to that work we must now turn. It was not his only book. "He looked on himself primarily not as a geographer", writes Mr Leaf, "but as a philosophical historian. It was to History that he had given his life; the *Geography* was the work of his old age, destined to be an appendix to his histories."[2] But the *ὑπομνήματα ἱστορικά* (c. 13), which were used by Plutarch, Josephus and Arrian, and are supposed to have been a continuation of Polybius—not the only one, by the way—have perished. The fact that his first work was on History explains the richness of historical matter in the book that happily survives. A Geography—to English ears it does not promise half what it gives us. Mr H. F. Tozer calls its composition in the Augustan age "a piece of extraordinary good fortune", not merely for its intrinsic merits but for the fact that we are chiefly indebted to it for our acquaintance with his predecessors.[3] "No more picturesque book", writes Mr W. W. Tarn,[4] "remains since Herodotus."

Geography, he says, is a sphere of Philosophy as much as any other science; indeed to treat of it aright the geographer needs philosophy as well as knowledge of facts, history,

1 On the dates of the book's composition, see J. G. C. Anderson in *Anatolian Studies Presented to Sir W. M. Ramsay*, a shrewd examination of the text in the light of epigraphy, which brings out some errors of the geographer.

2 Walter Leaf, *Strabo on the Troad*, p. xxx.

3 H. F. Tozer, *History of Ancient Geography*, ch. xii.

4 W. W. Tarn, *Hellenistic Civilization*, p. 236.

natural history and what we nowadays call economics—with a preference, as in duty bound, for the world as it exists (c. 574), but a love (as we have seen) for antiquity. He should not be tied down too closely to delimit frontiers—he is not a land-surveyor (c. 629); he is allowed the "more or less" of which he spoke; and he need not really go outside the inhabited world (c. 131, 132). He must inevitably borrow a good deal of his material, and there may be errors in it, which may be forgiven, if his treatment is on the whole better or fuller (c. 465)—the spread of the Roman and Parthian empires, like that of Alexander, has added immensely to knowledge (c. 14). But, of course, there are what Polybius criticized in other writers as λαοδογματικά—"popular notions", e.g. hearsay statements or estimates of distances (c. 317), though Polybius did not quite always avoid them himself (c. 465), to say nothing of the opposite fault of that great man, τὸ περισκελές,[1] abstruseness and stiffness in matters really simple (c. 107). Strabo means his book to be useful to the statesman, to men in high station,[2] and also to people of ordinary culture, who have had the usual round of letters and philosophy (c. 13). His task, he says, anticipating a phrase of Dr Johnson's, is "carving a colossus"—κολοσσουργία τις; he has to think of the general effect of the thing on the scale planned, and minutiae are of very minor importance (c. 13, 14). Like Homer who never mentioned his native land (c. 30), he has to learn to omit; and omission is not proof of ignorance—though he gives himself away a little perhaps by saying that, if Homer had known about India, he must surely have mentioned it (c. 39).

Every geography has to be in some measure a compilation, to depend on authorities. It is needless here to make a list of Strabo's authorities. It is obvious that they are not all his contemporaries; they hardly could have been; and he has to depend for India on men who combined what is recognized

1 Compare c. 636; and also Sophocles, *Antig.* 475, σίδηρον ὀπτὸν ἐκ πυρὸς περισκελῆ.

2 This passage to some seems to hint at his relations with Queen Pythodoris and her government.

to-day to be true with what no one outside medieval and Mandeville circles could have believed (c. 711). In two cases, however, he refuses to look at very interesting figures. Following Polybius, he dismisses Pytheas, the explorer of Britain and the North Sea shores about 320 B.C., as a liar of the most portentous type—a "Bergaean" (c. 47). Modern critics who know more of Britain and the shores of the North Sea, even than Polybius (who explored the Atlantic coast of Africa), recognize from the fragments of Pytheas which Strabo gives us that he really had been where he claimed.[1] The other man's case is rather different. The voyages of Eudoxus to discover the extent of Africa Southward Strabo sums up in a most attractive page; it is a first-rate tale, and the reader would wish it to be true; but this Strabo will not allow, and he points out improbabilities and tears it to shreds, though the great Posidonius had accepted it (c. 98–102). Mr Tozer and Mr Warmington lean to a friendly opinion about it; "it has often been treated with scepticism", says Mr Tozer, but "he must have contributed largely to the stock of knowledge".[2]

From time to time Strabo comments on the historical sources available for his work, with some generalizations. "The ancient historians tell us a great deal that is not true; they became accustomed to falsehood, through writing myths; and the result is that they contradict one another" (c. 341). Olympia is the centre of stories told in many ways, and not very credible (c. 355), and we can neglect matters which merely lead to controversies about myths (c. 596). Old Persian history, too, is unreliable for the same reason—an excessive love of myth (c. 507). Some stories are repeated suspiciously often—so many images are brought from Troy, and the captive Trojan women so often burn their captors' fleets on the voyage from Troy (c. 264)—at the mouth of the river Neaethus in Southern Italy (c. 262), the very name

1 On Pytheas, see c. 11, 45, 63, 104, 201. See also H. F. Tozer, *History of Ancient Geography*, ch. VIII; and T. Rice Holmes, *Ancient Britain*, ch. IV.

2 H. F. Tozer, *Hist. Anc. Geogr.*, pp. 189–190; E. H. Warmington, *Commerce between Roman Empire and India*, pp. 49, 61, 74; G. F. Hudson, *Europe and China*, p. 177.

being suggestive of blazing ships, and in the neighbourhood of Potidaea, where the name Phlegra has the same temptations (vii, fragm. 25). Many rivers in many parts of the world flow underground—and he chronicles a good many of these *katavothra*—but that does not warrant such nonsense as Alpheius flowing under the sea and coming up again at Syracuse, or the absurdities of the great Sophocles about the Inachus, and of Ibycus about the Asopus (c. 271). There are still regions unknown (c. 294, 493), and there were in the past; and where peoples were barbarian and remote, cut up into small kingdoms, etc., their records are few and unsafe; and the farther from Greece, the greater our ignorance. Greeks have come to be the most talkative of men; but the Roman historians imitate them, they translate from the Greek, but they have not much love of knowledge, so, where the Greeks leave a gap, there is very little done by the Romans to fill it; most of the most distinguished names are Greek (c. 166). And then a shrewder comment; how many migrations have there been since the Trojan War—of Greeks, Trêres, Cimmerians, Lydians, and so on to the Galatians? These migrations have disturbed and confused everything, and not these only; for the historians have used different names for the same people, calling the Trojans Phrygians as in tragedy, and the Lycians Carians, and so on (c. 572, 573); and the Macedonians too have changed the names of places (c. 518). History has been tampered with to glorify Alexander—the Caucasus, Prometheus and all, shifted into India (c. 505). There was indeed great confusion about the names of the mountain ranges even without the design of flattery. Names undergo many changes among barbarians (c. 549); and the civilized peoples lump the natives of a little-known region together—the tribes are all Scythians in Russia, all Celts or Iberians in the West, or, worse still, are compounded and become Celtiberians and Celtiscythians; and probably Ethiopian was as vague a term in the past (c. 33). We know the wild use that the West has made of "Indian" since the Renaissance, and the East of "Frank", and the dreadful profanity of American purists who, to avoid confusions with

Hiawatha's kindred, will talk of a Mohammedan Hindu. After all this, it seems an almost lovable vanity that would emend the text of Homer to connect a pedigree with Nestor (c. 339).

Still, with all these difficulties, it is remarkable how much History his book carries with it, like the many streams he tells of that wash down the gold dust, with the chance every now and then of a nugget (*βωλάριον*, c. 778). But the gold comes as naturally as in the river; he does not, like the modern poet, try to cram every rift with gold. His wide range of interest, reading and observation allows endless variety, and whether it is art or nature, or both, his story moves easily. There must be many a reader who takes some time to realize how gracefully it is written, and how well the author handles an immense amount of learning that in another's hands might have been unsufferable. The Greek world preserved his book without abridgement, and well it might. I shall not attempt an analysis of the work, beyond saying that, after a discussion of longitudes and latitudes very proper for a prelude, and some argument on Homer as a geographer—how could a Stoic pass the flippant suggestions of Eratosthenes that the aim of every poet is to charm (*ψυχαγωγία*) not to instruct[1] (c. 7), and that we shall find the lands Odysseus saw when we have caught the cobbler who stitched the bag in which the winds were tied up? (c. 24)—he proceeds to describe the various lands from West to East, gives us a mass of collectanea about India, tells of Egypt as he saw it himself from end to end with Aelius Gallus, makes a brief survey of North Africa, and concludes with some paragraphs on the Roman Empire. It will be generally felt by his readers, as I have already hinted, that he gives us less on Greece than on any land—perhaps because we know more of Greece than of the rest of the ancient world. Here I propose to consider very briefly certain lines of observation which one finds in every part of his work. To the student of Geography it will be important to weigh the facts presented to him, but even he, like ourselves, must study the geographer. What is the geographer

1 On this see E. E. Sikes, *Greek View of Poetry*, pp. 31, 175.

looking for in this broad world he writes about, what does he see, what does he think significant? If we can answer these questions, we shall have a better idea of the man, and be more able to understand the value of his work.

He begins with a long section on scientific Geography, familiar to every student of ancient science, but with surprises for those who have confined themselves to the great central Classics and not wandered much upon byways. "The reader of this book ought not to be so simple-minded (or so lazy) as never to have looked at a globe or the circles drawn upon it, some parallel, others at right angles to the parallels, and others again oblique to them; or, again, not to have observed the position of tropics, equator (*ἰσημερινοῦ*) and zodiac—through which the sun is borne on his course and by his turning determines the differences of zones (*κλιμάτων*) and winds. Anyone who has learnt so much, and about horizons and arctic circles, and what else belongs to elementary mathematics—even in a general way—will be able to follow what is said here" (c. 13). So much for a beginning, and the modern reader will notice at once that Strabo, here as elsewhere, holds fast to a geocentric universe. He does not, I think, so much as mention Aristarchus of Samos, who propounded that the sun is the real centre for us; his Aristarchus is the other, the Homeric critic (c. 103). Another vestige of ancient astronomy, held by the Stoics and used by Lucan,[1] is the notion that the stars were fed by evaporation from the sea (c. 6). The astronomy and the mathematics I will leave to the better informed reader, who may wish to pursue them; but one or two outstanding points, of great significance, may be noted before we pass on.

First, then, Strabo starts and continues, as Aristotle did, with a spherical world. In the decline of learning in the middle ages this was lost;[2] and Theology for the time being, on the assurance of Hebrew poets, decided for a flat earth. It was the recovery of the ancient Greek geographers that gave the impulse to fresh speculation and at last to the

1 *Pharsalia*, VII, 5.
2 Cf. Sir Raymond Beazley, *Dawn of Modern Geography*, I, 39f.

voyaging of Columbus.[1] Strabo's prime argument is from the senses—from what anybody knows who has made even a very short voyage; "it is obviously the curvature of the sea that prevents people on ships from seeing distant lights that are set on a level with their eyes. At any rate, if the lights are raised above the level of the eye, they are visible, even though at a greater distance; or, if the observer is at a higher point, he sees what before was hidden"; and he clinches it by a quotation from Homer—how Odysseus "with a quick glance, as a mighty wave heaved him high", saw the land (c. 12; *Od.* v, 393). Aristotle—I may interpolate this, for, while I was at work on this essay, there was a total eclipse of the moon—Aristotle added the argument that the shadow of the earth on the moon during an eclipse proves the rotundity of the earth. Strabo was convinced that the Ocean covered the globe, except where the land stood out above it; that was the work of Providence, as we saw (c. 810); the habitable world is surrounded by water (c. 5, 6) and is in fact an island of immense size (c. 6). The highest mountains will be negligible on the surface (c. 112).[2]

Now, he suggests,[3] make yourself a globe (c. 109)—he recommends a ten-foot diameter for it (c. 116), or the habitable part will show too small; mark on it Iberia (Spain) and India—they will be, as measured partly by land travel, partly by seafaring from West to East, 70,000 stades apart (c. 116). There will obviously be a great deal of Ocean. One mistake, by the way, not made by Herodotus, is made by Strabo, his Caspian is open to the Ocean on the North (c. 507); but that is a minor point. But look at your globe the other way, and then turn to an earlier page of Strabo, where he quotes Eratosthenes in a most significant sentence which we should never forget—"if the size of the Atlantic Ocean did not make

1 Cf. Justin Winsor, *Christopher Columbus*, p. 107, who specially notes the printing of Strabo in a Latin version in 1469, several times reprinted in the next few years. See also Sir Clements Markham, *Columbus*, pp. 33–35.

2 Polybius (cited in c. 209) had told the Greeks that the Alps were vastly higher than anything they knew.

3 On this globe of Strabo's see E. L. Stevenson, *Terrestrial and Celestial Globes*, I, p. 8; Crates is credited with the first globe.

it impossible, we could sail over the rest of the circle along one parallel from Iberia to India" (c. 64). How much of human history has been made by definitely trying the experiment of Eratosthenes! and how strange to find in a geographer of Alexandria two centuries before Christ the actual plan of Columbus! And Eratosthenes was called *Beta*, because he was nowhere quite first class.[1] The "rest of the circle" added to the length of the habitable part made, according to Eratosthenes, the circumference of the globe roughly 252,000 stades (c. 113), or 24,662 miles, which implies a diameter of 7850 miles or 50 miles less than the value of the polar diameter.[2] That it should have been calculated at all, and a result so amazing reached, is worth consideration. Ptolemy afterwards gave the measurement as 180,000 stades; and, Ptolemy being the standard, it prevailed. Perhaps we may be glad that it did; it reduced the prospective voyage of Columbus by a good half or more, and it was terrible enough at that.

Certain homely suggestions for our globe are added by Strabo. We habitually think of Italy as shaped like a boot; in a memorable phrase the Marquis d'Azeglio said, about 1830, of the divided Italy that "the railways would stitch the boot"—as the Roman roads had done. Strabo suggests that our habitable world will be the shape of a Greek *chlamys* or sleeveless cloak (c. 113, 118); he is helped to this view by an immense error as to the Southern extension of Africa which he makes far too small. The city of Alexandria is another *chlamys* (c. 793). Another section of the world is like a cook's knife (c. 519), and the Nile's course is like the letter N (c. 786).

Nature and Providence, as we saw, left the globe fit for man's habitation and well-being, but with possibilities of changes between land and sea (c. 810)—changes brought about by the action of water and fire, earthquakes and volcanoes (c. 49). How else is it that mussels, oysters and scallop-

1 W. G. de Burgh, *Legacy of Ancient World*, p. 165; but perhaps it was jealousy, he adds. Mahaffy, *Ptolemies*, p. 249, calls him "the best man of his time".

2 J. L. E. Dreyer, *Planetary Systems*, pp. 174–178; cf. also H. F. Tozer, *History of Ancient Geography*, p. 172; and Sir T. Heath, *Aristarchus of Samos*, p. 339, following Dreyer. See Pliny, *N.H.* II, 247, who gives Eratosthenes' figure, *improbum ausum verum ita subtili argumentatione comprehensum ut pudeat non credere.*

shells are found in masses sometimes as far as 3000 stades from the sea—and salt marshes, too? (C. 49). The modern perhaps does not class these together; but, from Xenophanes onward (*c.* 500 B.C.), the ancients were familiar with the idea of great changes of level at one period or another in the earth's surface (C. 49–51; 102). There are minor changes, easier to note; the Achelous is the standard instance of a river bringing down silt and linking islands to the mainland (C. 458),[1] while the delta of the Nile is, as Herodotus said,[2] the gift of the river. "Then," says Strabo, "there are Bura and Helice [towns of Achaia]; Bura disappeared in a chasm of the earth, Helice in a wave of the sea" (C. 59).[3] The country all about the river Maeander is "well-earthquaked"—a most ingenious adjective (*εὔσειστος*, C. 578); there is fire below and water—witness the hot springs of Hierapolis with their quick deposit of stone, and the strange cave near by, the Plutonion with its deadly vapour ("we threw in sparrows and they dropped dead", and so will a bull) (C. 629, 630), and the constant disasters to cities throughout the region, which Augustus and Tiberius helped to rebuild (C. 579). The Straits of Messina are evidence, he says, and many other Classical writers also hold the view, that Sicily was ripped[4] off by earthquake from Italy; and there are islands that have risen in the open sea (C. 258). He records the belief that wind has something to do with volcanic eruption; wind at least accompanies it and ceases with it; and winds are begotten by evaporation from the sea and fed by it (C. 275, 276).

But turning to the solider earth, on which we can more or less rely, and to man's life on that earth, he remarks with Ephorus how much the sea is the decisive factor for the Greek world (*ἡγεμονικόν τι*, C. 334). Living in a region of gulfs and headlands and peninsulas, with the Peloponnese as a sort of acropolis (C. 334), "we are in a way amphibious (*ἀμφίβιοι τρόπον τινά*) and belong no more to the dry land

1 Herodotus, II, 10; Thucydides, II, 102. 2 Herodotus, II, 5.

3 Cf. Pausanias, VII, 24; and H. F. Tozer, *Geography of Greece*, pp. 130ff., on Greek earthquakes.

4 He wavers as to the derivation of Rhegium from the Greek *ῥήγνυμι* or the Latin *regium*, which the Samnites might have given it (C. 258).

than to the sea" (c. 8). Havens and rivers naturally interest a Greek; even if he comes from the continent, Trapezus and Sinope are household words. He pauses to describe the mouths of the Rhone (c. 186) and the Nile; and it may be noted that he knows the cause of the Nile's summer overflow which so much perplexed Herodotus and the men of his time.[1] Alexander's admiral, Nearchus, had announced the explanation in the summer monsoon rains (c. 696); the ancients guessed, but in later days the cause was plain enough to those who went to the cinnamon country[2] and were engaged in elephant-catching—the overflow depended on the rains in the mountains of Ethiopia or Abyssinia (c. 789). Strabo pauses to pay a tribute to the scientific interests of Ptolemy Philadelphos which ancient kings had not shared (c. 790). And before we leave this region and forget about harbours, there is Myos Hormos to be thought of, the port on the Red Sea as we call it—Herodotus' Arabian gulf—whence in Strabo's day some hundred and twenty ships might sail in a season for the Malabar coast (c. 118; 815), though few would go as far as the Ganges (c. 686). He does not actually mention the monsoon, the Hippalos, so-called (they say) after the Greek mariner who taught sailors to trust it, but the numbers of the vessels surely suggest that it was already known, as it certainly was a very little time after Strabo's writing.[3] All this Indian traffic used Alexandria as its junction with the Mediterranean, a city brought near ruin by the later Ptolemies but restored by the Romans, and the greatest *emporion* of the world (c. 797, 798).

Strabo saw a good deal for himself, and he borrowed a great deal, borrowed wisely, and wisely owns it; what he saw developed in him the instinct to know what to borrow. He is interested to give the general sense of a countryside, to seize the significant features—the great alluvial plain of the Po

1 Herodotus, II, 20–24; note his own caution, *εἰ δὲ δεῖ...αὐτὸν περὶ τῶν ἀφανέων γνωμὴν ἀποδέξασθαι....*

2 But cf. G. F. Hudson, *Europe and China*, p. 94.

3 On Hippalos, see E. H. Warmington, *The Commerce between the Roman Empire and India*, pp. 44–48; H. G. Rawlinson, *Intercourse between India and the Western World*, pp. 109–112.

(c. 212, 218), the Russian steppes (c. 307, 493), the swamps of Boeotia (c. 406–7), and the Galatian plateau nearer home (c. 568). He takes note of climate; the tide washes out the water-ways of Ravenna and saves it from *δυσαερία*, as the Nile purifies the lake behind Alexandria in summer, and both cities escape the bad effects common where there are lagoons (c. 213, 793). South Russia is little known because of the cold and poverty of the country; the natives can bear it, living on flesh and milk, but other people cannot (c. 493). Ierne—or Erin, as some have since spelled it—again, away to the North of Britain, is a miserable place to live in because of the cold (c. 72), the abode of utter savages (*ἀγρίων τελέως*, c. 115), gluttons, cannibals, indecent—"though we have not indeed reliable witnesses for all this", there are parallels that make it probable (c. 201). It may be the humidity of India that prevents Indian hair from curling (c. 690). But fertile though North India may be (c. 73), the Nile productive above all other rivers (c. 695), and Arabia "happy", it is Europe and especially the Mediterranean basin that are most favourable to the development of men and politics (c. 126). Europe is most independent of other lands, whether in peace or war; her fields are safely tilled, her cities are secure, she produces the best of fruits and crops, she has all the most useful minerals, she has abundance of cattle and is largely free from wild beasts. All she needs to import is spices and precious stones, "and life is no worse for those who lack these things than for those who have plenty of them" (c. 127). For history, culture, arts and government, the Mediterranean lands are well ahead of all others (c. 122). And so they were.

The natural products of these lands interest him—timber for building Rome, as we have seen, ship-timber in Cyprus (c. 681), cedars in Cilicia (c. 669), finer woods for furniture (c. 546, 826),[1] ebony from Ethiopia (c. 822); and he pauses to tell us of the Persian "Song of the Palm" and its three hundred and sixty uses (c. 742–3); of lucerne or Medica (c. 525), of which Servius tells us Virgil's country was full; of

1 "Mauretania supplies the Romans with the one-piece tables of the greatest size and most beautiful grain."

the medicinal drugs of Cyprus (c. 684), and Indian cotton and cotton seed (c. 693, 694). Earth has other products, and we have seen his interest in the quarries of Italy; and there are others on Scyros (c. 437) and at Mylasa (c. 658). He speaks of oil-boring in Asia near the Ochus river (c. 518), and of asphalt Eastward and elsewhere (VII, fr. 55; 743, 763–4, 830). But to anyone interested in mining his book is a revelation. I have collected more than a score of references to gold-mining alone,[1] and I resist with regret the desire to quote at length his accounts of various processes, from the primitive fleeces of Colchis (c. 499) to the joyous page on Spain (c. 146)—but I must not imitate "the flowery style of Posidonius, who drew his language as it were from the mine", even if Posidonius was, as is probable, Strabo's authority here. There are also the silver mines of Attica—exhausted, he is told, with piles of mining rubble round them (c. 399, 447), copper mines in Africa (c. 830), and plenty more; and he does not ignore the bad conditions of labourers in some of the mines (c. 561). Ruddle (c. 540), potash (c. 529), and the topaz (c. 770)[2] may conclude a sadly truncated paragraph.

At the beginning of his book Strabo states his view that, in addition to all other multifarious knowledge, "polymathy", the geographer must take account of the natural history of animals, sea-beasts and land-beasts (c. 8). He fulfils the implied promise; and a very interesting thing he makes of it. Take his account of the animals of Spain (c. 163)—Spain is one of his best sections—or of Egypt (c. 823). He is perhaps the first to tell us what a plague rabbits may become—a Spanish animal; "Spain has hardly any destructive animals except the burrowing hares, which some call *lebêrides*; for they damage both plants and seeds by eating the roots". This pest covers Spain and spreads to Marseilles. Some one brought a couple to the Balearic islands, with the result that the inhabitants at last called on the Roman government to find them a new home, where there would be

1 Let me at least copy my list in a note: c. 142, 146, 156, 187–8, 190, 205, 208, 214, 218, VII, fr. 34, c. 499, 506, 509, 511, 529, 625, 680, 700, 711, 718, 726, 778. See pages 75–77.

2 Cf. Job xxviii, 19, the topaz of Ethiopia.

no rabbits. Ferrets from Africa, well muzzled, are put down the burrows, and drive the rabbits before them to be caught and killed as they come out (c. 144, 168). He notices plague spread by field-mice, and the ruin of crops, and the necessity for the government offering a bounty for the killing of the mice (c. 165, cf. 604, 613). Spain has many deer and wild horses; its marshes team with swans and other waterfowl, and the beaver builds in the rivers—though luckily for the beaver its Black Sea cousin is more useful medicinally (c. 163). So he goes on, noting the big cetaceans in both Oceans, Atlantic and Indian (c. 145, 725) and perhaps the narwhal, if it ever came so far South and if it is the oryx; the habits of the tunny, its life in the Black Sea (c. 320), its fancy for an acorn abundant on the shore of Spain (c. 145), and plenty of places where the fishermen have look-outs for it; seals in the Caspian (c. 513, 776)—the square-faced animals of Herodotus;[1] the little dogs of Malta[2] (c. 277); the horses of Arcadia (c. 388), of Media (c. 525), of Cyrene (c. 837). And to all this, and the natural history of the Black Sea (c. 312), we have to add of course the elephant in India and Africa, and how he is hunted (c. 710), with some dubious stories about the Indian being larger than the African (c. 705) as Polybius also said, and about the wells he digs with his tusks (c. 773), and how he sleeps standing because his legs have no joints (c. 772), which Aristotle had already refuted;[3] but he refuses the mere fables of Artemidorus about the olive branch, etc. (c. 829). He speaks of the giraffe (c. 775, 827) and tells us how he saw a rhinoceros, but apparently not of the biggest (c. 774), and how the Egyptians feed the sacred crocodile at Arsinoe (c. 811). Perhaps he ought not to have brought up the gold-mining ants again (c. 702, 706, 718, 782), though they may come from some Sanskrit literature; but he is surely right in reprobating Megasthenes for his dwarfs and mouthless men, the folk who sleep in their own ears and the notorious dog-headed (c. 711); but national associations may make one glad to read of Indian "horses with one horn and

1 Herodotus, IV, 109. 2 Cf. page 173.
3 Cf. page 143.

the head of a deer",[1] coupled with the wondrous bamboo (c. 710). The big crabs and the pearls of the Persian Gulf must end an incomplete list.

The primitive peoples of Europe from Gibraltar to Moscow claim his attention, and he makes a great contribution to Anthropology. The migrations of the races, Cimbric, Spanish and others (c. 102, 166, 305) are noted as imperfectly known, and the shrewd observation is made that, where a tribe remains stationary to the point of being *autochthonous*, as in Attica, it means differentiation in speech and custom (c. 333). His treatment of Spanish ways is a capital passage (c. 154, 163); and the Celts match it—a tall race, with a strong dash of *ἄνοια*, mad on war,[2] *ἀρειμάνιον*, especially good as cavalry, honest and not ill-mannered but quite *αὐθέκαστον* (the type that calls a spade a spade, as Philip of Macedon almost put it[3]), keen on education and culture, especially on Greek—"they even write their contracts in Greek" (c. 195, 180). The Greek influence came from Marseilles, and lasted for centuries; Greek names abound in Christian Gaul, and even the British heretic Pelagius must turn Morgan (they say) into Greek. The Germans are savages, and treacherous (c. 291)—he came too early to be able to read Tacitus' *Germania*; but he writes something of the kind of his own about the Scythians, using them with their primitive virtue (c. 300, 302) as a foil to the luxury of the Roman world. Savages sleep on the ground like the Selloi of Homer (*χαμευνεῖν*, c. 164[4]), and allow much influence to their women; the rule of women, *γυναικοκρατία*, is not civilization (c. 165). Nomads clearly interest him, and he notes how the Ethiopians watch over their flocks by night, "singing a song of a sort by the

1 Cf. page 147.

2 Cf. Polybius, II, 20, 7, the Celts and their *λοιμικήν τινα πολέμου διάθεσιν*.

3 Plutarch, *Apophthegm. Reg.* 15, 178B, says that, when certain Olynthians complained to Philip that some of his friends called them traitors, the king rejoined that the Macedonians are a rude and rustic people, *καὶ τὴν σκάφην σκάφην λέγοντας*. Cf. Lucian, *Hist. Conscr.* 41, 54, *τοιοῦτος οὖν μοι ὁ συγγραφεὺς ἔστω...παρρησίας καὶ ἀληθείας φίλος, ὡς ὁ κωμικός φησι, τὰ σῦκα σῦκα, τὴν σκάφην δὲ σκάφην ὀνομάσων*. Contrast Plutarch, *Solon*, 15, on the Athenian habit *ἀστείως ὑποκορίζεσθαι*.

4 Cf. *Iliad*, XVI, 235.

fire" (c. 776). The cowboy in Canada and the States has to ride round his bunch by night and, if they begin to rise, he has to sing to them till they settle down, for otherwise there is the risk of a panic rush. Arab polyandry (c. 783) and African polygamy (c. 835), the Nabataean plan of fining a man who reduces his property (c. 783), and a great mass of information about India with its castes, its *suttee*, its Brahmans and its ascetics, show the range he traverses and how thoroughly he fulfils the promises of his opening pages.

But by now the civilized world, at least the world of the Mediterranean, is Roman; and, as we survey land after land, we see what the change means. Piracy with its atrocious slave trade is put down. The kings of Syria and Cyprus, who countenanced the pirates, have ceased to be (c. 669); and Delos is no longer the horrible market, where ten thousand captives would be landed from the slave-ships in a day (c. 668). It is once again the possession of Athens (c. 486), and it is forbidden to keep dogs there—happy isle! Bandits and brigands, East and West, are stamped out by the Romans. Strabo tells of one bandit chief, Selurus, who called himself "son of Etna", and harried Eastern Sicily, but was caught, and publicly torn to pieces by beasts in Rome—εἴδομεν, "I saw it", he says (c. 273). He has a more amusing story of another, Cleon by name, whose headquarters were on Mount Olympus in the Troy country, who had better opportunities and used them aptly. In Antony's interests he countered the extortion of money from the district for the renegade Labienus, and was duly rewarded; but at the time of the battle of Actium he was discreet enough to choose the winning side. Augustus made him Prince-Bishop of the Mysian god Zeus Abrettenus—a change from being a brigand, says Strabo drily. But whether the goddess of the temple did not like him eating swine's flesh, which was taboo in her precinct, as the temple people said, or whether it were mere ordinary over-eating, he died in a month (c. 574, 575). There is no longer a sanctuary at Ephesus, it had become a nuisance, and Augustus stopped it (c. 641, 642). Roads and *emporia*, centres of distribution, were taken care of by the

Romans, suitable places strengthened with "colonies"; and all is noted in due course by Strabo. Athens and Sparta are free cities (c. 398, 365); but the helots of Sparta are also free now (c. 364). Fifty thousand Getae from over the frontiers are settled in Thrace (c. 303); the Allobroges are turned farmers (c. 186); the Britons are left to themselves. There was nothing to fear from Britain, and nothing to be gained by annexation; it seemed that more revenue was to be drawn from duties on imports from Britain and exports to it than from any tribute the country could yield, when the cost of occupation should be deducted (c. 116). His account of Britain is in our English history books, but one may note that among other taxed exports to the barbarous isle were ivory necklaces (c. 200).[1]

Side by side with all this civilization and prosperity Strabo brings to our notice a great amount of desolation—Sicily, Southern Italy, and, above all, Greece are empty and forsaken as compared with the days of old. No doubt there was great emigration from old Greece to the cities and camps of the Hellenistic kings, and perhaps there still was emigration. But Strabo reminds us of Polybius' statement that Aemilius Paullus sold one hundred and fifty thousand of the people of Epirus into slavery[2] (c. 322). That was nearly two hundred years ago, but there is no creation of population *ex nihilo*. The barbarian in Tacitus may well say *solitudinem faciunt, pacem appellant*. Most of the old languages of Asia Minor have disappeared (c. 565); not a trace of Lydian is left (c. 631).[3]

But it was peace, and that Strabo emphasizes along with

1 It is interesting to learn that in crossing to Britain you embark at night on an ebb-tide and land next day at 2 P.M. (c. 193; cf. c. 199, and Caesar, *Bell. Gall.* IV, 23; V, 8). The ships are flat-bottomed, high-prowed, high-sterned (c. 195).

2 To understand this, see Sir Edwin Pears, *Turkey and its People*, p. 108, on the Turkish massacre and enslavement of the Chiots in 1822; or Finlay, *History of Greece*, VI, pp. 255–260.

3 It is very odd to find Rostovtzeff, *History of Ancient World*, I, p. 378, saying that "we have the express evidence of Paul the Apostle that the natives of Asia Minor still spoke Phrygian and Galatian". St Luke (Acts xiv, 11) says the priests at Lystra spoke Λυκαονιστί. Sir William Ramsay has shown us that this town was in the Roman province of Galatia. Strabo does not allude to any Lycaonian dialect.

the Emperor's care for the well-being of the Empire. The Roman citizenship is being gradually extended; it reaches to the Alps in Italy (c. 210). Prosperity is found in friendship with Rome (c. 140). "The Romans took over many nations savage by nature on account of the regions they inhabited, regions rugged, harbourless or cold, or otherwise little suited for human life; and races that had been isolated they interwove with one another, and taught the wilder kinds to live like citizens"; and each sort helps the other, one supplies arms, the other food, arts and culture (c. 127). The movement, as in the Rhone region, is toward the Roman *type*, *τύπος*, in speech, in habits of life, and in some cases in city life (c. 186). The cost has been great; the Empire was initially won by force (c. 401[1]). "Italy was long torn by factions, but since it came under Roman rule, it has been saved, like Rome herself, from utter ruin and destruction by the excellence of Rome's polity and the excellence of her rulers. But it would be a difficult thing to administer an Empire so great, except by entrusting it to one man as to a father. Never in fact have the Romans and their allies had such abundance of peace and prosperity as Caesar Augustus gave them, from the time when he assumed absolute rule, and as Tiberius, his son and successor, gives them now, making Augustus the model of his administration and decrees, as his sons Germanicus and Drusus make their father their model and work with him" (c. 288).

1 Some simple reflections on the relations of power and finance (c. 415).

THE DAEMON ENVIRONMENT

ONE of the most striking effects of the French Revolution was the reaction against it in the sphere of religion. The eighteenth century had been an age of Reason, and the early nineteenth century saw the glorification of Faith, the rehabilitation of Authority and the return of Miracle. In the ancient Roman world a similar change followed the establishment of the Imperial system. The conquests of Alexander had turned men's minds from the state to the individual, and the long wars of the Macedonian despotisms, incessant and purposeless, intensified the natural craving of man for order, for inward peace, for unity in the world without and in his own soul. The last hundred and fifty years of the Roman Republic had been at once a period of rationalism and individualism, of lawlessness and civil war. The Macedonian period had seen the rise of Stoicism and Epicureanism; the Empire was to see the restoration of religion.

The contemporaries of Augustus realized the political value of religion. The propositions were freely made that "the whole belief in immortal gods was invented by wise persons in the interest of the state"; that "the myths of Hades, though pure invention, contribute to make men upright" and that "it is for the good of states that men should be deceived in religion".[1]

But serious people, free from the cynicism and shallowness which characterize such judgments, came, on looking over the history of their own times, to another conclusion on this connection between religion and morals, a conclusion very different in tone and in consequences. They argued the other way. Greek speculators had moved away from polytheism, from ritual and ceremony, and finally from all belief in deity as an effective thing at all—and the result was conspicuous in the disorder of national and individual life. Working back-

1 Cicero, *N.D.* I, 42, 118; Diodorus Siculus, I, 2; Varro *ap.* Augustine, *de Civ. Dei,* IV, 27; VI, 5.

ward, however, from the union of good morals with traditional belief, and the clear effect of atheistic and sceptical philosophy upon character, men now began to surmise that truth lay rather with the beliefs of their fathers than with the disastrous speculations which human experience, in spite of logic, had by now hopelessly discredited.

It was impossible, however, to go back at once to the old days when there was no philosophy, nor did it seem necessary. There had been fine and impressive utterances upon the nature of the divine, which had rooted themselves in the hearts of men. The goodness, the grandeur and the unity of the Supreme and Ultimate God had offered too strong a ground of hope and consolation to be discarded, and in the story of the revival of paganism the emphasis on Providence is one of the constant features.

But when once speculative philosophy has been abandoned for the safer method of noting the practical values of beliefs, suggestions and traditions, Eclecticism is inevitable. Men drew freely upon all the schools of thought for material with which to piece out the data of experience, conceding points in one place for which they meant to recoup themselves elsewhere. Thus, when it became clear that the logic of the philosophers forced men step by step to negate every quality which they had once associated with divinity—and this, as they realized, in the interest of God's absoluteness, a matter closely bound up with his value to them; when it was evident that this process ended in a God of whom nothing whatever could be predicated, not even being, a God "away beyond existence" (*ἐπέκεινα τῶν ὄντων*), between whom and the universe intercommunication was logically quite impossible in any way whatever; it was also obvious that, unless they could recover elsewhere what they had here given away, all was over with religion.

Homer[1] had spoken of two jars on the threshold of Zeus, one full of good and the other of evil, out of which God gave men their destinies good, bad, and mingled. "I the Lord create evil" says a writer in the Old Testament. But a later

1 *Iliad*, xxiv, 527.

age shrank from attributing evil to God. "We must not accept Homer or any other poet who makes such a mistake", said Plato.[1] God and evil were mutually exclusive terms; and, if they were not, the Supreme was in any case, beyond the thought of man's destiny good or evil.

Yet good and evil were in the world. The order, the law, and the beauty of the Universe, of sun and star, of the earth and its seasons, implied Mind and Providence. So argued the Stoics. "When we look up", wrote Lucretius himself, "to the heavenly regions of the great universe, the aether set on high above the glittering stars, and the thought comes into our mind of the sun and the moon and their courses; then indeed, in hearts laden with other woes, that doubt too begins to wake and raise its head—Can it be perchance that after all we have to do with some vast divine power that wheels those bright stars each in his orbit?"[2] In Nature, too, and in its power of self-reproduction, there lurked, as Eastern religions taught, a divine power. All was law, unity, Cosmos. And Stoic pantheism would not serve to explain it. That a God should submit to change and extend himself through land and sea, winds and animals, and "the strange experiences of both animals and plants", that he should make and unmake, would prove him poorer than the child in Homer's simile, building sand castles, and knocking them down to build them up again. So said Plutarch.[3] But if God is not in the universe, whence come all these manifestations of mind?

Evil was in the world—pain, hunger and bereavement, cruelty and lust, abundant evidence for them all. Even in the sphere of religion there was evil; there were foul rites, obscene legends, human sacrifices,—*tantum religio potuit suadere malorum.* Whence came evil? Stoic pantheism involved that God was the author of sin, the inspiring and operative agent in every deed of shame. The very idea was revolting to the religious mind.

Once more it was remarked that the consensus of mankind was in favour of belief in gods. Such a consensus could not be accidental; it was attributed to Nature, and it was taken

1 *Rep.* II, 379D. 2 Lucretius, v, 1204. 3 Plutarch, *de E.* 21

therefore as reliable evidence for the matter concerned. "Of all customs", says Plutarch,[1] "first and greatest is belief in gods....You might find communities without walls, letters, kings, houses or money, with no knowledge of theatres or gymnasia; but a community without holy rite, without a god, that uses not prayer, nor oath, nor divination, nor sacrifice, no man ever saw and no man will ever see....This is what holds all society together and is the foundation and buttress of all laws."

Further still, when the Stoic said that the gods care for mankind, and "sometimes even for individuals", once again there was the evidence of men. Marcus Aurelius, in the first book of his Journal, thanks the gods, as many must in every age, for his "good grandsires, good parents, a good sister, good teachers, good associates, kinsmen, friends, good almost every one"; but when he goes further and thanks them "for help vouchsafed in dreams, more particularly for relief from blood-spitting and dizziness", he suggests a special providence of a type very familiar in the literature and monuments of his day.

A presumption might then fairly be granted in favour of divine interest in the universe, and of relations between the world and the divine; and yet the Supreme could not be conceived as susceptible of any relations whatever. The common solution of the difficulty is perhaps nowhere given with such clear vigour—certainly nowhere with such wealth of phrase—as in the book of Apuleius on the God of Socrates, written perhaps about 190 A.D.

Plato, he says, for he classed himself as a Platonist—Plato groups the gods in three categories. Of the celestial gods some we can see—sun, moon and stars; and on these he digresses with characteristic rhetoric, which we may omit; what follows will suffice. Others the mind alone can grasp—incorporeal natures, animate, with neither beginning nor end, eternal before and after, exempt from contagion of body; in perfect intellect possessing supreme beatitude; good, but not

1 Plutarch, *adv. Coloten*, 31, 1125D, E; cf. Seneca, *Ep.* 117, 6, on consensus, and Tertullian, *adv. Nationes*, II, 1.

by participation in any external good, but of themselves. Their father, Lord and Author of all things, free from every nexus of suffering or doing—him Plato, with celestial eloquence of language commensurate with the immortal gods, has declared to be, in virtue of the ineffable immensity of his incredible majesty, beyond the poverty of human speech or definition; while even to the sages themselves, when by force of soul they have removed themselves from the body, the conception of God comes, in a flash in the darkness, in a flash only and is gone. He is probably thinking of mystical experiences, in which it seems that he himself practised.

"To whom then shall I recite prayers? to whom tender vows? to whom slay victims? on whom shall I call, to help the wretched, to favour the good, to counter the evil?... Shall I swear by Jove the Stone (*per Iovem lapidem*) after the most ancient manner of Rome? Yet if Plato's thought be true that never God and man can meet, the stone will hear me more easily than Jove.

"Nay! not so far (for Plato shall answer, the thought is his, if mine the voice), not so far, he saith, do I pronounce the gods to be sejunct and alienate from us, as to think that not even our prayers can reach them. Not from the care of human affairs, but from contact, have I removed them. But there are certain mediary divine powers, between aether above and earth beneath, situate in that mid space of air, by whom our desires and our deserts reach the gods. These the Greeks call daemons, carriers between human and heavenly, hence of prayers, thence of gifts; back and forth they fare, hence with petition, thence with sufficiency, interpreters and bringers of salvation."

To cut short this rhetoric, we may turn to Plutarch, who sets forth substantially the same view in quieter language. "It is one Reason that makes all things a Cosmos, one Providence that cares for them, with ancillary powers appointed to all things, while among different nations different honours and names are given to them as customs vary." Stoics raise the question whether there are many universes or one, as if many universes would require many Zeuses; but he asks, Why should there not be in each universe a guide and ruler with mind and reason, such as he in our universe whom we call lord and father of all; and all of them subject to the destiny and providence of which Zeus is lord, all of them receiving from him the beginnings and seeds and principles (λόγους) of all things achieved in each of their spheres, all of them responsible to Zeus?[1] Why not?

"Are not all things," Celsus asks the Christians,[2] "ruled according to the will of God? Is not all Providence from him? Whatever there is in the whole scheme of things, whether the work of God, or of angels, or other daemons, or heroes, all these have their law from the greatest God." "I do not think it makes any difference whether you call Zeus the Most High, or Zeus, or Adonai, or Sabaoth, or Amûn like the Egyptians, or Papaios like the Scythians." "Probably all things are allotted to various rulers (ἐπόπταις) and distributed into provinces and so governed. Thus among the various nations things would be done rightly, if done as those rulers would have them."

The Stoics and others suggested that these deputy gods might be natural laws, or even natural objects, wine and grain and the like.[3] But, says Plutarch, "we must not turn the gods as it were into queen-bees, nor keep them shut up in the prison-house of matter, as the Stoics do, when they change the gods into conditions of the atmosphere, fire, water, etc., and thus beget them with the universe and burn them up with it". This was a reference to the Stoic doctrine of the final conflagration of the world and its re-creation which should both periodically recur throughout eternity—and in which, as Plutarch elsewhere says, the Stoics' gods were to "melt like wax or tin". Meanwhile the Stoics "nail the gods down" like statues to matter, yes! and fuse them with it and rivet them to it.[4]

1 Plutarch, *de defectu oraculorum*, 29.

2 Celsus *ap.* Origen, *c. Celsum*, VII, 68; V, 41; V, 25.

3 Cf. Cicero, *de Nat. Deorum*, II, 23, 60ff., the gods of popular religion are names of benefits received from the gods, or personified virtues and passions, or spirits of departed benefactors, or personified forces of nature.

4 Plutarch, *de def. orac.* 29, etc.

Under the Supreme is a hierarchy of gods, and beneath them and above men is an intermediary order; for, as Apuleius says, it would have fitted ill with the majesty of the celestial gods that one of them should paint a dream for Hannibal or turn prophecy into verse for the Sibyl. It is not their function to come down to such detail; all that is assigned to the daemons.[1] The daemons, it is agreed, are of mingled nature—"not so brute as the terrene, not so light as the aetherial"; like clouds they keep a mid distance between earth and sky. They are of the purest liquid, of air, the serene element, and thus scarcely visible to men, save of their own choice; they are of a matter so infinitely fine, "as by its rarity to transmit the rays of our sight, by its splendour to turn them back, by its subtlety to frustrate them". They share immortality with the gods above and passion with men below.[2] Plutarch says the same, and alleges it can be proved on the testimony of wise and ancient witnesses, though he is less clear that the daemons are eternal. If, he says, the atmosphere were abolished between the earth and the moon, the void would destroy the unity of the universe; and in precisely the same way "those who do not leave us the race of daemons destroy all intercourse between gods and men, by abolishing what Plato called the interpretive and ancillary nature—or else they compel us to make confusion and disorder of everything, by bringing God in among mortal passions and mortal affairs, fetching him down for our needs, as they say the witches in Thessaly do with the moon".[3]

The intermediary position of daemons has interesting results. Some daemons have by their virtue risen into the ranks of the gods—Isis, Osiris, Herakles and Dionysos, for example.[4] And similarly the souls of good men "when set free from re-birth (γένεσις) and at rest from the body" may become daemons;[5] and as old athletes enjoy watching and encouraging young ones, so the daemons, who through worth of soul are done with the contests of life, do not despise what

1 Apuleius, *de deo Socr.* ch. VII.
2 Apuleius, *de deo Socr.* 11, 13.
3 Plutarch, *de def. orac.* 13.
4 Plutarch, *de Iside*, 27.
5 Plutarch, *Romulus*, 28; *de def. orac.* 10.

they have left behind, but are kindly-minded to such as strive for the same goal,—especially when they see them close upon their hope, struggling, and all but touching it. As in the case of a wreck, landsmen will run out into the waves to help the sailors they can reach, so the daemons help us as the waves of life break over us.[1] The expression will cover not only this life, but the whole cycle of many lives, however long. But why, asks the Christian Tatian (§ 16), should they be more effectual (δραστικώτεροι) after death?

The fact is, we are told, that there is little difference between a daemon and a human soul. A daemon, says Apuleius, may be a human spirit that has earned its discharge from life and abjured the body—just like the Lares and Lemures of Roman belief. Conversely the human spirit may be a daemon for the present in a body.[2] Emperor-worship is not to be explained, I think, apart from this belief. Augustus is like Hercules; Horace says so much; each is the incarnation of something divine. From this kinship of soul and daemon comes the ready communication between men and the powers above them, in prayer and revelation.

"There is nothing unreasonable in it", says Plutarch, "or marvellous, if souls meeting souls make on them impressions of the future (φαντασίας τοῦ μέλλοντος)", for even men with men communicate by many other methods than speech.[3] The body indeed dulls this faculty, and some souls only shake off its influence in dreams, or even at the approach of death. But sometimes the body is thrown by some cause or other into such a condition as to allow the soul to see. This condition is called "enthusiasm"[4]—it is caused, for instance, by "the enthusiastic spirit" which the earth sends up as an exhalation at Delphi; and the Egyptians again blend a potion, called *Kyphi*, in a very mystic way with sixteen drugs—sixteen being the square of a square carries some remarkable properties or suggestions—and this drug when inhaled calms the mind and

1 Plutarch, *de gen. Socr.* 24.
2 Apuleius, *de deo Socr.* 15; cf. Plutarch, *de def. orac.* 38.
3 Plutarch, *de def. orac.* 38–40 for the whole subject.
4 See page 231.

reduces anxiety, and "that part of us which receives impressions (φανταστικόν) and is susceptive of dreams, it rubs down and cleans like a mirror". So cleaned and set free the soul is open to receive what will come to it. Perhaps the vapour may "by heat and diffusion open pores (πόρους) that can take such impressions". "The words of the daemons are borne through all things, but they only sound for those who have the unruffled nature and the quiet soul."[1]

The daemons have wings, says Tertullian, they are everywhere in a single moment; the whole world is as one place to them; and all that is done all over the world, it is as easy for them to know as to report. Dwelling in the air, among stars and clouds, they learn readily what the weather will be, and can promise rain, which is coming in any case. When sorcerers call up ghosts and make what seem the souls of the dead appear; when they cause even goats and tables to divine; it is the work of daemons. Yet it was curious that Cybele left her priest in Carthage in ignorance of the death of Marcus Aurelius for a week.[2]

Plutarch lays great stress on the oracles. The theory of the "enthusiastic spirit" or exhalation—with its strange blend, as it seems to us, of spiritual and material—was liable, he says, to be attacked on the ground that it took divination out of the sphere of the gods and of reason.[3] But he rejoins that there are double causes for everything—the ancients derived all things from Zeus; moderns, natural philosophers (φυσικοί), wander away from "the fair and divine cause" and make everything depend on bodies, impacts, changes and mixtures—and both err in degree. Thus in the oracle there may be the exhalation from the earth, but Earth is a goddess, and so is the Sun who gives her this power; "and then we leave daemons installed as lords and warders and guardians" of the oracles. If Apollo was a god, there were many on the border line between gods and daemons who had oracles of

1 Plutarch, *de genio Socratis*, 20.
2 Tertullian, *Apol.* 23–25.
3 Plutarch, *de def. orac.* 48.

their own—Asclepios, Amphiaraos, Trophonios, etc.[1] Clear proof of the truth that gods and daemons exist, and care for men and give them oracles, is to be seen in the great shrines. Men were "in anguish and fear lest Delphi should lose its glory of three thousand years", but Delphi has not failed. On the contrary, though hard to believe and much tested, the Pythian priestess has never been convicted of error; and she has filled the oracle with offerings and gifts from barbarians and Greeks and adorned it with beautiful buildings.[2] This was not man's doing; "the god came and inspired the oracle with his divinity". *Esto perpetua.*

Pausanias, writing about 170 A.D., tells how men consulted the oracle of Trophonios; and then he says, "I did it myself". What he learnt in his strange adventure in the pit, he does not say. But a remark let fall in his eighth book is significant.[3] He had seen many strange things, and now he says: "When I began this work, I used to look on these Greek stories as little better than foolishness; but now that I have got as far as Arcadia, my opinion about them is this. I believe the Greeks, who were accounted wise, spoke of old in riddles and not straight out; so I judge that this story of Cronos [swallowing a foal instead of his child] is a piece of Greek philosophy. In matters concerning the divine I will hold by what has been said"—by tradition, in fact.

Tertullian gives a list of places where there were temples in which men slept to obtain dreams of revelation.[4] Miss Mary Hamilton in her book on *Incubation* shows how the practice still survives in the Greek islands. Thus, in Ceos, where once men slept in the shrine of Artemis, to-day they sleep in the church of St Artemidos.[5] Strabo says the practice was an essential feature of Judaism, and he compares Moses to Amphiaraos, Trophonios, and Orpheus, etc.[6] But

1 Cicero has a strange commentary here: *de Nat. Deorum*, III, 19, 49. *An Amphiaraus erit deus et Trophonius? Nostri quidem publicani, cum essent agri in Boeotia deorum immortalium excepti lege censoria, negabant immortales esse ullos, qui aliquando homines fuissent.*

2 Plutarch, *de Pyth. orac.* 29.

3 Pausanias, VIII, 8, 3.

4 Tertullian, *de anima*, 46.

5 *Incubation*, p. 174.

6 Strabo, C. 761–2; see page 233.

the most famous of these shrines was that of Aesculapius (Asklepios) at Epidauros—a god whose miracles are recorded in wonderful inscriptions and in the orations (as wonderful) of Aelius Aristides. Celsus,[1] in his attack on Christianity, brings up the oracles given by gods and daemons and fulfilled, as evidence to the truth of traditional religion. But he goes further; for "let a man go to the shrine of Trophonios, or Amphiaraos, or Mopsos, and there he may see the gods in the likeness of men, no feigned forms but clear to see",[2] "not slipping by them once, like him who deceived those people [the Christians], but ever associating with those who will". "Multitudes, Greeks and barbarians, testify that they have often seen, and still do see, Aesculapius—not a phantom of him, but himself healing men, doing them good and foretelling the future."

Here it may be suggested that there is some caution needed. Is Aesculapius a god or a daemon? Hardly a god, in the strict sense, if he consents to be visible to the eye of flesh—but then there is no strict sense in this region.

Explanations may be offered of various kinds, sleight of hand, hypnotism, sheer credulity. A curious illustration will be found in Lucian's pamphlet called *Alexander*, where he shows how a man of that name founded a new oracle at Abonoteichos in Cappadocia—and with the aid of a tame snake, and his native gifts of cunning and impudence, drove a roaring trade in prophecy. As for the miracles of Jesus, says Celsus, ordinary quacks on the streets will do greater for an obol or two—"driving devils out of men, blowing away diseases, calling up the souls of heroes, and displaying sumptuous banquets which are not there".[3] Tertullian admits all these operations—they are done by the aid of daemons—"it is no great thing for him to cheat the outer eyes, who finds it quite easy to blind the sight of the soul within".[4] Marcus Aurelius records with gratitude that Diognetus taught him

1 Celsus *ap.* Origen, *c. Celsum*, VII, 35; III, 24.

2 Criticism of such anthropomorphic views in Cicero, *de Nat. Deorum*, I, 27, 76ff.

3 Celsus *ap.* Origen, *c. Celsum*, I, 68.

4 Tertullian, *de anima*, 57.

to neglect such miracles.[1] Lucian, in his *Lover of Lies* (Φιλοψευδής), draws a wonderful group of people revelling in the wildest displays of the supernatural; and the strange thing is that, as one reads the literature of the age, the parody loses its extravagance; for one thing after another is paralleled by sober writers.

But now we must turn to another aspect of the subject. Plutarch quotes with approval a couplet from Menander, omitting the lines which follow, as they did not suit his purpose.

> By each man standeth from his natal hour
> A daemon, his kind mystagogue through life.[2]

Aristotle was also quoted by Isidore the Gnostic as an authority for the belief.[3] "Our ancestors", says Seneca, "gave every individual man and woman a Genius or a Juno."[4] The genius or daemon is not merely Greek and Latin. It appears in Persia as the *fravashi*, the spiritual counterpart; in Egypt as the *ka*;[5] in the Syrian Gnostic's *Hymn of the Soul* it is represented as a robe exactly reproducing the likeness of the man—

> Two in number we stood but only one in appearance;

and it is quite possible that Peter's "angel" and "the angels" of the little children in the New Testament are nothing else. "Zeus", says Epictetus, "has placed by every man a guardian, every man's daemon, to whom he has committed the care of the man, a guardian who never sleeps, is never deceived. For to what better and more careful guardian could he have intrusted each of us? When then you have shut the doors, and made darkness within, remember never to say that you are alone, for you are not, God is within and your daemon is within, and what need of light have they to see what you are doing?"[6] The daemon when our life is done,

1 Marcus Aurelius, I, 6.
2 Plutarch, *de tranqu. animi*, 15; cf. Tertullian, *de anima*, 57.
3 Clement Alex. *Strom.* VI, 53.
4 Seneca, *Ep.* 110, 2.
5 Cf. Adolf Erman, *Handbook of Egyptian Religion* (tr.), p. 86, with a picture of a king and his *ka*, exactly alike; and J. H. Breasted, *Development of Religion and Thought in Ancient Egypt*, pp. 52 ff.
6 Epictetus, *D.* I, 14.

Apuleius says, carries his *custodia* to our trial, and by his report goes our doom.[1] This daemon-guardian can of course give word in dreams and omens, and more, he can appear in person. The Pythagoreans, Apuleius says, used to wonder if any man said he had never seen a daemon. An Egyptian priest in Rome went to the Iseum outside the city walls, on the Campus Martius, the only "pure place" he could find in or about the city, and there he sought to see the daemon of Plotinus; but he saw more than he dreamed of—for, when it came, it was a god and not a daemon. So great a man was Plotinus.[2] Plutarch doubted such appearances, as he did an Egyptian theory that the spirit of a god could have a child by a human woman.[3]

Empedocles however, Plutarch says, held that we each have two daemons. The Egyptians said that the human body is assigned, part by part, to six and thirty gods or daemons of the air; and they knew their names, too, Chnumen, Chnachumen, Knat, Sikat, Rhamanor, etc.; and, by calling on the daemon concerned, they said they could cure any part that was sick.[4] Basilides, the Gnostic, is credited with describing man as a sort of Wooden Horse, with a whole army of different spirits within him.[5] Plutarch uses the same figure in taunting the Stoics with turning the virtues into personal beings—they made a man "a paradise[6] or a Wooden Horse".[7]

It is not strange then to find a series of significant words like theolept, nympholept, lymphatic, enthusiasm, daemoniac, theophorete and the like, all testifying to the power that daemons, nymphs, Pans, gods and other beings had of seizing upon and occupying human beings. "Unclean spirits hover over waters", says Tertullian, "as shady fountains know, and hidden streams, and the public baths, and water-pipes in

1 Apuleius, *de deo Socr.* ch. xv.

2 Porphyry, *vita Plotini*, 10.

3 Plutarch, *Numa*, 4. Cf. the stories referred to on page 135 about animals fertilized by wind.

4 Celsus *ap.* Origen, *c. Celsum*, VIII, 58.

5 *ap.* Clement Alex. *Strom.* II, 113.

6 In the Persian or Greek sense, in which Xenophon uses it.

7 Plutarch, *adv. Stoicos*, 45.

houses, cisterns and wells".[1] They could give mere disease; they might remain and ensure lasting madness. And again it was possible that all sin and uncleanness was the work of daemons inhabiting a man, for a legion could hardly be idle inside an individual. Was every act the result of a spiritual impulse from a good or bad daemon? Was marriage essentially a daemonic thing? Whence came the beginnings of life? Here we touch a great question on which Folklore may yet have much to teach us.

But we have come now to the question of evil, for every candid person owned that daemons were to blame for a great deal of mischief. Celsus[2] himself has a warning against magic and the daemons connected with it. "One must be on one's guard not to get entangled in these matters through over-occupation in them, and so, through love of the body and by turning away from better things, to be overcome by forgetfulness. For perhaps we should not disbelieve the wise who say that, of the daemons who pervade the earth, the greater part are entangled in re-birth (γένεσις)—fused and riveted to it—and being bound to blood and smoke and chanting, etc., they can do no more than heal the body and foretell the future." Again, there were strange and revolting religious rites, in which the eating of raw flesh, Plutarch says, the rending asunder of animals, fasting, and the narration of obscene legends, were a part. These could not be attributed to gods, but must be the institution of evil daemons. Human sacrifices, he says, could not have been welcome to the gods, nor would kings and generals have been willing to sacrifice their own children unless they had been appeasing the anger of ugly, ill-tempered and vengeful daemons, who would bring war or pestilence otherwise. Ill tales of the gods—rape, suffering, wandering, servitude—are not true of gods, but of daemons who usurped their names.[3] And yet, Plutarch has

1 Tertullian, *de Bapt.* 5. Cf. J. C. Lawson, *Modern Greek Folklore and Ancient Greek Religion*, ch. II, §9, especially p. 131, where Mr Lawson describes how he and his muleteer escaped from a Nereid.

2 Celsus *ap.* Origen, *c. Celsum*, VIII, 60. Cf. Tertullian on sacrifices, *Apology*, 22; "What else", asks Clement of Alexandria, "would cats ask for if they could speak?" (*Protr.* 41).

3 Plutarch, *de def. orac.* 14, 15, 21.

apologies for animal-worship in Egypt, and for the traditional obscene image of Osiris which still stood; and in general he offers no means of telling which were the rites ordained by a god and which by a bad daemon. Christians pointed this out with some emphasis. None the less philosophic paganism found God acquitted of sin, at once by his remoteness from human contacts and by the energies of evil daemons. Whence comes the evil that makes daemons evil, is not explained. God was good; and that God should be good was the chief concern of religious philosophers.

The system of ideas here set forth was consistent. It rested on ancient tradition and on philosophy—on association and reflection. It was confirmed every day by oracle, theolepsy, theophory, trance and mystery, while, more and more as time went on, the subtlest and the most religious of Greek thinkers took pains to show how inevitable it was on the side of thought. Yet complaints are heard from various quarters that the daemon theory and the religion that rested on it were cruel; men knew of human sacrifices that recurred; that they were unclean; the hierodules and the Galli of the temples are only part of the proof of this charge. Cicero, Horace, Epictetus, Plutarch himself—and they are not alone—emphasize how superstition paralyses the human mind. But if the daemon theory was true, this was inevitable. Lucretius and the Christian apologists have the same criticisms to make here, and all the evidence shows their justice. The system did dwarf the intellect of men—it worked out in cruelty, lust and paralysis. But it broke down; and it is worth remembering that it did not yield to the attack of philosophy or science, for in truth it was very largely the construction of philosophers accepting popular beliefs; and it held its own among the early Christians, bred as they were among the people and educated, as we all are, to accept contemporary philosophy as final; but it faded away at last before the ideas and the personality of Jesus of Nazareth.

THE STUDY OF ANCIENT HISTORY

A man must be very vain to write history, for to do so requires imagination.
ANATOLE FRANCE

Historians are usually professors or other simple-minded people.
BENEDETTO CROCE

DR JOHNSON was speaking of Goldsmith: "Whether, indeed, we take him as a poet, as a comick writer, or as an historian, he stands in the first class". Boswell: "An historian? My dear sir, you surely will not rank his compilation of the Roman history with the works of other historians of this age?" Johnson: "Why, who are before him?" Boswell: "Hume, Robertson, Lord Lyttelton". But Johnson will not have it; and as for the superiority of Robertson and the gifts which Boswell claims for him,—"Sir, you must consider how that penetration and that painting are employed. It is not history, it is imagination. He who describes what he never saw draws from fancy. Robertson paints mind as Sir Joshua paints faces in a history piece; he imagines an heroic countenance".[1] The great Cham[2] frequently spoke of History, and generally in the same vein:—"Great abilities", said he, "are not requisite for an historian; for in historical composition all the greatest powers of the human mind are quiescent. He has facts ready to his hand; so there is no exercise of invention. Imagination is not required in any high degree; only about as much as is used in the lower kinds of poetry. Some penetration, accuracy, and colouring will fit a man for the task, if he can give the application which is necessary".[3] "There is but a shallow stream of thought in history."[4] As for motives, they are generally unknown.[5] "That certain kings reigned, and certain battles were fought, we can depend upon as true; but all the colouring, all the philosophy, is conjecture."[6] Boswell:

1 Birkbeck Hill's Boswell, *Life of Johnson*, II, 236.
2 *Ib.* III, 312.
3 *Ib.* I, 424.
4 *Ib.* II, 195.
5 *Ib.* II, 79.
6 *Ib.* II, 365.

"Then, Sir, you would reduce all history to no better than an almanack, a mere chronological series of remarkable events"; and the biographer adds that Mr Gibbon was present, but did not step forth in defence of that species of writing. He probably did not like to *trust* himself with Johnson![1]

Johnson was not alone in this view. Even Hume wrote to Robertson, who was meditating a History of Greece:—"What can you do in most places with these (the ancient) authors but transcribe and translate them? No letters or state papers from which you could correct their errors, or authenticate their narration, or supply their defects".[2] What seems still sadder is that Aristotle himself, with Herodotus and Thucydides before him, says something of the same sort. History, he says, tells us what Alcibiades did or suffered; Poetry is a more philosophic and a more serious thing than History.[3] More serious, not necessarily more solemn, but it takes more mind, more earnestness, more concentration. Some readers to this day hardly realize that in *The Jolly Beggars* Burns was serious, far more serious and in earnest than in some of his more sabbatic pieces, or his high-stepping letters.

It is hard on Thucydides; for he did put mind into his work; he was earnest in inquiry, and complains of men's indifference to truth. By one of Time's revenges, he has undergone attack, and suffered damage in some quarters as an historian, on the ground that his history was what Aristotle and Johnson imply it could not be—a work of art. Polybius, again, conceived of History as a philosophic thing; the "philosophy of history" happily does not appear among his innumerable abstract nouns, but it is that essentially which engages him. As for Herodotus, he is so enjoyable that you cannot credit him with philosophy, seriousness or art, unless you think twice.

But, for a great part of the field, Johnson and Hume describe only too faithfully how history has been written. There are the authorities, and your first and chief task is to select the one you prefer to trust. That seems to have been Livy's way; and after a great deal of transcription (by which indeed

1 Birkbeck Hill's Boswell, *Life of Johnson*, II, 365.

2 *Ib.* II, 273, note.

3 *Poetics*, 9, 1451 b.

the narrative gains) he does allude to Polybius, gracefully dismissing him as "a quite reliable author".[1] Reliable, perhaps, but, the Greeks said, not too readable. There Livy shone; "il parle d'or", as Paul Louis Courier said. Choose your authority; pare down his statements if need be, using probability as your guide; and write as well as you can. Those were the rules; and the last was by far the hardest. The ancient critics, Longinus, Dionysius, Polybius, and others, had much to say of historians who confounded tragedy with history, who wrote emotionally, or carried the tricks of the school too far. Johnson, again, made fun of Sir John Dalrymple's way of telling how people had thought and talked a hundred years before; and Boswell recalls a parody made on their journey when they delayed Sir John's dinner. "Stay now.—Let us consider! Dinner being ready, he wondered that his guests were not yet come. His wonder was soon succeeded by impatience. He walked about the room in anxious agitation; sometimes he looked at his watch, sometimes he looked out at the window with an eager gaze of expectation, and revolved in his mind the various accidents of human life. His family beheld him with mute concern. 'Surely (said he with a sigh) they will not fail me.' The mind of man can bear a certain pressure; but there is a point when it can bear no more. A rope was in his view, and he died a Roman death."[2] The "Roman death" was the historian's own term.

But, if desire for a fine style could lead a man astray, there was another peril. Did not someone define history as "philosophy teaching by examples"? Might not Plutarch's precedent, his great series of *Lives*, be used to defend such procedure? But not every moralist can tell as good a tale as Plutarch; and morals are of various kinds, the patriotic and political kinds not least dangerous. Livy perhaps idealized Rome, and Mitford was shocked (they say) by the French Revolution. Bury, no doubt, had provocation enough when

1 Livy, XXX, 45, *Polybius haudquaquam spernendus auctor*; XXXIII, 10, *Polybium secuti sumus non incertum auctorem cum omnium Romanarum rerum, tum praecipue in Graecia gestarum.*

2 Boswell, *Tour of the Hebrides*, 20 November.

he spoke of History trailing along with literature and moral philosophy, and insisted so severely that History was a science, nothing more and nothing less.

In the nineteenth century the whole conception of History was so enlarged and developed as to be almost transformed. Immense additions were made to knowledge from sources for centuries untapped; and the adjustment of the new facts with the old meant a fresh study of method and new canons of criticism. The accepted story was always liable to be challenged and to be upset; the new archaeologist had facts that were, or seemed to be, more solid than the statements of the old historian. Every fresh discovery opened up new questions and led on to fresh investigations, to further exploration and to intensive criticism. The spade, as someone said, ceased to be the emblem of mortality and became the symbol of life. But History had other tributaries, other confluents, than Archaeology; they were many and powerful; and its stream became turbid and dangerous, a very Mississippi whose pilots had to chart it again with each fresh voyage.

Five of these tributary streams it will be well for us to survey; and first, Archaeology. From the days of Bonaparte and Champollion in Egypt the nineteenth century saw an ever-increasing mass of material, fresh, authentic and perplexing, accumulated from grave, monument and papyrus. The Rosetta Stone gave the key to hieroglyphic; and the books and documents of Egyptian literature, and endless royal records, were read more and more freely. Down to Napoleon's day Herodotus was the chief source, almost the only source, for the story of ancient Egypt. Now its history is read from Egyptian sources at immensely greater length, with far more detail, and naturally with much closer accuracy. Herodotus was not an Egyptologist; he neither spoke the language nor read its hieroglyphics, nor did he pretend to do either; it was his business, he said explicitly and more than once, to write down what he was told.[1] What he observed for himself is another thing; he watched with curious eyes the ways of living Egypt, and there he stands on firm ground.

1 Herodotus, VII, 152; cf. II, 123; VIII, 94.

But for the ancient history he could depend only on his informants, Greek or Egyptian, or half-breed, as might be; and they, it is clear, fell short of modern standards of knowledge. History was not for them a science, but a genial and leisurely Muse, fond of human interest and not much tied to art. It was Herodotus who had the art. However, it is all changed by now. Egyptian dynasties are sorted out, and their chronology is more exactly known than could have been believed. It is supplemented by wide knowledge, ever deepening, of Egyptian literature, religion and art. One side of Archaeology is concerned with the history of pottery. The broken earthenware is thrown aside by the woman who breaks it; and the archaeologist gathers it from a hundred heaps, and studies it; and at last he can give us a surprising chart of the movements of taste and skill and design over thousands of years. But remains of Egyptian pottery and imitations of Egyptian designs are found far outside Egypt's borders, still bearing on them their date for the student of ceramics—dated débris among the undated wreckage of other civilizations. To have two more or less exact, two careful chronologies running through the ancient world, correlated by occasional data in the historians, and checked by the history of art, means that everything is on a surer foundation, or will be when all is known.

For Egyptian chronology is not the only one by which Greek history has had to be checked and tested. Persian inscriptions are deciphered; and from the full inscription of Darius, carved on the precipice face at Behistun,[1] this at least emerges, that the Persian princes and nobles, with whom Herodotus consorted, knew their history better than his Egyptian acquaintance knew theirs. They told him different stories; the account of Cyrus, he says (I, 95), goes three ways, and he chooses the variant of those who do not wish to glorify Cyrus. Babylon and Nineveh, too, have become household words; and it was an unlooked-for boon for

1 The English reader may well be proud of Henry Rawlinson's work. An officer in the Bombay army in the '30's and '40's of the last century, he transcribed and translated this remarkable document.

the historian that, in each case, the last kings of Babylon and Nineveh had a taste for literature and history, and their libraries survived—myriads of inscribed clay tablets, indestructible and useless, under the mounds that marked the site of the ancient cities. No one could want them, and they could not perish; so the history of the great Euphrates region became known, its kings and chronologers, and, again, the story of its art.

Still more significant for Greek history is the series of surprising discoveries begun by Schliemann's excavations. Schliemann's story is interesting. A schoolboy with an imagination set on fire by Homer and a passion stirred for Greece; long years in a grocery business acquiring the fortune needed for his project; and then freedom, Greece, a Greek wife, the spade; and Troy, Tiryns and Mycene came to life again. Modern archaeologists may deplore the rough and ready digging of Schliemann; they dig by science, he dug by nature; but he was the pioneer. From his work and from their work comes to light something like a millennium of Greek civilization—Greek, we say, but was it Greek as the age of Pericles was Greek? When did the Angles and Saxons become English, or were they always English? The result is a new Mediterranean world, a new story of culture, a vastly larger circle of light touching darkness at so many more points.

Other excavations, other discoveries in Asia, make other undreamed-of additions to our framework. The Hittites were a by-word; Andrew Lang used their name to poke fun at Sayce—"where Professor Sayce is, the Hittites will not be far off"; but Sayce was right. The Hittites have become a people, with a capital at Boghaz-Keui on the Halys, and a foreign office full of clay documents in perhaps eight ancient languages; and we shall hear more of Herodotus's White Syrians, and perhaps learn who were Homer's Ketaioi.

This is not all. Beside the great outlines newly written into ancient history, there is endless detail—political, social, economic. Here is an inscription telling us that Cleon in 424 B.C. doubled the tribute of the allies of Athens; here is a batch of family letters on papyrus; here the collected accounts of an estate in Hellenistic Egypt. And Westward it is the same sort of story. The Romans in England and in Africa built temples, palaces and baths, set up mile-stones, ceaselessly carved inscriptions, above all upon grave-stones. The wealth of information available is enormous. There are drawbacks, however, in all this gain, for a man may be swamped with fresh facts till he cannot realize them—cannot, that is, group and understand them—cannot see the wood for the trees. In dealing with the private letters of ancients and their public records we have to remember that, much as they tell us, they do not necessarily tell us what most matters. A learned English historian, or perhaps he was a Scot, spent a lifetime in the English Record Office, and wrote on the Lollards and the Reformation. From the records (perhaps his own outlook also affected him) he concluded that there was not in England much need or much desire for a reformation of the church. If he is right in his deduction, it surely follows that the real movement of a people, the surge and trend of opinion, may not be prominent among its official records. Who would expect officials to understand or to register new ideas? And, again, the study of a small town's churchyard might lead us to over-estimate the virtue of the inhabitants, as much as the study of its police-court records might lead to a gloomier view; neither would be quite right; and neither source would tell us much of the factors working for national development. The newspapers may be every bit as useless. The object of the journalist, all over America and generally (in these times) in England, is to tell the less reflective members of the middle and lower classes what is already in their own minds. In both countries the journalists are the enemies of education; they are only valuable to the historian as the echoes of the unthinking. Plato's description of the rhetorician exactly fits the journalist; "he has made a study of the opinions of the multitude", in complete indifference to truth and right.[1] The real life of a nation may be felt by contemporaries, as it shapes them, but it is their way to miss its force and its direc-

1 Plato, *Phaedrus*, 260 D, *δόξας πλήθους μεμελετηκώς*.

tion. We notice and record the insignificant by preference; it is easier to note, and it comes home to us, and we are not bound to do posterity's philosophic work for it. The London evening papers are evidence of this. So contemporary records have to be noted or neglected.

But now for another great tributary to history. Anthropology is a new science, feeling its way, but already contributing much to our understanding. Herodotus tells us (I, 146) how the women of Miletus would not eat with their husbands nor call them by their names—all because long ago the Ionian conquerors killed off the Carian menfolk, and this was the revenge of the Carian women in usages handed down to their daughters. But the legend of Lohengrin, the fairy tale of Tom-Tit-Tot, the practices of savage races all over the world, suggest another reason. Why is the name concealed? For fear of magic and enchantment. On the Congo a man will change his name to cure his sleeping-sickness, which he assumes comes from a devil set on to him by name. There are countless other usages that folklore can explain or at least illustrate. As we see in *The Golden Bough*, men and women do the same sort of things the world over; beliefs repeat themselves; and sometimes, when they are compared, they become more intelligible—not that the ultimate reason necessarily appears at once. Legends and usages—do they, or does philology, help us more, if for once one may include the science of language in Anthropology, a little daringly? The aid of philology is not to be rejected, but its contributions, like all others, must be examined. The Irishman and the negro speak the same language, though with different tones; they are not, in consequence, of the same race; the language is foreign to both, though they live in the same American town. If philology helps History, it has to be helped by History. The Irish and the negro have different histories, and their physical structure is different. This may remind us of yet another phase of Anthropology—the anthropometric study of living and dead races. Much was to be hoped from the precise and scientific measurement of skulls, etc.; it promised "quantitative thinking"; but again caution is needed. A skull seems objective enough, but the label on it may be wrong because the man of science has forgotten to verify his history. I was told once by a charming old expert, very categorically, that there are no Pelasgian skulls found in Attica. But for Herodotus Attica was one of the chief homes of the Pelasgians (I, 57). Had the Pelasgians then no skulls, like those pleasant African people in his fourth book (IV, 191), whose eyes are in their breasts; or what did they do with their skulls when they died? or was the old gentleman's label not quite scientific? Later research to some extent invalidates older conclusions as to permanence of a skull type; it seems possible, not perhaps proved, but worthy of study, that soil, climate and diet may modify a skull type. One researcher tells us of minute differences between gophers in consecutive areas of California; another says that in Africa every parish has its own type of zebra. It used to be remarked that the New Englander approximated gradually to the Indian type, a hatchet-faced man, and it was put down to climate; to-day he is of a broader gauge—perhaps due to the crossing of his parents or to better feeding; Charles Dana Gibson's young men are not quite like Uncle Sam. Long heads and round heads, dolichocephalous and brachycephalous, may be a useful basis of classification; but again further research may give us surer canons.

This has brought us to our third confluent, Geography, and the influence of the habitat. Crétinism, we are told, need not belong to mountains, unless something is wanting in the soil, and as a result in the water, which the human system needs. Ranges and rivers dispose human settlements and fix the location and direction of roads, and with them determine where the great cities shall be. The fortress will be, like Newcastle, on the ford, where the road crosses the river; the great port will be, like New York, at, or, like Marseilles and Alexandria, more safely near the mouth of the river, the great waterway into the heart of the land; and Rome will be both port and fortress on the Tiber. The constitution of the United States still bears the marks of its oldest map. The rivers dictated the placing of the settlements, and communications were for long easiest by sea. Governor Andros could not unite New York and New England to oblige James II. The nature of the country and the absence of easy roads baulked him, as it nearly did George Washington. The framers of the constitution had to recognize that their new states were kept apart by a hundred and fifty years of History made by Geography, and that Geography was still potent. It is only since the Civil War that Westward expansion to the Pacific, the railroad, and the telegraph and the newspaper have made one country of it. Greece had none of these things. Much else is determined by Geography; and here Herodotus was some two thousand years ahead of some of his critics. He saw with interest the close relation between climate and man's clothing and diet; soil and climate determine the natural products on which man must live, and Herodotus always notes them, and the effect of water on health, the effect of the seasons and of uniform temperature; why else are the Egyptians so healthy, and the Libyans (IV, 187) too, with their queer diets? The Greeks settled in swarms on the Black Sea in spite of the severe cold of those regions, which Herodotus notes; but they avoided the Adriatic, its lands were rainy, the Balkan mountains intercepted the rain and came too close to the shore, while Eastern Italy south of Venice is deficient in harbours. So far there was no need for Venice, there was no hinterland yet in Germany calling for the wares of the Mediterranean and the Orient; so not yet did she hold the gorgeous East in fee.

From this it is but a step to the next confluent. The study of Economics is modern. Apart from Herodotus and some hints in Polybius, ancient historians ignored it. Next to nothing is told us of commissariat in ancient war; we pick up the trade routes almost by accident, from speeches made in the law-courts and other stray allusions. Commodities, their sources, their manufacture and their distribution of course did interest men in the past, as we see in Strabo; one or two tracts on the matter survive, notably the *Poroi* long attributed to Xenophon; but the idea of an economic history seems not to have occurred to anyone. The military history predominates. But to-day every endeavour is made to collect economic data, to weave them into a connected story, and to find the economic motive in ancient wars. Professor Bury would have it that the economic motive weighed less in antiquity; and in some degree he is right. There was less realization in general of the ramifications of trade; and it was not then a popular form of literature, nor indeed until the seventeenth century with its pamphlets; books came in the eighteenth. But the bread-and-butter issue, the "full dinner pail", is an issue that can never be escaped for very long. The very scene of Greece, its geographical breakage into small plains among mountains, its very limited arable land, shaped all its problems and coloured all their solutions. The outstanding type of Greek soldier, the heavy armed hoplite, was developed by the need to fight for a small area of wheat; no manoeuvres were required, only massacre. The population perhaps doubled every fifty years—a fact constantly forgotten by historians; but the food-supply scarcely increased. On the contrary with deforestation and loss of soil, with diminishing productiveness, it would tend to decrease; but the value of land would rise. Hence some large part of the bitterness of Greek politics, the hatreds of oligarch and democrat—though not all of it; ideas seem to have counted more among them than among us. Decline in food-supply relative to population had to be met; and it was met in three ways—by methods of food preservation (*ταριχεία*), by importation of food, and by export of consumers to new colonies Northward and Westward. City life had its own problems; not every legislator realizes that difficulties of food, water, housing and sanitation do not increase in exact arithmetical progression with the growth of population; far from it. Even on a prairie the surface of the town area may show variety; elsewhere it will confuse town-planning, even when it is thought out, which it was not in most ancient and medieval towns. The distribution of good springs is done very irregularly by Mother Earth, and a predestined great commercial centre may be terribly short of water. Athens, Megara and Samos are cases in point. All these very elementary needs of man are written all over Greek history. The problems take varying shapes in different regions and periods; and whatever stress ancient thinkers or politicians might lay or not lay on economic motives, economic factors are as significant in ancient history as in modern—if you can only find them. Three at any rate of the tyrant dynasties appear to have been interested in questions of water-supply, notably Pisistratus and Polycrates. The Cypselids and Pisistratus himself had colonial policies which clearly imply expansion of trade; and the histories of Miletus and Megara, if they could be written, would be full of commercial issues and economic questions. Solon is the greatest of ancient economists.

Last of all, in our brief survey, we may set the comparative study of politics and constitutional history, in which Aristotle deserves the honours of the pioneer. Polybius at all events would not allow Plato to claim them for an imaginary republic; it would be like comparing a statue, he said, with a living person. But constitutional history is rather like morphology, a study of structures, forgetful of life.

So far is the historian to-day from having the "facts ready to his hand". If he has not in ancient history "letters or state papers", he has much that will serve the same purpose. History has a far wider scope to-day, and requires more intensive application. The study of natural science, with its methods, had inevitably to affect History, as it has all branches of intellectual activity. Two or, perhaps, three features of scientific thought have passed over into history—a closer attention to fact with a higher standard of verification; a new insistence on the objective as opposed to the subjective treatment; so far everybody must endorse Bury's dictum; but a third feature, common to scientific study, has to be noted in history to-day, a limitation of range. Philosophy to be itself must be universal; it must be the contemplation or study of all time and all existence, as Plato put it.[1] The scientist abandons any such project; his affair is with the phase of things, mathematical or chemical, not with the whole; science and its advancement require him to be a specialist.

1 Plato, *Republic*, VI, 486A, θεωρία παντὸς μὲν χρόνου πάσης δὲ οὐσίας.

And he has given the historian the new ambition to be a specialist rather than a philosopher. In scientific studies, even in philosophy scientifically treated, style is suspect; what place could it have in algebra? A great anthropologist practically admitted to me that in his scientific work he cultivated a style which could almost be called algebraic.

No one will quarrel with the man of science or the historian for his closer attention to fact—or, at least, for his more determined verification of his facts. It is what distinguishes Thucydides from the rhetorician, the modern historian from the journalist. Not the absolute truth, but what might generally be taken for it, was according to Plato the rhetorician's ideal.[1] But in human story it is very hard to isolate facts so as to have them in concrete objective shape; it may reduce you to Boswell's almanack or a shop catalogue. *O nata mecum consule Manlio*, writes Horace, which gives us the objective fact that he was born in 65 B.C.—a fact perhaps important to know, when he adds in another poem that he was forty-four years old when Lollius had Lepidus for his colleague. "Are not five sparrows sold for two farthings?" we read elsewhere. The question gives us an economic fact; and the price is confirmed in an official document. But does the date of Horace's birth much matter, or, in itself, the price of sparrows? There is a real danger in this pursuit of objective facts; they may cease to be valuable in becoming isolated. A man may be so devoted to detail as to lose all sense of perspective; all facts may become equally important to him. But when all facts are of equal importance none can be of much importance; perspective or proportion is essential to understanding, and anyone who wishes to understand History (or anything else) has to begin all over again. The bones in Ezekiel's vision of the Valley of Dry Bones were equally important till the movement began that gave them life; then their relative importance was greatly changed.

History is movement, and movement implies spirit; and in his passion for detail the historian becomes more and more likely to lose sight of the movement and to disbelieve in the

1 Plato, *Phaedrus*, 260 A.

spirit. The attitude of that type of man constantly seems to imply that he knows the laws underlying human nature and human society as a chemist may claim to know the laws of chemical combination. With all his multiplication of facets and factors, he simplifies too abruptly. The laws, whatever they are, that guide and control human affairs are not so simple as he seems to suppose; there is a wild variety in human life and human temper which the innocent elements lack. Measurement, "quantitative thinking", is of the essence of scientific research; it is less possible in History. The apparatus for determining the force of the human spirit, or the exact weight of human character, is yet to be devised. The objective treatment of History has led to attributing more significance to the situation than to the individual; which is so generally right that in the crucial case it is disastrously wrong and means the falsification of the whole thing.

Again, this procedure implies a feeling that History is what happened, "what Alcibiades did or suffered". Polybius is wiser; he conceives it to be History's task to explain rather why what happens follows and must follow from what has happened;[1] and Cicero says the same; not events but their causes appeal to him.[2] Surely the serious thing in any historical situation is the factor, or group of factors, that is making the next stage possible, or even a stage more remote. No sepulchral inscription, no legal document, no imperial edict, no newspaper, is likely to record this force that makes for change. It is imponderable and unobserved, or, if observed, it will often be treated as trivial. Was any event between 1850 and 1860 so serious, or so epoch-making, as Darwin's publication of *The Origin of Species*? Was it noticed, was it realized? It was sixty years before Tennessee woke up to the fact that the book had altered the manner of approach for every man who thinks at all. Even yet we do not know all that it means in Theology or all that it will do—and by "do" I mean write into history by way of change and impulse—in

1 Polybius, v, 21, 6, *βουλόμεθα δὲ πάντες οὐχ οὕτως τὸ γεγονὸς ὡς τὸ πῶς ἐγένετο γιγνώσκειν.*

2 Cicero, *ad Atticum*, IX, 5, *semper enim causae eventorum magis movent quam ipsa eventa.*

political and international thinking. Is it English history, if you omit Darwin in that decade? But does any History of England yet signalize that book as the thing of chief significance in that decade? In the same way the agriculturists note that even yet the historians of the eighteenth century hardly realize what Jethro Tull and Lord Townshend did for England; who among their contemporaries saw what that work would mean?

If History is movement, surely it is better to treat of History as movement. But the common way of writing "scientific" history almost compels a man to cut out the movement. The mass of knowledge is so great, the detail can be so full and so overwhelming, that a man cannot cope with it over any extended period. Every teacher of history knows how set "periods" are shortened to make it possible for students to master them, with the same result for the student as for the writer of history; the period is known, but not the history. If we may borrow a simile from a necklace, is History the bead or the string? The tendency is to emphasize the bead, the chapter over the story. Conscience that makes cowards of us all, especially of scholars, bullies us with the value of detail; the fragments must all be gathered, nothing must be lost. But to save the ship, some part of the cargo must be jettisoned. The story is the thing, and the chapter must be sacrificed to it. But we are very reluctant to do it; it means ceasing to be "scientific", and becoming philosophic.

A Natural History in chapters—each chapter by a separate specialist, each chapter devoted to some genus or species—may be tolerable; it will probably be rather too full of detail to merit Johnson's forecast of Goldsmith's *Animated Nature*, "entertaining as a Persian Tale";[1] it will not make the cow shed her horns every year;[2] but it will still be a compilation, and lack something that a bolder, deeper and simpler treatment might secure. It may have that "shallow stream of thought" which Johnson attributed to history;[3] for thought

1 Birkbeck Hill's Boswell, II, 273.
2 As Goldsmith made her do; Boswell, III, 85 note.
3 Boswell, II, 195.

is susceptible of various meanings, and work that is done with the most meticulous care may yet lack thought. "Sir, I like that muddling work", said Johnson himself of dictionary making,[1] where surely concentration on accurate detail can be most securely independent of broad constructive thought and intelligence.

But a history that is to illumine the past, to make it significant, to bring out not merely its meaning, but what it really is, cannot be cut up in this way. A great movement has a certain unity, whether it reaches over months or centuries; you cannot with real truth make monthly records of it. Such records might be of use, like the "almanack" of Boswell's jest, but only in a subsidiary way. The man who makes them has to be a hodman, the scientific historian to the philosophic, the scholar to the thinker, the "original" researcher to the man who uses his researches,—the brick-maker, in fact, to the architect. It is a favourite absurdity with beginners in literary criticism to pick some line from a poem (Wordsworth's, very often) and insist that it is prosaic. Very likely it is; but the procedure is almost as wise as to pick a brick from St Paul's and to shake one's head over the architect. "Peter the Great," said Johnson, "had not the sense to see that the more mechanical work may be done by anybody, and that there is the same art in constructing a vessel, whether the boards are well or ill wrought. Sir Christopher Wren might as well have served his time to a bricklayer, and first, indeed, to a brickmaker."[2] Research is as essential to History as brick-making or stone-cutting to architecture, and as distinct from it. Surely it is time that there was a reaction to a larger and profounder conception of History, to the study of movements and their causes rather than events and their dates—a study (if one may stray to other pursuits for an illustration) more akin to biology than to morphology, a study of the living rather than of the dead. It will be more difficult and more dangerous; the supreme and compulsive factors are harder to determine than the matter for the almanack; there is far greater risk of mistake, and of bad

1 Boswell, II, 204 note. 2 *Hebrides*, 23 September.

mistake; but to be dead is perhaps the most hopeless of mistakes; and the mere chronicle is dead, however scientifically and with whatever original research its details are discovered and embalmed.

Though it is not always wise to challenge Aristotle, let us say for once that we shall regard History as "a thing more serious and more philosophic" than poetry. It is the function of poetry to show us the universal in the particular—the story of mankind in Mary Morrison, let us say, or in Wordsworth's leech-gatherer. May not the function of History be something similar, while it takes, not the individual perhaps, but the race, and with the same passion for truth, the same happiness, brings out the real laws of our nature, the real significance of life? Here is, not a chapter, not an almanack, but a story—of a movement, of a development, of the play of forces ethnic, geographical, economic, yes! and of forces human and spiritual, discovered through the generations of a people. It was so, with lapses and digressions, but with earnestness and no small success, that Polybius treated of Rome; fifty-three years of movement, and the face of the Mediterranean world was changed—and why?

> Dull would he be of soul, who could pass by
> A sight so touching in its majesty!

No doubt, moral judgments will be involved, but this is not to make the historian the moralist at whom Bury laughed. But why Bury's laughter should decide the case, it is hard to see. There have been historians profounder than Bury, and it is only too plain that some of his judgments lacked sympathy and fell short of finality. Moral judgment there must be when life is handled with any real grip; and if History be treated as is here suggested, and treated by the master mind, the moral judgments will be as great as the rest of the work—not explicit, perhaps, but written into it, and vocal for those who understand. It is a modern opinion that Thucydides had no feeling, because he did not unpack his heart with words; the wiser ancients felt in his austere restraint the master of pathos.

What is more, there will be more emphasis on the personal

element in history. It is strange to think how long certain historians would have it that the situation made the man, very often the economic situation, and then to recall the years 1914 to 1920, when the decisive factors in the world's history were individual men, when the quarrel of Woodrow Wilson and Henry Cabot Lodge, like that of Agamemnon and Achilles in the dawn of history, made a decade of unhappiness for Europe—perhaps, it will yet be decades. A plague on both your houses! Bury wrote a volume interpreting St Patrick's work in Ireland as part of the design to extend the Roman see's authority; the features of the man he dismissed in a paragraph—his writings "do not enable us to delineate his character, but they reveal unmistakably a strong personality and a spiritual nature", etc., etc. for two or three lines; "subtle analysis might disclose other traits".[1] Very possibly it might. But in the case of men who move and make the world, as Patrick did, and Paul, and Garibaldi (to vary our instances), it is playing with words, dodging the issue, to say that their personality achieved what they did. We need something "more philosophic" than that; and with it the temper that can recognize the Hero (let us go back to Carlyle's word)—a temper that must be able to respond to the heroic and to love it, as old Plutarch loved it. Mr G. M. Trevelyan handles Garibaldi in this way, and the reader feels the warrior's spirit at every stage, as his soldiers did, and understands the story. Finally, it is to be remembered, whatever is said about literature as a dangerous ally to History, that the great historians have been masters of style; that "style is thought", and comes of itself when men think deeply and truly enough.

What was it that "friend Sauerteig" said?[2] What were the two pinions on which History soars—or flutters and wabbles? Were they not Stern Accuracy in discovering the facts and Bold Imagination in interpreting them?

1 J. B. Bury, *Life of St Patrick*, p. 206.
2 Carlyle, *Essay on Cagliostro*.

THE VITALITY OF GREECE[1]

SUPPOSING that the sturdiest of all opponents of Greek studies—the man (if it is not too wild a flight of fancy to count him quite human) who is most uncompromising in his opinion that "history is bunk" and that modern days need no ancient tongues—suppose that this man had been standing by when the Venus di Milo was discovered in Melos in 1820,[2] would he have wished her to be buried again? Might not even he have conceded that, useless and dangerous as dead tongues and old ideas are to mankind, there might be little harm in a thing of beauty, and that it (for he would hardly have said "she") might be allowed to stay above ground, damaged and broken as she was? And when mankind has multiplied the beautiful goddess in a hundred thousand copies, and found in her gracious presence a charm and a quiet that have enriched life, might not even this practical person be willing to concede again, that, useless and dangerous as dead tongues are, the Greeks had, apparently—though he saw little in it himself—given a good deal of pleasure to a lot of innocent people—in other words, done something for us? And when further exploration adds other statues, to say nothing of architecture, will not our debt to Greece grow larger? The Venus di Milo has not had a long history; so she serves my purpose the better. Here is a thing in itself, which, without associations, with never a Greek word to add to it or subtract from it, untouched by history, has, by its unexpected and inherent beauty, made life for modern people a fuller and a happier thing. Then the Greeks did do something for us, when they made those statues, even if they were lost to the sight and knowledge of men for a millennium and a half.

1 A paper read to the Hellenic Travellers on the *Lotus*, 12 April, 1928, off Sunium. It is based on a former lecture given to Indian students at Poona on 16 August, 1916.

2 See Michaelis, *A Century of Archaeological Discoveries*, p. 49. The statue was found, in pieces, by a peasant, Georgios. It was originally made in several pieces.

A further step. When a boy of four is overheard talking to himself as he walks by his nurse, and out of his imperfect speech, as he stumbles over certain letters, as children do, a fragment of a tale emerges—"And I, standing above, leant with all my force upon the stake, and turned it about, as a man bores the timber of a ship with a drill. And the burning wood hissed in the eye, even as the red-hot iron hisses in the water, when a man seeks to temper steel for a sword"—what does it mean? For him the *Odyssey* has no history at all, but the tale of Odysseus and the Cyclops is good—is better for the time than all other tales—with the scene, the adventure, and the ringing words. And the Greeks gave us this tale; and once again, quite apart from history or association, quite apart from the music of Greek word and Greek rhythm, the great old tale captures the living heart, and sets it free in a larger world—gives a gladness of its own and enriches life; and once again the thing in itself, the mere story unsupported by tradition, is the work of the Greeks. They gave it to us.

"I cannot do without Plutarch", wrote Montaigne. Why? for one thing because Plutarch is so good to read, so full of genial wisdom and splendid story. Man cannot live by bread alone: he must have something to feed his soul, or his spirit, or whatever our contemporaries wish us to have instead; and, like the wine in the Gospel, the old is better; and Montaigne, and many with him, "cannot do without it". For, as an ancient critic put it,[1] the test of "the real thing" in literature is that you can read it often, that you can keep on reading it. Here I am perhaps anticipating a little, but I would remark at once that, when it is not you, but mankind that goes on reading and reading and reading, Plutarch and Herodotus, and Euripides and Plato, and will not take our great living contemporaries instead—no, nor even the greater Victorians either—it looks as if Greece again had left us something worth while, something of real value. And once again, just as you can and do enjoy the Venus di Milo in a plaster cast (I for one have never seen the original), and as you could

1 Longinus, *On the Sublime*, ch. VII, 3. "The real thing" is a very rough translation of *ὕψος*, but not far wrong.

and did enjoy Homer in Mr Church's *Story of the Odyssey*, and can and do enjoy him in "Butcher and Lang" or in Worsley's Spenserian stanzas or Mr Mackail's Rubaiyat—so the Persian War in Jacob Abbott's setting, and the story of Alexander in any garb, appeal to you, and you realize that Herodotus and Plutarch have enriched your life, as they made your heart beat with the stories of the War for Freedom and of the Great Adventure. And these again the Greeks have given us. The statue, the poem, the story—what is it they do, coming, as we have imagined, anew to a new discoverer—what else but what the old critic said?[1] "The soul is given wings by the true sublime and soars on high with glad uplift, proud as if she had herself given birth to the beautiful thing." So we have gone to the Greeks again, to learn the meaning of our enjoyment of their gifts.

Before long we shall go to them yet again and find in Euripides that "interpretation of life", which Matthew Arnold counted the gift of literature—and from him, even in translation, we shall gain a truer and deeper insight into the human heart. And we shall go to Plato and learn in his school to think of the foundations of human life—of God and justice and the human soul.

So much for the actual gifts of Greece to us to-day, whether we pursue the study of dead tongues or not, whether we know or do not know, how these men lived, and how their works and gifts have shaped the world that has made us, how they have trained those who have taught us, and given us the minds, the hearts, and the capacity for thinking and feeling, by which we enjoy them, judge of them, and live in them.

For we are not living in a new world after all, where great statues made by unknown hands and great poems translated from forgotten tongues are dug up or dropped on us from the sky, like Diana's image at Ephesus. We are living in a very old world indeed, made, and made over again, by generations of earnest men, who put mind and heart into the problems of government, of physical law, of beauty, of the spiritual side of things, and of God. And when we come to know their

1 Longinus, *On the Sublime*, ch. VII, 2.

story, we are not long in getting back to the Greeks. East and West, these wonderful people made the world new for those whom they met and who would look and listen.

Alexander the Great entered Asia and took with him, as a modern historian has said, that strange and potent thing, a body of ideas—Hellenism.[1] Asia Minor, Syria, Egypt, Babylon and even India felt the magic of the Greek spirit. It is disputed whether Indian architecture in stone was a new thing brought in by Alexander's Greeks; but kings ruled in Bactria for generations, who bore Greek names, and Greek titles, and coined gold money with Greek devices and Greek legends. Significant evidence of what Greece did for India you will find in the Museums of Lahore and Calcutta. There are gathered endless variants of the Buddha's story in stone; and while later Buddhist art, from which the Greek influence has passed away, is stereotyped and stiff enough, in these relics of old days from the Swat Valley, in the far North-West, the touch of Greece is visible in the life and energy and variety of the figures, in the grace of pose, the freedom of limb, the truth and vigour of the whole. Pass on from the first rooms in the Calcutta Museum, and, in the last, on your right are the Buddhas and Taras from the North, slowly hardening in treatment, and on your left are the gods and goddesses of the Hindus; and, by seeing Indian art as it is by itself, and as it was when Greek life breathed upon it, you learn what Greece does for the world. Quite apart from art it is held certain that no Indian scientific work can be dated with probability before the time of Alexander;[2] and there are those who say that he brought to India the very conception of an ordered empire.

But the influence of Alexander, and of Greek dynasts and artists, died away in the East. The Parthian rose to power in the lands between, and the Greek influence in the regions beyond flagged and died; and the old ways and the dead hand reasserted themselves. Westward it was another story —here was a virgin soil, and the cutting from the Greek

1 Edwyn Bevan, *House of Seleucus*, I, chapter I, a fine presentment of Hellenism.

2 J. Burnet, *Greek Philosophy*, Part I, p. 9.

stock took root and throve. The Roman met Greece as a conqueror and a master; but, as Horace says, "captive Greece took the fierce victor captive, and brought the arts into rustic Latium".[1] About two hundred years before Christ, "the Muse with winged foot", as another Roman poet says, entered Rome; and there was a change in every aspect of life that depends on thought. Architecture came, and painting, and all the arts that make life pleasant; the arts, that Socrates and Plato had despised, came along with the rest, Rhetoric and Cookery. Poetry came, and the Roman wrestled manfully with Homer and Euripides, and hammered them doggedly into Latin that scanned if you were not too particular; and then he read the originals again, and laughed at his copy, and tried once more. After that, he tried his hand at original composition, never getting quite out of reach of some Greek poet, from whom he might draw inspiration and ideas, telling sentence and bright phrase. With Poetry came Philosophy, a little later, and making her appeal more slowly. "The stolid race of Aeacus' line", as a Roman poet said in those days—and it was still truer of his own people—"are bellipotent rather than sapientipotent", or, in plainer terms, better at fighting than at thinking. But, just as Roman poets left off coining such monstrous terms as the Greek spirit lifted them past imitation into original life, so the stolid race began to see that the earnest eager Greek meant something by those subtleties—that his criticism was not mere quibbling or sneering—that he had seen something which his blunt host had missed. What was it?

The Romans never spoke of a Renaissance, but precisely what Europe caught from Greece in the fifteenth century of our era, Rome had in the last two centuries before Christ. What was it? Will it seem fanciful to borrow what Wordsworth says of his sister?—it is historically true:

> She gave me eyes, she gave me ears;
> And humble cares, and delicate fears;
> A heart the fountain of sweet tears;
>   And love, and thought, and joy.

1 Horace, *Epp.* II, i, 156.

The proof of this? Is it not all in Virgil? I am not forgetting Pindar's conviction that it is nature and not education that makes a poet;[1] but poets, even great poets, learn from poets; where, then, did Virgil learn to see and to hear, to think and to feel, as he did, but from Greece? Why, with all their gifts, did the great Latin poets before him—great they were, and poets, too—why did they fail of the music and the feeling, the depth and the truth, that we find in Virgil? *Sunt lacrimae rerum*; but they missed those tears. The making of a poet requires "leaf-mould", as an American critic has suggested—a soil of depth enough to afford nourishment to the deepest reaching roots of the imagination and the intelligence;[2] and the soil of Latium had been thin and hard enough. English education, following the practice of nineteen centuries and more, puts Virgil into the hands of the boy;[3] and the man too often is content not to revise the judgments of his immaturity and never realizes what he has lost. But look at the long story of European culture—read Domenico Comparetti's *Virgil in the Middle Ages*—and what a new place Virgil takes before the mind! He is the teacher of all who think and feel—from St Augustine[4] who wept for

Didonem extinctam ferroque extrema secutam

and

ipsius umbra Creusae,

to Dante, who called him Master and took him for his guide in the other world. St Augustine and Dante—in one field and another, are there names of more significance in the history of a thousand years of Western thought? or spirits of more beauty and power? And Virgil, taught by Greece, had them for his pupils.

To turn to a sterner side of life, Greece taught the rulers of the world. The Romans thought in terms of Law; they were a race of lawyers and state-builders. The Roman lawyer met

1 See page 112. The Romans, at least, recognized the part that a great tradition plays, when they would praise a poet as *doctus*.

2 C. E. Norton, writing on Longfellow.

3 R. L. Stevenson to Colvin, March 1886 (*Letters*, III, 279), "Virgil is one of the tops of human achievement; I never appreciated this; you should have a certain age to feel this; it is no book for boys".

4 Augustine, *Confessions*, I, 13, 20–22; *Aeneid*, VI, 457; II, 772.

the Greek Stoic, and he recognized his peer. The Stoic took him outside the bounds of the Forum, outside Latium, outside Italy itself; he introduced him to a new conception of Law, beyond even that Law of Nations which he had been building up for himself—the Law of Nature. The Stoic made him think anew—every old Roman notion was dragged into the light of the impressive concept of a Law written by Nature herself in the heart of man, in the life of nations, in the very fabric of the Universe itself. Small and pitiful enough some old Roman ways looked in the new setting, and yet they were his own; and, building on them and moving upward, the Roman lawyer made a new thing in the world —the stately structure which we know as Roman Law. Greece had achieved no such thing; yet she breathed her spirit into the Roman and made him free of a larger world; and he did it. So it always is, with this Greek spirit. Many and many a thing that the Greek never achieved—came nowhere near achieving—was accomplished by his pupils, in whom his spirit stirred. Caesar himself—the author of the new government of the world, which in one form and another lasted for centuries and then lingered for centuries more in the minds of men, of thinkers and dreamers, yes! and of kings and of emperors—Caesar, too, is the foster-child of Greece. She taught him to think, to feel, to know, to imagine—and made him the greatest of all Rome's political thinkers, the greatest of all her master-builders.

Alexander had planted the seeds of Greek life in Asia Minor; and the Rome, that Greece had taught and Hellenized, ruled Asia Minor and safeguarded that higher life. From the Graeco-Roman Asia Minor and Thrace grew the Byzantine Empire, for centuries the safeguard of the West against Asiatic, Moslem, Turk, and barbarism—the *Greek* Empire. Byzantium, when the Northern barbarian submerged culture for the time in the West, was the guardian of Greek thought and Greek letters—keeping them safe for us, till the time should come when Europe would be of an age to understand. Meanwhile in Gaul and Spain and Britain the Roman had been laying foundations, never quite washed away by the Northern deluge. That culture, whose soul was Greece, was what Rome gave in turn to the Western lands. The speech was Latin, but the thought in more ways than one was Greek. The Greek language was lost; but Greece had given Western Europe other gifts than her own tongue; and these were not lost.

For since Greece and Rome together had made themselves sovereign in the world, a new force had come into being. The Christian church, with its Gospel of the Galilaean peasant in whom was God, reconciling the world unto himself, had set out to conquer mankind again. In the forefront of the battle was the Greek spirit once more, facing the young church. The struggle was long and hard; the line wavered and swayed, but in the end the church triumphed—but not quite the church that had begun the contest—a church, scarred and stained and injured in many ways, but a church of larger outlook and profounder insight—taught by the Greek spirit which it had fought. Every question that the human mind could raise had been hurled at the Christian; "Answer this, and this, and this." Slowly and stumblingly he began to try to answer them; and some of his answers were as clumsy and impossible as the Roman's earliest attempts at translating Homer. But the discipline was more valuable than its early products. The Christian was forced into thinking out the relations of Jesus with all time and all existence—into clearing up for himself the bearing of his new experience of God in Christ upon every problem of thought and conduct, of society and government—a long and dreadful discipline. But it was not all a hideous mistake, as some hurried natures suppose. It meant a clearer view of God, and a firmer grasp of Christ—a Christ greater than they dreamed, richer, ampler, "very God and very man", the Redeemer. The struggle had given the church its thinkers and teachers, all touched directly or indirectly with the Greek spirit—Origen and Athanasius, Tertullian and Augustine. This church held Europe through the difficult times and educated the Northern races; and when a fresh impulse was needed, Constantinople fell to the Turk, and Greeks and Greek manuscripts and

Greek thought once more began the training of the world in what we call the Renaissance.

Many things go to make a great movement;—long time, the gradual progress of human thought, the exhaustion of all impulses; and in the fifteenth century all the factors were there for a great change, a new development. Many things combined to bring it to pass. The old world of the Mediterranean began to be closed, at the very moment when the new world of the Atlantic was thrown open by the discoveries of Columbus and Vasco da Gama. Constantinople fell; and just when the mind of man was stirring with the consciousness of a new age, the Greek spirit once again touched Europe. What followed was a great emancipation. Outside the known limits of the world men were looking seaward to strange lands; and in the region of thought, it was the same. Greek learning brought old lands and old ways under survey, introduced to men's thoughts the challenges of a by-gone day and a brilliant race.[1] The surprise, the questioning and the emancipation that Egypt had meant for the early Greek, Greece meant for Europe—it was all so strange, so different, so wonderful and so brilliant.

The Greek poets were so great; they wrote with such mastery of words, with such insight, with such an unimagined feeling for beauty and humanity, that the poets of the new-born Europe, touched by this new inspiration, stand far from their medieval fore-runners. They have a new freedom of spirit; they look at the world with new eyes; they try new experiments with their own mother-tongues, and win from them tones of a beauty that no one had dreamed could be. In England, for instance, alone, how much have Spenser and Milton drawn directly from the Greek—and Shakespeare indirectly, through North's *Plutarch* alone, to name no other source?

Religion, too, felt the touch of the Greek spirit. At first it

1 Linacre and his contemporaries had learned Greek, and the study of the books of ancient Greece, whether Hippocratic or philosophical, opened their minds to the true source of natural knowledge—Nature herself and not books. Norman Moore, *Medicine in the British Isles*, p. 55.

was reaction to paganism—a revolt from the medieval church, its dogmas, its traditions and its schoolmen—the running riot of young spirits set free. The church was challenged indeed; there had been other faiths in those old days, when the human mind had achieved such triumphs—and might they not be achieved again, if the cage could be broken, and the human heart, like a captive bird, regained its native element? What songs might men not sing again? What triumphs of thought might they not reach, to match a Plato and a Plotinus, if once they were free? And this craving for freedom, this faith in the human soul once set free, came from the books the Greek scholars brought Westward with them. The books, with the great examples of what man's mind had done, set men on fire to do it again, and to do still more. They not only gave the longing, but with it the hint how to achieve it. But the bondage of the church must end; and everywhere, despite the frenzy of the monks against Greek, it showed signs of being ended.

The second stage was reached when Erasmus, in 1516, published the Greek Testament that he edited at Cambridge. This was another stroke for freedom. For centuries Jerome's Latin translation, the Vulgate, had been the New Testament of Europe, the last court of appeal for those who sought the letter. But now behind Jerome there rose a greater authority that set men free from him; and the reaction was amazing. A small discovery in Greek by a monk of Erfurt—the correction of the mistranslation of a single Greek word—how could it matter? But from Luther's realization that μετανοεῖν did *not* mean *facere poenitentiam*, how much followed! Here, in the Greek phrase, he caught again the real spirit of Christianity. "Do penance," the church had said with Jerome, giving the phrase generation by generation a more mechanical significance; "think again!" said the Greek;—what a difference! Then the teaching of the Gospel is after all to do what men are doing—"to think again". Luther thought again, and Europe thought again with him; and the Reformation was the result. The Latin version was relegated to those who knew no Greek, to those who feared the new life, to those who preferred ignorance and darkness; but the peoples of Europe, in Luther's German and Tyndale's English, got at the heart of the "divine oracles", and first the religious life of the world, and gradually the political, became a new thing.

For politics, too, felt the breath of the new Spring; they too were born again. There had been a Europe of nobles and kings, of emperors and popes; but long ago, before the night fell, men had been free, they had governed themselves, and done it nobly. A new ideal of political life, of social order, of justice, rose before men's minds, as they read of the Athens of Pericles, of the Sparta of Lycurgus, of that great *Republic*, which Plato drew, copying as best he could the great type laid up in heaven. A new world-order might be—if the bad ages could be forgotten, and man might live again as the Greek had lived. That was the new ideal; and when men caught again in the New Testament, each in his own tongue, intelligible and unmistakable, the clear teaching of God that for each man and every man, of whatsoever rank or name, Christ had died—equally for all, and that One Great White Throne, one great Assize, awaited all men equally—men rose to a new conception of the value of the human soul, the old distinctions lost meaning, a new manhood dawned—and Democracy began. Peasant risings against oppression there had been before Luther was ever born. Once he and Tyndale had gone to the Greek and given the spirit of the old Greek book to the world, the movement grew more serious, as men acted with a deeper sense of their dignity and their responsibility. Two centuries later, when the French Revolution came, men turned again to the Greek, and in Plutarch read of a state's regeneration, when Lycurgus gave laws, equality and grandeur to Sparta; and the young men set about doing the same—not so happily.

So the Greek spirit has worked in our history. Wherever it has come among men, it has been life. But let us come more closely to the matter, and ask how this life manifests itself, and what this spirit has given to men, and may give to us in our turn. We find that, where the Greek spirit has been a living influence, it has manifested itself in a new passion for

Inquiry, a new freedom in Criticism and in Experiment. Let us take them in turn.

The instinct for Inquiry, as we all know, is native to man, but, as we also know, it can be stamped out where conservatism is strong enough in church, or public school, or polite society. But with the Greek, and with those whom he has influenced, the instinct has its full freedom and becomes a passion. *Historia* is the Greek word—"getting to know"; and it involves or carries with it the habit of Interest, the habit of Truth and the habit of Clearness. "You Greeks are always boys; there is not an old man among you; you are all young in your souls", says the old Egyptian priest in Plato's dialogue.[1] It is true; they keep the boy's habit of curiosity, of interest; they cannot let things alone; they notice; they want to know. For how many ages had there been fossils in the rocks before Xenophanes noticed them in the hills of Sicily? How had they come there? That was the question. They had always been there; perhaps we were not intended to know; and, in any case, it did not matter. But Xenophanes wanted to know; and he hit on what modern geologists tell us is the real explanation. That is characteristically Greek. In Africa, again, Xenophanes noticed that men made black images of the gods; then the gods, it would appear, are black; but the Greeks make them white; what colour are they? Does it matter? men asked; why not let everybody go his own way, his father's way, and leave such things alone? But Xenophanes was too much interested to do that; and he thought the thing out, and in satiric lines suggested that if cows and horses could carve gods, they would represent them as cows and horses, in their own image. "To whom then will ye liken Me?" is the question of God, as the Hebrew prophet put it. That habit of interest never died out while the Greek spirit lived. Herodotus could not keep his mind off soils and climates, and the reasons for things. Egypt—it was "the gift of the river",[2] he saw; the Delta was made by that "river with its passion for work".[3] Men's customs and their physique—all the variations between race and race—do not

1 Plato, *Timaeus*, 21. 2 Herodotus, II, 5. 3 Herodotus, II, 11.

climate and the soil and its products make them? He wants to know; he has the habit of interest; and even if he cannot reach cause and explanation, he will inquire and note—nothing escapes him. He is interested in everything—sowing, boating, gold-getting, the flow of rivers, the lie of ranges, the circumnavigation of Africa, the hot dawns and cold afternoons of India—surmise here, and not experience!—primitive peoples of South Russia and of Tunisia—the marriage-customs of the races, their ways of worship, their conceptions of the divine. Nothing human is alien to him; it all appeals; he is a boy in heart.

With the habit of Interest we may put the habit of Truth. Greeks were not remarkable for their practice of telling the truth in daily life, but the quest of intellectual Truth is the badge of all their tribe. The *real* explanation, not the passable one, is what they want. The Magians, when the great storm was wrecking the Armada of Xerxes, set to work, and "with their sacrifices and their chants they stopped the storm—or else", adds Herodotus, "it left off of itself".[1] Was it a god or an earthquake that made the gorge of the Peneios river?[2] Herodotus said it was plainly an earthquake—which, however, he hints, may not altogether exclude the god. "We must always tell the truth about God", said Plato, "in no case lies—whether they are allegories or whether they are not allegories."[3] In India one is constantly confronted by the assertion that the *rishis*, the holy men of old, knew about flying machines, and it would appear that men believe it. One day it occurred to me that the Greeks too had a story of a flying machine—in the legend of Medea; but they knew that it was a fable. It seemed to me that this contrast was symbolic of much. The whole movement of Illumination, that marks Greece in the sixth and fifth centuries before Christ, from the old days of Thales and Heraclitus down to Plato, is a long steady campaign against tradition, and for the discovery of Truth.

1 Herodotus, VII, 191.
2 Herodotus, VII, 129.
3 Plato, *Republic*, II, 378D, E.

The habit of Clearness is above all the characteristic of Greek thinking.

> This is the truth I saw then, and see still,
> Nor is there any magic that can stain
> The white truth for me, or make me blind again.

So says Phaedra in the play of Euripides.[1] She is always clear; and once clear, her mind is not to be clouded over again; once she has seen a thing, she has seen it, and there is no escape from it. It is a Greek habit of mind, and not all nations share it. A preference for intellectual vagueness and confusion, for half-knowledge and mysticism—the sentiment that a "religious light" will be "dim"—the habit of deliberate self-deception practised by other races for the sake of religion or polity—these are utterly alien to the Greek mind. The Greek is interested in the world; he will know the truth of each thing; and, once he knows, he does not try to persuade himself that he really does not know, or that it is something else. So far the instinct of Inquiry, with its concentration in interest, truth and clearness.

The instinct of Criticism—and of self-criticism—possessed by the Greeks has affected mankind for ever. "The unexamined life", says Socrates (or Plato says it for him), "is un-live-able for a real human being."[2] A man must look into life in earnest, and understand all its relations—father and son, citizen and state, man and God; and the comparative method was one to which, as we have seen, the Greeks took at once; —were the gods black or white? Herodotus contrasts Egyptian and Persian ideas, and even Scythian ideas, of the gods with the beliefs of Greece. This and that the Greek did, but not the Egyptian. The Greek burnt his dead father, the Indian ate him. And every divergence of idea or custom was of value. "Everyway", he says, "it is plain to me that Cambyses was greatly mad; or he would never have taken in hand to mock at sacred things and customs."[3] No, the custom of the stranger is a criticism of your own. The common mind, the conservative, knows that and resents it; but the Greek spirit sees its significance. "Opinion" for the

1 *Hippolytus*, 388–390. 2 Plato, *Apology*, 38 A. 3 Herodotus, III, 38.

Greek, as for Milton, "in good men is but knowledge in the making".

Self-criticism is the real antithesis to provincialism. "Home-keeping youth have ever homely wits"; and whenever a people carries a *Swadeshi* doctrine into the realm of thought, it is a step backward. "Our village, its food, its garb, its thought, its god"—is not the watchword of any people with a future. When Greece declined, a sure sign of it was contempt for the foreigner. It is remarkable how thorough a respect for the Persian marks such minds as Herodotus, Xenophon and Alexander—the men who knew and understood the Persian best; and it will hardly be contended that they were un-Greek. When Plato says in his *Laws* that the young men in his ideal state should be told that the customs of the foreigners are not as good as their own[1]—is he joking for once at his ideal, or is his Republic to be provincial, a parish? In the better days, the Greek mind ranged outside Greek notions, and grew strong and clear, as it criticized itself, and used the foreigner to find the weak spots of Greece.

Analysis—definition in language—close accuracy in thinking—these distinguish the Greek mind. Men were grateful to Socrates because he forced them to explain to themselves, while they did it to him, exactly what they meant, and the precise significance of the words they used. He would not tolerate "roughly speaking"—"more or less"[2]—"that sort of thing"—the slovenliness of speech that means slovenliness of mind.[3] Aristophanes makes a jest of "that native way of ours, that 'Just what mean you?' that always pops out". And a very good native way![4]

Greek criticism definitely committed mankind to philosophy, to thinking things out, to the freest and to the utmost use of intellect and of every God-given faculty. And Greece showed men how to do it—and taught the world to think. If a year spent in India gives one the right to hazard a tenta-

1 Plato, *Laws*, XII, 951 A.

2 See page 227.

3 Marcus Aurelius, I, 7, is grateful to Rusticus for teaching him "to read exactly and not to be satisfied with a general notion".

4 See page 109.

tive opinion, I would say that what India needs above all things is a strong injection of the Greek spirit that will lead her to self-criticism, and a long course of discipleship to the Greek mind. Nor is India the only country whose needs lie this way; there are other lands to the West of Greece where self-criticism is sometimes dormant.

I have alluded already to Greek political life and thought, and when I speak of Experiment as a mark of the Greek spirit, it is to politics that I would turn. "The city teaches the man", said Simonides, in a fragment of three words that survives from some poem—*πόλις ἄνδρα διδάσκει*. So men believed in those days—the City, the State (for they were synonyms) was the real education; and they were right; the City-State made Greece, so long as it was the natural expression of Greek life. "A wondrous thing is man", wrote the poet Sophocles,[1] "none more wondrous"; and he runs over man's achievements, dwells with emphasis on "speech and wind-swift thought and all the moods that mould a state" (*ἀστυνόμους ὀργάς*)—as if the essential thing in man is that social instinct that makes the life of a community real, inevitable, educative and splendid.

The range of Greek experiment in politics is very wide—perhaps no race has ever approached it. Mountain and sea played their part here. The mountains cut up Greece into small communities, and the sea kept them together. Independence and intercourse mark the political story of Greece. No despot was ever able, before Alexander, to rule all Greece at once. No vast Empire swallowed up the small states in the characterless slavery of the East from the Halys to the Brahmaputra. No priesthood ever controlled the life of a Greek city.[2] No caste system ever strangled a Greek community.[3] There was no uniformity among Greek types; the Greek spirit is everywhere and it makes for independence, and the Greeks never cared for anything else. Hence a small

1 Sophocles, *Antigone*, 332.

2 Cf. page 220, where Professor Bury's theory, that there was a risk of Orphism doing this, is considered.

3 Caste in Egypt astonished the Greeks, cf. Herodotus, II, 41; 164.

race in a small land has the widest range of political variety to show—from tyranny to a democracy of which we can hardly conceive, where a Chancellor of the Exchequer is elected by lot—and between the extremes is every grade of nobility, oligarchy and popular government, tempered and extreme.

It is Athens that gives us the most wonderful example of Greek political achievement. Here City and Citizen are an equation more than in any other state the world has known. "L'état c'est Moi", they tell us the French king said; and every Athenian citizen could have said it. He ruled, himself; he judged his own cases, himself. The Assembly of Athenians, in one form or other, is Prime Minister and Supreme Court. There was no Greek state where government was so successful; and, it must be remembered, it was the government of a confederacy of two hundred and fifty states, with foreign relations all over the world. There was probably none where Justice was more apt to rule. In Athens men did not carry arms; there was less faction there than elsewhere, and fewer revolutions;—why should you wish to disobey the laws you have made to please yourself? or the unwritten laws, which all keep from good feeling?[1] Democracy, as Athens teaches us, is the most exacting form of government; it asks more than any other of every citizen. It calls for enlightened and intelligent service, no mere acquiescence in law and public resolution, but for the active contribution of intellect to the state's needs, for self-dedication with open eyes, for the humanizing of life, for devotion to the beauty of the city and to her intellectual life, as well as to her prosperity; it asks for all your gifts, poetry, art, music, mind; and when you have given Athens all, she asks for yet more lavishness in self-sacrifice, self-control, and (above all) self-development—she calls on you to be more than ever the best, and more than the best, of yourself, for the sake of all, *αἰὲν ἀριστεύειν*. Where in political history is the like of it? Do we not owe something to Greece for such an ideal?

Think of what is implied in it. It is essentially the dis-

1 See the Speech of Pericles, Thucydides, II, 37, 3.

covery of the Individual and his value—the realization that a man's chief contribution to national life is his personality developed to the highest degree and consecrated in that degree. No less. No man liveth to himself there. It was no mere dream, either; it was in measure achieved. Compare Greek history with Roman, British or Indian; and one thing stands out. Greeks had many most obvious defects, but Greece, in proportion to its population, was far richer than other races in distinct characters and striking personalities. For good or evil, the man, especially the Athenian, is *himself*, and no mere copy of another, no reproduction of some fancied ideal type; and he brings into Greek history, for good or for evil, the greatest thing that a man can bring—a living, energizing personality, as individual as can be.

By the soul
Only, the nations shall be great and free.

And the miracle of Greek politics is that men really did believe in the soul,[1] and captured and used and enjoyed it, and made the world over again in their faith.

The last great characteristic of the Greek spirit with which we have now to deal is, in a way, the strangest—its gift for the union of Form and Freedom. Loyalty to Form we know well. Egyptian, Assyrian and Indian art became early stereotyped. When I once suggested to some Indians that Art did better when Religion did not tell it what to do—I do not mean that Art should lack the inspiration of Religion, not at all, but that Art achieves more when religious tradition does not prescribe its limits, and its methods,—I was told that the *rishis* of old knew best, and that Art should follow the lines they laid down, perhaps some thousands of years ago. A god, for instance, should be painted blue, because he is infinite. I would not say that they were Indian artists who so thought; but Indian art has been hampered by the interference of the priest as Greek was not. The dog-headed Anubis, the elephant-headed Ganpati, the many-armed goddesses, represent no doubt religious tradition or symbol; but,

1 Perhaps the author does not use this word with the same meaning as the reader.

considered as Art, they go far outside anything the Greek allowed himself. He was amazingly loyal to Nature, to the form she gave—and to the freedom she inspired in his own spirit. He and she understood each other; she told him what to do, and he did what he liked; and the result was beauty that lived, and lives still to our lasting joy.

In Poetry there is the same amazing twin-loyalty to Form and Freedom. Modern times have hailed with ecstasy the unchartered and uncontrolled rambling of Walt Whitman, the vagueness of Tagore, the sentimentalism, the unchastened fancy and chance desires, the ingenuity and contortionism, of a dozen others—revolts all of them against Form, a reaction for Freedom against convention. But the Greek was wiser. Instinct or study, or both, guided him to a surer sense of the laws of metre and their spiritual values—subtle, wonderful and true; and he obeyed those laws with amazing fidelity, or, when he broke them, it was to enlarge them, to interpret them and re-assert their power. His poetry, lyric, tragic or comic, is based on truth to human nature, loyalty to the dominant instincts and passions of men and women. He interprets them also, and again heightens Nature's wonder for us and her glory. The thing is real throughout; he never breaks loose into the fanciful, but imagination gives him a higher freedom; and in that blended Freedom and Loyalty he achieves for us all a real happiness, and gives us a new sense of wonder which makes the world our own in a new way.

So it always is with the Greek in his great days. He will use Tradition and he will keep Freedom. He will absorb all that the past has to teach, but he will not accept it blindfold; he will look for himself, and he will understand. He will be bound by the laws of experience but he will enlarge them. He will claim the utmost of freedom, and challenge himself, while he does it, as to his right to be free. In Art, in Poetry, in Philosophy, in Religion, he asserts the right of the individual to think, and (what is more) the duty of the individual to think, and will remind him further of the duty of sanity in every exercise of the mind. In all such antitheses there is danger on one side and on the other; but of all men the

Greek avoided both; and the wonder grows as to how he did it. Was it instinct given by Nature, or the challenge of his peers? However he attained to this high fortune, one thing stands out—the keynote of all was the sense of Truth as his deepest, sanest, happiest and most glorious characteristic.

Such were some of the gifts of the Greeks. These have been their contributions to mankind in the past; and they seem to be of value still. The question to-day would appear to be: Does our modern world need them, and will those, who are appointed to control our education and (where possible) our thinking, allow us, who do want the gifts of the Greeks, to accept them and to hand them on to our children? Everything seems conspired to standardize us nowadays; in every English-speaking land, the press, the boards of education, the gramophone, the ecclesiastical statesmen, the public schools, the wireless, all work toward one result; and the Greek offers us that dangerous gift, that individualizes and isolates a man, freedom of mind.

INDEX

For EU product safety concerns, contact us at Calle de José Abascal, 56–1°, 28003 Madrid, Spain or eugpsr@cambridge.org.

www.ingramcontent.com/pod-product-compliance
Ingram Content Group UK Ltd.
Pitfield, Milton Keynes, MK11 3LW, UK
UKHW010350140625
459647UK00010B/960

* 9 7 8 1 1 0 7 4 3 8 4 9 1 *